Women at Sea

Women at Sea
Travel Writing and the Margins of Caribbean Discourse

Edited by

Lizabeth Paravisini-Gebert and

Ivette Romero-Cesareo

palgrave

First published 2001 by
PALGRAVE™
175 Fifth Avenue, New York, N.Y. 10010 and
Houndmills, Basingstoke, Hampshire, England RG21 6XS.
Companies and representatives throughout the world.

PALGRAVE™ is the new global publishing imprint of St. Martin's Press LLC Scholarly and Reference Division and Palgrave Publishers Ltd (formerly Macmillan Press Ltd).

ISBN 0-312-21996-2 hardback

Library of Congress Cataloging-in-Publishing Data
     Women at sea : travel writing and the margins of Caribbean discourse / edited by Lizabeth Paravisini-Gebert and Ivette Romero-Cesareo.
          p. cm.
     Includes bibliographical references and index.
     ISBN 0-312-21996-2 (cloth)
  1. Women travelers—Caribbean Area. 2. Travelers writings—Caribbean Area. I. Paravisini-Gebert, Lizabeth. II., Romero-Cesareo, Ivette.
  G155.C35W65   2000
  917.2904'082—dc21   99-37439
                                                                          CIP

A catalogue record for this book is available from the British Library.

Design by Westchester Book Composition

First edition: January, 2001
10 9 8 7 6 5 4 3 2 1

To
The memory of my godmother
María Magdalena Paravisini de Vilá
And my aunt
Angelina Paravisini de Baerga
—LP

To
The memory of my grandmother
Evarista Cáceres
And to my mother
Victoria Martínez Cáceres
—IR

Contents

Acknowledgments   ix

Permissions   vi

Introduction   1

Chapter 1: Itinerant Prophetesses of Transatlantic Discourse   9
    José Piedra

Chapter 2: Violence and Awe: The Foundations of Government
    in Aphra Behn's New World Settings   41
    Richard Frohock

Chapter 3: Cross-Dressing on The Margins of Empire:
    Women Pirates and the Narrative of
    the Caribbean   59
    Lizabeth Paravisini-Gebert

Chapter 4: When the Subaltern Travels: Slave Narrative
    and Testimonial Erasure in the Contact Zone   99
    Mario Cesareo

Chapter 5: Women Adrift: Madwomen, Matriarchs,
    and the Caribbean   135
    Ivette Romero-Cesareo

Chapter 6: A "Valiant Symbol of Industrial Progress"?:
    Cuban Women Travelers and the United States   161
    Luisa Campuzano

Chapter 7: Colonizing the Self: Gender, Politics, and Race
in the Countess Of Merlin's *La Havane*   183
Claire Emilie Martin

Chapter 8: Travels and Identities in the Chronicles of
Three Nineteenth-Century Caribbean Women   203
Aileen Schmidt

Chapter 9: Journeys and Warnings: Nancy Prince's Travels as
Cautionary Tales for African American Readers   225
Cheryl Fish

Chapter 10: Decolonizing Ethnography: Zora Neale Hurston
in the Caribbean   245
Kevin Meehan

Epilogue

Chapter 11: Haiti's Unquiet Past: Katherine Dunham,
Modern Dancer, and Her Enchanted Island   281
Joan Dayan

Contributors   293

Index   297

Acknowledgments

As a collaborative effort, this book would not have been possible without the generosity, inspiration, and patience of all the scholars whose essays appear on its pages, and to them go our most sincere and heartfelt thanks and admiration. Kristi Long and Donna Cherry, our editors at Palgrave, have been models of patience and graciousness, for which they have our enduring thanks.

LP & IR

I must thank, first and foremost, my relentless and most resourceful research assistants, Malian Lahey and Jennifer Romero, for an extraordinary effort and for the joy and enthusiasm they have brought to my projects in the last two years. Among the friends and colleagues who generously assisted with their expertise and support in the completion of the work, I must single out Joan Dayan, Consuelo López Springfield, Elaine Savory, Margarite Fernández Olmos, and Carmen Esteves. My young friend Aryeh Palmer-Gold shared with me his collection of pirate books and enthusiasm for piratical lore. Ivette Romero was, as always, a wonderful collaborator and friend. To her, and to little Mario Sur, who very patiently waited through many a long telephone call, my most affectionate gratitude.

My stepdaughters, Carrie and D'Arcy—who were present when we first envisioned the project during a leisurely chat at a riverside Oxford pub during a family vacation several years ago—have in the intervening years gone off to college and to travels of their own. I miss them—and although I know they must sally forth, I wish they were home.

And to my two Gordons—husband and son—as always, my deepest love.

LP

Many thanks to "Odysseus" for his travels, and for bringing me the gifts of warmth, laughter, and music.

My warmest gratitude to Irma Blanco Casey for her editorial skills and enthusiastic encouragement; to Rose De Angelis for her incisive comments on the subtleties of the English language, her supreme patience, and her limitless energy; to Lizabeth Paravisini-Gebert for being supportive and equanimous, even in the most stressful times, and for being a model of a hard-working scholar with a zest for life; to Mario Cesareo for his comradeship and continued support.

Thank you all for the splendorous gift of your friendship.

And all my love to my son Mario Sur, the star that guides my travels.

IR

Permissions

Women at Sea

Introduction

TRAVELING THE MARGINS OF CARIBBEAN DISCOURSE

mar·gin (mär′jin) n. *The blank space bordering the written or printed area on a page.*

—American Heritage Dictionary

Can the subaltern travel?

—Mario Cesareo

*W*omen at Sea seeks to address two questions rarely posed in the ever-growing scholarly literature on travel, travel literature, and gender: Can the exploration of travel (and its genre, the travelogue) be expanded to include those traveling the social and economic periphery, the margins of colonial societies? And if so, what form do these travels and their chronicles take? The travelers in whose wake we initially followed when we envisaged this collection—pirates Anne Bonny and Mary Read, and the heartbreaking Adèle Hugo—were marginal creatures. As pirates emerging from eighteenth-century working-class English societies, Bonny and Read cross-dressed their way into male occupations that brought them to the West Indies. As a "madwoman"—and thus not bound by the constraints of respectability and decorous observation of "the Other" characteristic of women travelers of her race and class—Adèle Hugo could travel the margins of colonial societies with deranged impunity. These women were undoubtedly travelers—but not known as writers. The stories of their adventures and misadventures, fascinating as they have proven to be, enduring as they have through the years, have been left to others to shape. Illiterate and "mad," they are the quintessentially marginalized—silent, requiring to be taken "into custody," and female— they most decidedly inhabited "the blank spaces bordering the written or printed area on a page."

In the modern field of scholarship that investigates travel writing—for which studies such as the oft-quoted Mary Louise Pratt's *Imperial Eyes* have quickly become classics—there has been no space for nonwriting travelers, or indeed for writers who are not imperially bound. By this we mean that the field has defined itself, perhaps narrowly, especially as it concerns women travelers, as one interested in how chronicles of travel can be read as glimpses into colonized societies, as articulating colonial viewpoints and racist assumptions, and as constructing and reacting against the notion of "the Other." As such, the field has made most important contributions to colonial and postcolonial studies. It has brought subjectivity and nuance to our understanding of relations between colonizer and colonized; it has provided a much-needed framework for our interpretation of the speci- ficities of those race- and class-bound relationships on which colonialism was grounded; and it has brought to our attention a multiplicity of texts bringing fresh documentation to our reconstruction of colonial histories.

This field of study, however, by privileging the travelogue—a text avowedly resulting from a stated desire to chronicle the displacement of travel, whether meant for the public as a book or designed to inform a closer and more intimate audience, as in the letter—has imposed a double silence on that "Other" who can either not write about her travels (as in the case of Bonny, Read, and Hugo) or writes with a purpose other than that of chronicling displacement as a means in itself (as in Mary Prince's slave narrative or as in Nancy Prince's cautionary tales for potential African American settlers in Jamaica). In this collection we look within the mar- gins—the poor, the illiterate, the slave, the mad, the black, the displaced Creole, the African American anthropologist—for ways to redefine travel and the traveler, seeking to demonstrate that there are broader ways to travel, and that the discourse of travel coming from the margins of the written or printed page can yield extraordinary instances of contestation of colonial and racial discourses. "Women at sea," traveling "the margins of Caribbean discourse" as voices of contestation, turn their gaze upon the very aspects of colonial existence from which the "center" and their trav- elogues have averted their eyes.

The essays of *Women at Sea* are organized chronologically by the date of travel. Thus the book opens with José Piedra's witty re-reading of Alvar

Núñez Cabeza de Vaca's sixteenth-century account of his misadventures following a shipwreck in the Caribbean, *Castaways*. Piedra, in "Itinerant Prophetesses of Transatlantic Discourse," recovers the figure of an Afro-Hispanic prophetess, la Mora de Hornachos, and of the often-silenced women who accompanied Nuñez de Vaca's expedition, as being at the very center of *Castaways* despite their marginality in and outside the text. They—the women, that is—provide a model for "adopting and adapting to gender-pending and gender-bending professional mediations" that make existential survival possible. In their roles as "traders of faith, fate, and fetishes," but "also [in their] generalized ability to accept differences, to test, and even to taste them," they can negotiate their Caribbean exile "into knowledge and safety, even 'discovering' the harbor haven which eventually only four castaways were able to reach."

Piedra's "itinerant prophetesses," nameless and unsung, voiceless except through the margins of Núñez de Vaca's narrative of survival, contrast sharply with Aphra Behn's bold assertion in her seventeenth-century novel *Oroonoko*—based on events observed during her prolonged sojourn in Surinam—that "I was myself an Eye-Witness to a great part of what you will find here set down." Behn inhabits a different Caribbean margin; writing "at the beginning of the first great age of English imperialism," her novel, like other New World accounts, offers "an emplotment and narration of experience," in a remote, embattled, and ultimately abandoned colonial outpost, "imagining the forms and qualities of just colonial governance in the New World." In Richard Frohock's insightful reading of *Oroonoko*, "Violence and Awe: The Foundations of Government in Aphra Behn's New World Settings," Behn's efforts to turn her experiences as traveler—the veracity of which has been questioned unsuccessfully by some twentieth-century scholars—into an illustration of the atrocities inflicted on slaves in an imperial setting are revealed as grounded on a series of unresolved tensions, chief of which is her evasion of an acknowledgment that "political order in the New World colony has its origin in violence and force."

In Lizabeth Paravisini-Gebert's exploration of the careers and interpretations of women pirates Anne Bonny and Mary Read, "Cross-Dressing on the Margins of Empire," we see how the deployment of violence and force decried by Behn as resulting in an unjust society leads, by the early years of the eighteenth century, into the closing of the social and economic freedoms provided by the increasingly less marginal (to colonial coffers) territories of the Caribbean region. Framed by the most intense period of English efforts to eradicate piracy in the Caribbean and establish political order over the increasingly profitable colonies, Bonny and Read emerge as symbols of the subjugation of the margins to the necessities of the colonial enterprise. As such, they emerge, in the many accounts of their adventures, as protean figures, literally "blank spaces" at the margins of written texts, who are made to bear the burden of myriad paeans to the loss of freedom from colonial rule.

In "When the Subaltern Travels: Slave Narrative and Testimonial Erasure in the Contact Zone," Mario Cesareo examines "the historical and institutional (im)possibility of [a slave's] travel writing" through his reading of Mary Prince's nineteenth-century slave narrative, *The History of Mary Prince: A West Indian Slave,* as a travelogue. Through a theoretical investigation into the "organicity obtaining between the narrated experience and the generic form that structures it," Cesareo links Prince's testimony not to the genre of the travelogue, but to that of the picaresque. Prince's "picaresque appropriation of writing as an instance of the Other in the self-production of an otherness," he argues, "lays bare the possibilities, agency, and restrictions, of the subaltern, once irrevocably installed, and writing, in the contact zone."

Writing as a form of agency for the marginalized is central to Ivette Romero's "Women Adrift: Madwomen, Matriarchs, and the Caribbean," an examination of Adèle Hugo, Mary Seacole, and Céline Alvarez Baa as eccentric/ex-centric travelers whose "marginal positioning enables them to circulate from margins to center and back again despite the physical obstacles and societal constraints" they faced as mad Frenchwoman and native Caribbean woman in mid- to late-nineteenth-century society. Romero-Cesareo reviews the construction of the figures of Hugo and Alvarez Baa by others against Seacole's complex construction of herself in *The Wonderful Adventures of Mrs. Seacole in Many Lands,* concluding that it is the latter's writing that "enables her to address and reconform the paradigms of both margins and centers."

Luisa Campuzano, in "A 'Valiant Symbol of Industrial Progress'?: Cuban Women Travelers and the United States," expands the narrow generic limitations of the travelogue to examine the various texts—poetry, letters, reports on educational programs, political essays—through which Cuban women in the mid-to-late nineteenth century narrated their experiences of travel to the United States. Building upon the notion of writing as agency, the women about which Campuzano writes seek to insert themselves into the political and social discourse of their native island through their engagement with the nation to the north, whose influence and presence loomed so large in the determination of Cuba's future at the time. It is Campuzano's goal to elucidate the ways in which, when visiting the United States, "the concentration of these writers' gaze on public life and on the system of government that sustains it, and the audacity of the opinions on politics they expressed," represented protofeminist approaches responsible for the development of feminism in Cuba and for the entering of Cuban women into the political sphere.

Campuzano's essay serves as a fitting introduction and finds its complement in the two essays that follow: Claire Martin's "Colonizing the Self: Gender, Politics, and Race in the Countess of Merlin's *La Havane*" and Aileen Schmidt's "Travels and Identities in the Chronicles of Three Nineteenth-Century Caribbean Women." Martin analyzes the ways in which the public letters through which the Countess of Merlin narrates her return to her native Cuba after an absence of many years articulate "the dissonant discourse of her imperialist ideology and her avowed longing to belong to the island." It is perhaps because of this unresolved tension, Martin argues, "that *La Havane* succeeds as a personal narrative, a travel and a metaphor for the conflictive beginnings of the new American nations." Schmidt, in her turn, looks at another form of "travel"—that forced upon the Cuban and Puerto Rican sent into political exile by the Spanish colonial authorities because of their seditious and revolutionary activities. Through her examination of various chronicles of exile/travel, Schmidt seeks to demonstrate the importance of travel "as a liberating discourse for women" that reveals "the historical value of personal experience." Schmidt scrutinizes the generic identity between autobiography and the travelogue to show how the autobiographical narratives of Lola Rodríguez de Tió, Aurelia Castillo de González, and Catalina Rodríguez de Morales "are expressions of an anti-hegemonic literature" that demonstrate "how the trajectory of the feminine subject contributes to the formation of a concept of nationhood."

Notions of nationhood—of either belonging to or being marginalized from the nation—are at the heart of Cheryl Fish's "Journeys and Warnings: Nancy Prince's Travels as Cautionary Tales for African American Readers." For Prince, who, like Mary Seacole, traveled "within the limited parameters of viable social and economic roles open to black women," travel is part "of a dialectic on what it means to be a free and mobile ethical subject with a complex relationship to nationality, class, and public discourse." Through her focus on "the significance of embedded warnings to African American readers regarding emigration schemes that characterized Prince's hybrid writing about Jamaica," Fish illustrates how Prince's narrative authority—which derives from her position both inside and outside American society—is "enhanced by a struggle that comes in part from the tensions between marginality and defiance."

The blurring of the boundaries between self and others is, according to Kevin Meehan in "Decolonizing Ethnography: Zora Neale Hurston in the Caribbean," one of the most significant accomplishments of Hurston's account of her visit to Jamaica and Haiti, *Tell My Horse.* In *Tell My Horse,* the "shared reality of living gendered female experience as alienation, negation, and displacement figures as a possible condition for Hurston being able to see and write about kinds and degrees of difference among Haitian, Jamaican, and North American women." In his analysis of Hurston's text, Meehan shows how the text "exposes the tension between theory and practice of representing colonial encounters and, ultimately, subverts the existing production modes of high theory" through the displacement of the discourse of social science in favor of spirit possession, and "by voicing a critique of ethnography as an institutional practice designed to reinforce stereotyped conceptual models of dependency and modernization." For Meehan, Hurston's most groundbreaking contributions, revealed through the examination of the text as an account of travel, are those of addressing "the role of cultural theory as a key problem in articulating cross-cultural dialogue" while insisting on seeing writing "as a form of social action."

If for Hurston writing becomes a "form of social action," for Katherine Dunham dance paves the way to social commitment and responsibility. Dayan's account of Dunham's engagement with Haiti in her essay "Haiti's Unquiet Past: Katherine Dunham, Modern Dancer, and Her Enchanted Island," examines Dunham's autobiography, her tale of her relationship with Haiti as traveler/visitor/houseowner, as a "disturbing and transformative" text whose courage resides in Dunham's "refusal to limit her choices, [in] her willing embrace of the syncretism that is so much a part of African-based religions in the New World, taking on the entire range of images of the diaspora in her dance and in her writings." In Dayan's account of Dunham's possession of the house built by an earlier traveler/exile, Pauline Bonaparte, she evokes the profound, albeit romantic, connection to colonial history that fuels Dunham's relationship to Haiti; while in Dunham's "willingness to submit to the risks of the life of the spirit, mixing the gods and risking their anger in testimony to a longed-for 'reconciliation' of 'these wandering, jealous siblings of different nations but of the same ancestors,'" Dayan reads the transformation that Haiti has produced in this African American visitor who, like Zora Neale Hurston before her, must needs discover in Haiti the shared realities of diasporan history.

At the center of these narratives of travel is the Caribbean region—imagined, historical, coveted, fragmented, multilingual, hybrid—at once object of desire and confined space from which to escape. When traveled by empire-bound subjects—when seen through imperial eyes—it emerges as homogeneous territory, peopled by "Others" of distinctly separate race and culture, easily fitted into colonial hierarchies and within rigid categories. Through the prism of imperial eyes, there is a sameness from island to island born of the colonial institutions—slavery, the plantation, the colonial bureaucracy, the pigmentocracy, the expatriate versus the Creole—that empire-bound travelers have been taught to recognize as created in the image of themselves. The Caribbean islands, when seen as islands in the stream of colonial history, lose a great measure of their individuality and uniqueness—they become part of a territory coveted because it can produce wealth; despised perhaps because their cultures and languages have borrowed too heavily from African models; and dependent, like a child is dependent, on the wisdom and guidance of those who have assumed, for better or worse, a parental/colonial role. The natives, when not silent, are ill-judged—when not silenced, they are banned.

Women at Sea seeks to offer a glimpse, through the metaphor and reality of travel, of the cacophony of contestatory voices coming from the margins of Caribbean discourse. The Caribbean, if we look from the printed page of officialdom to the margins traveled by native women, Creole countesses, mad daughters of illustrious French writers, African American dancers and anthropologists, low-class pirates, itinerant prophetesses, revolutionaries in exile, and black higglers, emerges as a chaotic space of possibilities, a polyphonic expanse of potentiality—nuanced, multifarious, eclectic, heterogeneous, whole. Freed from the constraints of empire, offering mediation and negotiation, the peripheries—the margins—are both inside and outside the bounds of the colonial enterprise. They exist in a symbiotic relationship with the page, with official space, but provide a space for contestation and escape. Any notation on the margin can at any moment transform the truth of the official page.

Chapter 1

ITINERANT PROPHETESSES OF TRANSATLANTIC DISCOURSE

José Piedra

Dear fellow women travelers throughout my life:
    Nadie es profeta en su tierra. *(No one becomes a prophet at home.)*
—Saying often heard in the Spanish Caribbean.

Te he inscrito en la vida; te queda tiempo para la mía. (I have inscribed you into life; you have time left for mine.) So answered my mother in her golden-gray years in Miami exile to my question "Why don't you write the story of your life?" To a certain extent I have heard this before, such as when quoting the Bible (11 Corinthians, 3:3), Christopher Columbus felt forced to embrace Queen Isabella's transatlantic life story just as Christ had done with his own Father as He signaled to him "You are our epistle . . . written not in ink, but . . . in fleshy tables of the heart . . ."

1. Caribbean Crossroads

Such shapes, such gesture, and such sound, expressing . . . a kind /
Of excellent dumb discourse.
—William Shakespeare,
The Tempest (III. iii, 37-39).

The Bible they had been taught, thus they spoke their panic in the prophetic language of the Bible. The moment the earth began to shake, horror among blacks peaked.
—José Martí, "El terremoto de Charleston"
(Charleston's Earthquake).

As the Caribbean became an Atlantic crossroads between Europe, America, and Africa, it became the locus of unfair exchanges. Under whatever name—encounter, discovery, conquest—transatlantic voyaging imposed a variety of colonialisms and imperialisms in the area. Whether unwillingly or strategically, Caribbean exchanges also promoted the blurring of boundaries between Selves and Others, and between the different sides of the Atlantic. The events in question eventually led to the kind of hybridity that I proudly represent.[1] The roots of the situation are far deeper.

Even at the outset of the Spanish-sponsored Caribbean, Selves and Others were not always so easy to tell apart. The situation applies to the mix of peoples that converged in the Iberian territory since time immemorial, passing through the Muslim-inspired, Arab-speaking, North African period of Al-Andalus, and peaking with the foundation of the Spanish nation as a heterogeneous group of "converts"—at the religious, linguistic, and national levels. We can deduce from this picture the crossover nature of the transatlantic crews.[2]

Some of the Caribbean colonizers were Others, including women, slaves, citizen apprentices, converts, and fellow travelers. I treasure among them Afro-Hispanic prophetesses who tended to be symbolically enslaved and factual ex-slaves, relatively Hispanicized and Christianized, capable of standing by their male partners as well as challenging their ideals. I am thinking of La Mora de Hornachos, in Alvar Núñez Cabeza de Vaca's sixteenth-century chronicle *Naufragios (Castaways: The Narrative of Alvar Núñez Cabeza de Vaca)*, who leads a team of itinerant prophetesses interpreting the heterodox Atlantic fate of the Caribbean.[3] The women of *Castaways* were capable of providing alternative transatlantic ways in and out of the Caribbean; in many cases they saved or could have saved those who paid heed to them, and could doom those who would not. These women trusted their own free spirit and mind-set more than the perilous sea and transatlantic rhetoric of adventurous men in search of glory, gold, and God's faraway lands. It was precisely the men at the helm and in charge of the pen who invited the women in question to become characters in their travel chronicles. I believe that deep down the itinerant authors recognized the importance of their sponsored prophetesses as readers of the destiny of the Caribbean. The prophetesses represented a measure of freedom and engagement with circumstances that many soldiers would envy. Even from within the captivity of Euro-Christian male texts, they show the gift of sifting through multiple discriminations and restrictions, ranging from those applied to women in their "original" African cultures, through the symbolic "unofficial" status as textual partners of transatlantic men.

In a parallel fashion, some of the colonized in the Caribbean remained feisty and self-righteous Selves, including men and women who, given the right opportunities and circumstances in rhetorical milieus, would have become themselves conquerors and converters in their own right. I count among these colonized Selves the cannibals and Amazons whose lifestyle became a source of attraction and repulsion to the Spanish in voyaging throughout the Atlantic into the Caribbean. In the imagination of the Spanish voyagers from Columbus onward, cannibal men and Amazon women were for them, or rather, against them, waiting at every turn.[4] These icons of difference were also sample and examples to behold and to be held.

Cannibals ate their male enemies and Amazons killed practically every man in sight as they raided neighboring communities. Consequently, the very Spaniards who lived and fantasized the Caribbean phenomena felt compelled to kill or assimilate cannibals and Amazons, or be assimilated and killed by them. A third possibility also enters the picture. Spanish voyagers may have taken the opportunity to sample notions of difference in the archipelago of alternative value systems that spread before them across the Atlantic. After all, the Caribbean and surrounding Atlantic areas symbolically floated in terra incognita from the imagining angles and actualizing perspectives of itinerant Selves as well as Others. Practically everything was possible "overseas"—or many wished it were.

Even nominally, the term "Caribbean" embodies the transatlantic challenge. The fantastic etymology of the word is indeed far-reaching, ranging from the intended goal of the trip (the fabled treasure of the real Grand Khan) to the mistaken goal of the trip (meeting people in whose language [Arawak] the word "carib" signifies "gifted"). Thus, transatlantic discourse inadvertently exchanged a human appetite for problematic riches for a problematically rich human diet. Contributing to the making of the Caribbean, the term Antilles adds an important note as the "anti-" or "ante-islands," standing in the way to the other end, antipodes, or simply *the* end, of the world. The civilized men's attraction and repulsion connected to the area required the presence of monsters and mediums, such as the cannibals at the core of the Caribbean. But, as we shall find upon reading Columbus and his heirs, Amazons were never far behind. As challenges to Euro-Christian principles, cannibals and Amazons have had a long tradition: male figures ranging from Kronos, through the Cyclops, to the cannibals, and female figures ranging from the Atlantides, through the Medusas, to the Amazons. As part of the Caribbean exchange, monsters and mediums were put within reach, both through the auspices of the Afro-Hispanic prophetesses.

The lure of the New World and the Old World's fear of monsters and mediums went hand in hand, as befitting relations between iconic extremes of civilization and savagery, particularly when the latter produced homosexual panics in the former. It is by now traditional to assume Amazons to be lesbian warriors and, as I have said elsewhere, it should be equally plausible to assume cannibals to be gay warriors.[5] Columbus himself recognized both groups living on side-by-side islands of the Caribbean and dividing among themselves the girls and boys they officiously procreated once a year. In the end, cannibals and Amazons became Self-imposing Others of the post-Columbian Caribbean. The situation becomes particularly engaging and frightening when Afro-Hispanic prophetesses begin to act as guides into the realms of cannibals and Amazons.

Having lived among cannibals or knowing about them from afar, the itinerant prophetesses portray these men as far more omnivorous in questions of food as well as mates than the master encoders would have admitted. As we shall find out in our review of Castaways, Spaniards are much more apt to eat each other than their Indian counterparts. Having lived among Amazons or acted like them, the shipwrecked women emerge as far more accommodating in terms of behavior and sexual practices. The exceptions included living arrangements and organized conquests with males, which exceeded these women's occasional mating rituals and the woman-conquering habits. In their capacity as mediators and mediums—ranging from commercial transactions to transnational, transgendered, and transcendental matters—the "Amazons" or merely feisty women revisited in Castaways have a thing or two to teach their Euro-Christian male captives.

Note to satisfy my editorial friend and ad hoc medium, who prefers to remain anonymous: "transnational" is a concept I have adopted and adapted from an unpublished Cornell thesis by Mayra Santos Febres. To my mind, it does not imply giving up one's nation for another, but rather transcending national exclusivity as a means of achieving utopian globalization. I cannot determine where "transgendered" comes from, but it is certainly a concept both Mayra and I would trust, and even cherish, sharing; it does not actually imply giving up one's gender or notion thereof for another's, but rather to transcend gender exclusivity as the sublime means toward heritage making. Finally, the old-fashioned term "transcendental" does not imply giving up one's "inferior" reality for another person's "superior" ideal, but rather to transcend one's given circumstances in order to seek visceral opportunities beyond the status quo. This is also a "secular" means to achieve a "sacred" social end. Prophetic women—such as the editor, Mayra, Mother—have helped me come to terms with addressing transcendental, transgendered, and transnational issues.

It would not surprise anyone, at least those familiar with Freudian theory and practice, that the relationship between transatlantic voyagers, prophecy-makers, man-eating men, and women-conquering women, would be a complex one, combining matters of sex, aggression, orality in all its digestive faces, death, and destiny. This is certainly the panorama I have found in the Caribbean primal scene of transatlantic discourse. A few questions remain in light of this paradoxical search for transatlantic compromises between Spanish Selves and Caribbean Others that would justify and rationalize colonial takeovers.

I have narrowed down my present work to the study of a team of Caribbean-centered transatlantic women whose surprise appearances, loquacious whispers, overreaching desires, and fertile wombs learned to partner, when they would not part with, the pens and penises of master colonials. However, I have kept in mind that not everyone privileges writing and procreating or, for that matter, any relatively permanent form of rhetorical inscription or biological heritage, as proof of identity.

The Columbus-inaugurated transatlantic discourse of which these women became martyrs/heroines does not seek as strategic excuses the polarization of the Atlantic encounter at any level: as a matter of the conquerors versus the conquered, men versus women, straight versus gay "behavior," the oral versus the written, the graphic versus the agraphic, the "Western" versus the non-Western. In theory, in practice, and in print—not to mention on the grounds of gender-coding in the spaces of sexual behavior—the more overt the intent to conquer, the more readily the conqueror appears to benefit from disguising the intended takeover as a two-sided exchange. Thus transatlantic discourse emerges as an eminently transnational, transgendered, and transcendental exchange that lies both within and beyond colonial restrictions. Such a series of transgressive strategies inform the Euro-Christian construct of the Caribbean.

After a long hiatus in temperate academic climates, there I was, nearly bare and belly up at the edge of a pool in what the official brochure proudly claimed as the site of the original cemetery of a sixteenth-century Dominican nunnery, now a modest hotel.

"You shall burn," said to me in passing an anonymous Afro-American tourist with a warning tone to her voice and a cynical smile on her face.

Welcome to the realm of female prophetesses, guardian angels, devilish witches, or sassy bitches whose voices appear to be stranded in, but not strangled by, male words, and thus apt to enjoy transatlantic exchanges. They avoid falling into colonial traps, at least not without pre- and/or post-factum knowledge and a measure of self-benefiting. It should not come as a surprise that the women I have studied inhabit colonial chronicles in which the whiteness and machismo of the conquerors struggle against an overwhelming Caribbean reality that defines the advantages of being white and male—not to mention European and Christian. And yet, prejudice overcomes these women's rhetorical condition: black prophetesses would never be admitted into the category of messiahs, a position traditionally reserved for light-complexioned men.

To what degree should the Hispano-Caribbean icons of libidinal exchange and means of reading destiny be considered heroic or martyred figures of transatlantic space? Could an Afro-Hispanic woman and her team of prophetesses skirt the white master's code and become avowed mistresses of transatlantic discourse? Are these transient informers eminently capable of the "excellent kind of dumb discourse" advertised by Shakespeare as the insidious way of the most alluring of Others? Is there an Euro-Christian epidemic of cannibals and Amazons that reached geographically as far afield as Shakespeare's Caliban and the prophetess Sycorax or, critically, as far as today's Caribbean culture? And above all, could the Caribbean crossroads be considered as a permissive closet for transatlantic discourse and intercourse outed by Christopher Columbus?

2. Transatlantic Discourse

For the islands wait for me, and the ships of the sea in the beginning: that I may bring thy sons from afar.
                    —Isaiah 60:9a, quoted by Christopher Columbus,
                                    Libro de las profecías (1502).

Of the New Heaven and Earth which Our Lord has made, and
as St. John writes in the Apocalypse, after he had told of it by the
mouth of Isaiah, He made me the messenger for it and showed me
where to find it.
    —Christopher Columbus, *Libro de las profecías* (1502).

In the search for a system that would put in perspective the multiple
Caribbean exchanges that we have come to know through colonial Spanish-
American literature, we find Christopher Columbus to be an odd pioneer
of transatlantic discourse. However, his mid-Atlantic posturings are unavoidable to the understanding of the hybridity he left behind, and this is only
the tip of the iceberg, for his posturings were not merely rhetorical. I have
come to think of transatlantic discourse as the result of the human
exchanges occurring behind the scenes and between the sheets of the
Atlantic takeover—be they expressed rhetorically or through intercourse. I
also think of this promotional form of discourse and intercourse as a liberal paradise of sorts intent on finding, or bound to find, a middle
ground—if not always an equitable compromise. In that sense Christopher
Columbus is not such an odd pioneer of transatlantic perspectives.[6] It
makes sense that an improvised member of the Euro-Christian elite who
pioneered the expansion of Euro-Christian principles overseas against the
rules and regulations of the status quo, would apply the same strategy combining challenge and assimilation to those he claimed to oversee in the
name of Spain and Christ. It might be harder to view Columbus as the natural ally of Afro-Hispanic prophetesses, much less their model. And yet we
shall find out that in the making of America, Spain shared much with
Africa and with a prophetic tradition, and that perhaps, given Columbus's
recounting of his transatlantic deeds at the end of his life as a fated fact, he
may have had time to meet one or more Afro-Hispanic prophetesses.

Following the line of Columbus's own life, the Atlantic led to Africa
and Asia (although not admittedly by way of America). Columbus tentatively called the space of his exploration "Mar Océano [which] is between
Africa, Spain and the Indies," a title derived from "occidit nobis" ("new
Occident" or "new West").[7] Thus Columbus himself suggested his having
been as far as the Indies—time would tell whether the East or the West
ones. The explored body of waters eventually bore the name Atlantic
Ocean, thus corroborating its subliminal connection to Plato's utopian
Atlantis and eventually to the Euro-Christian construct of the Atlantic as
an international means of worldly, wordy, and certainly worthy proportions

for the right voyagers. Thus, the history of Columbus's voyages and the history of the Oçéano Sea (or Atlantic) become intertwined and highly dependent on the notion of prophecy—not to mention classical and scriptural destinies, African mediation, and the world's border-spaces.

Atlantis had appeared and disappeared during Greece's classical period as a mid-continental landmass "bridging" Europe to Africa and Asia (plus onward to India). To what degree the bridge was actual, symbolic, or mercantile, we shall never know. Legend places Atlantis somewhere in the Mediterranean (Midland Sea), which the Europeans considered their *Mare Nostrum (Our Sea)*. Under the name Atlantic, the utopic land-bridge was eventually pushed beyond the pillars of Hercules, the Atlas Mountains, or the titanic Atlas holding up the sky or the entire globe of the world. For all intents and purposes Atlantic exploration helped redefine the confines of the European world in terms that are eminently attached to classical prediction concerning the fate of the site of Selfhood in the hands of the impending commercial and exotic need (India among other Asian lands) and the digestive, cultural, faithful, and fatal menace of Otherness. The issue of attraction and repulsion closely followed, including the experimental extremes: as the most desirable and the deadliest of sites, both appraisals were unavoidably linked to one another. The ensuing sense of doom and redemption of the American hell and paradise further engaged African mediation, the world's border-spaces, and scriptural prophecy.

I have counted in the making of the Atlantic, by way of Atlantis, at least nominal allusions that relate at once to African mediation and to the world's border-spaces. I am thinking of the pillars of Hercules at the entrance of the Mediterranean, straddling Europe and Africa, the Atlas chain of mountains in North Africa—traditionally in Spanish the border between North and sub-Saharan Africa—and, specifically the Atlas region of Lybia, presumably the scene of the Herculean Atlas's titanic deed. In fact, from Libya westward the name Atlantic, "of Atlas," was given to the ocean that lay beyond the columns of Hercules—or *Non Plus Ultra* of ancient times which led to the modern *Plus Ultra* engraved on the first transatlantic coin.[8]

Moreover, the word Atlas (from the Arabic word for "smooth") derives from the cloth on which maps were drawn in ancient times, and this is the concept related to the essential flat surface on which the world was "scripturally" projected—at least among Muslim Arabs and Christian Europeans. Finally, the Atlantic is associated with the four Atlantides, daughters of Atlas, who inhabited wondrous yet treacherous gardens on the extreme western edge of the world, where they guarded flocks, apples, or clouds against the attacks of male gods. The African-born Atlantides, unlike Eve, did not cause man to fall from grace.

I find that the appearance and disappearance of Atlantis and its Atlantic replacement also have scriptural overtones. Atlantis and the Atlantic were signs of destiny—be it good providence, bad fate, or a combination of both. From an Old Testament perspective, Atlantis was likely the scene of a worldwide deluge leading to the coming of the definitive Messiah; from the New Testament's perspective, the Atlantic would also lead to a complementary reversal of sorts: the triumph of man over waters, leading to the Second Coming of that same messiah. Just as Atlantis iconized the linkage of the world under one faith, the Atlantic promised the world under one empire—or at least a series of Euro-Christian empires. At a more religious level, the Atlantic would lead Judeo-Christian Europe with its lost flock overseas, in time for the apocalyptic end of the world which, according to millenarian predictions, was about due at the same time as the opening of transatlantic routes.

If exploration, commercial ventures, and the Crusades into Africa and Asia had not been able to secure the transport of the world of Christ to the infidels, perhaps Christopher Columbus might facilitate Europe's last chance for global outreach before the End and the New Beginning. Illusory as such mediators and proposals might be, they made Europeans hope for, as well as justify, the prophetic destiny of the messianic desires to converge in America and serve as the New World that would provide the Old World with an antidote to the apocalyptic millenarianism that threatened to annihilate the globe. This junction benefits Caribbean itinerants, such as Columbus in his fated voyage and his prophetic sisters in their own.

Columbus nominally and scripturally embraced the prophetic Atlantic course as a strategy of Self-justification vis à vis overseas Others that lies at the core of transatlantic discourse. Early on in his quest he "reassigned" himself the first name *Christo ferens* (Christ's bearer), hopefully counteracting the more auspicious connection of his Hispanicized last name, Colón, to the term "colonial." In the text in question, *El Libro de las profecías,* Columbus encounters a messianic personification of his prophetic destiny in the voice of Christ speaking directly to him. Such scriptural impersonations alternate with less orthodox ones, particularly references to womanly messengers with whom the Admiral deeply empathizes. In this regard I can think of two roles that exemplify the range of Columbus's emphatic impersonation.

In the Second Voyage Columbus finds a Caribbean child carrying arrows, while looking and acting part lonesome American Cupid and part budding American cowboy, to whom he sends "a woman that had come here from Castile," to raise him properly (Varela/Gil, 238). This anonymous Castilian woman (presumably white) should be able to transform the innocent angel of love into a good Spanish Christian, rather than a free-wheeling devil of eroticism. In contrast with the Spanish woman adopting a Caribbean charge, the episode from the Third Voyage, which I have come to know as "the floating breast," shows Columbus adopting at the edge of the Caribbean an American Mother:

> I began to think out the shape of the world, and arrived at the conclusion that it was not round as it had been written, but in the shape of a very roundish pear, except where the pear had its nipple, which is elevated, or like having a ball but instead of being round it would be like a woman's breast, whose nipple will be higher and closer to heaven, beneath the equinoxial line in this Ocean sea at the end of the orient (calling orient the place were all land and islands end). (Varela/Gil, 377)

This prophetic woman reduced to a heaven-pointing nipple, carved on the northern Caribbean coasts of South America, inspires the voyager to reshape the globe, and thus his own reading of a destiny that is—and should definitely remain—in his hands. This episode comes closer than any other of this time and space to suggest America herself as a prophetess offering intellectual direction as well as sexual freedom that cannot be found anywhere else. The sexy yet nurturing breast of the Caribbean profile acts as a virtually unscribable sign of transatlantic discourse that prophetically insinuates itself to the mouth of a great river (likely the Orinoco), to Columbus's itinerant imagination, and to the world's destiny. The severed breast is also a sign of Amazonian proportions, as befitting the female challenge at the core of the Caribbean.

It does not surprise me that between the passage of "the floating breast" and a similar one that follows—confirming the utopic nature of Columbus's self-assigned task of climbing the nipple of the world's pear—the chronicler transfers the notion of Paradise from "The sources of the Nile in Ethiopia" to the Caribbean (Varela/Gil, 379-381). Once again the notion of African border-spaces, scriptural predictions, women's means, and Columbus' ends, converge in the interpretation of prophetic sites of transatlantic discourse.

Increasingly throughout his life, Columbus adapts his own life to suit the

Christo Ferens signature nominally declaring him as transatlantic prophet. Recounting a vision he had in his youth, the voyager addressed in the third person the issue of his destiny: "[God] caused your name [Christopher Columbus] to be wonderfully resounded through the earth . . . and gave you the keys of the gates of the ocean which are closed with strong chains" (Varela/Gil, 322-323). By the time he wrote this passage in a letter to King Ferdinand and Queen Isabella describing his Fourth Voyage, he desperately needed to reconcile not just his discoveries but himself with a fated Hispano-Christian tradition that legally and ecclesiastically disputed his role in the transatlantic affair. No wonder Columbus imbues several of his mature writings with scenes in which Christ himself speaks to him, particularly during his last transatlantic trip.[9] Even his own son Ferdinand, who is not always complimentary toward his dead father, admitted to his being a humble Christ-like sailor who went on "publishing His [God's] name on distant seas and shores [rather than] . . . in cities and palaces."[10] There were subsequent Vatican talks of elevating Columbus to the category of saint, even while the rest of the world doubted the effects of the Columbian transatlantic balance between fate and fatality.[11]

In the midst of all of these live and posthumous evidences concerning Columbus's fated and fatal destiny, I find the most revealing to be his own last gesture. The old man weaves both apocalyptic fatalism and prophetic redemptionism into his life and that of his followers by arranging for the communal effort titled *Libro de las profecías*.[12] This work is a compendium of "classically" Euro-Christian scriptures on apocalyptic millenarianism and messianic prophecy, commentaries by Christians and non-Christians alike, and the author's own views as well as accomplishments on the subject. The book itself is written as the world's—or at least Columbus's—last chance against the end of the world, a fact that is rhetorically enacted in the text.

The *Libro* becomes increasingly cryptic and climaxes in a fragmentary sequence of biblical citings—mostly from the Book of Revelations. This sequence eventually leads to schematic references from New Statement sources—which readers presumably would search in order to compose their own personal narratives guided by the apparatus that frames Columbus's imaging. After this scattering of textual seeds, we finally encounter the voice of Columbus, as the poet of messianic prophecy, born out of necessity from the text itself, the critical redeemer of transatlantic discourse.

Like the Euro-Christian climate at the time, Americans themselves tended to prefer compromise to collapse of the Atlantic human, cultural, and geographic space. The Caribbean attitude in question was rather one of respect toward receptivity and fate capable not only of consoling them as conquered people but of guaranteeing their survival under siege and within the necessary compromises with the conquerors. Their strategy also included improving their success rate in negotiating transatlantic contracts. Above all, by expecting the arrival of Euro-Christians from overseas, Americans set their own course in assimilating those intent on assimilating them.[13]

For all the above-mentioned reasons, peoples of the Atlantic and beyond saw fit to process their destinies in a common course through means ranging from transnational intercourse to transcendental discourse. And in this form of processing, the notion of a Western bias is counteracted by the impact of border spaces and border crossers with deep ties with Africa and beyond, as well as by biblical predictions and predictors with deep ties to the Middle East and beyond. In all regards, Afro-Hispanic prophetesses emerge as model performers of transatlantic destiny rivaling Columbus's own existential impersonations. Above and beyond Columbus's feat, desire, and acknowledgment, his sisters in destiny are the ultimate border crossers and challengers of border spaces. They adopt and adapt libidinal practices at which Columbus could merely hint. They might not be as frankly committed to biblical quoting, but their animistic soothsaying comes in handy in their own work as well as that of post-Columbian males, such as Núñez Cabeza de Vaca.

3. Castaway Prophecy

After my African-American friend left the chaise lounge next to mine, another foreigner joined me at the edge of the hot Dominican pool. He was not very interested in talking. Eventually I realized that his basic needs were sated at a nearby hotel, the Colón, where he lodged as part of his sex tour of the Caribbean. "I take it as a people-to-people exchange," said he after my stated objections, with a self-serving tone of well-rehearsed sincerity to his witnessing voice.

A Cuban family bottled up their Castro anxieties and threw them to the waves—just as Columbus had done upon returning from the first voyage; and just as one does during the feast of Yemayá, Yoruba-American goddess (potencia) of waters. In both cases the sea was fierce, but so was the will of the scriptural vessels. A month later, a letter arrives from California. A school had intercepted the bottled Cuban message and offered to sponsor the ship-

*wrecked family's United States exile. Miraculously, the family had
already begun to learn English.*
> —From news read during 1996 in Miami's
> *El Diario de las Américas.*

The very title *Naufragios* proposes Cabeza de Vaca's novelized chronicle of
his experience of conquests, shipwrecks, captivities, and rescues as a text
bound to exhibit forced and/or willful bouts of cooperation with the Others, both residents of and willfully or forced travelers to the Caribbean area.
Written between 1527 and 1542—date of the first edition—and finally
revised for the definitive authorial publication of 1555, *Castaways* presents an
author, who is also protagonist and narrator, tightly bound to the values of the
Others, if only for his own survival as a human being, as well as to vouch for
the record of his transatlantic deed. Moreover, the chronicle of these "shipwrecks" allowed Cabeza de Vaca to exonerate himself from any shame that
might be associated with perceived deficiencies as a colonizer or conqueror.

Cabeza de Vaca is neither the official chronicler nor the head of the
expedition, but eventually becomes a bit of both, as other records and leadership are lost or lacking. These voyagers do not become "castaways" in the
Caribbean hinterlands because of shipwrecks, of which they suffered
many. The adventurers are prompted to plunge inward by a mixed bag of
motivations, circumstances, and opportunities that both forced and freed
the group to take certain chances beyond the norm. The author summarizes his fate with laconic fatalism: "And such was the land to which, for
our sins, we had come . . ." (29). The American land and the Spanish souls
were not much to speak of, and yet, for the sake of the in-depth exploration, these issues provided as good an excuse as any.

Castaways begins with Cabeza de Vaca acting as treasurer and judicial
officer *(alguacil)* of the expedition who starts taking on new responsibilities
as other authorities begin to fail, particularly Pánfilo de Nárvaez and the
anonymous scribe—both of whom ostensibly follow Euro-Christian codes
and Spanish mandates. As character, author, narrator, and self-made authority, Cabeza de Vaca makes sure that we doubt all other sources of authority—with the exception of the itinerant prophetess who comes later on in
the text. Even in that case, her belated appearance might seem to belittle
her importance, as if a last chance or afterthought. Other authorities are
treated to far more cutting forms of belittling.

For instance, Nárvaez appears unreasonably obsessed with the idea of
proceeding inland, pretending to have his men's backing. Moreover, Cabeza

de Vaca insists on calling him Governor, alluding to Narváez's previous post in Cuba or to his future post in the territory to be settled. The text circumvents Narváez' actual role in the expedition and, thus, his leadership, as it were, is put on hold. The author does as much with the scribe, whom he not only leaves anonymous but transforms into Narváez's infelicitous lackey. The scribe even serves Cabeza de Vaca as amanuensis for his complaints against Narváez, and ostensibly as an unacknowledged source from whom to borrow material for the *Castaways*. As far as the fated destiny of the expedition is concerned, neither Narváez nor Cabeza de Vaca—and much less the scribe—come close to setting the course of conquest or, for that matter, achieve independence of action. On the contrary, they weave in and out of each others' means and ends, converging and diverging, so as to create the polyphonic fabric of transatlantic discourse.

No matter how tenuous the sense of authority achieved by Cabeza de Vaca or any other men, a veiled self-apologetic yet self-serving, first-person singular form of address predominates in the book. Only the last chapter is written in the first-person plural and ostensibly from the "neutral" and "communal" perspective of an authorizing apparatus. When the perspective abruptly shifts, Cabeza de Vaca seems to abandon the tentative role of "replacement author in charge." He becomes instead a guest character, one of the four "survivors" alluded to as well as included in a collective form of address that I assume to be the voice of the transatlantic recording system itself. Other improbable voices included/alluded to are those of Pánfilo de Narváez, who has been long dead, and La Mora de Hornachos, who does not quite speak, and if she exists at all, she is in faraway Spain at the time.

Both the self-serving author and the mastercode-serving text flirt with a plethora of official and unofficial Others and, above them all, with a pervasive sense of fate. In fact, officially speaking, the narrative centers on precisely such a fated space, the Isla de Malhado (Isle of Ill Fortune—today Galveston Island in the Gulf of Mexico, at the edge of the Caribbean). This site appears approximately in the middle of the text and is the scene of Pánfilo de Narváez's death. The vessel in which the leader of the expedition was attempting to get back on course—and which had been improvised by a team of castaway Spaniards and hosting Indians—overturned. It drowned him, the friars, and possibly also the scribe who is never heard of again. Meanwhile, Cabeza de Vaca is aboard another improvised vessel, which merely sank, sparing his life. In command of the rest of the vessels, the official ones ostensibly left behind, are the beta males and the anonymous females. At the end of the text we find out that this whole misadventure had been predicted by La Mora, the Afro-Hispanic "oracle" who had organized the "stranded" women according to their own sense of identity, and indeed saved them from the men's failures. Consequently, at least unofficially speaking, La Mora de Hornachos is at the temporal and motivational center of the narrative, while the Isle of Ill Fortune remains the spatial center, or the vortex of transatlantic disgrace.

Whether La Mora leads us to and back from that ill-fated island symbolically or factually—that is, in real or narrative time and space—or viceversa, that the Isle inspires La Mora's leadership or the author's reverie on the subject, we shall never know. I perceive a rhetorical parallelism between the space that marks the writer's transatlantic center and the timing that marks the Afro-Hispanic prophetesses' central reading of that destiny. At any rate, I felt compelled to reread *Castaways* from the spatial and temporal viewpoints. That is, after finishing the book, I returned to Malhado guided by *Castaways* and Mora, reminded that the authority of Narváez and the scribe, which had been taken over by Cabeza de Vaca, is now under the auspices of a communal authority guided by a group of itinerant prophetesses that enact the word of an Afro-Hispanic oracle.

The entire island adventure that follows Malhado might be a mere figment of the Mora's prediction of Alvar's imaginative conditions. There are reasons to support both "rereadings": Mora allegedly predicts that most men would perish in their inland plunge, and Alvar's first text of the narrative ended in Malhado. Presumably from that island onward, it is up to us readers to trust La Mora's factual directions or Alvar's fictional intentions in order to survive the catastrophic Caribbean adventure. No official authorities or authors are watching over our shoulders as we improvise ways and means of travel, survival, and even success, in what appears (if only in name alone) to be a forbidden rhetorical site caught between worlds, words, fate, and fatality.

The same deceiving mix of temporal and spatial reading choices emerges in the realm of transportation. Ostensibly, deep-sea navigation is the macho's forte; the shoreline is the realm of the scribe, the friars, the traveling women, and tentatively Cabeza de Vaca; while the hinterlands are the castaways' terra incognita in Indian hands. However, all of these agents are prone to infringe upon each other's territories. For example, throughout *Castaways* Spanish men of the high seas get the urge to settle on the coast or plunge inward to conquer it. Likewise, American men who inhabit the coast or depend on it are forced by Spaniards to go inland, while inland Americans take over the stranded Spaniards who invade their hinterlands. Finally, home-hugging women drawn to the coast or to margins are forced to move wherever the men take them; they also travel by other means.

Although this situation is eventually tentatively systematized by La Flota's route, there is no such system at the time of the action. Prophetic mediators such as La Mora de Hornachos, indirectly through texts that are not theirs, become active participants in forging alternatively transatlantic systems of communication—and the type of course, recourse, and intercourse—that we have come to associate with transatlantic discourse. La Mora, like other transatlantic prophetesses, is adept in unconventional forms of transportation, perhaps by transmutation, flights of fancy, or actual flight that bypass all of the other narrative and actual itineraries. She could also be Alvar's transatlantic alter ego—the kind of woman Columbus's needs carved from the Caribbean coasts.

Questions of manliness assail both Alvar and Columbus throughout his trips. Indeed, manliness becomes associated with taking chances at the edge of the status quo and mastercode and on behalf of a fate and fatality sailors conventionally attached to womanly forces. Thus what began as a question of voyaging choices ends up tainted with gender codings and sexual performances. Transatlantic discourse tends to blur all of these boundaries, but not without considerable pain and resistance.

For instance, early on in the text, navigating off the coast of Cuba, Cabeza de Vaca observes the ominous signs of an impending tempest, and reluctantly opts to abandon ship, advising others to do likewise and to proceed to the island without loosing sight of the boats and the coast. The phenomenon in question occurs "naturally" enough in the Caribbean, but the Spanish reaction is not quite so natural. The improvised leader and his advisees survived on dry land by holding onto each other in silence while listening to the voices and percussive music of unseen Indians. We shall never know whether these Indians "supernaturally" provoked and/or swayed the forces of destiny and of nature, or whether Cabeza de Vaca only thought so. Perhaps Spaniards "unnaturally" longed to join the Indian fiesta, but instead held to each other in quiet expectation of the worst.

The climax to the passage comes about through the post-factum reading of transatlantic signs. The author finds "a ship's boat up in some trees" as the group recovers from the effects of the tempest (9). Not just Spaniards but an official Spanish vessel has been pushed out of line. Is this natural, supernatural, or unnatural? Is this a transgendered, transcendental, or merely transnational approach to the Euro-Christian interpretation of their Caribbean cruise? The point is that the tempest in question, presently known as a hurricane—from the Arawak goddess of winds—was likely read as an ominous sign of the upcoming deluge, a topsy-turvy time for all human matters. Anticipation of the worst not only puts the Euro-Christian crew helplessly in the hands of Caribbean powers, but also unleashes their own repressed desires. The group's reaction, as represented by Alvar, speaks—or should I say refrains from speaking?—about such a helpless sense of new-found freedom: "íbamos mudos y sin lengua," literally "we traveled mute and without tongue"—that is, without a proper language to express themselves or to communicate with Others. The itinerant Selves had not a clear way of voicing destiny, or of interpreting their desires and needs to themselves or to Others.

Unlike the men, the women on board would have likely been fully prepared to engage in transatlantic discourse, if only they would have been allowed to. As mentioned, the women have known since before leaving Spain about the negative outcome of the white men's American plunges. This is most evident when Narváez, rather than Cabeza de Vaca, is the one deciding to go inland and, unlike the author, losing sight of the boats and the coast. Practically every man agrees with their official leader:

> everyone who was there thought that this was the best thing to do, except for the scribe, who said that rather than leave the ships unprotected they ought to be left in a known and safe harbor, in a place that was populated: that once this had been done the governor could march inland and do whatever seemed best to him. (15)

If the women behind the scenes are not acknowledged at the time, the anonymous scribe and, in turn, Cabeza de Vaca, impersonate, take over, and take temporary credit for the women's prediction. As record-keepers, the scribe, his male substitute, and female counterpart remain fully aware of transatlantic lines that should not be violated, namely the safe-haven provided by the Spanish boats, the Caribbean coast, and the group's setting—or nesting—instinct at the edge of the Atlantic. And yet, at Narváez's insistence, Cabeza de Vaca has to take rhetorical command:

> The governor followed his own inclinations and the advice of the others; seeing his determination, I adjured him in Your Majesty's name not to leave the ships unless they were in a harbor and safe, and requested it in writing through the scribe that we had with us. (15)

The author may side subliminally with the scribe and with La Mora, but does so factually with the Crown. Moreover, if the governor acted out the manly conquering instinct, the author acted out, on the one hand, the womanly art of persuasion and, on the other hand, the transgendered act of recording the transatlantic contract. Cabeza de Vaca emerges from this passage as both dictated to and dictator.

Finally, in order to justify his position, the Governor not only seeks to represent the official voice of the stranded males ("the opinion of the majority of the other officers and the commissary"), but in so doing questions Cabeza de Vaca's wherewithal ("I had no right to make these demands on him") and commands the scribe to manufacture some lame reason for the inland plunge:

> he asked the scribe to write in the record that, because there were not sufficient food supplies in that place to establish a colony, nor a harbor for the ships, he was breaking up the settlement that he had established there and going to look for a better harbor and better land. (15)

Furthermore, in what I consider a poignant show of infantile machismo, Narváez "effeminizes" those who oppose his plan, Cabeza de Vaca in particular: "he told me that because I had made so much trouble and feared going inland, I should stay and take charge of the ships and the crews who remained in them, and set up a settlement *(poblar)* if I arrived before him. I refused to do this" (16). Narváez's ploy to shame Cabeza de Vaca into following his order backfires. Instead it officially transforms the treasurer and legal officer into leader and scribe, but not without hitches.

Cabeza de Vaca states that the majority would have thought that he "had stayed behind out of fear" and consequently his "honor would be impugned." He preferred to risk his "life rather than place my honor in that position" (16). Out of what seems to be an excessive if cynical preoccupation with appearances and honor—or illusory sideshow of machismo (but secretly, for he had little choice as an underling)—Cabeza de Vaca joins the march of the hard-headed males.

4. Caribbean Family Romance

> *Typical male behavior: they could not ask for directions, much less from some women.*
> —Heather Finlay, ex-Cornellian from California who specializes in the lesbian undertones of Renaissance witches, and with whom I chatted about this paper.

There is justice in the fact that the work of an author who, even if for strategic reasons, has repressed acknowledging inspiring women, ends with a chapter in which the plural narrative format rescues the voice of such women. For the record:

> After our departure the three ships—for the other had already been lost off the rugged coast—were in great danger, and nearly a hundred persons staying in them with few provisions. Among them were ten married women, and one of them told the governor many things that happened to him on the voyage before they occurred; and when he was preparing to explore the country she told him not to do so, for she believed that neither he nor any who went with him would ever leave that land, and if someone did escape it would be because God would do mighty miracles for him; but she believed that few would escape or none. (125)

The itinerant gang of Others who ostensibly stayed behind ends by gaining the subliminal recognition of having been always ahead. Penless and penisless leaders find their own way to fulfill their destiny. And, in the long run, the author had to survive as best he could, and bend the rules, in order to lend pen and penis to an adventure that the women would have spared him.

Pánfilo de Narváez is not quite as accommodating as Cabeza de Vaca in accepting the women's partnering of destiny. The Spanish Governor of Cuba literally comes back from the dead in *Castaways'* last chapter in order to explain to the readers of the text how he blocked the women's way. To that effect:

> he beseeched her to tell him about the things she had said, past and present: who had told them to her? She answered and said that a Moorish woman of Hornachos had told it to her in Castile, that she had reported it to us before we left Castile, the whole voyage had happened just as she had told us. (125-126)

Hispanic women in the Caribbean organize under a leader who becomes the transatlantic vessel for the messianic advice of a virtually anonymous African prophetess. The whole female system avoids relying on the stubborn tyranny of self-sufficiency, male bravado, and mastercodes. But as we have mentioned earlier, the mechanics of the libido and those of messianic prophecy go hand in hand, particularly as they connect to women's desires to become means and mediums of destiny.

The communal text or the actual author, acting as spokesperson for the rescued males, adds a sexual twist to female fate:

> At the time when all of them gathered in the ships, they say that people who
> were there saw and heard that woman saying very clearly to the other
> woman that because their husbands were going to explore the interior and
> were placing their persons in such peril, they should by no manner or means
> count on them, and that they should look for the men they were going to
> marry, because that was what she was going to do; and so it was done, for she
> and the others either married or served as concubines for those who
> remained on the ships. (126)

If kept hidden as masters of the Atlantic, at least the voyaging women
refuse to become merely the men's mistresses once in the Caribbean. The
males having abandoned these women to their own destiny, the female
crew decided to settle in and mated at will with their cowardly guardians.
Women justify their rhetorical silence and their erotic freedom according
to unofficial prophecy and even official marriage.

There could also be a further justification of these women's taking sexual freedoms under separate circumstances: procreation (sometimes
euphemistically referred in transatlantic colonial terms as "to settle"—
poblar) might be a sensible tool of survival for the stranded group. At the
same time, women might also "settle" men's homosexual panics or break
up and render "fertile" the dead-end male bonding that prevails among the
warring cultures of both the Spaniards and the Indians.

At a time in which miscegenation was not officially considered as the
right imperial choice, exogamy with the natives was out of the question.
Adversity and destiny back up the fellow women travelers' decision to mate
with fellow Spaniards—their husbands'"brothers in arms," as it were. In this
instance Cabeza de Vaca would excuse symbolic or legalistic incest. The
multicultural message of *Castaways* becomes clearer as we compare the
Hispanic women's attitude to that of their Indian sisters. The author could
have had the notion of comparative mores and international politics of
mating in mind, as this becomes evident elsewhere in the text.

Whereas, according to Cabeza de Vaca, certain Spanish women chose to
mate with the presumed weaker and only available males left behind, this
behavioral choice contrasts with Esquivel's version of the behavior of
Indian females—told by the Indian captors to Dorantes and transcribed by
Cabeza de Vaca in his text. This third-hand account refers to certain Indian
men mating the ostensibly weaker females of an enemy group with whom
they had established a system of mercantile exchange of wives. Or, to put
the situation in terms of the Indian women, they mate the presumed
stronger and only available males who are able to buy them. This type of

arranged "marriage" insures some Indian women relative independence from erotic or ethical commitments to a specific group. Heterosexual men remain much more indebted to traditional erotic and ethical demands:

> We asked them [the Mareames], why did they not marry with themselves and also among themselves? They said that to marry women to their kinfolk was a bad thing [*cosa fea*], and it was much better to kill them than to give them to their own kin or to their enemies; and both they and their neighbors the Yguazes have this custom, but only they, for none of the other tribes in the land practice it. (60)

There is hardly any difference between this native practice and the lingering European exchange of dowries between the families of the bride and groom, except that in the case of the natives it is the groom who buys the bride from a designated outside source—as is still the case in the business of male-order brides. The traditional American transaction leads the way in terms of the telling nature of the currencies of exchange. "And when these Indians want to marry they buy wives from their enemies, and the price each man gives for his wife is a bow, the best that can be procured, with two arrows, and if perchance he does not own a bow, a fishing net two cubits wide and one long" (60).

The wife, the warring, hunting, and fishing equipment, as well as the dowry or payment to a mating agency are all male-centered means to insure the balance of powers. Not surprisingly, Malhado Indians (otherwise known as Mareames) trade bows and arrows or nets for wives, that is, instruments of aggression and nutrition for parallel instruments of biological survival. The choice of mate, or for that matter the prevention of incest, is not a matter of love and ethics, but rather of the need to preserve a heritage through the purchase of spousal allegiance.

In comparison with the Indian ways with miscegenation, Spanish adaptation to the same American circumstances, including cannibalism, seems rather extreme. At one point the chronicler cynically comments as to how:

> five Christians who were encamped on the beach came to such straits that they ate one another until only one was left, who survived because there was no one left to eat him. (46)

In contrast with the Mareames' ingenious ways of preserving their heritage, the Spaniards appear as rather inept; they eat each other out of existence. The Malhado site in which this event occurs nominally iconizes the

Spanish mishandling of their heritage. Worse yet, the mishandling jumps from a matter of desperate need to one of systematic preservation of human food. A Christian learned how to preserve human flesh and survive by eating it (58).

In spite of the fatal Spanish mishandling, Malhado is still a fated site. It becomes a virtual transatlantic utopia, one that works only for insiders, those who are "born," or intuitively drawn, to it. The two cultures who live on the island are big, beautiful, peaceful people and, even though they have warring equipment, men do not use it against each other, but rather on themselves—in a ritual piercing of their breasts, which presumably shows their manly valor. The woman, instead, suckle their children virtually into puberty. Couples are monogamous, joyful, classless, and loving of each other and their children. They easily express their emotions, crying in public to show vulnerability to their fellow humans. They are charitable and share property. There is among them an open choice between hetero- and homosexuality.

As members in a matriarchal society the males of the Mareames have more ritual restrictions than females, while females carry the burden of the work and presumably also the responsibility for government and certainly for peace—only women know how to control men's occasional temper tantrums. Even cannibalism among them is actually symbolic: drinking the diluted dust of ancestral bones. They would rather die of hunger than eat what or when they are not supposed to eat. Together, Spaniards and Indians improvise their own hybrid version of life as lived in transatlantic ships, one that, as already mentioned, eventually kills Narváez and his men while saving Cabeza de Vaca and his men. This is a matter of destiny, but also, I suspect, of the flexibility of our hero and company to handle hybrid vessels. Should we consider as part of the Spaniards' mishandling of their heritage the fact that they built inept ships? Should the demise of the ships be considered as sabotage by the Mareames who worked on the project?

In spite of the success of the group of Spaniards in accommodating to the island circumstances—including their enticing, if fatal, decision to engage Indians to help them build a boat to move on—the transgressors find themselves in a sociocultural dilemma. The surviving Spaniards have to learn to cure the very ills they have imported. To that effect, the islanders invest the Spaniards with the role of *físicos,* a mixture of medicine man, magician, witch, physician, and psychiatrist, but also as factotum mediators: capable of making real, physical, or possible. In short, Spaniards provide both the source and the cure of alien ailments. The role also achieves certain transgendered quality, as befitting men who invoke bigendered or sexually-neutral deities and cure patients of both sexes. *Físicos* finally achieve a transcendental stage; upon death they are burned, rather than buried, and their charred bones transformed into powder that they feed to the community in a watery drink.

Perhaps more important for our present purposes, *físicos* become transnational and transcendental beings. Spanish practitioners gain freedom beyond the national and religious boundaries of the American as well as the European worlds—something that only women are allowed in either of these clusters of cultures. For instance, the newly minted professionals combine Catholic and Animist practices with a good dosage of self-serving wishful thinking: "The way in which we cured was by making the sign of the cross over them and blowing on them and reciting a Pater Noster and an Ave Maria; and then we prayed as best we could to God Our Lord to give them health and inspire them to give us a good treatment" (49).

In the end Spaniards, feeling trapped and compromised, plan their escape from the island of Malhado, taking the opportunity that the islanders have gone inland to feed on wild tunas that, in season, they traditionally consume alongside other groups, which the text visits before and after Malhado. It would seem indeed that the Spanish group came in contact with the Malhado culture during one such season; and during another season they escape this culture to join the next, and so on. The first moment of freedom amidst the tunas was likely possible because the Spaniards had begun to be trusted in their new hypocratical, if also hypocritical, oath to their patient group.

There is further significance to this transgendered, transnational, and transcendental male-bonding ritual built around the consumption of wild fruit. If nothing else, the ritual serves Cabeza de Vaca as a comparative perspective from which to give his amateur anthropological assessment of the cultures visited. Such a classificatory strategy suits well a chronicler well-versed in the Hispano-Christian policy of finding a place for all their charges and challenges found in the course of transatlantic voyages and recorded in transatlantic discourse.

5. Life Beyond Ill Fortune

The cultures found before the ill-fated Malhado season correspond to today's Florida and the coastal areas west of the peninsula. Spaniards share with these peoples a bucolic, if precarious, understanding as the newcomers become objects of the Indians' pity. Furthermore, the inhabitants of the area in question seem ready to assimilate the Spaniards, or at least their "currency" of exchange, from the most emotionally charged—crying for and with them—to the most artificially charged—cherishing the trinkets introduced by the newcomers. Needless to say, before the Malhado experience, Cabeza de Vaca's experiences or memories remain rather vague.

The cultures found after Malhado are largely organized as variants of that of the Mareames from the Isle of Malhado, living in what is today the coastal areas of the Southwestern territory of the United States. Spaniards find these peoples either threatening or appealing, depending on what version of the captivity we take into consideration: Baltasar Dorantes de Carranza's version as reported by Cabeza de Vaca or Cabeza de Vaca's own. But, no matter which version we chose to privilege, the Spaniards become objects of piety or opportunistic and pitiful merchants of Indian symbols.

Dorantes' version of the culture of the Mareames is of a warring, paternalistic society that is compulsively heterosexual and misogynous: treating men as partners in war and women as merchandise for peace. The Mareames people do not treat their offspring any better: some sons might be killed as predicted by dreams, while all daughters are fed to the dogs. They sell the children of others. Men divorce their wives by merely signaling it with an amulet—the *figa,* a sexualized allusion to a female version of *figo, higo* (fig), which is still in use, as *fica,* in Portuguese and Italian. Members of the culture in question are not particularly big, but rather handsome—ostensibly improving their looks by piercing their breasts and lips. They are hunter-gatherers but ill prepared for both activities. Out of desperation they are omnivorous, feeding even on feces and stones—if they could find the latter in the deserts they inhabit.

Whatever the people of this culture cannot digest as is, they pulverize for consumption. Only when *tunas* (which the text says are like "figs") are plentiful do they cease to be hungry and become relatively happy. Their occasional joy is marred by the seasonal invasion of mosquitoes, whose bloodsucking habits make this otherwise hungry and beautiful people look like swollen "lepers." Besides the plague of mosquitoes, the rare times of plenty are also marred by inadvertent show of emotion and rampant sexual aggression—is it the result of the figlike *tuna* or "forbidden" fruit? The smoke they continuously produce in order to get rid of mosquitoes makes people cry, and this justifies the Spanish captives' taking refuge in the coastal areas away from their captors' smoke. Spaniards actually use the smoke as a smokescreen. The fig-eating orgy may very well have libidinal connotation—a festival of freedom of sorts. While satisfying themselves orally in their male-bonding rituals, Indians also make sexual demands of their women. This scene reminds me of the once-a-year procreative ritual endorsed by Amazons and cannibals. At such times in *Castaways* there is fighting over women (the best?) in another example of the Darwinian "survival of the fittest" that hovers over the entire text. Finally, I wonder whether the fig-ritual gives a window of opportunity for Spanish escape because of the licentious character and the Indians' orgiastic and/or transcendental self-absorption rather than due to a mere question of smoke inhalations or other equally fanciful smokescreens.

In his own version of the culture of the Mareames, Cabeza de Vaca refers to this group by sexually evocative names, which appear nowhere else in the history of North American Indian cultures. The names include: Susolas, Yguaces, Acubadaos, Atayos, Avavares, Mendicas, Quitoles, Comos, Quevenes, Camoles, and Maliacones. Anyone willing to stretch Spanish morphology would detect composite words that signal a propensity to, among other things: softness/aloneness, sameness/equality, cowardice/cupidity, attachment/service, avarice/silliness, begging/proselytism, stealing/defeatism, gluttony/mimicry, bedality/heaviness, readiness/complacency, and mischievousness/queerness. At any rate, the text suggests the incidence of at least some of these behavioral patterns among the peoples of the Caribbean periphery. I do not quite know how to interpret the classification of this culture as a Fig People, unless it is a veiled allusion to the ubiquitous "forbidden fruit."

The text is explicit about two salient characteristics of the post-Malhado Mareames. They all exhibit partial or total blindness and are tolerant or embracing of homosexuality—respectively in the group in general and in the Fig People in particular. Could we combine these two notions in one and think of these men as able to build a smokescreen from behind which to blindly "succumb" to homosexuality? I assume that this double sign about human perception and erotic pairing makes sense as a common indicator of how a people, or a people's castaways, handle judging Others: he "turns a blind eye," as it were, toward issues of sexual tolerance and/or smokes up the hot issue. At the core of the explanation is the chapter entitled "Of the Tribes and Their Languages," in which the witness points out that:

> During the time that I was with them [Indians in general, some Indians, the Mareames, the Fig People among the Mareames?] I saw a devilish thing, and it was that I saw a man married to another man, and these are the effeminates [*amarionados*] and impotent and go about covered like women and do the work of women and do not shoot arrows, and carry heavy loads; and among these folk we saw many of them who were thus effeminate [*amarionados*], as I have said, and they are heavier [*membrudos*] and taller than the other men; they can bear extremely heavy loads. (85)

In spite of the adjectivization of homosexuality as "devilish," this passage is extremely nonjudgmental. The witness seems more interested in the impact of such a practice on the future of society than in questions of aesthetics and ethics. There are no overt negative effects from the legalization of male homosexuality on the rate of procreation—as there is still a heterosexual contingent. Besides, there seems to be a positive effect on other forms of "productivity," as the strongest males and most females are still busy at work. There are also unexpected transgendered challenges to aesthetics, as the males in question do not all take womanly roles, marrying others who presumably "look"—if not necessarily "act"—in traditionally masculine ways. In fact, those who take womanly work roles are defined as "heavier" and "taller" than most men and substitute, or take their rightful place alongside, women in the workforce. Furthermore the original qualifier of these men as *membrudos,* literally "big membered," may lend itself to genital implications that also defy the "feminization" of queer male behavior. Finally, God only knows how Cabeza de Vaca found out or assumed that the effeminate Indians were impotent. Perhaps there is a built-in form of birth control in this sexually permissive society.

In short, the text virtually forces its readers to consider at length, and as a fairly natural deviation from the norm, a transnational and transgendered view of human nature that is legally and emotionally accepted by the society at large. The assimilated "difference" also affects language, at least that of the Fig Men who "call to other men by saying 'Look here, hurry here,' and to dogs they say 'Ho'" (84). Queer or not, the very language of the society of males retains, or exacerbates, the patriarchal ways of compulsive heterosexuality. Words, classifications, and forms of address divide people between masters, on the one had, and servants, slaves, or "dogs," on the other. Dog and bitch *(perro* and *perra)* have connoted since that time "deviants," prone to be penetrated, likely at a price.

Women in this group remain very much on the periphery, relegated to being beasts of burden, virtual sex puppets, procreating and feeding machines. Incidentally, men's heterosexual behavior is connected with heavy smoking and drinking, ostensibly for the sake of bolstering their desire for women. Yet, there is a curious dependency of men upon women: boys literally remain mama's boys, breast-fed, until they can fend for, or feed by, themselves. Perhaps symbolically even more misogynous than either female servility and male reliance on it, is the fact that the men assume the responsibility to decide what is best for women, particularly in light of their diet. The text even discusses how men control women's water intake—ostensibly to conserve water, a precious commodity in this desert climate.

The savage and paternalistic habits of the heterosexually compulsive tribe of one version raise their ugly head within the otherwise civilized and bisexual interpretation of the same tribe favored by the author. This might inspire other readers, like myself, to be more openly critical and motivated to develop gender-equitable heterosexual and homosexual alternatives to those listed as part of the Hispano-American colonial environment. For all the above-mentioned reasons, the women's reading of destiny, inscription of social ways, and proclamation of freedom under the remote control of La Mora de Hornachos emerges as the best alternative.

The gender roles and sexual practices among the Mareames and their "tentatively engendered" behavioral variations have a further effect on the discourse of messianic prophecy. Indians appear destined to a social behavior commensurate with their "reading" of the reigning deity Mala Cosa, or Evil Thing, who, in spite of its ominous name or because of it, challenges its believers with the relativity of maleness and femaleness, as well as good and evil. The divine persona is construed as a trickster force, a transgendered deity common to many cultures—particularly many of the African ones imported and fusing into the Caribbean cultural arena. The ugly, hairy, and small shape of this nightcrawling, forever ambivalent, questioning, rewarding, and punishing force of nature, is a well-known figure to Caribbean children and beyond—often referred to as Coco or Boogeyman.

Whereas Indian males had their choice of following the model of Malhado or that of Mala Cosa, women fare much better in the text of *Castaways*. Our author far from relegates women to the position of embodying objects of transaction, destined to enact men's words of agreement, as well as to provide wombs to further male-determined expansion of power. Women become merchants in their own right, even though the merchandise they handle might include their own flesh and blood. Previously we have seen how the Spanish women stranded in the Caribbean use their bodies and beliefs to express their freedom—namely, they engage in the kind of sexuality that they believe is rightfully theirs. Likewise, Indian women risk their lives by trading with the enemy, but gain something in the exchange. These go-betweens make compromises with both the men of their own and of the enemy tribe, but while carrying out their assigned task, female envoys enjoy a measure of freedom and power unavailable to males:

> And so they [the Indian men] sent two, one from their tribe and another whom they were holding captive [presumably for the purpose of marriage], and they sent these because women can parley even in times of war. (98)

These women are not held responsible to a particular group, dependency, or commitment, much less to a single man. They not only supplement the fact of being traded with their becoming tradespeople par excellence, but also supplement their being "male-ordered" brides by sharing with men the right to divorce: "their marriage lasts only as long as they are happy together, and they dissolve marriages by the use of an amulet *(figa)*" (60).

Through their mastery of the policy of exchange, the women in question transform not just themselves, but also men-controlled objects of consumption, including Animist fetishes, into the province of their merchandising. They trade on icons of tribal belief, ostensibly including those related to marriage and divorce. Cabeza de Vaca's attitude toward female "tradesmanship" becomes obvious when he himself considers its benefits and actually engages in similar transactions (adding the role of merchant to his role of *físico*) in the hinterlands of America. Like many a woman before and after him, the author manipulates objects of passion and belief, as well as bodies and souls, in order to survive, compromise, commerce, make a profit, and thrive, by influencing destiny. By now castaway men had gained considerable experience in the appreciation of women—after all, at least one of them had neglected and lived to regret his nonchalant attitude toward the Spanish women's advice.

Indian women in *Castaways* influence reality through their prophetic dreams. Cabeza de Vaca illustrates this effect as: "a woman [who] had dreamed that he [a Spaniard] was going to kill her child; and the Indians went after him and killed him . . ." (60). We find a similar observation in Columbus' *Libro,* which paraphrases the Bible (Joel 2:28-32): "And it shall come to pass after this, that I will pour out my spirit upon all flesh: and your sons and your daughters shall prophesy: you old men shall dream dreams . . ." (196-97). Not unlike the dreams Columbus projected onto his Spanish, American, and Spanish-American heirs, Cabeza de Vaca zeroes in on the destiny of the Spanish and Hispanicized inhabitants of the Caribbean basin. However, whereas Columbus's view of transatlantic progeny is largely paternal and symbolic, Cabeza de Vaca's allusion to progeny is largely maternal and actual.

Male liberation is not only a by-product or recipient of female liberation, but it also occurs as a parallel, if not entirely independent, textual trend. Under precarious circumstances, such as those narrated in *Castaways,* gender liberation responds to a basic instinct or a complex strategy of survival. Both genders liberate themselves by exploiting the possibilities of the margins, the center, and points in between. As a result, the four surviving males find a transatlantic niche in the gender-ambivalent profession of *físicos* as well as in the traditionally womanly position of traders. All iconic male authorities in the text appear and disappear in crucial moments, learning along the way gender-flexibility and female-trusting as a form of survival. In total I have counted four male authorities, each of whom had an odd way of surviving. They are not necessarily the actual survivors listed in *Castaways.*

Recapitulating, Alvar is rhetorically born as a writer from the pages of the text itself. He specifically appears as an author (improvising on male failures and female knowledge) at the moment in which the prophetic path of women and the traditional path of men part ways. As we know, the author officially "disappears" as an author in the last chapter of the book and reemerges as a surviving character in the adventure failed by the Governor and rewoven by La Mora. In turn Narváez is rhetorically born as a Governor of the territory explored in *Castaways* (only) from the pages of the text itself. He begins to disappear as the leading authority from the very beginning of the narration, until he fatally sinks into the Caribbean toward the middle. In the end, he reappears as a questioning authority in an episode of questionable memory in which the Governor's authority is finally revoked and La Mora's is definitely invoked. In a sense, Narváez survives as a "bad" example in history. The scribe, rhetorically speaking the "original" or "basic" male authority in *Castaways,* is not only left anonymous but phased out—first, virtually without a job, and then existentially without an individual presence—as Cabeza de Vaca takes over the leadership from Narváez and the record from such a scribe. However, the scribe survives not only by providing "raw materials" to the author, but also as the official icon co-opted as an officious third-person plural in the last chapter. Finally, the "last" surviving male authority is Estebanico the Black, who comes closer to parallel (and likely impersonate) La Mora de Hornacho's prophetic posture as the absent female voice of the oracle. Estebanico is literally, rhetorically, and socially "the last"; he not only likely occupies the lowest official level of engagement in the expedition and in the Euro-Christian transatlantic hierarchy, but the text ends with a note on him—as we shall visit later on. Estebanico must have been a silent and blind presence in the text from the beginning, and yet he only emerges as a character during the episode of the Isle of Ill Fortune, and virtually stays in the text adopting and adapting to forms of transatlantic mediation until he nominally closes the narrative with a biographical note, part epitaph and part eulogy: "an Afro-Moorish man born in Azamor" (in Spanish-held Morocco).

By adopting and adapting to gender-pending and gender-bending professional mediations, each of the four "surviving" male authorities—which are not necessarily among the four who appear to be alive at the end of the text—engenders his own lasting authorial imprint on transatlantic discourse. The mediating abilities that determine whether or not these four authorities would existentially survive their sojourn in the Caribbean area is precisely the most gender-pending and gender-bending of professions of faith and fate. I am referring to the role of traders of faith, fate, and fetishes, but also to a generalized ability to accept differences, to test, and even to taste them. Even in such a situation there is an obliging and religiously aware sense of ethics overseeing the realm of Caribbean freedom of choice. At the core of the trading skills of the transatlantic mediators lies the iconic figure of Mala Cosa, patron/ess of all social mediation—ranging from medicine to mores. The transgendered and transcendental guiding light finds a transnational niche in Caribbean belief, at least from the perspective of either the symbolic or factual surviving castaways.

Those who decide to fight the transatlantic system invariably perish. The only one who neither opts for professional "freedom" nor a "fatal" fight is Doroteo Teodoro, perhaps not arbitrarily described as a Greek sailor and implicitly named for his god-loving attributes. I did not include him among the symbolic survivors or, for that matter, the factual ones, because he becomes irremediably lost and/or assimilated in his pathway into America's hinterland—history assumed that he joined an Indian culture. Doroteo Teodoro, the "classically" if not "divinely" classical envoy who "goes native" bears in his very name the double jumbled-up reference to his God-dependency. *Castaways,* however, is sympathetic to this iconic character; it pairs him up with Estebanico as part of the symbolic search team for a transatlantic pathway ultimately ruled by La Mora. The classical Greek approach to transatlantic destiny, and love, does not quite work, although there is a lot of both floating in the Caribbean archipelago. The classical Euro-Christian joins the Euro-Pagan, the American, and the African traditions or icons thereof in the problematic mix of transatlantic discourse.

In spite of their survival rate, mediatory qualities, and authorial importance, there is at least a hint of prejudice in the portrayal of Estebanico and for that matter of La Mora. Not only are they relegated to the margins in more than one way, but their service as go-betweens with Americans suggest the Afro-Hispanic ability to communicate and assimilate at a generic level of "savagery"—Other to Other. Yet Cabeza de Vaca appears to counteract the negative effect of homogenizing Otherness as he becomes an Other himself for the duration of his forced Caribbean pilgrimage. The author bonds with both the Mora de Hornacho (in absentia) or the women who represent her (in situ), as well as with Estebanico, the former by listening and the latter by similarly accommodating to circumstances.

La Mora de Hornachos could be said to be the woman behind *Castaways;* in spite of her belated recognition, she guided her sisters in Caribbean exile into knowledge and safety, even "discovering" the harbor haven that eventually only four castaways were able to reach. She anticipates and closes full circle the trajectory of the text and the round-trip transatlantic voyage. Likewise, in spite of Estebanico's stated differences and compromises as a member of the transatlantic colonial troops, he becomes the pragmatic prophet of Father Marcos de Niza's messianic explorations of what is today the Southwestern United States. Estebanico even anticipates his own post-*Castaways* destiny as a provider of a posterity of sorts for his fellow shipwrecked sailors. His presence and that of his Afro-Hispanic peer also throw a singular prophetic light over Cabeza de Vaca's own post-*Castaways* life: as he was sent by the Crown into exile in Africa and eventually pardoned, he emerged in Spain as a minor historical figure who published a work about an ostensibly black agency mediating the off-white destiny of the Atlantic passage.

NOTES

1. I explore the political implications of this subject at length in my "The Game of Critical Arrival." *Diacritics* 19:1 (Spring 1989): 34-61.
2. I address the historical background of this issue in "Literary Whiteness and the Afro-Hispanic Difference." *New Literary Theory* 18:2 (Winter 1987): 303-332.
3. *Relación o Naufragios de Alvar Núñez Cabeza de Vaca* (Madrid: Editorial Castalia, 1992). All quotations are from the English translation: *Castaways: The Narrative of Alvar Nuñez Cabeza de Vaca.* Edited by Enrique Pupo-Walker and translated by Frances M. Lez-Morillas (Berkeley: University of California Press, 1993).
4. See my discussion of the eroticization of cannibals and Amazons in my "Loving Columbus." In *Amerindian Images and the Legacy of Columbus.* Edited by René Jara and Nicholas Spadaccini (Minneapolis: University of Minnesota Press, 1992), 230-265.
5. See "Loving Columbus" and "Nationalizing Sissies." In *¿Entiendes? Queer Readings, Hispanic Writings.* Edited by Emilie L. Bergmann and Paul Julian Smith (Durham, NC: Duke University Press, 1995), 370-409.
6. I explore Columbus's mid-Atlantic perspective in "The Game of Critical Arrival."

7. "Memorial de la Mejorana," in Cristóbal Colón, *Textos y documentos completos.* Edited by Consuelo Varela and Juan Gil (Madrid: Alianza Editorial, 1982), 337. All further references to this work will be indicated in the text by the parenthetical notation (Varela/Gil).

8. I discuss this issue in "The Value of Paper." *Res* 16 (Autumn 1988): 84–104.

9. For this and other instances of Christ speaking to Columbus, see Varela/Gil, 492.

10. Fernando Colón, *Vida del Almirante Don Cristóbal Colón, escrita por su hijo Hernando Colón* (Mexico: Fondo de Cultura Económica, 1947). Quotations are from the English edition: *The Life of the Admiral Christopher Columbus, by His Son Ferdinand.* Translated by Benjamin Keen (New Brunswick, NJ: Rutgers University Press, 1959), 3.

11. For a novelized version of the affair, see Alejo Carpentier's *El arpa y la sombra* (Madrid: Editorial de la Universidad de Alcalá, 1994).

12. *The "Libro de las Profecías" of Christopher Columbus.* Translated by Delno C. West and August Kling (Gainesville: University of Florida Press, 1991). The original manuscript (1502) is found in the Biblioteca Colombina in Seville, Spain.

13. The sense of destiny among the peoples of the Americas was surprisingly parallel to that of the Euro-Christians in general and Columbus's in particular. Some Americans foresaw the prophetic potential for a messianic common end and a new beginning; others foresaw their destiny in the explicitly fatal terms of an apocalyptic millennarism. As far as many Americans—not to mention Asians and Africans—were concerned, some sort of clash with the overseas world was not only "in the cards," but also a prelude to a fresh crop of people, ideas, methods, and goods, which would optimistically lead to fair conditions of exchange, renewal, and even convergence.

Chapter 2

VIOLENCE AND AWE:
THE FOUNDATIONS OF GOVERNMENT IN APHRA BEHN'S NEW WORLD SETTINGS[1]

Richard Frohock

Aprolific and successful poet, playwright, and novelist, Aphra Behn (1640-1689) holds the distinction of being the first English woman to earn a living off the proceeds of her writing. Her popularity among her contemporaries carried over into the eighteenth century, and her collected works went through eight editions by 1735. Behn's prose works eventually fell out of favor with scholars—the writer of the entry on Behn in the *Dictionary of National Biography* calls her prose works "decidedly less meritorious than her drama and the best of her poems." Yet, this judgment obscures the fact that it was Behn's *Oroonoko,* a novella, that contributed more than any other single work to the formation of her literary reputation among her contemporaries. (The renown of Behn's *Oroonoko* increased in 1695 when it was transformed into a successful play by Thomas Southerner.) In recent decades, Behn's *Oroonoko* has once again become popular with readers, and has generated a new body of criticism and scholarship. An indication of *Oroonoko*'s success with today's readers and its increasing status in the canon of English literature is its recent inclusion in the sixth edition of the *Norton Anthology of British Literature* (Vol. I).

Behn presents *Oroonoko* to her readers as "The History of the Royal Slave," and she claims to have witnessed many of the events she depicts during a prolonged sojourn in the English Royalist colony of Surinam: "I was myself an Eye-Witness to a great part of what you will find here set down."[2] Although her contemporaries never questioned the veracity of her narrative, some twentieth-century scholars have, most notably Ernest

Bernbaum, who declared Behn a "liar" who never traveled to Surinam, but instead took her details about the colony from contemporary accounts, such as George Warren's *An Impartial Description of Surinam* (1667).[3] More recently, however, various scholars, including Behn's three biographers, have determined that external evidence available in a variety of colonial records indicates that Behn did indeed travel to Surinam.[4] Although the records are not conclusive, it is probable that Behn traveled there in the fall of 1663 and remained there until early in 1664, during which time she experienced, in some form, the events she depicts in her novella.

The purpose of Behn's journey is a matter of speculation. In the preface to *Oroonoko,* Behn states that her father was taking their family to Surinam where he was to assume the post of lieutenant-general (48); Duffy suggests that Behn's father may have been nominated as captain general, rather than lieutenant, or that he may have been responding to an appeal for planters to travel to Surinam.[5] More recently, Janet Todd has suggested that Behn, who would have been in her early twenties at the time, may have gone to Surinam "as a spy or agent" of the government; Behn later served Charles II in such a capacity when she was sent to Antwerp during the Dutch war.[6] The relationship of fact to fiction in Behn's *Oroonoko* cannot be settled conclusively in many points, but the same is true of many of the European accounts of the New World that proliferated in the late seventeenth century. When approached from a different angle, Behn's *Oroonoko* presents the reader and scholar with many issues in addition to the question of the veracity of its details. *Oroonoko* is, like other New World accounts, an emplotment and narration of experience; as such, it constructs and invents, as well as describes, the New World that is its setting. In particular, Behn's narrative puts much energy into imagining the forms and qualities of just colonial governance in the New World. In this essay, I argue that Behn's perspective on colonial governance in the Americas can be understood largely in terms of her royalist sympathies.

In 1975, George Guffey called attention to the political topicality of *Oroonoko,* finding in it evidence of Behn's avid Toryism and parallels to the issues leading up to the Glorious Revolution.[7] Recently, political readings of Behn's novel have become more frequent, though they constitute a different kind of political reading, attending to the ideological issues of race, class, and gender.[8] *Oroonoko* is resituated in its colonial context and attention is focused on colonial politics, slavery, trade, and gender. Such work makes clear that Behn's New World setting is more than a vehicle for commenting on post-Restoration domestic politics: it serves to theorize English colonial authority.

Behn writes her novel at the beginning of the first great age of English imperialism,[9] and clearly she is enthusiastic about the possibilities of New World colonization. She describes the pleasantness and fruitfulness of the land in detail: it "affords all things both for Beauty and Use . . . the Trees bearing at once all degrees of Leaves and Fruit, from blooming Buds to ripe Autumn: Groves of Oranges, Lemons, Citrons, Figs, Nutmegs, and noble Aromatics, continually bearing their Fragrancies" (48-49). Convinced of the beauty and value of Surinam, Behn laments the loss of this English colony to the Dutch: "had his late Majesty, of sacred Memory, but seen and known what a vast and charming World he had been Master of in that Continent, he would never have parted so easily with it to the Dutch" (48). Similarly, discussing the possibility of abundant gold in South America, Behn writes, "'tis to be bemoan'd what his Majesty lost by losing that part of *America*" (59). The New World offers rich possibilities for the English nation if they can lay claim to it.

Behn also provides a theoretical justification for the English appropriation of the New World, recognizing that establishing and maintaining an English colony inevitably involves conflict, and not only with European nations such as the Netherlands. Surinam is occupied by Caribs and, under the colonial plantation system, the goods of the land are extracted through the labor of enslaved Africans. Any justification for English colonialism in South America must therefore negotiate and legitimate the relationships between the English and the other racial and ethnic groups.

As the principle of mere force might indicate the absence of a more just foundation for colonial order, Behn grounds colonialism in something other than the violence apparent in her novel. Locke formulates the general problem in his *Second Treatise:* a demonstration that government is more than the product of brute force requires showing the "Original of Political Power" and a way of "knowing the persons who have it."[10] Behn's novel can be read as attempting to fulfill both of these requirements. Behn, a royalist, grounds colonial power in what she identifies as the natural privilege of noble blood lines. This natural privilege is readily apparent in those who enjoy it, even when it is not culturally marked. The recognizability of nobility, regardless of the circumstances in which it appears, seems in turn to confirm the naturalness of noble privilege. Behn thus represents "proper" colonial government as an assertion of nature's order.

It follows that improper colonial government would constitute an inversion of nature's order, and Behn's work includes such a model of New World misgovernance. Surinam's lower-class council members, mainly transported convicts and a "wild Irishman," rule through physical coercion, including torture and execution. The upper-class colonists, by contrast, base political power on perceived natural differences between races and classes. They emphasize the body's capacity to function as a sign, an index of innate privilege or of subhuman essence, and they attempt to distance themselves from physical coercion. Behn thus aestheticizes "legitimate" colonization by attributing violence and the less palpable acts of imperialism to the "other" immoral and lower-class whites. This class division is central to the book's justification of imperialism, yet Behn has difficulty asserting it consistently. This distinction between the governing rights and methods of the two colonial classes collapses in places. Ideological tensions appear in Behn's justification of colonial government because the "natural" signs of noble privilege often turn out to involve various cultural fictions.[11]

Behn describes the Native Americans she encounters during her stay in Surinam in complex, and sometimes contradictory, ways. In the opening pages of the novel she depicts the Caribs as embodying a prelapsarian innocence; she compares their clothing to that of Adam and Eve, and their unadorned modesty to "our first Parents before the Fall" (2, 3). She describes their innocence in romantic courtship: "I have seen a handsome young *Indian,* dying for Love of a very beautiful young *Indian* Maid; but all his Courtship was, to fold his Arms, pursue her with his Eyes, and Sighs were all his Language" (3). Although these terms are deeply embedded in European cultural myths, Behn herself attributes American virtues to nature: "these People represented to me an absolute *Idea* of the first State of Innocence, before *Man* knew how to sin: And 'tis most evident and plain, that simple Nature is the most harmless, inoffensive and vertuous Mistress" (3). Behn thus elevates and praises the Caribs for what they lack: the corruptions that accompany religious and political institutions. Nature, she continues, "better instructs the World, than all the Inventions of Man: Religion wou'd here but destroy that Tranquility they possess by Ignorance; and Laws wou'd but teach 'em to know Offence, of which now they have no Notion" (3-4). Behn, for the moment, defines these Caribs as Noble Savages, living more virtuous lives than "civilized" Europeans. She can criticize European corruption by relating the anecdote of the English Governor who finds himself caught in his lie by a people who have no notion of "Vice, or Cunning" (4).[12]

Yet the association of the Caribs with nature allows Behn to exploit other rhetorical possibilities: ties to nature subordinate, as well as elevate, the Native Americans. Paradoxically, in a land of eternal spring and fruitfulness, the Native Americans are indispensable to the colonists in procuring food. English colonists, consciously contrasting themselves to Spanish colonists, often imagined themselves getting Native American service nonviolently, trading trifles or "toys" for goods or labor.[13] Such is the case in *Oroonoko:* the colonists trade small items—"Beads of all Colours, Knives, Axes, Pins and Needles"—in return for essential supplies—"Fish, Venison, Buffalo's Skins, and little Rarities" (2).[14] Amicable relations grounded in mutually beneficial free enterprise are thus maintained without violence.

Yet for Behn the nonviolent trade relation is not simply the result of economic supply and demand. In acknowledging Native American hunting prowess, Behn goes a step further by metonymically linking the Native Americans to the nature they hunt. The Caribs

> supply the parts of Hounds, by swiftly scouring through almost impassable Places, and by the mere Activity of their Feet run down the nimblest Deer, and other eatable Beasts; but in the water one wou'd think they were Gods of the Rivers, or Fellow-Citizens of the deep. (4)

Behn implies that the Caribs' position in the colonial economy is suited to, if not determined by, their very natures, rather than by colonialist need. Yet clearly the narrator's rhetoric, rather than anything inherent in the Caribs, makes them "citizens" of nature, naturalizing their function as food-gatherers and hunters.[15] Behn here reads, or rather writes, the Native American bodies to justify subordination and the exploitation of their labor by natural difference.

While Native Americans serve the colonists as hunters and gatherers, Africans are used as domestic laborers: "Those then whom we make use of to work in our Plantations of Sugar, are *Negroes,* Black-Slaves all together" (5). As with the Native Americans, Behn sees the blacks—"a gloomy Race" (6)—as essentially subhuman. Black bodies signify aesthetic inferiority: the beauty even of Oroonoko is lessened in her eyes by his skin color, a prejudice Behn embeds in an ostensible compliment: "bating his Colour, there could be nothing in Nature more agreeable and handsome" (8). More important, Behn's narrative implies that the vast majority of enslaved Africans are naturally suited to their position in the colonial economy. Under the test of battle, the majority of the slaves prove to be completely tractable and "slavish" in their actions.[16] First swayed to rebellion by the forceful words of Oroonoko, they are quickly overcome by the whips of the overseers, turn on their prince, and whip him (67). Because of this reversibility, Oroonoko scorns the other slaves and criticizes himself for trying to raise them above their natural station: "he was ashamed of what he had done, in endeavoring to make those free, who were by Nature Slaves" (66). The incident serves to justify the exploited position of the slaves in the colonial economy, a reflection of their perceived natural ignobility.[17]

In *The Widow Ranter,* Behn's only other work set in the New World (in Virginia), a similar incident reinforces the representation of lower-class "others" as natural slaves. The play has important parallels to *Oroonoko* and helps define Behn's perceptions of colonial governance and racial divisions. The Indian King is represented as a monarchical and military leader with aristocratic sentiments and some European education (in the gentlemanly art of swordmanship, for example).[18] Initially, his situation is similar to Oroonoko's: Europeans have taken away his right to rule and have enslaved his people: "We were Monarchs once of all this spacious World," the Indian King tells Nathaniel Bacon, a rebel fighting the Native Americans without official permission, "Till you an unknown People landing here . . . Abusing all our Charitable Hospitality, Usurp'd our Right, and made your friends your slaves" (36).

Like Prince Oroonoko, who rallies his fellow slaves with a speech about the injustice of their condition only to despise them later, the Indian King speaks out against slavery, but later reverses his opinion and concludes that his fellow Native Americans are fit only for subjection. The Indian King in fact reacts even more violently against his fellow countrymen than Oroonoko does. Leading his troops in battle against European forces, he is outraged when the cowardly Indians flee; he chases his retreating warriors, calling them "fugitive slaves," shooting at them himself with poisoned arrows "as they Fly" (87). Bacon, an aristocrat in his own mind and thus sympathetic with the Native American monarch, reinforces the Indian King's view of the Indians, calling them "slaves" on various occasions (87, 112). In Behn's representations, the slavish nature of common-class Africans and Native Americans asserts itself under the strain of battle; their enslavement seems just even to the leaders who had defended their rights. For Behn, the base nature that determines a slave's station is observable: those who deserve to be politically subjected ultimately can be identified by their physical attributes or by their cowardly and tractable actions.

Just as a slave is naturally suited to his lowly social condition, Behn takes pains to show that princes are naturally and essentially, not semiotically, distinguished from the common classes. Wearing distinctive clothes, Oroonoko looks like a prince when he arrives in the New World; yet, even after he changes into a slave's garb, he is recognized universally as a person of quality: "he shown thro all. . . . The Royal Youth appear'd in spight of the Slave, and People cou'd not help treating him after a different manner, without designing it" (39). Royalty does not need the codes of a "rich Habit" as signal (39). Nature's pen, not man's, writes political privilege onto the body.

Michael McKeon has argued that aristocratic ideology claims for the prince an elevated, external authority.[19] Behn grounds Oroonoko's aristocratic status in a source higher than his own language. The Africans whom Oroonoko had formerly sold into slavery refuse to recognize Oroonoko as a fellow slave and pay homage in spite of his leveling modesty: "he besought 'em to rise and to receive him as their Fellow-Slave; assuring them he was no better" (41). The source of the prince's status supersedes even his expressed will, and can require actions in others contrary to the prince's desire. Nobility, requiring no invented human signs to mark itself, defies even the prince's own language to deny its presence.

Similarly Trefry, who finds Imoinda exceptionally appealing and is "transported with passion even above Decency," refrains from raping her because he perceives her quality. Her very presence, he explains, strikes "Awe into the Hearts of her Admirers," and, on the verge of using force to subdue her, he is overcome by her modesty and weeping (42–43). Oroonoko praises Trefry for his restraint, of his recognition "that Slave might be noble, or, what was better, have true notions of Honour and Vertue in her" (43). Despite her status, Imoinda's quality, like Oroonoko's, is essential, not circumstantial, and evident to Trefry. Persons with a claim to political privilege can be identified through strongly perceived sense-experiences (such as "Awe"). Trefry's restraint further suggests that human relations in the colony are governed not by brute force and desire, but rather are grounded in a transcendent, self-evident order. Right, not might, is the governing principle of moral persons of quality.

Behn's fiction supports class divisions as well as race divisions by naturalizing them, grounding noble privilege in nature rather than in force or in fiction. Nobility is represented as substance, not code, in this representation of colonial government. Behn's fiction of nobility denies its own fictionality, denying, moreover, its very need to be told.

Yet Behn's attempt to ground nobility in nature contains two unresolved tensions. First, nobility relies on signs to denote itself: the very leveling language that Oroonoko uses when addressing the other slaves could be interpreted as the rhetoric of royal courtesy, which marks Oroonoko as noble in the very instant that it denies his distinction. Furthermore, African nobles, as the narrator at first forgets to mention, are elaborately tattooed, "delicately cut and raised all over the Forepart of the Trunk of their Bodies" (45). Class privilege is written into the body itself. The visible tattoos on Oroonoko's temples make it less remarkable that he is seen as royal after having changed into a slave's clothes. The body in its unadorned state seems to be an inadequate sign of natural privilege after all, and must be dressed with cultural symbols of power. Royal authority depends on sign systems—such as tattooing or speech—to manifest itself, a point that other examples in the novel try to elide.

A second tension in the naturalization of royalism results from the fact that in spite of the argument that nobility is self-evident, the sense-experience of "awe" is unreliable, or unavailable to many. The submissive reactions to Oroonoko and Imoinda are not shared, for example, by the criminal members of the colony's council. Oroonoko's praise of Trefry's restraint with Imoinda directly contrasts with his fear that the "Multitude" will rape Imoinda in the event of his death (71). This misrecognition of, or disregard for, the signs of authority creates a conflict in the colony.

Of the three ideological concerns of race, class, and gender, it is the conjunction of race and gender that writers on *Oroonoko* have explored most thoroughly.[20] Class division among the English colonists, however, is also central to Behn's representation of colonialism.[21] In her New World texts, Behn employs a class binary to aestheticize English imperialism: the atrocities of New World imperialism are not committed by the upper-class plantation owners.

As in many New World narratives, Behn wishes to impose order upon chaos, and in her view the English colonial structure already in place is in disarray. The state of the colony's government is perhaps best captured in the fact that the Lord Governor is absent and the Lieutenant-General has been killed in transit: somewhere between England and the New World, governance has died. Similarly, in *The Widow Ranter* a missing governor is the cause of political turmoil. As Friendly explains, "for want of a Governour" the colony is ruled by a council of suspected criminals. The absent governor, according to Hazard, "has all the Qualities of a Gallant Man, besides he is Nobly born" (14); of course the council members that rule in his place lack these qualities of breeding and birth. In both texts, then, the lower-class colonists have inverted the "natural" order of government.

They serve Behn as a negative model of colonial government because the origin of their power is in violent force, not nature.[22]

In the Lord Governor's absence, Byam, the brutal Deputy-Governor described by the narrator as "not fit to be mentioned with the worst of the Slaves," takes limited command over Surinam (63-64).[23] Byam does not disguise the fact that he governs with brute force: when Oroonoko revolts, Byam is "the only violent Man against him" (63). After persuading Oroonoko to surrender, Byam brutally whips him, "rending the flesh from his bones" (67). Byam writes with a whip rather than the ink of tattoos, marking Oroonoko's body with signs of political subjection rather than political privilege.

The colony's council is politically aligned with Deputy Governor Byam, and he calls upon its members to help him gain access to Oroonoko after the Parhamites create an asylum for the prince. Behn, in spite of her disclaimer that she does not intend "to disgrace them, or burlesque the Government there," describes the members of this council as "notorious Villains as *Newgate* never transported; and possibly, originally were such who understood neither the Laws of God or Man, and had no sort of Principles to make them worthy the Name of Men." The Council meetings are models of disorder: "at the very Council-Table they wou'd contradict and fight with one another, and swear so bloodily, that t'was terrible to hear and see 'em." More fit to be governed than governing, the Council members might appropriately be called Lords of Misrule. Whereas Byam may be unwilling, they are clearly unable to read natural privilege in Oroonoko's body, and instead choose to deal forcefully with it; they resolve to circumvent the Governor and hang Oroonoko, intending to use his body as a sign of warning to other slaves (69-70).

Behn satirizes the incompetence of a colonial Council even more extensively in *The Widow Ranter*. As Friendly explains, the council members in the play "have been perhaps transported Criminals, who having Acquired great Estates are now become your Honour, and Right Worshipfull, and Possess all Places of Authority" (14). While *Oroonoko* attacks historical individuals such as Byam and Banister, *The Widow Ranter* generalizes the problem Behn sees when the lower classes are put into positions of authority. The allegorical names—Dullman, Timorous, Whimsey, Whiff, Boozer, Bragg, and special advisor to the council Parson Dunce—universalize their incapacity.

The council sessions in the play are models of self-indulgent disorder: Whiff begins one meeting by making a motion for a council punch-bowl of larger circumference (64). At Hazard's trial (for drawing his sword during an altercation with Timorous, Dullman, and Boozer), the Council demonstrates its misuse of legal terms and concepts, rendering Hazard's "se defendendo" ("in self defence") as "in defiance" (68). As an indication of their inverted perspective, the Council members ridicule English nobles and propose that Virginia could teach England good manners and breeding, and supply all positions of power there to save that "lost nation" (48). Behn wishes to fill positions of power in the colony with English gentlemen of breeding to save the "lost nation" of Virginia from self-destruction.[24]

As in *Oroonoko,* these Lords of Misrule govern by force rather than law. Deliberating what to do with the rebel Bacon, several members advocate hanging him directly without trial. Parson Dunce proposes entrapping Bacon by first officially sanctioning his actions and inviting him to be general, but then "as soon as he shal have render'd himself . . . seize[ing] him and strik[ing] off his Head at the Fort" (25). This ruse is similar to Byam's use of flattery to lure Oroonoko into surrender. Notably, in *The Window Ranter* two Council members, Wellman and Downright, reject the Parson's proposed deception, insisting instead on giving Bacon a trial in England or when the Governor returns. These two alone hold out against letting the colonial government collapse into a contest of force regardless of right. By deferring authority to the absent noble Governor, these two Council members exemplify Behn's view of proper civil order.

Behn's two New World narratives are full of force and violence, but Behn generally blames the brutalities on "others." The colonized themselves perpetrate much of the violence: the Caribs inflict terrible wounds on themselves in the course of electing war captains, and after the departure of the English from Surinam, the Caribs dismember a Dutch footman and hang the parts of his body in trees (57-58, 54). Oroonoko also mutilates; he decapitates his own wife and partially disembowels himself before being captured (72, 75). Behn displaces the violence committed by Western colonizers onto "others": the burlesqued, lower-class Council members who finally execute Oroonoko in gruesome fashion. Banister, a "wild Irish man" and "a Fellow of absolute Barbarity" (76), dismembers the hero at the novel's end and sends Oroonoko's body parts to four plantations to be put on display.

Throughout the novel the only group that does not commit overt atrocities is the aristocratic white faction with which Behn identifies herself. Colonel Martin's refusal to accept a quarter of Oroonoko's body as a bloody warning to other blacks is an important example of the upper-class colonists' desire to distance themselves from the violence of the slave trade and English imperialism. The colonel swears that he "could govern his

Negroes, without terrifying and grieving them with frightful Spectacles of a mangled King" (77). The upper class thus washes its hands of imperial violence by rejecting its symbols: for them the body of the prince had exemplified the law of nature, which grounds their own right to rule, but Banister turns it into an index of the principle of force.[25]

Yet a tension remains: plantation owners cannot separate themselves as cleanly as they wish from the brutal lower class. Colonel Martin has the same end in mind—controlling his slaves—as Byam and the Council members, even if he insists on different means. This tension generates important unresolved questions. What type of coercion can the upper class oppose to the Council's violent force? How does one govern an unruly colony without spectacles of mangling? Colonel Martin does not specify, but other parts of the novel suggest some answers.

Behn writes herself into a double bind. On the one hand, she wishes to argue that a proper colonial government is grounded in a natural order that precedes human manipulations and impositions. On the other hand, the uprisings and disorders in the novel plainly show that some type of coercion is necessary to create colonial stability. Of course the upper-class colonists do not wish to embrace openly the misrulers' physical brutalization and coercion; Colonel Martin's scruples may be said to reveal what Mary Louise Pratt calls the colonial "desire to subject without violence."[26] As a way out of this dilemma, the upper class needs a method of control that is not overtly forceful. One solution for them is in the manipulation of the signs, or articulations, of authority: they work to narrate their own political privilege convincingly.

The upper-class strategy of marking their own political authority can best be seen in their relations with the Caribs. As we have seen, Behn represents these Native Americans ambivalently: as prelapsarian noble savages and as capable warriors. The outnumbered colonists dare not attempt to enslave the Caribs (3, 5), and when the Caribs threaten war with the colonists, it gives them "many mortal Fears" (54). Behn describes a Carib attack on the Dutch: they "cut in pieces all they could take, getting into Houses, and hanging up the Mother, and all her Children about her; and cut a Footman, I left behind me, all in Joints, and nail'd him to Trees" (54). The colonists thus have strong motives for communicating their noble status and evoking in the Caribs an experience of "awe" that will prevent them from attacking.

The visit to the Native American village at the time of impending war is intended to produce such awe in the Caribs. "Diversion in gazing" and conversing with the Caribs ostensibly motivates the excursion (54), but the visiting whites quickly show that they wish to be seen more than they wish to see. The colonists carefully stage their entrance to the village to increase their visual impact: the narrator explains that "we, who had a mind to surprise 'em, by making them see something they never had seen, (that is, White People) resolv'd only myself, my Brother and Woman should go" (55). Oroonoko and the dark Fisherman hide behind bushes so that they will not detract from the theatrical effect of the entrance of the whites. The colonists thus fully exploit the opportunity to present their white bodies as a sign of difference and, by implication, superiority. The visual impact is heightened by their elaborate clothing, which the narrator describes as "very glittering and rich; so that we appear'd extremely fine. . . . I had a taffety Cap, with black Feathers on my Head; my Brother was in a Stuff-Suit, with silver Loops and Buttons, and abundance of green Ribbon" (55). Both skin and clothing—the body as sign and sign bearer—succeed in evoking responses of "Wonder" and "Amazement" (55). The "admiration" of the Caribs grows when the narrator and her brother play their flutes (56). Through careful staging and performance, the excursion party makes a spectacle of itself and produces politically advantageous responses.[27]

The most powerful spectacle of the visit, however, is the demonstration of a burning-glass. Such demonstrations of European technology are often central moments in colonial writings. Eric Cheyfitz, for example, discusses Captain John Smith's demonstration of a compass and a pistol as a means of making a powerful impression on Native Americans.[28] Similarly, Columbus convinced Native Americans of his divinity by predicting a solar eclipse. Edmund Burke praises Columbus as "truly ingenious," and concludes that there is "no people who have not some points of ignorance, weakness, or prejudice, which a penetrating mind may discover, and use."[29] In *Oroonoko* the narrator's kinsman makes a similar impression on the Native Americans when he lights a piece of paper with his burning-glass. The Caribs "were like to have ador'd him for a God, and begg'd he would give 'em the Characters or Figures of his Name, that they might oppose it against Winds and Storms: which he did, and they held it up in those Seasons, and fancy'd it had a Charm to conquer them, and kept it like a holy Relique" (56–57). The kinsman's technological theater elicits the kind of "awe" that apparently subordinates the Caribs without the use of force. Like Trefry, who submits to Imoinda when he could have forced her, they cannot but pay obeisance to a nobler nature. Behn reinforces the impression that the Native Americans have been subordinated when she makes her first and only reference to "Indian Slaves" immediately after this visit to the village (59).

This successful evocation of "awe," however, leaves the colonists with two problems, one theoretical and one practical. Theoretically, it reveals the possibility that government is grounded in imposed fictions rather than in nature. Observing the Caribs' reactions to the flutes, the narrator concludes that "by an admiration that is natural to these People, and by the extreme Ignorance and Simplicity of 'em, it were not difficult to establish any unknown or extravagant Religion among them, and to impose any Notions of Fictions upon 'em" (56). Behn, who elsewhere in the novel argues for the authenticity of power hierarchies by asserting that they are in no need of cultural signs to denote them, here introduces the possibility that the upper-class colonists' narrative of power is only a construct of signs, with no authentic referent. Certainly the kinsman does nothing but impose a fiction with his burning-glass. The upper-class colonists, in trying to avoid making government the product of force, fail to make it the product of nature and risk exposing government as the product of fraud. Power becomes the product of neither right nor might, but merely convincing storytelling.[30]

The practical difficulty is that despite colonial claims, an imposition of fictions is not in itself powerful enough to maintain order in the colony. Cheyfitz points out that John Smith presents himself as a "consummate storyteller or dramatist" in his writings, claiming for himself "the power to persuade of power," yet concludes that "this portrait of Smith as a grand manipulator of fiction, as an eloquent orator of absolute command . . . is a fiction."[31] Behn's observation that admiration comes "naturally" to the Native Americans already constitutes a fiction: they are not likely to be so gullible, nor is European storytelling so convincing that imposed fictions can keep them indefinitely subordinated. The fiction of European superiority, imposed with the signs of skin, clothing, and technology, does not prevent the Caribs from later warring against the Dutch and sending the colony back into a contest of force. The production of "awe," then, finally does not solve the upper-class colonists' problem of how to "subject without violence"; the dilemma generated by Colonel Martin's statement persists.

The methods used to control the Africans on the plantations also reveal practical and theoretical shortcomings. As with the Caribs, the upper-class colonists rely partly on displays of force to govern their slaves. Living on the slave plantations, indentured servants—themselves "*slaves* for four years"—stand as a visible presence of force over the Africans. They wear swords that are rusted into their scabbards, and their guns are equally corroded. Their supposed technological superiority in this instance is a fraud: the Africans in fact have superior weapons in the bows and arrows that they are skilled in using (60).

The upper-class colonists make an exception, however, in the case of Oroonoko. With him they try another strategy for coercing without violence: that of surveillance. The same indentured servants who guard the other Africans also spy on Oroonoko when he is on the plantation (60), and whenever Oroonoko leaves a certain compass he is accompanied by "some that should be rather in appearance Attendants than Spies" (48). Ironically Oroonoko thinks his special attendants confer on him a mark of distinction, when in fact their presence undermines a difference between Oroonoko and other slaves: he has his overseers, just as they do.

The colonists hope to prevent a violent mutiny led by Oroonoko by keeping him under watch (46), yet as with the production of "awe," the nonviolent method of surveillance is in itself insufficient to maintain subordination. Surveillance has inevitable lapses: Oroonoko eventually eludes his spies and convinces the other Africans, who are equally successful in escaping their overseers, to flee. To be effective, surveillance and the display of force, like the production of "awe," require violence to complement them: it is up to Byam's militia to put down the slave revolt. The upper-class colonists distance themselves from Byam's action, but clearly they are implicated in it, and benefit from it.

The upper-class opposition to the Council's violence, voiced in Colonel Martin's refusal to accept a piece of Oroonoko's body, is finally unconvincing because slavery in the colony is routinely administered with spectacles of mangling. Oroonoko details the practice in his antislavery speech to the other Africans: on "Black Friday" all the slaves, "whether they work'd or not, whether they were faulty or meriting, they, promiscuously, the innocent with the guilty, suffer'd the infamous Whip, the sordid Stripes, from their Fellow-Slaves, till their Blood trickled from all Parts of their Body" (60-61). The alternative to governing slaves with the spectacle of a mangled king seems to be the brutalization of all slaves. Plantation owners like Colonel Martin have no moral high ground on which to stand: their methods of subordination are neither different in principle nor distinguishable in degree of violence from the methods of the Council.

The methods of coercion of the upper-class colonists—arousing "awe," displaying force, and surveillance—are not opposed to, but rather are compliant with, the Council's violence. The noble colonists do not show different principles of governance, but at best a reversal of emphasis: whereas the Council might use fraud (flattering words to Oroonoko) to make its exercise of force more effective, the upper-class colonists must rely on force to keep their fictions in place. The fictions and vigilance of the upper-class colonists and the violence of the lower class work together to maintain the subjection of blacks and Native Americans in the British colony of Surinam.[32]

Behn's New World writings—the product of her observed experiences as a traveler—while having much to do with the domestic politics of post-Restoration England, must be understood as addressing seventeenth-century England's foreign policy as well. Behn directly supports colonization, and her texts work to aestheticize British imperialism. While it might appear that Behn works to expose some of the horrors of slavery in the New World, she consistently attributes unpalatable imperialist acts to colonial misrulers who, in the Governor's absence, temporarily exercise control. She represents colonial violence as resulting from the turmoil that comes from mixing natural stations: force rules when princes are enslaved and sub-human criminals hold positions of political might. For Behn, proper imperialism, the assertion of nature's own hierarchy, can only be dismantled, not created, through force. As such it is free from atrocities.

Yet to illustrate atrocities in an imperial setting, while justifying imperialism itself, inevitably results in unresolved tensions. First, the upper class' nonviolent means of coercion raise the theoretical problem that colonial power is grounded in fiction rather than nature. Second, since even the imposition of fictions cannot maintain lasting order, the upper-class colonists must rely on the very violence from which they wish to disassociate themselves. As a result of these unresolved tensions, the book ultimately cannot conceal an uncomfortable aspect of the issue with which it grapples: political order in the New World colony has its origin in violence and force. Other claims are storytelling.

NOTES

1. An earlier version of this essay appeared in *Eighteenth-Century Fiction* 8:4 (July 1996): 437-452.

2. Aphra Behn, *Oroonoko: or, the Royal Slave*. Edited by Lore Metzger (New York: Norton, 1973), 1. Parenthetical references are to this edition.

3. Ernest Bernbaum, "Mrs. Behn's *Oroonoko*." In *Anniversary Papers by Colleagues and Pupils of George Lyman Kittredge* (Boston: Ginn, 1913), 419-35.

4. Maureen Duffy, *The Passionate Shepherdess: Aphra Behn, 1640-89* (London: Jonathan Cape, 1977), 30-41; Angeline Goreau, *Reconstructing Aphra: A Social Biography of Aphra Behn* (New York: Dial Press, 1980), 41-69; and Janet

Todd, *The Secret Life of Aphra Behn* (New Brunswick, NJ: Rutgers University Press, 1996), 35–66.

5. Duffy, *The Passionate Shepherdess,* 31–32.
6. Todd, *The Secret Life of Aphra Behn,* 41.
7. George Guffey, "Aphra Behn's *Oroonoko:* Occasion and Accomplishment." In George Guffey and Andrew Wright's *Two English Novelists: Aphra Behn and Anthony Trollope* (Los Angeles: University of California Press, 1975), 1–41. Guffey argues that "Behn makes a strong argument for the absolute power of legitimate kings, and that, through a series of parallels between James and the mistreated royal slave Oroonoko, she attempts to gain the sympathy of her reader for James (16–17). Maureen Duffy further explores this link, arguing that emotionally Oroonoko, Imoinda, and the unborn child are James II, Mary, and an unborn child. See *The Passionate Shepherdess,* 275.
8. Call for such political readings can be found in the introduction to *The New Eighteenth Century: Theory, Politics, English Literature.* Edited by Laura Brown and Felicity Nussbaum. (New York: Methuen, 1987), ii; the introduction to *Rereading Aphra Behn: History, Theory, and Criticism.* Edited by Heidi Hutner (Charlottesville: University Press of Virginia, 1993), iii–iv, vi; and Laura Brown's *Ends of Empire: Women and Ideology in Early Eighteenth-Century English Literature* (Ithaca, NY: Cornell University Press, 1993), 26–27.
9. Brown designates the period "from the Restoration to the fall of Walpole" as "the first major age of English imperialism," *Ends of Empire,* 3.
10. John Locke, *Two Treatises of Government.* Edited by Peter Laslett (Cambridge: Cambridge University Press, 1960), 2:1.
11. Anita Pacheco, in "Royalism and Honor in Aphra Behn's *Oroonoko." SEL: Studies in English Literature* 34 (1994): 491–506, gives a cogent account of the royalism that is forwarded in Behn's novella, but that never achieves "ideological closure" (491). My work parallels Pacheco's in asserting that the royalism Behn promotes in the novel is riddled with tension. Brown also identifies the combination of aristocratic and bourgeois systems as the "ideological contradiction which dominates the novella" (*Ends of Empire,* 48).
12. Behn's portrayal of Carib innocence is not entirely consistent: the Caribs are feared by the English colonists, who do not dare to command them (2); they are also slave-holders and warriors (4).
13. According to Jeffrey Knapp, the English operated according to the principle that "trifling and not torture would best obtain their [the Native Americans'] labor." *An Empire Nowhere: England, America, and Literature from "Utopia" to "The Tempest"* (Berkeley: University of California Press, 1992), 4.
14. Similarly, Captain John Smith reports trading pins, needles, and beads for berries, bread, and fish in *A True Relation of . . . Virginia, The Complete Works of Captain John Smith (1580–1631).* Vol. 1. Edited by Philip L. Barbour (Chapel Hill: University of North Carolina Press, 1986), 23–108.

15. Robert L. Chibka discusses how the Caribs are subordinated and made sub-human in "'Oh Do Not Fear a Woman's Invention': Truth, Falsehood, and Fiction in Aphra Behn's *Oroonoko.*" *Texas Studies in Literature and Language* 30:4 (1988), 516.

16. Lore Metzger discusses the "slavish" representation of the Africans in her introduction to *Oroonoko,* xii.

17. There has been much dispute about Behn's attitude toward slavery. See Pacheco; Hutner (1); Charlotte Sussman, "The Other Problem with Women: Reproduction and Slave Culture in Aphra Behn's *Oroonoko.*" In Hutner, *Rereading Aphra Behn,* 217; Moira Ferguson, *Subject to Others: British Women Writers and Colonial Slavery, 1670-1834* (New York: Routledge, 1992), 27-49.

18. Aphra Behn, *The Widow Ranter: or, The History of Bacon in Virginia.* Edited by Aaron R. Walden (New York: Garland, 1993), 88. Parenthetical references are to this edition.

19. Michael McKeon, *Origins of the English Novel, 1600-1740* (Baltimore: Johns Hopkins University Press, 1987), 178.

20. Since Brown first treated the subject in "The Romance of Empire: *Oroonoko* and the Trade in Slaves" (chapter 2, *Ends of Empire*) several critics have considered the politics of race and gender in *Oroonoko.* See Stephanie Athey and Daniel Cooper Alarcon, "*Oroonoko*'s Gendered Economies of Honor/Horror: Reframing Colonial Discourse Studies in the Americas." *American Literature* 65:3 (September 1993): 415-443; Ros Ballaster, "New Hystericism: Aphra Behn's *Oroonoko:* the Body, the Text, and the Feminist Critic." In *New Feminist Discourses: Critical Essays on Theories and Texts.* Edited by Isobel Armstrong (New York: Routledge, 1992), 283-295; and Margaret W. Ferguson, "Juggling the Categories of Race, Class and Gender: Aphra Behn's *Oroonoko.*" *Women's Studies* 19 (1991): 159-181.

21. See Guffey; Pacheco; Margaret W. Ferguson; Wylie Sypher, *Guinea's Captive Kings: British Anti-Slavery Literature of the Eighteenth Century* (New York: Octagon Books, 1969), 108-116; and Moira Ferguson, 27-38.

22. See Goreau, *Reconstructing Aphra,* for contemporary accounts of the lower class that populated the colony (47-48).

23. Guffey makes the important point that though the historical Byam was a royalist, in Behn's novel "he is over and over identified with the rabble" (34). Pacheco also observes that historically Byam and Banister were "high royalist officials," but in the narrative Behn works to associate them with the lower class. See Lizabeth Paravisini-Gebert, *Phyllis Shand Allfrey: A Caribbean Life* (New Brunswick, NJ: Rutgers University Press, 1996), 6-7, for an overview of the history of Byam's activities in the Caribbean.

24. For a discussion of Behn as an "avid Tory," based on evidence from a series of her writings, see Guffey, 8-15. In her pindaric "To the Most Illustrious Prince Christopher Duke of Albemarle, on his Voyage to his Government

of Jamaica" (London, 1687), Behn also endorses the idea of sending a nobleman to the plantations to manage affairs first-hand: "How must that Wondring World rejoyce to see/ Their Land so Honour'd, and themselves so Blest,/ When on their Shores (Great Prince) they Welcome Thee" (5).

25. Brown discusses the relationship between the dismemberment of Oroonoko and the execution of Charles I, 55-63.

26. Mary Louise Pratt, *Imperial Eyes: Travel Writing and Transculturation* (New York: Routledge, 1992), 50.

27. Stephen Greenblatt discusses Columbus's rhetorical use of wonder "as a redemptive, aestheticizing supplement to a deeply flawed legal ritual of appropriation" in *Marvelous Possessions: The Wonder of the New World* (Chicago: University of Chicago Press, 1991), 24.

28. Eric Cheyfitz, *The Poetics of Imperialism: Translation and Colonization from "The Tempest" to "Tarzan"* (New York: Oxford University Press, 1991), 64–65, 79.

29. Edmund Burke, *An Account of European Settlements in America*. 2 vols. 3rd ed. (London: R. and J. Dodsley, 1760), 59.

30. This discussion of the fictions imposed on the Native Americans through technology is indebted to Stephen Greenblatt's discussion of Thomas Harriot's *A Brief and True Report of the New Found Land of Virginia* in "Invisible Bullets: Renaissance Authority and its Subversion, *Henry IV* and *Henry V.*" In *Political Shakespeare: New Essays in Cultural Materialism* (Ithaca, NY: Cornell University Press, 1985), 18-47, esp. 18-25. Greenblatt argues that the subversive elements in Harriot's narration are almost entirely contained; in Behn's text, however, I find that the subversive doubt raised is never effectively contained.

31. Cheyfitz, 79.

32. See Pacheco's discussion of how the opposing groups of colonists are "collaborators as well as competitors in the British colonial enterprise" (503).

Chapter 3

CROSS-DRESSING ON THE MARGINS OF EMPIRE:

WOMEN PIRATES AND THE NARRATIVE OF THE CARIBBEAN

Lizabeth Paravisini-Gebert

> *To my young friend Aryeh Gold-Parker,*
> *who so kindly lent me his copy of*
> The Man Whose Mother Was a Pirate

Nearly 300 years after they sailed the Caribbean Sea from the Bahamas to Jamaica with "Calico" Jack Rackam's crew, pirates Anne Bonny and Mary Read remain the region's most infamous women at sea.[1] Their piratical careers, which ended with their capture and trial in November 1720, have fascinated writers from Captain Charles Johnson (the first chronicler of their adventures, once thought to be a pseudonym for Daniel Defoe) to the present, being recounted in countless stories, songs, novels, plays, movies, and children's books.[2] The enduring fascination of their story has been doubtless the result of their gender, of their irruption into a quintessentially male world, and of the titillation of their adventures in a highly eroticized environment. They have retained their hold on the popular imagination because of the protean nature of what is known of their personalities and adventures: just enough documentation of their escapades has survived to anchor them firmly in the history of the Caribbean at a specific time and place; enough remains tantalizingly in mystery to give the imagination endless wings.

Writers throughout the last three centuries have woven countless narratives around the erotic possibilities of Anne Bonny and Mary Read's cross-dressing adventures in that most male and most lawless of possible settings—the eighteenth-century pirate ship. I would like, however, to claim them for the Caribbean margins in which popular versions of early colonial history begin to be told. Taking my cue from the earliest interpretations of their story and from their connection to a crucial period in West Indian history—when the pressures of European competition are brought to bear on the Spanish empire and the region begins to define itself in more complex terms—I would like to examine the ways in which the various retellings of Bonny and Read's piratical careers become ways of narrating and interpreting the Caribbean.

The earliest extant sources of the Bonny and Read story, *The Tryals of Captain John Rackam and other Pyrates* (1721),[3] a pamphlet printed in Jamaica within days of their arrest and trial (and sent by the Jamaican governor to London in lieu of his official report), and Johnson's *A General History of the Robberies and Murders of the Most Notorious Pirates,* published in 1724,[4] make much of their being women. Their tales are most decidedly "engendered" by the thrill of their male attire, by the play of concealments and disclosure of their breasts that punctuates the narrative of their adventures, and by their ultimate reprieve from the gallows by the plea of "their bellies" (the fact that they both claimed to be pregnant at the time of their conviction and sentence to execution). The constant shifting of the boundaries between their male activities and their female essences will always be at the center of any narration of their real or imagined adventures—ideal canvases on which to deploy the constant shifting of national and geographic boundaries that typify Caribbean history in the early decades of the eighteenth century.

The salient points of their story, as given by Johnson, whom we must trust (despite many obvious inventions) as their earliest biographer, are as follows. Mary Read, an illegitimate child, had been raised as a boy by her mother in a fraudulent attempt to pass her off as the legitimate infant she had lost just prior to the girl's birth. At thirteen she had been put into service as a footboy in a brothel, but soon tiring of this employment had sailed in a man-of-war to become a soldier in Flanders. Smitten with love for a fellow soldier, she had disclosed her true gender, and having refused a sexual liaison outside of marriage, they had been married with great fanfare. After her husband's premature death, however, she had again joined the army, but seeing very little possibility of advancement, sailed for the West Indies. En route she was kidnapped by pirates, whom she joined. When her ship was captured by a Jamaican warship in 1720, Anne Bonny was among her companions. It is quite clear from the tone of Johnson's narrative that of the two pirates, Mary Read was his favorite, "for he could always find some means of excusing her actions or praising her purity."[5]

Bonny was the illegitimate daughter of a parlour maid and a prosperous Irish lawyer who, faced with the scandal of his adulterous relationship, left Ireland and his wife for South Carolina with his lover and daughter. There he had become the owner of a plantation, and Anne enjoyed very comfortable circumstances until her rebellious ways (exemplified primarily by her penchant for cross-dressing and preference for male companions and manly pursuits) and a misguided marriage to a poor seaman led her to be cut off from home and fortune. Having gone to Providence Island, then a refuge for pirates, with her husband, Anne encountered "Calico" Jack Rackam, who enticed her into leaving her husband and coming aboard his ship dressed as a man, thus beginning her career as a cross-dressing piratical marauder.

There is in their stories, which Johnson inserts in the picaresque tradition that produced, in the same year, Daniel Defoe's *Moll Flanders,* an emphasis on disguise and guile, on masquerade and subterfuge, that rests on the calculated concealment and unveiling of the women's true gender identity. The allure of their tale for the mass public of the period, as culled by Johnson from various newspaper accounts and bestselling pamphlets, rests on the skillful structuring of his narrative around carefully spaced incidents of near-discovery or intentional revelation of the women's true nature. Their story, chroniclers would write later, is particularly remarkable for the extraordinary circumstance of the "weaker" sex assuming (through its adoption of male piratical attire) a character "peculiarly distinguished for every vice that can disgrace humanity, and at the same time for the exertion of the most daring, though brutal, courage." Of Mary's mother, Johnson writes that she "bred up her daughter as a boy, and when she grew up to some sense, she thought proper to let her into the secret of her birth, to induce her to conceal her sex" (131). Anne's father had likewise "put [her] into breeches as a boy" in order to deceive his legal wife, leading the child into regarding male attire as the easiest way to subvert the limitations of female life. Their subsequent adventures, as soldiers and pirates, would only be possible once cross-dressing had become second nature to them.

Cross-dressing, Marcus Rediker reminds us in his article "When Women Pirates Sailed the Seas," was a "deeply rooted underground tradition" in Read and Bonny's time, somewhat common to young, single, usually illegitimate women of humble origin.[6] Society offered few opportunities for women to break out of their sharply defined positions, and cross-dressing opened fantastic vistas in comparison. Bonny and Read, Rediker argues, perfectly exemplified what other researchers have identified as the two main reasons women chose for impersonating men: for Read it meant the possible escape from a life of poverty, for Bonny the satisfaction of her instincts for love and adventure.[7] The little that is known of Mary Read's career underscores the link between economic necessity, cross-dressing, and piracy. There were few careers in eighteenth-century England open to illegitimate young women with no connections or "characters": servitude, if they were fortunate; crime and prostitution if they were not. The threat of illness, starvation, or the dreaded workhouse was always before them. Cross-dressing gave Mary Read access to itinerant occupations such as foot or errand boy, which provided helpful and sometimes profitable connections to the criminal subculture,[8] and later soldiering.

Although not a widespread practice, cross-dressing was by all evidence common enough in reality, fiction, and drama. The London press occasionally reported on real-life heroines who dressed *en cavalier* to follow their lovers into adventure and battle; and biographical works such as the *Life and Adventures of Mrs. Christian Davies* (1740) or *The Female Soldier: Or the Surprising Life and Adventures of Hannah Snell* (1750) gave a peculiar notoriety to the cross-dressing heroine. Likewise, in fiction, Daniel Defoe's popular picaresque heroine, Moll Flanders, was a frequent cross-dresser; and it is obvious, from the number of cross-dressing heroines we find in the plays of Shakespeare, Aphra Behn, William Wycherley, George Farquhar, and other leading dramatists of the preceding period, that the theatergoing public found the type diverting enough. Cross-dressing women were often celebrated in popular ballads, then at the height of their popularity, and Anne and Mary's adventures would themselves be the subject of many such ditties. "With pitch and tar her hands were hard/Tho' once like velvet soft," claims one, "She weighed the anchor, heav'd the lead/And boldly went aloft."[9] Dianne Dugaw, in her various studies on women and popular balladry in England, writes of these sailing and soldiering women disguised as men—"rambling female sailors," as in the title of a popular ballad—as "a gender-confounding ideal of womanly behavior which defies simple-minded explanations of human sexuality."[10] In her assessment, these ballads, which spoke to an audience of common people, open a space for the type of heroine "whose stories rarely surface in the annals of 'history'" (183).

There is also ample evidence in the period of our heroines' adventures, moreover, of a fascination with the earthiest aspects of female cross-dressing. The anonymous *The Life and Adventures of Mrs. Christian Davies*

(1740), the biography of Mother Ross, who saw service under the Duke
of Malborough in the Low Countries—a book also attributed to Daniel
Defoe—tells in great detail "how women performed a certain natural operation without being discovered."[11] This feat Mother Ross had accomplished through the use of a "urinary instrument" whose description defies
the imagination. Another historian of piracy will excuse his interest in the
most prurient aspects of female cross-dressing by arguing that "it is impossible to discover the truth about these unique women pirates without some
consideration of the usual sanitary arrangements on a sloop."[12] The
detailed inquiry into the minutest details of cross-dressed life on board
pirate and navy ships is indicative of the prurient interest in the materiality of the female body and the intricacies of its concealment that has contributed to the lasting appeal of Read and Bonny's tale.

> *I confess I am malicious enough to desire that the world should see,*
> *to how much better purpose the* Ladies *travel than their* Lords;
> *and that, whilst it is surfeited with Male travels, all in the same*
> *tome, and stuft with the same trifles; a lady has the skill to strike*
> *out a new path, and to embellish a worn-out subject, with variety*
> *of fresh and elegant entertainment.*
>
> —Mary Astell, *Letters* (1785)[13]

Bonny and Read, although travelers, were not writers—their legacy is
not among the numerous travel books produced in the eighteenth century,
some of them by women. As Thomas Curley writes in *Samuel Johnson and
the Age of Travel,*

> The number of travel-books issuing from presses underscores their over-
> whelming popularity in the 18th century. Between 1660 and 1800 eight
> encyclopedic collections and forty five smaller compilations appeared in
> England. Besides the major works, there were thousands of individual
> accounts and miscellanies of local tours, distant expeditions, and Continen-
> tal travels. If we include publications from the Continent, the number of all
> European collections of voyages and travels would alone mount to well over
> a hundred voluminous productions in several editions and translations.[14]

Most of these travelers, however, were men. Women did not travel as
often as men did, since they could not do so independently, nor could they
venture safely (or so was the belief at the time) into what were considered
dangerous or far-away destinations.[15] It was forbidden by social conven-

tion. Women are thus at a disadvantage as potential writers of travelogues, as they were at a disadvantage as travelers. Those women who wrote about their journeys belonged to the middle- and upper classes—Aphra Behn, Mrs. Hester Lynn Thrale, Mary Morgan, Mrs. Mary Ann Hanway, Ann Radclife, and Mrs. Kindersley, among others[16]—worlds apart from the milieu that produced an at-best semiliterate Mary Read. Mrs. Hanway, writing in the preface to her *A Journey to the Highlands of Scotland* (1776), speaks of her reasons for traveling as stemming from a "sentimental" impulse:

> I resolved to travel rather critically than casually, rather to accommodate my friends with information than merely to gratify the greediness of vacant curiosity. The consequences were, I did not suffer the postilion to indulge his professional passion, to pass briskly through any parts of cultivated country, or rattle rapidly over the pavement of towns, that were fertile of remarks, but ordered him to move *sentimentally;* in a word, I rode pencil in hand, employing myself in drawing a sketch of the landscape, whether of hill or valley, morass or mountain, as it lay before me . . .[17]

The statement is a remarkably revealing one, as it speaks volubly of class and privilege; she is in a position to instruct her friends, give orders to the postilion, and survey the landscape proprietarily. Bonny and Read's relationship to the landscape traveled is of a different sort altogether. They must propel themselves forward without aid from postilions and—having undertaken their journeys without "a view to writing and publishing their observations for the benefit of travellers and the information of the curious"[18]—are without the means to instruct. As pirates they inhabit the margins of society and discourse; as sailors—workers, albeit criminally employed—they lack the leisure to travel *sentimentally* across the landscape and therefore are not at liberty to write. Their tales come to us second-hand, as multiple interpretations of the stories they wrote into history. Not having written their own accounts, they have become the heroines of a multiplicity of fictions.

Bonny and Read, like Hannah Snell—the unlettered daughter of a Worcester hosier who saw service in both the navy and army between 1745 and 1750 and whose adventures were narrated in *The Female Soldier*—must rely on the "hacks" of their period, balladeers and pamphleteers writing for immediate public consumption, for the shape their stories would take. Their story sprang into the public imagination at a time when sensibilities were shifting away from the picaresque transvestite heroine who embodied "the trope of masquerading as a pastime and as a way of conceptualizing identity"[19] to the ethos of female delicacy embodied in the sentimentality of the Richardsonian novel.

The contemporary accounts of their story—the anonymous pamphlet *The Tryals of Captain John Rackam, and Other Pyrates* . . . and Captain Charles Johnson's *A General History of the Robberies and Murders of the Most Notorious Pirates*—faced with two cross-dressing heroines, assign each to a different model of womanhood. Mary is made to fit into the developing bourgeois ethos of the reluctant transvestite, able in love and war, who nonetheless aspires to a life of genteel virtue; Anne must, by way of contrast, embody the gritty despair and unheroic stance of one who has turned her back on chastity and opted for sexual titillation and "manly" savagery. Both renderings of womanhood, however, underscore how gendered identities—the various versions of maleness and femaleness open to these cross-dressing adventuresses—are self-generated rather than "natural," based on perceptions and relationships and not inherent. In *Making Sex: Body and Gender from the Greeks to Freud,* Thomas Laqueur argues that the public's understanding of gender and sexuality had undergone a profound change in the early eighteenth century, a period that corresponded to that of our heroines' adventures: "An anatomy and physiology of incommensurability replaced a metaphysics of hierarchy in the representation of woman in relation to man . . . the female body came to be understood no longer as a lesser version of the male's (a one-sex model) but as its incommesurable opposite (a two-sex model)."[20] This oppositional model of gendered identities, Catherine Craft-Fairchild argues in her turn, "depended for its stability upon the maintenance of a clearly visible line of demarcation between the roles of man and women; cross-dressing, in violating the boundaries between separate spheres, came increasingly to be perceived as a threat" (177). Bonny and Read, living in a world where gendered identity is increasingly constructed by means of external signs—clothing, stances, manners, voice—must manipulate what remains of flexibility in these perceptions to navigate the sea of possibilities that cross-dressing opens for them.

> The pirate queens before the judge
> Each pleaded for her life.
> "I am about to have a child;
> I am a pirate's wife."
> —Jane Yolen, *The Ballad of the Pirate Queens*

Cross-dressing is as necessary to Bonny and Read's negotiation of the limitations of their gender as the revelation of their "true" gender identity is necessary to the resolution of their tales. Their hold on the popular imagination stems, after all, from the dramatic revelation of their female-ness during their trial, exemplified by the witnesses' references to "the largeness of their breasts" and their sensationalized announcement of their pregnancies. Beginning with Johnson's 1724 account, the disclosure of their gender identity through the exposure of their breasts becomes an essential plot device in any narrative of their adventures. This breast-revelation motif may have been suggested to Johnson and later chroniclers by the 1721 semi-official account of the trial, in which captives called as witnesses make much of having been led into a belief that the two fierce pirates were women by their possessing distinctly female breasts. This, cou-pled with their dramatic life-saving revelation of their being "quick with child," emphasized for the contemporary audience their gender-bound true constitution, which, measured against their quintessentially male activ-ities, led to their overshadowing the till-then famous John Rackam in the popular imagination.

Their own "essential" womanhood—literally embodied in their breasts and pregnancies—is effectively counterpoised to a witness' accounts, as quoted in *The Tryals* . . . , of the prisoners at the bar as wearing "Mens Jack-ets and long Trouzers, and Handkerchiefs tied about their heads; and that each of them had a Machet and a Pistol in their Hands, and cursed and swore at the men, to murder the Deponent." Their breasts and bellies—evidence of their purportedly true female nature—are also juxtaposed to, and serve to counter, their reported statements of a wanton cruelty and disregard for life of which only males should be capable. Mary, a witness reported, had replied to his asking whether she was not afraid of death by hanging (the usual pun-ishment for a conviction for piracy), by saying that "she thought it no great hardship, for were it not for that, every cowardly fellow would turn Pirate, and so infest the seas that men of courage must starve."[21] Annie, receiving a visit from her lover John Rackam hours before he was executed, was said to have told him "that he was sorry to see him there, but if he had fought like a man, he need not have been hanged like a dog."[22]

The breast-revelation motif is particularly crucial to the telling of Read's tale. The story of her adulthood is traditionally centered around three episodes of intentional disclosure of her sex, two built upon her "suffer[ing] the discovery to be made, by carelessly showing her breasts, which were very white," to both the soldier in Flanders whom she would eventually marry and the pirates' captive by whom she is smitten and who will become the father of her unborn child.[23] (In John Abbott's 1874 account, for example, Mary, pretending to be asleep in the tent she shared with her "fair-faced, flaxen-haired" Flemish comrade, "allowed her drapery so to fall as partially to expose her fair and beautiful bosom.[24]) The third episode is the revelation in court of her gender and pregnancy. Subsequent writers have embellished Johnson's tale of a duel she fought with another pirate in her efforts to save her lover's life by expanding on this motif. In Johnson's version, Mary's lover, a captive turned reluctant pirate, found himself engaged to fight a duel with a fiercer and better-trained opponent. Fearful for her lover, Mary quarreled with the pirate and challenged him ashore two hours before the pending duel, where she fought him with sword and pistol and killed him upon the spot. To this, later writers have added two variations of the breast-revealing motif, the use of the breast emphasizing the underlying gist of the episode. In one, Mary, about to be slain by her opponent, tears open "her rough sailcloth shirt" and reveals her breasts. "For an instant only the pirate forgot his guard," Jamaican folklorist Clinton Black tells us, "forgot his peril as he stared in utter astonishment at what he saw. But that instant was his undoing."[25] In another, having vanquished him, she pulls aside her clothes, baring her breasts as she cries to his opponent, "You thought me a woman and struck me on the cheek. Well! It is in truth a woman to-day who kills you that she may teach others to respect her"[26] (see figure 3.4 below). Then she coolly proceeded to pull the trigger, blowing his head to pieces, thus juxtaposing feminine weakness and male deadly power.

Not surprisingly, episodes connected to the unveiling of their breasts—as the most salient feature, no pun intended, of their "true" gender identity—are most common in the numerous illustrations that have accompanied the various retellings of the tale. The earliest known illustration of Bonny and Read is that accompanying Charles Johnson's *A General History. . . .* It approaches the depiction of gender through female attributes (long hair, an intimation of roundness of breasts, and slimness of waist) and a softness of pose (tilted heads, hands extending gracefully away from the body, demure glances that turn away from the artist/viewer) that counter the swords and hatchets waived, the wide trousers and background of pirate ships that are emblems of their piratical careers (see figure 3.1). It serves as the basis for two illustrations (see figures 3.2 and 3.3 below) that reproduce the same basic elements while claiming the viewer's attention to the open jackets and intimations of naked breasts.[27]

Likewise, the lithograph that accompanied Maurice Bresson's *The Scourge of the Indies: Buccaneers, Corsairs, and Filibusters* (1929), dramatizes,

The two women Pirates, Mary Read and Anne Bonney.

Figure 3.1. From Charles Johnson's *A General History of the Robberies and Murders of the Most Notorious Pyrates* (1724).

through the revelation of Mary's breasts at the conclusion of her duel, one of the central devices of this cross-dressing plot.[28] In turning the viewer's gaze to Mary's breast, the illustrator evokes the erotic component of her tale as the dominant message: the visual depiction of the naked breast intensifies the tension between Mary's male attire, violent gestures, and her victim lying prone and dying on the ground.

Margaret R. Miles, in "The Virgin's One Bare Breast: Female Nudity and Religious Meaning in Tuscan Early Renaissance Culture," underscores the power of the image of the naked breast (particularly the representation of the nursing Virgin) as signifying the "power to conceive, to nourish, shelter and sustain human life, a power that may well have been understood by . . . people threatened by famine, plague, and social chaos as 'the body's best show of power.'"[29] This power was seen, however, "as [one] that must be firmly directed to the socially desirable ends of a patriarchal society, that is, to keeping women 'in their place'"—the very message behind the duel depicted in the illustration, fought to preserve the life of the man Mary loved and with whom she hoped to fulfill her dream of domestic happiness. As in the representation of the Virgin's nurturing breast, the emphasis on Bonny and Read's breasts in the illustrations of their tales acts always as a visual reminder of how women "must be guided to accept the model

Mary Read

Figures 3.2 and 3.3. From Clinton Black's *Pirates of the West Indies* (Cambridge University Press, 1989).

of the nursing Virgin without identifying with her power—a power derived from her body, but ultimately a social as well as a physical power."[30]

Most recently, In Jane Yolen's *The Ballad of the Pirate Queens,* a book

Anne Bonny

Mary Read blows out the brains of the sailor who had insulted her. (Lithograph of the romantic period.)

MARIE READ.

Figure 3.4. An image from c. 1828 (described by Maurice Besson in *The Scourge of the West Indies* (Routledge & Sons, 1929) as a "Lithograph of the Romantic Period").

intended for children, the nurturing power of the female body is depicted through David Shannon's illustration of the defiant pirates flaunting their power to procreate, standing before the judge in profile, their breasts eclipsed by their protruding bellies—the judge's disapproving stare and the crowd's astonished gasps as a backdrop (see figure 3.5).[31] The illustration's affirmation of Bonny and Read's essential femaleness—doubly underscored by their breasts and bellies—returns us to Johnson's contemporary account, in which the pirates' dramatic plea of "their Bellies" propels them out of history into a multiplicity of fictions having at their core the tensions between true female identity and the freedom afforded by the assumption of male attire.

> *Today's lessons were math and geography. In math we learned*
> *about angles. (You use them when aiming a canon.) In geography*
> *we learned where the West Indies are and how to read treasure*
> *maps.*
> —Colin McNaughton, *Captain Abdul's Pirate School*

The sensation caused by the women's cross-dressing piratical career, as revealed after their apprehension and trial, must needs be seen in the context of England's efforts to eradicate piracy in the Caribbean. "Piracy is frequently (but far from always) against foreigners (and so has links with war); . . . [it] is often not committed randomly by individuals but is part of a complex structure of trade and territorial power."[32] The Golden Age of piracy, the period between 1650 and 1730, included the years of the Spanish War of Succession (1701-14), whose end left the soldiers from disbanded armies looking for ways to survive; piracy became one of the few job options. The surplus of labor at the end of the war had produced an immediate reduction in wages and greater competition for available seafaring jobs. It was followed by a slump in trade beginning in 1715, extending well into the 1730s. The extraordinary growth of commerce in the colonies before this slump had, however, "made it a tempting field for depredations of every kind, and the result [had been] that high-handed proceedings on the open sea [were] the rule rather than the exception"[33]; the slump intensified the competition and tempted pirates to move against those communities that had previously shown extreme leniency toward them. Pirates had been until then more often than not tolerated by otherwise law-abiding communities. Charleston, South Carolina, Anne Bonny's hometown, had been particularly notorious for its forbearance. Pirates of all sorts walked its streets with impunity; if arrested by the English authorities and brought to trial, juries rarely managed to return a negative verdict. The juries "were made of the people, and then, as now, public sentiment ruled, the law to the contrary notwithstanding."[34] Moreover, the Charleston authorities had sought the aid of the pirates in the colony's defense when under attack by the Spanish, as it had done in 1706. It was not until the pirates began to plunder the colonists themselves that stricter measures were enacted and hangings of pirates became more common. Governments shifted from tolerance or indifference to active suppression only when legitimate trade was disrupted. These efforts at suppression had peaked in 1720 following offers of general pardons to any pirate renouncing (his or her) profession. These pardons, however, offered in 1717 and 1718, had failed to rid the sea of pirate vessels, as acceptance of the pardon meant merely a return to the dismal economic conditions from which pirates had sought to escape. Aware of their failure, English colonial authorities intensified their campaigns against piracy, with the result that probably 500 to 600 pirates were executed between 1716 and 1726,[35] among them Jack Rackam and most of his crew. Rackam's most grievous sin—for which he and his followers had to be made an example—was that of returning to piracy after having purportedly announced his renunciation of piratical activities.

Pleading their Bellies

Figure 3.5. From Jane Yolen's *The Pirate Queens* (Harcourt Brace & Company, 1995). Illustrations by David Shannon.

Eradication efforts were centered primarily on the colony of New Providence in the Bahamas, one of the chief pirate headquarters. In January 1708 British merchants and planters had petitioned the British Crown to take the government of the Bahamas into their "immediate protection and government" in order to safeguard West Indian trade, which included at the time a profitable slave trade threatened by piracy—there had been too many incidents of pirates displaying their humanitarian feelings by giving chase to slave ships and freeing their cargo. The 1710s witnessed a struggle for control between settlers engaged in the extremely profitable production and shipping of cotton, wood, sugar, indigo, salt, tortoise shell, and whale oil, and the pirates who had made of the Bahamas their capital. Settlers complained of being forced into cooperation with the pirates and argued that "without good government and some strength" the Bahamian islands would always be a "shelter for pyrates."[36] Their successful attacks upon international commerce between 1716 and 1726 created what Marcus Rediker has called "an imperial crisis."[37] In 1717, many complained, Nassau "was in the hands of professionals," and as a result a year later the English Government sent a squadron to the Island of New Providence, led by Captain Woodes Rogers, offering a general pardon as a first step in turning the "pirates' nest" into a law-abiding colony.

The English government's struggle to seize and retain control of the islands, the conflict between lawful and piratical commerce, between the embryonic settler establishment and the anti-establishment pirate population against which Bonny and Read's stories play, is "embodied" in the many tales of their adventures that circulated after their trial, conviction, and escape from execution. Their tale became emblematic of the Bahamian struggle between lawfulness and lawlessness, between their "true" nature as domestically bound women needing to reveal their breasts, pleading their bellies, and their unnatural incarnation as bloodthirsty pirates. A trial of pirates, Julie Wheelwright has argued, was "an expression of the power of social leaders as well as of their needs: freedom to move goods without impediment; the acceptance of their values; freedom to expropriate wealth in whatever way they chose, supported by a flexible and acquiescent work force."[38] Bonny and Read's trial has to be seen as part of the "greatest wave of such trials." Their story, Mary Read's particularly, embodied the strife between the settler's Puritanical notions and the pirate's love of life, "for when ashore, they spent their nights in riotous living, drinking, dancing, and carousing."[39] Johnson insists on Mary Read's desire for domesticity, thus incarnating the central conflict of the Caribbean as a locus of Empire in the early decades of the eighteenth century. In her capacity for an amorous passion leading into self-forgetfulness—she, for example, neglects her arms and accouterments, previously kept "in the best order," when she falls in love, following her loved one into danger "without being commanded," only to be near him—in her proving "very reserved and modest" as well as steadfast in her resisting an illicit liaison with her future husband, in her resolution to leave the life of piracy to live honestly with her new lover (a decision thwarted by her arrest and trial), in her being able to "plead her belly," she proves her true nature, thereby legitimizing for her contemporaries the economic and political battles being waged in the Caribbean. She was, after all, a pirate by accident, and fierce and determined as she was in the defense of her ship and crew, looked forward to a life of domesticity. Although she was a "daring pirate," as a nineteenth-century historian of piracy reminds us, "she was also a woman, and again she fell in love."[40] What better symbol for English aspirations for control and order in the region than this English young woman (she was then 28), who had patriotically fought for her country in Flanders before sailing to the Caribbean, and who yearned for domestic prosperity? The unveiling of her breasts (in Johnson's version) was always in the guise of a "confession" that would eventually lead to marriage and the possibility of assuming her true identity. Her story demonstrated that "the heroine's flight from domestic commitment was a temporary state"—she would ultimately contradict the rules under which she played.[41] Among the many apologies for Read's career as a pirate, the typical one reads thus:

> [Mary] was vain and bold in her disposition, but susceptible of the tenderest emotions, and of the most melting affections. Her conduct was generally directed by virtuous principles, while at the same time, she was violent in her attachments. Though she was inadvertently drawn into that dishonorable mode of life which has stained her character, and given her a place among the criminals noticed in this work, yet she possessed a rectitude of principle and of conduct, far superior to many who have not been exposed to such temptations to swerve from the path of female virtue and honor.[42]

Anne, by contrast, was a pirate by choice, and in her tale contemporary audiences could read the need for the eradication of piracy. Of a fierce and courageous temper, she renounces the very life of domesticity that Mary craved—and that Anne enjoyed as the daughter of a prosperous South Carolina planter—in order to embrace a life of seafaring marauding. In most accounts of her adventures her link to Charleston, a city considered too embracing of piracy by Royal authorities, and her familiarity with the many pirates who visited the city with impunity, are underscored as evidence of her wicked tendencies and deficient upbringing. Anne, a colonial—as she had not only been raised in America but was marked by an "American" rashness and impudence—was said to have killed an *English* servant maid in a passion with a case-knife. Johnson claims to have found this story groundless upon further inquiry, but added that she was so robust that once, "when a young fellow would have lain with her against her will, she beat him so that he lay ill of it for a considerable time."[43] Her unfemale robustness, in this context, bears comparison with Mary's more feminine physique, as exemplified by the whiteness of the latter's breasts—particularly as Anne's physical strength exemplifies the roughness of the colonial as against the comparative daintiness of her English counterpart. A later chronicler would describe her as a "desperado, as robust in person as she was masculine in character."[44] Anne, an illegitimate child herself, growing up in a colonial culture not necessarily particular about legitimate unions and the strength of marital vows, had soon after her marriage found the means of "withdrawing her affection from her husband" and agreeing to elope with Rackam; further proof, in case we needed it, of the unmaidenly behavior and unnatural tendencies linked by writers of pamphlets and ballads to precisely those very elements of colonial licentiousness and piratical wickedness that it had become so necessary to eradicate. Anne's unwomanly nature is further attested to in her abandoning in Cuba the first child she had conceived with Rackam—as if the Caribbean, as a region, facilitated the unnatural abandonment of newborn babes.

> *When her snow-white breast in sight became,*
> *She prov'd to be a female frame,*
> *And Rebecca Young it was the name*
> *Of the Rambling Female Sailor . . .*
> *On the river Thames she was known full well,*
> *Few sailors could with her excel*
> *One tear let fall as the fate you tell,*
> *Of the Rambling Female Sailor.*
> —"The Rambling Female Sailor" (1830).[45]

The play of concealment and unveiling of these pirates' female bodies proved as fascinating to their contemporary readers in their literal and symbolic aspects as it would prove, encoded in new symbolic contexts, to later audiences, to which their tale has been presented to dramatize political and social ideals from Lockean liberalism to lesbian liberation. These accounts—most of them twentieth-century novels, plays, and films—seek meaning in the juxtaposition of the protagonists' femaleness against a "violent, ruthless enterprise, apparently drenched in masculinity" and linked to a particular geographic and historical space, notable for profanity, heavy drinking, and "thinly-veiled brutality and violence."[46] Standing, so to speak, between anarchy and domesticity, they are ever-repeating symbols of riotous freedom.

Julie Wheelwright, in her essay "Tars, Tarts and Swashbucklers," claims for Johnson's *A General History of the Pyrates* the use of poetic license to mold the historical Bonny and Read into the figures of the "rapacious lady pirates who still appear in women's fashion magazines and on screen today."[47] In her view, Johnson's central contribution to the reinvention of these questionable heroines is that of transforming them from "accepted members of the pirate crew into exceptional, bloodthirsty amazons." His version, for better or worse, with all the inventions for which he claims historical veracity, remains the "official," most accessible narrative, and is often quoted by most experts on piracy as fact. Johnson's version of Bonny and Read as cross-dressing "desperadas" with a soft romantic side was reinforced in a popular London chapbook of 1755 dedicated to adventurous women, the anonymous *The Lives and Adventures of the German Princess, Mary Read, Ann Bonny, Joahn Philips, Madam Churchill, Betty Ireland and Ann Hereford.*

The Bonny and Read story received a variety of treatments throughout the nineteenth century. The anonymous author of *The Daring Exploits of Henry Morgan,* published in 1813, for example, embellishes Johnson's version with an ambiguous account that appears to refer to Mary and Anne's relationship as lesbian—during their trial Mary will argue in her defense that "she entered the service of the privateer purely upon the account of Anne Bonny, who was her lover."[48] This unconventional assertion, however, is most explicitly contradicted by the rest of the text, which underscores Mary's sexual virtue—"she had behaved very modestly among the men"—and argues that Mary had assumed her male disguise "to prevent her being ill used by seamen; and being taken in that disguise, she continued in it for fear of being worse used by the barbarous crew of the pirates."[49] This is a view underscored in another nineteenth-century work, the anonymous *Les Aventures et l'héroïsme de Mary Read,* in which Mary, and her companion Anne, are depicted as "possessing a rectitude of conduct far superior to that of most women."[50]

These nineteenth-century accounts of Bonny and Read as models of virtuous comportment are balanced by portraits that underscore their unnatural occupation and unwomanly sensuality. The anonymous *History*

of the Lives and Bloody Exploits of the Most Noted Pirates . . . (1855) portrays
Anne as a spy with whom Jack Rackam develops "a criminal acquaintance," after which he became "very extravagant, and found it necessary, to
avoid detection and punishment, to abscond with his mistress."[51] Of Mary,
this account says not a word. A nineteenth-century French version—that
found in P. Christian's *Histoire des marins, pirates et corsaires* (1846-1850)—
underscores Mary's devotion to her would-be lover, but does it through the
highlighting (with a vivid and revealing illustration) the moment in which,
after defeating her lover's enemy in a duel, she displays her bosom to the
dying man to let him know that he has just been defeated by a woman (see
figure 3.5).[52]

These nineteenth-century versions of their adventures, however, have
little to say about the Caribbean setting of their tales, other than as a background that makes their adventures as pirates possible. None of them purports to be anything other than a rewriting of Johnson's account with
some harmless embellishments added for the interest of the reader. They
reinterpret but do not recast the narrative provided by Johnson into new
molds. Twentieth-century accounts, by contrast, provide seemingly endless
reimaginings of Bonny and Read's piratical adventures, treating them as
canvases on which authors can superimpose, with heavy doses of fiction,
everything from feminist ideology to 1960s-style alternative societies.[53]

One of the earliest of these is Frank Shay's 1934 *Pirate Wench*,[54] a novel
that builds an elaborate fiction around Mary as the de facto captain of her
pirate vessel, a figure owing more to Hollywood corsair fabrications than
to history. In his account, Anne emerges, not as a pirate, but as the weak
and jealous lover of the dissolute Rackam and as such, Mary's enemy. Shay
has frequent recourse in his text to allusions to the female body as emblematic of either English virtue or colonial licentiousness—assigning virtue, as
it has become traditional, to the English Mary and lewdness to Anne and
the many prostitutes of mixed race who inhabit the Caribbean space. He
explains Read's incursion into piracy, for example, as stemming from her
need to protect her body and virtue. Held prisoner by pirates, with other
members of the crew of the ship to which she belonged, she refuses to join
them until they order all prisoners to strip, whereupon a "blush crept to her
cheeks and her heart sickened with a great fear as she began unbuttoning
her jerkin" and she finally relents (49). Anne, by contrast, is not only an
adulteress, but a rabidly jealous one who does not hesitate to attack Mary
with a knife when she suspects Rackam of an interest in her or to
denounce her as a woman before the crew, knowing full well that the arti-

cles state plainly that the first wench on board goes to the captain, but the second must be sent down to the men, forcing Read to defend her body and honor from them. Despite her virtue, the myth engendered by Mary Read's piratical career is that of an eroticized woman "dressed in the clothes of her sex, amorous, voluptuous and bedizened with gems," her hands bloodied, and "more rapacious than any man" (244).

In *Pirate Wench,* the Caribbean is identified with the space where domestic happiness is possible for the likes of a disenfranchised working-class young woman such as Read was:

> What she wanted most of all was to go ashore and settle down and be a gen-
> uine housewife, taking care of husband and home and children if such there
> were. She might, she thought, like the Bahamas; she had heard the soil was
> fruitful and that there were no cold foul winters as in England. Too, land was
> cheap in addition to being fertile. She had over a hundred guineas in prize
> money and more was due her on the sales to be made in port. (77)

Read's first glimpse of the Caribbean, however, conjures up imperial notions of disdain for the "valueless" small islands of "rank and riotous verdure" that dot the West Indian seascape, and an identification with the conquerors who, like her, preferred "controlled loveliness." The social landscape of the Caribbean is invoked, ironically, through the sexuality of those non-English women whose bodies, unlike Read's, are available to the crewmen panting to go ashore, thus underscoring colonial notions of relative human (and womanly) value through the reference to "conquest":

> She listened to the ribald jests of her fellows as they told each other of their
> previous conquests ashore and talked or rum and women, two of life's ele-
> ments that were seemingly inseparable in their minds. There was a yellow
> girl here, she heard, a Spaniard there; all about her were men who declared
> that only black women knew the art of love, that the darker the meat the
> richer the quality; still others desired the fire of the Frenchwomen. [Read's]
> problem was not theirs. (83)

Conqueror-like, Read will establish a settlement, organized around the labor of African captives rescued from a slaver, through which she intends to create a sort of colonial utopia, with a form of government, specific tasks for all, and protection for the slave women from the advances of the whites. To this settlement, which resulted from her unconscious impulse for a home and children, she intended to enlist white women and merchants so as to turn it into a substantial colony of which she would be as much a mistress as she was of her vessel. Torn between her desire for home and domesticity and her habit of power, at a pivotal moment in the text Mary stands atop the high hill behind her settlement, surveying her domain, momentarily forgetting her desire for power before the vista of natural beauty before her, ironically unaware that her very proprietary surveying of the landscape is the gesture of imperial domination. From the vantage point of the hill, however, she will glimpse the British ship whose taking will be her undoing, as her success in capturing it unleashed against her the force of true and legitimate imperial power that will dismantle her unlawful settlement.

Shay's *Pirate Wench* is grounded on a detailed historical background that anchors Read's story in the British government's efforts to eradicate piracy. Read herself takes her place in the text as the ambivalent incarnation of these efforts, a character whose deficiencies as a pirate—stemming from her own ingrained desire for domesticity and control, for "settling" herself and others—leads her to collude with the forces of Empire who are destroying piracy and the freedom it represents. As she is seduced into dreams of being a lady through her love affair with the governor's son, her settlement—formed from "the human flotsam and jetsam that drifted hither and yon"—begins to shape itself architecturally along class lines: "The single street, at the head of which the wench had built her own house, was now crowded with various types of buildings, from those built with timber from captured prizes to the thatched huts of the negroes" (293). The ultimate irony, in Shay's interpretation, is that while Mary is tortured and condemned to hang, she must endure her ordeal with the knowledge that her erstwhile lover—"as piratical and vengeful a man as any she had met in her short life"—had been saved from torture and the gallows through the influence of his high-born family, and had claimed one half of her ship's treasure. He would go on—although death would spare her the knowledge of this—to lead the expedition that would raze her settlement at Grand Caicos. Mary Read's final victory, a hollow one at that, is that of relinquishing the expensive silk and brocade garments in which she had wished to die, in favor of her coarse sailcloth shirt, cotton hose, and rough boots: "I had thought to die as a woman but better judgement prevailed and I die as I lived" (329).

The Caribbean is but a barely-glimpsed promised land, offering possible riches and freedom, in *Mary Read: A Play in Three Acts* by James Bridie and Claud Gurney, produced for the first time in 1934, the same year that Shay's *Pirate Wench* was published.[55] The work, which follows Mary's story from her adolescence—when her mother successfully passes her off as her dead son—to her death after childbirth in Jamaica, adds to the familiar elements of her tale her romantic involvement with a painter and fellow soldier in Flanders who abandons her after their marriage and resurfaces in the West Indies as a spy of the government of the Bahamas in its efforts to apprehend Jack Rackam. The thematic focus of the play is Mary's ambivalent feelings about her gender, her discomfort with the sex and the limitations placed upon women, and the failure of every attempt she made to embrace her womanhood.

In Bridie's characterization of Mary Read, which supplements Johnson's contemporary account, her being "a bold, manly sort of wench" and her fierce and fearless temperament become the focus of her struggles to conform to the demands of womanhood (2). The text makes much of her courage and competence as a soldier and of her adherence to strict principles of honor and loyalty, even if these principles ultimately fall outside the law. Asked by the chaplain as she lays dying of fever if she is sorry for the life she led, her reply summarizes her peculiar code of honor:

No, I'm not sorry, I've led a gallant life. I've killed men, but always in fair fight and I've shown mercy to my prisoners. I've never robbed the poor nor wheedled the rich. I've never sold my soul for money or ease. I've never turned my back upon friend or foe. I've no woman's tricks, but I've no alderman's tricks either. I've never let cowardice stop me from doing anything under God's heaven. And I'll not go out of this life cringing to you nor to any man. (98)

Anne Bonny plays a very minor role in Bridie's *Mary Read,* serving primarily as a contrasting image of sensual womanhood placed against Mary's manly plainness. Described in the text as "a bundle of flaming sin," she stands in sharp contrast against a Mary who finally loses her virginity the night before Rackam's ship is ambushed. She is Mary's match in courage and daring and is endowed with a sense of humor that allows her to befriend the sterner Mary. She has, after all, also left her Virginia plantation home in search of freedom from the confines of genteel womanhood: "I had my fill of fine gentlemen in the sugar plantations, with their 'Pray Ma'ams' and their 'Oh Ma'ams' and their 'Madam, your obedients.' They can't ask a girl for what they want without wimpering and play-acting. And then along came Calico Jack like a great roaring stallion. I thought I'd died and gone to heaven" (76).

Flights of erotic fancy, however, are not a part of Mary's quest. If England, Flanders, and the army prove to be less than ideal spaces for her search for freedom from the confines of an understanding of womanhood for which she is ill-suited, the Caribbean emerges as the place of escape, idealized as "a dream of purple mountains and dark trailing jungles" (47). Her lover lures her toward the Indies as a place where she could "wrap petticoats round your legs" and leave behind a life of soldiering and pirateering. Pernambuco, he tells her, is a fine town "with broad tiled pavements, and great avenues of tall cocoanut trees" where "the sun shines all day long" and they dig out "dark, copper-coloured gold, and mint it into moidores" (47). But the Caribbean space toward which she entices her is rapidly becoming a space that no longer tolerates freedom and lawlessness, a space preparing for an assault on unconventionality and permissiveness in the name of Empire. The third act of *Mary Read* is plotted against the Government's proclamation of full-scale war against piracy. The governor of the Bahamas, commenting on the state of the colony, summarizes the official view of the situation: "I am here in the midst of a nest of cutthroats and expected to subdue them by proclamations. The island is packed to the foreshore with pirates, waiting till I drop an eyelid to disembowel me and every honest man-jack in the fort" (66). Bridie recognizes, and elaborates dramatically in his play, the startling historical coincidence of Bonny and Read's piratical adventure as unfolding against the canvas of Captain Woodes Rogers's arrival in New Providence bearing the official Royal pardon that would do so much to end piracy and establish firm colonial control over the Caribbean region.

Marie Read, femme pirate (1952) by Michel Candie[56] takes a novel approach to the retelling of the story of Read and Bonny by presenting the text as purportedly fragments of a journal drafted by Read herself.[57] Written in French, the tale that emerges from this pseudo-autobiographical narrative reflects Candie's protofeminist concerns, presented here through Marie's ambivalences about gender roles and reluctance to succumb to what her age considered appropriate womanly pursuits, a portrait that goes against the grain of the familiar characterization of Mary as the most genderbound of the two female pirates. Candie, in her retelling of Read and Bonny's tale, posits Marie's wavering between land and sea, femininity and masculinity, piracy and domesticity, as a paradigm of the contemporary female quandary. Her adventurous, masculine impulse always propels her toward vast spaces and openness; her yearning to share the joys of home and family becomes a catalyst toward confinement and death. "There is always a part of me which remains unavowable in my relationships with people who live on dry land. I can only find complete rapport with Anne Bonny," she claims (138). Standing as she is between one option and the other, she is never truly whole. Unable, like Anne Bonny, to be both mother and pirate, she ultimately wills herself to die.

Marie's relationship with Anne Bonny—the bond of friendship between them—is at the center of Marie's dilemma. As daring pirates they are unique and alone, only able to rely completely on one another. As women, they have followed opposite paths; while Anne has exploited her femininity and sexuality, giving full rein to both sides of her nature, Marie has repressed her sexuality, not trusting to the ambivalence of her vacillating bisexuality. Torn between manifold attractions of the comradeship of her fellow pirates and the comforting but ultimately treacherous sisterhood of the upper-class, empire-bound women among whom she is sent as a spy, she ultimately gives herself to Christian, a captive of the pirates with whose plight she identifies, only to discover to her bewilderment that she has surrendered to Guillaume de Rieuze and that the father of her unborn child is an aristocratic spy working with the enemies of piracy and the husband of her erstwhile friend Catherine de Rieuze. The betrayal, which she sees as a self-betrayal, as a failure of her divided self to act in concert and wholeness, leaves her unable to face life again:

> Before dying, I would like to pinpoint the breach through which my virtue drained away; there was but a fleeting instant in which I lowered my guard: the moment when I met Catherine in Manzanillo. Why couldn't I understand that she would become my unrelenting enemy? I loved that flawless face, the apparent rigor of her life. I relished the time I spent in her house. I came to find it natural to drink my coffee out of jade cups. Or maybe Corner was right: jade was not made to assuage our thirst. And then, afterwards, there was Guillaume. Those are the two poles between which my fate shipwrecked, and it is only now when I'm so close to the end, that I realize that only one face fills my heart: Anne's. She's the only one to whom my death will seem a betrayal, the only one who'll be unable to forgive me for its being voluntary, the only one who'll continue to love me even if she won't forgive me . . . (293)

Marie's quandary is the product of ethical principles challenged by her incursions into soldiering and piracy. Her behavior had been guided by the mentorship of the tutor her grandmother had provided for her after her mother had passed her off as a boy. Educated in the ways and principles of an English gentleman, she must translate the code of honor and rules of behavior of English middle- and upper-class manhood into the more disreputable environments into which her cross-dressing experiences propel her. Pitted against the decimation of the war in Flanders and the betrayal and savagery of the political and economic tensions of the early-eighteenth-century Caribbean, these principles betray their emptiness and irrelevance, their need to be replaced by a different system of values whose chimerical impossibility Marie must ultimately accept.

These new values are embodied in the romantic notion of a pirates' Utopia, the Republique des Frères de la Côte (the Republic of the Brethren of the Coast), a democratic nation built on the cooperative principles of the pirate community, one that would not recognize differences in class, race, and gender. The pirates' community is, in Candie's rendition and despite its obvious shortcomings, a society predicated on purity of principle, comradeship, and honor. The forces of government, on the other hand, rely on betrayal, seduction, and dishonor to accomplish their goal of territorial and political expansion. Marie's tragic destiny will hinge on the outcome of this unequal struggle between an outmatched Brotherhood and the combined force of the European powers, which can agree on nothing but their destruction.

Marie Read, femme pirate is rare among accounts of piracy in its explicit and detailed discussions of the issue of slavery from an abolitionist standpoint. Guided by Père Antoine in his role as her new mentor in West Indian social issues, Marie is instructed in the realities of plantation life through his tales of savage plantation masters and brutalized runaway slaves. Having heard from the highly placed wives of English noblemen and diplomats among whom she dwelled as a spy of the atrocities committed by the Jamaican Maroons against planters—one plantation had been "attacked by a horde of black demons, the crops set on fire, the [planter's] wife and children massacred"(114)—Père Antoine must offer the Maroons' side of the tale. The men of Nauny (Nannytown) have indeed become "ferocious beasts," the priest will admit, but only after enduring the sort of barbarous treatment that leads men to "disregard pity" (115).[58] A runaway slave who has found his way to Père Antoine's house had fled from a planter who fed his slaves nothing but rotten salted herring and who, having caught him out hunting for better food, had accused him of theft and "lashed him mercilessly." Having fled the plantation, he had made his way to Nauny, but only after having been pursued by a pack of dogs that had "torn up his calves and thighs" (116). Tales such as these have led Père Antoine to conclude that the slaves "had been well schooled" in pitilessness by their masters.

In Candie's somewhat sentimental presentation of the erotic elements of piracy, elusive visions of domestic bliss (such as Anne's bittersweet contemplation of the portrait of the young baby girl she had given birth to in Cuba and left in the care of relatives of Rackam in Jamaica) are countered by descriptions of wife-battering and rape. While in Cuba, Marie learns of a young married woman who is frequently battered by a husband to whom she is devoted but who cannot forget her admission of having been raped by the captain of the pirate ship who had attacked the boat in which she was returning to Cuba from Spain. Her husband "was convinced that a woman can never forget the man who has taken her virginity," a claim that is gleefully mocked by Marie's aristocratic companions, who claim that their wedding nights were best forgotten (128).

Candie exploits the complexities of the eighteenth-century Caribbean space as the dramatic backdrop against which she can portray twentieth-century feminist concerns and rapidly developing anticolonial thought. Her Caribbean is a space for enlightening Marie Read about the forces of oppression—patriarchal, colonial, racial, of class and social hierarchy—that shaped her life in England and Flanders and thwart her ambition for freedom and economic self-sufficiency at sea. Her relationship with the aristocratic Catherine de Rieuze, instrumental as it is in opening new vistas for social understanding, is also a perfect vehicle for Candie to explore a complex approach to feminism that takes into account class differences. For Marie Read, child of the London underclass, cannot find true sisterhood in an aristocratic companion who vows friendship only to become her bitterest enemy when their notions of political action diverge. It is ultimately Marie's realization that her life has played itself against seemingly insurmountable class-bound obstacles at home that pursue her relentlessly in the "frontier" space in which she hoped to escape that leads Marie to seek her death. Knowing they are behind her in fast pursuit, she wills herself to die.

Steve Gooch's *The Women Pirates Ann Bonney and Mary Read,* a play first produced by the Royal Shakespeare Company at the Aldwych Theatre in London in July 1978, seeks to place the Caribbean region as the centerpiece of the drama.[59] The work is technically and thematically an ambitious dramatic undertaking, intent on conveying the "broad panorama" spanned by Read and Bonny's lives through the techniques of the alternative theater and its expectations of a more active and engaged relationship to its audience. Gooch relies on a chorus of singers to offer the broader outlines of their complex story while structuring his scenes to highlight the salient points of the familiar story.

Gooch's reading of Read and Bonny's story is eminently political: he sees them as pursuing their "personal odysseys" in those very sites "where the European empire-builders of the eighteenth century were clashing: Ireland, Flanders, Carolina, the Caribbean" (iii). The broad geographical spaces in which their adventures unfold "reproduced the economic links and political hot-spots of their age" (iii). In Gooch's interpretation, the two women emerge as casualties not only of the restrictions imposed on women in their societies, but of "the development of English imperialism itself." When forced to leave Flanders after the war has ended and after her Flemish husband has been brutally murdered for having married an English-woman, Mary equates her fate to that of the devastated continent she is leaving behind: "If I stay now, I'll finish up like him. Battered and flattened like this whole continent. What's left is alive with maggots and fit only for the vultures in London and Paris" (28).

Gooch's Caribbean—particularly the pirate community of Nassau—is depicted as an "alternative society" of "anti-colonial rebels" that had the potential for becoming the site of a sort of piratical Utopia. One of the scenes of the play finds the pirates discussing the possibility of creating their own kingdom:

> We could build an empire here if we pulled together. Rome itself was started by sheep thieves and runaway slaves. Force is the key, and force we have. If we took the Indians, the labourers and settlers under our wing, we could make slaves of those who don't recognize our sovereignty. Declare ourselves a legal monarchy and every court in Europe would recognize us. They'd even send ambassadors! (38)

Gooch sees this pirate community—in which Read and Bonny can claim a role despite its intrinsic sexism—as engaged in a struggle to develop a new way of life; he sees the pirates themselves as community builders, "potential law-makers as well as law-breakers" (iii). They may have terrorized the settlers throughout the Caribbean and the Atlantic coast and interfered with legitimate trade, but they recognize their role as a force of resistance to the pressures of Empire. The last reckless voyage of Rackam and his crew is seen as a "desperate rearguard action, / a last defensive ploy, / Against a growing empire" (40). As the chorus concludes after Rackam's defeat becomes the symbolic representation of the end of piracy in the region, "We turn away, look for a new world, / and turn our back upon the old. / But all the time it's there behind us, / It pulls us back into the fold" (57). But their efforts are linked thematically—despite their failure—

to the origins, experiments, and weaknesses of comparable alternative movements in Europe and the United States in the 1960s (iv).

The Women Pirates Ann Bonney and Mary Read deals less successfully with the gender issues posed by Read and Bonny's story. Like many chroniclers before him, Gooch relies on the breast-revelation motif for those instances in the plot when Mary must reveal her female identity. One such scene finds Mary opening her coat to flash her breasts at a doubting comrade; another finds Rackam's crew, upon being told that Mary is a woman, crying "Show us yer tits, Readie!" (55). On the subject of motherhood, Gooch borders on the trite, as in the lines given to Bonny when she announces their pregnancies to the judge after they have been found guilty and sentenced to death: "Our only defence: motherhood. We've been chased from pillar to post, didn't fit in here, didn't fit in there. But we did find one place for ourselves. As mothers. You can't hang innocent life" (72). The chorus that closes the narrative is equally banal on the subject of the women's bittersweet triumph over the forces of empire: "So the case was stitched up tight / And England's growth was still called free. / But Law had been made impotent / By the pirates' potency" (73).

Piratical potency is at the core of John Carlova's *Mistress of the Sea,*[60] purportedly a biography of Anne Bonny based on extensive research but with no sources credited in the text, which bears mentioning in our context, not for its literary quality—which is at best questionable—but for the way it reiterates the many uses of the story outlined above. Having read all available interpretations of the Bonny and Read tale, Carlova weaves them together in a narrative hodgepodge of sorts to which he adds some interesting variations of his own. He sees his central character as a protofeminist figure who anticipated "her emancipated sisters of the 20th century by donning trousers and demanding the prerogatives that go with the pants" (11). But he also trivializes this female emancipation by speaking of her "voluptuous charms and cheerfully predatory nature" as worthy of "the gustier queens of Hollywood, Capri pants and all" (11).

Mistress of the Sea is a text intended for a popular audience, and as thus should not be taken to task for any unscholarly sensationalizations of which it may be guilty. The author's interweavings of narrative elements going back to Johnson's tale, however, seen here in their cumulative force, underscore the original story's malleability. Carlova, for example, returns with gusto to the breast-revelation motif as a means of eroticizing his character and her lewd pirate environment. "The bust," he explains, "in those days even as now, was considered of paramount importance in measuring a woman's glory"; and he claims for Anne a well-founded pride in her assets, which she herself proudly described "as milky white and of the size and strength of melons" (28). At "The House of the Lords," the New Providence tavern and pirates' haven, the corps of barmaids, "formidable females" and "hearty wenches," "took only token swats at the pirates who grabbed their precarious bodices, which needed only slight disarrangement to reveal the unabashed flesh beneath," with the result that after a while "all the flushed and busy barmaids were bustling about with breasts exposed and animated" (51). These passages—their racy vulgarity notwithstanding—are indicative of how variations of Anne Bonny's tale are driven by the erotic impulse.

Unlike those novels and plays that follow Mary Read's story—and that focus on the tensions between a piratical career and the yearning for domesticity, and as thus play directly into the stresses between piracy and colonial control—narratives based on Bonny's tale fit more narrowly into the picaresque tradition of the lewd cross-dressing heroine who uses her charms and willingness to engage in sexual activity as the means to propel her adventures. As such, Bonny is a less complex character. She is a more straightforwardly female figure, her story not as dependent on cross-dressing, her desires less torn between adventure and domesticity. Consequently, works like Carlova's, or Anne Gartner's *Anne Bonny* (1977), must depend for their narrative tension on a linear narrative peppered with erotic encounters as salient points. Gartner's, for example, offers one such episode per chapter, as Annie has heated affairs with many of the most vicious pirates of the day: her "torrid affair" with pirate Benjamin Hornigold she describes as "my downfall" (32); she delights in her erotic encounter with Stede Bonnet and seeks the young sailor Mark Read (Mary in her male attire) "as a bitch in heat." Likewise, Alison York's erotic romance, *The Fire and the Rope* (1979),[61] is dependent on erotic encounters to propel the plot. It follows Anne's adventures as reluctant spy after her release from prison as a series of somewhat masochistic sexual encounters from which she finally finds escape in the arms of a highwayman turned political rebel. Anne Osborne's *Wind from the Main* (1972) and *Sea Star: The Private Life of Anne Bonny, Pirate Queen* by Pamela Jekel (1983) follow similar narrative patterns in relating Anne's adventures.[62] *Wind from the Main,* like Gartner's *Anne Bonny,* Jekel's *Sea Star,* and Jacques Tourneur's film, *Anne of the Indies,* rely on the figure of a doctor (a character present in many other retellings of Anne's story) as the lover who ultimately saves her from the gallows (and from a life of sexual promiscuity) and brings her into the realms of domesticity for which Mary Read craved.

In Carlova's text, erotic encounters take center stage, and although the text purports to be the means of examining the 2,000-strong pirate republic of the Bahamas in the early part of the eighteenth century as a kind of idealistic community, sexual activity becomes paramount as the way of articulating these questionable republican ideals. Carlova, not content with depicting the Republic of the Brethren of the Coast as an orgiastic den of iniquity, uses homosexuality as an example of the "less healthy aspects of sex" that were ultimately to undermine the dream of a piratical utopia:

> Homosexuality was particularly rife among the pirates—as indeed it was among many seagoing men of those days—and some of the shipboard lovers had brought their rugged affections ashore. The most muscular and hairy brutes were hugging and slobbering over each other.
>
> The oil lamps flicker fitfully, and huge torches were lighted to supplement them. In this garish, leaping red light, the scene looked like a sideshow in hell. The scarred, battered faces of the pirates and their paramours, many devoid of eyes or teeth or even a nose, seemed symbols of evil. (53-54)

Mistress of the Sea, in its dubious rendition of homosexuality, features a flamboyant homosexual character, Pierre (more a parody of stereotypical gay exuberance than a realistic portrayal), who organizes a piratical raid on a ship loaded with precious fabrics. It also brands Rackam as an effeminate, potentially closeted homosexual as a way of preparing the reader for Annie's abandonment of him in favor of a more manly rival. Rackam is portrayed as a "handsome lad" who had, after joining the navy, become "a great favorite with homosexual ships' officers" (97). This had led to "a sexual detour, which later made Rackam's frantic heterosexuality suspect"; Rackam, the texts suggests, "may have taken to chasing skirts mainly to prove to himself he was really a man" (97). As further proof of his questionable manhood, Carlova argues that Rackam had a habit of "dousing himself with scent and spending hours trimming his hair and moustache [which] didn't exactly make him a man's man, either" (98).

In Carlova's text, erotic abandon—heterosexual as well as homosexual—does not prove to be a liberating force. Bonny will have to learn, if she is to achieve happiness, that Mary Read's dreams of domesticity are ultimately more conducive to contentment than the quest for fleeting erotic fulfillment. Thus the final pages of the text will find Anne, in the company of her chivalrous surgeon and child, leaving Norfolk in search of new frontiers in the American West. Carlova's text, for all its proclaimed intentions of depicting Anne as an example of the feminist heroine, reverts to traditional patriarchal notions of sexuality and domestic fulfillment in its conclusion—his reading of erotic abandon as evil and his condemnation of homosexuality being elements that justify his conclusions.

By contrast, Erica Jong's feminist erotic novel, *Fanny: Being the True History of the Adventures of Fanny Hackabout-Jones,*[63] a picaresque tale that narrates the sexual odyssey of its heroine across the seventeenth century's social landscape, finds in the figure of the female pirate a wondrous combination of gender attributes: as a pirate, Fanny fancies herself "neither Man nor Woman but a Combination of the noblest Qualities of the twain!" (428). Life at sea is depicted in *Fanny* as the essence of freedom: "my Spirit seem'd to soar at Sea. Each Night brought rapturous Dreams as I was rockt in the Cradle of the Deep, and I came to love the Water lapping at the Hull, the Gentleness of Sleep at Sea, and all the Sounds of Wind Thro' the Sails" (428). Fanny's encounter with Anne Bonny is but a brief passage in what is an extensive text covering a broad geographical canvas, but it is a pivotal one that comes near the end of the text and helps direct Fanny toward her own fulfillment.

The details of Bonny's story, as told to Fanny by Anne herself, follows Johnson's account almost to the letter, and bores Fanny to distraction. Anne's tale is told against Fanny's disparaging criticism, which underscores that the interest of a story is to be found, not in "Fidelity to fact alone" but in "Craft and Art" that can "stir the Blood" (441). Anne, however, accompanies her narrative with a slow and deliberate undressing that turns into an erotic dance and that eventually claims even Fanny's rapt attention. The scene leads to a riotous bisexual orgy that yields truly emancipating results:

> In the Debauch that follow'd, our own Annie was the Alpha and Omega of our Pleasure. We three scarce attended to our own Wants, but all to her Insatiable Appetites. Both Men had her, then did I almost devour her from her toes to her red Curls; then did she devour me! O what a clever Tongue our Annie had! Words she fumbl'd with, but Flesh flow'd for her as smoothly as a Springtime River. She could play the Man better than any Man, and the Key of her Tongue unlockt my Lock of Love that had ne'er been unlockt before! (445)

Fanny's erotic engagement with Anne Bonny allows Jong to address the concerns of female fetishism that were so prominent in feminist debate in the early 1980s. One reiterated motif in the chapter that narrates Fanny's encounter with Bonny is Anne's ability to make the penis unnecessary to sexual fulfillment. Anne's touch has a lightness "which more excites the female Blood than the heavy grappling most Men proffer," and brings Fanny to the "Ultimate Conclusion of Love's Pleasure" by "teazing, tickling, pressing, squeezing, licking" (446). Naomi Schor, borrowing from Sarah Kofman's *L'enigme de la femme,* argues that "by appropriating the fetishist's oscillation between denial and recognition of castration, women can effectively counter any move to reduce their bisexuality to a single one of its poles."[64] Female fetishism is thus not a perversion, but "rather a *strategy* designed to turn the so-called 'riddle of femininity' to women's account."[65] Elizabeth Berg, arguing for the political benefits to be derived from this strategy, sees Kofman's work as providing a "theoretical framework for reconciling two tendencies of feminism which have tended to remain in apparently irremediable contradiction: the claim for equal rights and the claim for acknowledgment of sexual difference."[66] The strategy, in its political dimension, provides a link between erotic fulfillment as a liberating force, as it emerges in *Fanny,* and the quest for a resolution of Bonny and Read's existential quandary.

The Anne Bonny of *Fanny* has survived her brush with potential execution and sails the sea with the daughters she is training as pirates, finding erotic pleasure as it comes while retaining full personal and financial autonomy—she is altogether queen of her domain. Fanny, who had felt torn between "the Lady and the Pyrate," as if "two people battl'd for Supremacy within my very Soul," finds in her passionate awakening in Anne's hands a revelation about true freedom (452):

> Perhaps I had resented Bonny because she alone of all the Women I had met had gain'd what we all seek: true Mastery o'er her Fate. She depended upon no keeper, whether male or female. She rais'd her own Babes and commanded her own Ship; and a Host of Pyrates listen'd when she spoke! If Women could master their Fates only thro' Pyracy sobeit! (453)

Fanny's fate, which brings her back to England as heiress to a grand estate and the financial autonomy and social position she coveted, rewrites Anne Bonny and Mary Read's tale, moving it from its historical tragic ending in prison awaiting the gallows—where historical documentation leaves them suspended—and inscribing it (and by extension, them) into the triumphant picaresque, a narrative of upward social mobility and moral rehabilitation. This return of the narrative to its original generic source—rendered through Jong's reinvention of the seventeenth-century picaresque as a feminist narrative that seeks success through female autonomy and true erotic liberation—vindicates Bonny and Read as cross-dressing heroines who serve as mentors for younger "pyrates" bent on seeking, like the Wife of Bath, whom Fanny quotes as an earlier mentor, "absolute Command/ With all the Government of House and Land;/ And Empire o'er his Tongue, and o'er his Hand!" (453).

"Command," "Government of House and Land," "Empire"—how apt the words of the Wife of Bath are as guidance through the maze of tales engendered by Bonny and Read's historical adventures, for they (the adventures and the women), in their relationship to the Caribbean, must be seen as emblematic of the Lockean imperative of full exploitation of land and territories for which "command," "government of house and land," and a full-blown empire are prerequisites. Bonny and Read, women seeking to assert their freedom from male command, government, and fledgling Empire, can never escape their symbolic potential as emblems for a region on which England will test its might as protoimperial nation and finesse its protocolonial institutions.

Yet the most engrossing aspect of Bonny and Read's tale, as told by Johnson and subsequent writers—whether the heroines' careers are seen as emblematic of historical social, political, gender, or feminist quandaries—continues to be their transgression of the lines separating men from women, as exemplified in their male attire. As Fanny learns when meeting Anne Bonny, "Ah, Men claim to be afraid of Women of Spirit, Women who can duel with Rapier like any Man, but i'faith, such Women fascinate 'em!" (435). Bonny and Read's cross-dressing—the tension between their male exterior and their "true" female natures—made them fascinating to generations of readers and writers, like malleable gender-bending figures on whose shoulders could rest a multiplicity of meanings. Their cross-dressing was a denial of the imperial and patriarchal imperative that must forever attempt to reduce them to that "floating breast" of which José Piedra writes in "Itinerant Prophetesses of Transatlantic Discourse"—"this prophetic woman reduced to a heaven-pointing nipple, which carved on the northern Caribbean coasts of South America, inspires the voyager to reshape the globe, and thus his own reading of a destiny which is—and should definitely remain—in his hands."[67] Bonny and Read's quandary is that of historical figures suspended between truth and fiction, femaleness and maleness, piracy and the law. As nonwriting travelers, their only testimony was that written on their body—the only words that can be fully attributed to them, without help from writers and pamphleteers are "Milord, we plead our bellies," a testimony that has left them forever suspended between notions of womanhood. The concealment and revelation of breasts that forms such a central element in the various retelling of their adventures points to a gender-bound "truth" that they struggled to redefine and control through cross-dressing in those geographical margins of Empire in which such freedom still seemed possible. And cross-dressed they had passed into history, vehicles for neverending tales of the struggle between reality and illusion, female potential and the patriarchy, the freedom of the frontier and the command and government of Empire, forever hovering between "the devil and the deep blue sea."

NOTES

1. Bonny and Read are not the only women pirates on record as having sailed the Caribbean. Edward Rowe Snow, in *True Tales of Pirates and Their Gold* (New York: Dodd, Mead & Company, 1953), includes the story, which he purports to be true, of "Fanny Campbell, Who Loved and Won," a young woman from Massachusetts who in 1773, in an effort to rescue her fiancé, mistakenly held in a Cuban prison on suspicion of piracy, became the captain of a pirate ship.

2. Johnson most definitely had access to the report on the trial of Rackam and his crew published by a Jamaican printer named Robert Baldwin soon after the proceedings. The records of the Vice-Admiralty at Saint Iago de la Vega are now lost, but the Baldwin pamphlet had been sent to the Council for Trade in England in lieu of the official trial report by the governor of Jamaica, who had presided over the Court, attesting to its authenticity.

3. *The Tryals of Captain John Rackam and Other Pyrates . . .* , (CO 137/14f. 9, Public Records Office, London).

4. Captain Charles Johnson, *A General History of the Robberies and Murders of the Most Notorious Pirates,* edited by Arthur L. Hayward (New York: Dodd, Mead & Co., 1927).

5. Miriam Williford, "Lost Women: Mary Read and Anne Bonney." Paper presented at the Ninth Annual History Conference at the University of the West Indies, Cave Hill, Barbados, 4–7 April 1997.

6. Marcus Rediker, "When Women Pirates Sailed the Seas." *The Wilson Quarterly* 17:4 (1993): 103.

7. Rediker, 103–104.

8. Jo Stanley, *Bold in Her Breeches: Women Pirates Across the Ages* (London: Pandora, 1995), 147.

9. Quoted in Clinton V. Black, *Pirates of the West Indies* (Cambridge: Cambridge University Press, 1989), 101.

10. Dianne Dugaw, "'Rambling Female Sailors': The Rise and Fall of the Seafaring Heroine." *International Journal of Maritime History* 4:1 (June 1992): 180.

11. Patrick Pringle, *Jolly Roger: The Story of the Great Age of Piracy* (New York: Norton and Company, 1953), 221.

12. Anonymous (often attributed to Daniel Defoe), *The Life and Adventures of Mrs. Christian Davies, Commonly Called Mother Ross; Who, In Several Campaigns Under King William and the Late Duke of Malborough, in the Quality of a Foot-Soldier and Dragoon, Gave Many Signal Proofs of an Unparalleled Courage and Personal Bravery* (London: C. Welch, 1740).

13. Mary Astell, writing in 1724 in her preface to the letters of Lady Mary Wortley Montagu, published posthumously as *Letters of the Right Honourable Lady M-y W-y M-e* (London: Osborne Griffin, 1785), vii.

14. Thomas M. Curley, *Samuel Johnson and the Age of Travel* (Athens: University of Georgia Press, 1976), 53.

15. M. Blondell, "Le Récit de voyage féminin au XVIIIe siècle." *Bulletin de la Société d'Etudes Anglo-Americaines des XVIIe et XVIIIe Siècles* 18 (June 1984): 104.

16. See Mary Morgan, *A Tour to Milford Haven* (London: Stockdale, 1795); Ann Radcliffe, *Tour of the Lakes* (London: Robinson, 1795); Anne Radcliffe, *Journey through Holland* (London: Robinson, 1795); Mrs. Kindersley, *Letters from the Island of Teneriffe* (London: J. Nourse, 1777).

17. Mrs. Mary Ann Hanway, *A Journey to the Highlands of Scotland* (London: Fielding and Walker, 1776).

18. Anna Riggs, Lady Miller, *Letters from Italy* (London: E. and C. Dilly, 1776), 24-25.

19. Dugaw, 181. See also Dianne Dugaw, *Warrior Women and Popular Balladry, 1650-1850* (Cambridge: Cambridge University Press, 1989), 121-143.

20. Thomas Laqueur, *Making Sex: Body and Gender from the Greeks to Freud* (Cambridge: Harvard University Press, 1990), 6, viii. Quoted in Catherine Craft-Fairchild's "Cross-Dressing and the Novel: Women Warriors and Domestic Femininity." *Eighteenth-Century Fiction* 10:2 (January 1998): 177. Subsequent page references will appear in parentheses in the text.

21. Johnson, 135.

22. Johnson, 141.

23. Johnson, 134.

24. John S. C. Abbott, *Captain William Kidd, and Others of the Pirates or Buccaneers Who Ravaged the Seas . . .* (New York: Dodd & Mead, 1874), 207.

25. Black, 113.

26. Maurice Besson, *The Scourge of the Indies* (New York: Random House, 1929), 45.

27. Figures 3.2 and 3.3 are held in the National Maritime Museum and are reprinted in Clinton Black's *Pirates of the West Indies,* 105, 108.

28. See Maurice Besson, *The Scourge of the Indies: Buccaneers, Corsairs and Filibusters* (London: G. Routledge, 1929).

29. Margaret R. Miles, "The Virgin's One Bare Breast: Female Nudity and

Religious Meaning in Tuscan Early Renaissance Culture." In *The Female Body in Western Culture: Contemporary Perspectives.* Edited by Susan Rubin Suleiman (Cambridge: Harvard University Press, 1985), 205.

30. Miles, 205.

31. Jane Yolen, *The Ballad of the Pirate Queens.* Illustrations by David Shannon. (New York: Harcourt, Brace & Company, 1995), n.p.

32. Stanley, 18.

33. Edgar Stanton Maclay, *A History of American Privateers* (Freeport, NY: Books for Librairies Press, 1899 [1970]), 30.

34. Maclay, 31.

35. Marcus Rediker, *Between the Devil and the Deep Blue Sea: Merchant Seamen, Pirates, and the Anglo-American Maritime World, 1700-1750* (Cambridge: Cambridge University Press, 1987), 283.

36. Sandra Riley, *Homeward Bound: A History of the Bahama Islands to 1850 with a Definitive Study of Abaco in the American Loyalist Plantation Period* (Miami: Island Research, 1983), 54.

37. Rediker, *Between the Devil,* 254.

38. Julie Wheelwright, "Working for a Living," in Stanley, 155.

39. Riley, 60.

40. Frank Stockton, *Buccaneers and Pirates of Our Coasts* (New York: Macmillan, 1898), 257.

41. Stanley, 177.

42. *The Pirates' Own Book: Authentic Narratives of the Most Celebrated Sea Robbers* (New York: Dover Publications, Inc, 1976).

43. Johnson, 140.

44. Abbott, 223.

45. From a broadside ballad printed in Newcastle by W. Fordyce, c. 1830. Houghton Library, Harvard University (Misc. Prints, no. 570784, vol. I, no. 536). Reprinted by Dianne Dugaw in "'Rambling Female Sailors,'" 178-179.

46. John C. Appleby, "Women and Piracy in Ireland: From Gráinne O'Malley to Anne Bonny." In *Women in Early Modern Ireland.* Edited by Margaret MacCurtain and Mary O'Dowd (Edinburgh: Edinburgh University Press, 1991), 53.

47. Wheelright, 182.

48. Anonymous, *The Daring Exploits of Henry Morgan* (London: n.p., 1813), 26. Quoted in Wheelright in "Tars, Tarts and Swashbucklers." I have been unable to locate any other bibliographic reference for this work.

49. *The Daring Exploits of Henry Morgan,* 27.

50. The work, a copy of which I have been unable to locate, is discussed briefly and quoted in Gérard A. Jaeger's *Les Femmes d'abordage: Chroniques historiques et légendaires des aventurières de la mer* (Paris: Clancier-Guénaud, 1984), 7.

51. *The History of the Lives and Bloody Exploits of the Most Noted Pirates: Their Tri-*

als and Executions. Including a Complete Account of the Late Piracies Committed in the West Indies (Hartford: Silas Andrews & Son, 1855), 189.

52. P. Christian, *Histoire des marins, pirates et corsaires.* 3 vols. (Paris: Cavaillé, 1846-1850.) See vol. III.

53. Of the Hollywood films inspired by the Bonny and Read story, which fall outside the scope of this essay, by far the best is *Anne of the Indies*, a 20th Century Fox production from 1951 directed by Jacques Tourneur. (In 1943, Tourneur had directed another classic set in the Caribbean, *I Walked with a Zombie*, based loosely on Charlotte Brontë's *Jane Eyre.*) As Anne, the dreaded Captain Providence, Jean Peters excels in the type of swashbuckling action that is usually the province of males. The plot finds Louis Jourdan, a French naval officer whose ship and wife are being held by the British, volunteering to capture Captain Providence. He manages to get aboard her pirate vessel and takes advantage of a natural attraction that springs up between them to trick her with a phony treasure map, thus leading her into a British ambush. However, Anne escapes the trap and takes her vengeance by kidnapping the wife, played by Debra Paget. The treacherous lover is a figure common to many twentieth-century reworkings of the tale, as is the rum-sodden doctor aboard the pirate ship, played here by Herbert Marshall.

54. Frank Shay, *Pirate Wench* (New York: I. Washburn, 1934; London: Hurst & Blackett, 1934). All quotations are from the American edition. Subsequent page references will appear in parentheses in the text.

55. James Bridie and Claud Gurney, *Mary Read: A Play in Three Acts.* London: Constable, 1936). Subsequent page references will appear in parentheses in the text.

56. *Marie Read, femme pirate* by Michel Candie (Paris: Gallimard, 1952). All quotations in English are my translation from the French original. A comparative study between this text and another roughly contemporary novel about Mary Read, *Mary Read, Buccaneer* by Philip Rush (London: T.V. Boardman & Co., 1945), would have perhaps yielded interesting results, but the latter is unavailable. The only copy I have been able to locate (at the New York Public Library) is listed as missing.

57. *Anne Bonny* by Chloe Gartner (New York: Morrow, 1977) also purports to be Anne's own narrative, written as a petition to the court to obtain a pardon. Subsequent page references will appear in parentheses in the text.

58. Candie's focus on Nannytown and the Maroons links *Marie Read, femme pirate* to the two novels Bahamian writer Sandra Riley has dedicated to the story of Bonny and Read, *The Captain's Ladies or Bloody Bay* and *Sometimes Towards Eden. The Captain's Ladies* offers a narrative inscribed in the tradition of the erotic romance. The latter work offers a most fanciful sequel to their tale of piracy, as it imagines Anne Bonny's career after her release from prison as that of a Jamaican plantation mistress pitted against Nanny and her maroon town in the Cockpit area of Jamaica, an interesting work in its own

right but one that falls outside of our purview here. See Sandra Riley, *The Captain's Ladies* (New York: Leisure Books, 1980) and *Sometimes Towards Eden* (Miami: Island Research, 1986).

59. Steve Gooch, *The Women Pirates Anne Bonney and Mary Read* (London: Pluto Press, 1978).

60. John Carlova, *Mistress of the Sea* (New York: Citadel Press, 1964). Subsequent page references will appear in parentheses in the text.

61. Alison York, *The Fire and the Rope* (London: W.H. Allen, 1979).

62. Anne Osborne, *Wind from the Main* (Columbia, SC: Sandlapper Press, Inc., 1972); Pamela Jekel, *Sea Star: The Private Life of Anne Bonny, Pirate Queen* (New York: Harmony, 1983).

63. Erica Jong, *Fanny: Being the True History of the Adventures of Fanny Hackabout-Jones* (New York: New American Library, 1980). Subsequent page references will appear in parentheses in the text.

64. Sarah Kofman, in *L'enigme de la femme: La Femme dans les textes de Freud* (Paris: Galilée, 1980). See Naomi Schor, "Female Fetishism: The Case of George Sand." In *The Female Body in Western Culture*. Edited by Susan Rubin Suleiman, 368.

65. Schor, 369.

66. Elizabeth Berg, "The Third Woman." *Diacritics* 12 (1982): 13.

67. See Piedra's essay in this volume.

Chapter 4

WHEN THE SUBALTERN TRAVELS:
SLAVE NARRATIVE AND TESTIMONIAL ERASURE IN THE CONTACT ZONE

Mario Cesareo

Travel carries wide implications in contemporary culture. In the field of cultural studies and, more generally, in the humanities, travel has become one of the predominant paradigms informing the political unconscious of current research. The concepts of border, deterritorialization, mapping, cartography, liminality, interlanguages, the intellectual-as-nomad, stand-point epistemology, hybridity, language-games theory, Otherness, pluritopical hermeneutics, and globalization, as part of an analytical repertoire that has come into prominence in the last two decades, attest to this ubiquity. The contemporary experience of heightened geographical mobility, the changing configuration of nation-states, the constant flux of ethnic, sexual, and gender identities, the rapid dissemination of information, and other phenomena associated with the globalization of late capitalism, present suggestive reasons as to why such notions have come to dominate current debates and scholarship. Under the garments of these analytical tools lurks travel as an all-powerful presence. Through its mediations we are to understand that new territories, communities, and paradigms are brought into focus, allowing for a cultural and historical negotiation of sorts: the nomad-intellectual would be the one to bring forth the tremendous difference of these spaces and practices allowing for a new understanding of this proliferation through the deployment of a critical apparatus that would seem to render this promiscuous materiality intelligible—in the process, I would suggest, textualizing the materiality of these practices, displacing the anthropological "body" of the nineteenth century by the "texts" of contemporary cultural studies, and replacing liberatory social practices with social exegesis.

From this perspective, a most prominent parcel of contemporary writing could be read as a form of travel narrative. The current scholarship, thus looked at, continues a notorious ancestry in the long tradition of travel writing that constituted the lettered arm of European imperialism from the fifteenth century onward—its more misty beginnings, taking us to antiquity. To write about travel writing, then, if from a critical perspective aware of such problematic affiliations, is to posit questions that go beyond the historical situatedness of the primary texts studied. It means to simultaneously reflect on the state of our scholarship and its position vis-à-vis the new political paradigms of a unipolar, globalizing world. To write about travel writing, therefore, becomes a form of travel: back and forth into the old and new practices of a colonizing enterprise still in the making.

The following pages engage one of these "travel" notions, Mary Louise Pratt's "contact zone,"[1] in relation to a particular form of writing that, although not usually categorized as travel writing, was the result of arduous travel (from the forced Diaspora of the Middle Passage to the northerly migrations of ante- and postbellum African Americans and the geographical wanderings of Caribbean slaves).[2] My purpose will be to scrutinize a narrative form (the slave narrative) by locating it within its material conditions of possibility (travel and the antislavery associations of nineteenth-century England) from the perspective of a hermeneutic category (contact zone), to gain some critical insights into all three.

The trouble with travel writing

From the material encounter of territories, peoples, and the natural habitats of travel, to the imaginative and experimental rehearsal of new logic that discourse makes possible, both travel and writing are practices that produce an other world. In this sense, travel and writing confront their primary materialities (a foreign world and the semiotic universe of a particular culture, respectively) as a referential. This "stuff" of travel and writing bring about the possibility of a playful passage (an entering and exiting) into the (un)known world. The dialectic of this nomadism of traveler and writer, this temporary (geographical, fictional, or theoretical) habitation in the realms of another world also constitutes the space of home, in the same manner as the apparition of the Other[3] (the one who inhabits that Other geography) and that of the other logic (the possible worlds lying dormant or repressed within the very world the One inhabits) posits anew the subject of home. In this respect, travel and writing are similar practices structurally situated between self, other, and discovery, the last of these constructs understood as the production of a certain knowledge, the opening up of a practical and/or theoretical space in which the self is recreated and repositioned in a new configuration. These similarities, plus the fact that European travel has been historically linked to the practice of travel writing, has recently led to a critical erasure of their differences.

Travel implies the removal of the subject from a known institutionality into new territories and political orders that make necessary a re-negotiation of his modus operandi—his institutional logic—vis-à-vis the newly encountered materiality and institutional reality of the foreign world being traveled. Traveling brings about a crisis in the subject's self-understanding by removing him from the accustomed uses and routines that tied him to a particular common sense and repertoire of cultural utensils that until then enabled his manipulation of his world. The space traveled crystallizes as an Other world: "Other," because it confronts the subject as a world alien to his needs, as an uncanny immanence[4] that questions his control over the world. The irruption of an Other, massive, and omnipresent reality, governed by unknown or poorly guessed human and natural laws, cultural customs, and geographical relationships, threaten to subject the traveler to a position of impotence—linguistic, material, and so on. The fear that results from the self's precarious position opens the way for the elaboration of symbolic mediations destined to render that radically Other reality into a discernible, pliable materiality.[5]

Thus, the destabilizing moment of travel calls for the elaboration of a discursive practice designed to explain the new experience. Recipe knowledge—the logic of the already known—as a practice derived from the discursive universe proper to the traveler's home culture and institutional experience, is quickly seen as a necessary but insufficient condition of understanding and survival. If the culturally and politically self-affirming character of his traveling necessitates the imposition of the homemade over the newly discovered, the consciousness of the material character of that (not always symbolic) danger, the daily and empirical corroboration of that world's uncanniness, mobilizes the traveler to adopt a learning stance that will allow him to successfully deal with the new reality. As Eric Leed notes:

> . . . travel retains its ancient significance and is given value by the fear that makes the individual "porous" and sensitive. . . . [T]he fear of the wayfarer,

the loss of security implicit in unaccommodated travel is a gain of accessibility and sensitivity to the world. Travel, from the moment of departure, removes those furnishings and mediations that come with a familiar residence. It thus substantiates individuality in its sense of "autonomy," for the self is now separated from a confirming and confining matrix.[6]

Travel, then, produces a radicalization of experience that forces the traveler into a double and contradictory gesture: an opening to the world—a learning destined to understand it—and a domination of both himself and that world—the imposition of an "autonomy" that constitutes his answer to that world, a strategy of (self) manipulation understood as survival and self-affirmation. As long as learning is inscribed in this politics of fear and survival, the auscultation of the new reality is an interested (instrumental) and reductive (allegorizing) act. The practice of metropolitan travel is, therefore, the exertion of a violence that is not only descriptive but constitutive. It is, on the one hand, a material violence: a disciplining of the self and the Other (as well as the Other's usufruct[7]); on the other hand, it is a representative violence: an aesthetic distortion exercised from a set of imperatives that is alien to the community, it names without interpolating.

Metropolitan travel is, in the last instance, a violence over the world. It presupposes two moments with an ensuing tension: an encounter of materialities (the Other beings that populate the world that is being traveled, that world, and its ecological structures) and a production of sameness and otherness. The first of these moments produces the *finding* (discovery's materiality), as well as the self's destabilization and fear in the face of the Other's irruption. The second moment is the result of the domesticating operations through which the traveler constructs his experience of that world: the semiotic conversion of that materiality into a datum, and the elaboration of the hermeneutics of its discernment. Traveling produces otherness. The latter, from this perspective, is the fiction through which the experience of human coexistence is thematized, conjured, and exorcised from an imperative of survival and domination. This is why otherness is more revealing of the order of the Same (of the self, the One, the I) than of the Other. It is more a formalization (an aesthetic rendering) of his fears, fantasies, and material interests, than a representation of the irreducible ecology it describes and reifies. In other words, the production of otherness presupposes both a perceptive sensibility (a reading) and a productive one (a writing) that function as a matrix of sameness, as an egology.[8]

The double character of otherness, a result of the tension between an opening to the world and the self's will to survival and domination, characterizes traveling as a crisis-ridden practice. But the traveler's discovery of a foreign world should not be understood simply as a production of knowledge (the writing moment). It is also the lived experience of a dramatic irruption of an Other into the order of the Same: the irruption of the Other carries with it the necessity of a reconfiguration of sameness, which has been thrown into a crisis as a result of that contact. What opens the gates to the dramatic irruption of the Other into the order of the Same is the face-to-face character of the encounter that traveling makes possible. Face-to-face communication[9] erodes the Other's anomie[10]—that renders the Other into an other—through the production of: (1) a shared present that affirms the Other's coevalness; (2) a continuous expressive exchange that makes visible the presence of the Other's subjectivity; (3) an orientation of expressivity toward the Other that allows the Other to become an interlocutor; (4) an intersubjectivity that is constructed from an abundance of symptomatic information, debunking the tendency to freeze communication in any one of its particular moments; (5) a massive presence of the Other, that militates against the Other's allegorical reduction; (6) a mutual proximity, an existential co-presence that produces the direct evidence of the Other and the self's consciousness of his own presence *to* the Other, the consciousness, therefore, of his own vulnerability. The face-to-face encounter makes this irruption of the Other possible, bringing about the crisis necessary for the production of an otherness that subverts the order of the Same. As Adriaan Peperzak explains:

> Another comes to the fore as other if and only if his or her "appearance" breaks, pierces, destroys the horizon of my egocentric monism, that is, when the other's invasion of my world destroys the empire in which all phenomena are, from the outset, a priori, condemned to function as moments of my universe. The other's face (i.e., any other's facing me) or the other's speech (i.e., any other's speaking to me) interrupts and disturbs the order of my, ego's, world; it makes a hole in it by disarraying my arrangements without ever permitting me to restore the previous order. For even if I kill the other or chase the other away, in order to be safe from the intrusion, nothing will ever be the same as before. (19-20)

The presence of the Other as a being-for-herself provokes a cataclysm in the traveler's experience. And yet, and this is a most important proviso, that perforation of the order of the Same will not effectively bring the Other into it. No negotiation with the Other is here enacted. The perforation of the order of the Same will be re-elaborated, but from the ruins of his order. This is why in the discourse produced by that encounter one does not find the native but the other: the phantasm, the relic, the remains of the cannibalized Other.[11] This double-edged mechanism of conjuration and exorcism establishes travel writing, insofar as an instance of historical writing, as a form of psychoanalysis,[12] re-establishing sameness into the Other's historical remnant. Here lies the irony of this practice of empire. While its newly constituted order rests upon the erasure and (not always merely symbolic) elimination of the Other, its very structure (its form and texture) remains captive to what it has eliminated:

> There is an "uncanniness" about this past that a present occupant has expelled (or thinks it has) in a effort to take its place. The dead haunt the living. The past: it "re-bites" [Il re-mord] (it is a secret and repeated biting). History is "cannibalistic," and memory becomes the closed arena of conflict between two contradictory operations: forgetting, which is not something passive, a loss, but an action directed against the past; and the mnemic trace, the return of what was forgotten, in other words, an action by a past that is now forced to disguise itself. More generally speaking, any autonomous order is founded upon what it eliminates; it produces a "residue" condemned to be forgotten. But what was excluded re-infiltrates the place of its origin—now the present's "clean" [propre] place. It resurfaces, it troubles, it turns the present's feeling of being "at home" into an illusion, it lurks . . . within the walls of the residence, and, behind the back of the owner (the ego), or over its objections, it inscribes the law of the other.[13]

This phantasmal persistence of the Other in the order of the Same (Certeau's "law of the other") alerts us to the discursive character of that order. As discourse,[14] then, otherness is able to articulate an imaginary where desire and experience are deployed experimentally:

> . . . literature is the theoretic discourse of the historical process. It creates the non-topos where the effective operations of a society attain a formalization. Far from envisioning literature as the expression of a referential, it would be necessary to recognize here the analogue of that which for a long time mathematics has been for the exact sciences: a "logical" discourse of history, the "fiction" which allows it to be thought.[15]

As such, otherness is an esemplastic playfulness, an essayistic, theorizing practice:

The literary text is like a game. With its sets of rules and surprises, a game is a somewhat theoretic space where the formalities of social strategies can be explained on a terrain protected from the pressure of action and from the opaque complexity of daily struggle. In the same way, the literary text, which is also a game, delineates an equally theoretic space, protected as is a laboratory, where the artful practices of social interaction are formulated, separated, combined, and tested. It is the field where a logic of the other is exercised, the same logic that the sciences rejected to the extent to which they practiced a logic of the same.[16]

Otherness functions as a fiction that allows for the reconfiguration of the world in its totality under new imaginary and institutional imperatives, restoring a sense upon the self while forcing it upon the Other and the ecological totality both self and Other inhabit and articulate (in this manner, for example, the voyage to the "New World," represented as a traveling-back-in-time, allowed for the resignification of the relations between European modernity and antiquity, placing the experience of mercantilism as a climatic moment of the civilizing process, thus legitimizing the exploitation of the Amerindian, the African slave, and their world, as an educational and tutelary practice[17]). For this reason, otherness, while itself historical, is neither fully nor exclusively about the history it narrates. It is a fiction that takes the place of an irrecoverable absence. This is why the "law of the other" (the law that emerges over the remains of the Other for Certeau and makes possible an unlimited opening-to-the-other for Levinas) is not the law of the Other.[18] The archaeological or psychoanalytical possibility of such an articulation is only to be found beyond all remnant, in an act of negotiation that European writing has left unfulfilled in all its travels.[19]

In short, while metropolitan travel is about a confrontation with an Other, travel writing is about the domestication of this encounter through the production of otherness. While travel is a most dislocating phenomenon of the "contact zone," travel writing happens, mostly, in an "incantation zone"—not the place of encounter but that of its substitute, the zone where the production of simulacra takes place. Travel writing, until the coming of the slave narrative, is not about a negotiation of the Other's appearance but an allegorical enterprise of symbolic restoration—where the conjuring of the Other results in an always-already exorcised appearance.

I therefore disagree with Mary Louise Pratt's construction of travel writing as a contact zone. Pratt does not differentiate the contact zone of the frontier with that of its textual remnant. While the former is anchored in the ecology of the frontier, bringing to the fore a reciprocal confrontation of diverse communities, materially engaged in strategies of domination, resistance, cooperation, survival, and extermination, in the unstable and contested realm of the frontier's materiality, the latter is the *result* of such a confrontation within the theoretical and imaginative confines of the Same's narrative logic. There is a subsuming, in Pratt's notion of "literature as contact zone,"[20] of these two spheres. On the one hand, there is an understanding of the contact zone as an ecological, material phenomenon:

> "Contact zone" in my discussion is often synonymous with "colonial frontier." But while the latter term is grounded within a European expansionist perspective (the frontier is a frontier only with respect to Europe), "contact zone" is an attempt to invoke the spatial and temporal copresence of subjects previously separated by geographic and historical disjunctures, and whose trajectories now intersect.[21]

On the other, textual production is posited, itself, as such a zone of contact. This lack of differentiation between the contact zone as a material territory and the discursive practices it generates is partly anchored in a linguistic understanding of literature coupled with a bourgeois/mercantile understanding of language:

> I borrow the term "contact" here from its use in linguistics, where the term contact language refers to improvised languages that develop among speakers of different native languages who need to communicate with each other consistently, usually in the context of trade.[22]

But, it is evident that, while in travel there is a constantly negotiated and open dynamic, in travel writing the negotiation does not happen amongst communities—it being a solitary elaboration performed within the discretion of the Same. These two practices cannot be subsumed without "textualizing" and rendering travel a metaphor, one of the predilect gestures of postmodern and postcolonial scholarship.

It is problematic to reduce a social practice (the encounters of the frontier) to a series of cultural objects (the texts that stand in its place). To do this obscures the meaning of their ecology: the analysis of cultural phenomena cannot leave their institutional dimension without becoming a hermeneutic of signs, textualizing its object of study, and missing from its purview the material conditions where that social semiotic takes place. The frontier that lies behind Pratt's narrative "contact zone" is an institutional practice: it presupposes an economic production of life, a geopolitics, a materiality that overflows and overdetermines any cultural artifact and its circulation. Pratt's lettered understanding of the contact zone substitutes the text with the communities that text articulates narratively, where, as John Beverley puts it:

> In Pratt's metaphor, literature . . . can serve as a kind of "contact zone" where previously disarticulated subject positions, social projects, and energies may come together. [23]

It would be in this literature as "contact zone" where subject positions, social projects, and previously diffused energies coalesce. I wonder, though, what escapes this "contact," what is it that is brought together, and where does this coalescing take place. In Pratt's textual substitution one can detect traces of the philosophical and imaginative poverty of poststructuralism's textualizing gesture, so preeminent in today's humanities.

Travel writing in the contact zone

As a practice of empire in its confrontations with its periphery, travel writing history attaches itself to that of the imperial frontier, from the imaging of the contours of the trade routes of early exploration, through the conquest of world territories and colonial settlement, to the appropriation of natural resources and expansion of capitalist technology and modes of production of the neocolonialist—or, in today's jargon, the globalizing—configurations of late capitalism. Its outline has therefore followed a movement from the forms of exterior exploration, carried through the fourteenth to the seventeenth centuries, to the interior exploration of the eighteenth century onward; from the logic of navigational charts to that of continental mapping; from the description of coastlines and landscapes to the systematic elaboration of ethnographic and natural histories. The narrative modes of travel writing have thus adopted their myriad forms as a literature of navigation, survival, monstrosities and marvels, civic description, textual mapping, and ethnographic manners-and-customs description. In all cases, pre- or post-Linnaean, the literature codes its encounters through an allegorizing process that rendered the Other as an instance of the Same, whether in the form of the heroic, Christianizing crusader, the entrepreneurial capitalist avant-garde, or the "neutral" eye of the naturalist. The organic character of this system of representation vis-à-vis the socioeconomic imperatives of capitalist accumulation has already been noted.[24]

As has been previously argued, to place travel writing in the contact zone implies an intercultural encounter and negotiation. And yet, although placed in the context of the frontier, travel writing's relationship between the narrative self (the traveler) and its Others (its travelees) has been one of calculated nonreciprocity: the target of its defamiliarization processes—the aesthetic operations through which what and whom is traveled assume the character of an other—have coincided, for the most part, with the relations of economic and military power attendant to each historical period. This delimitation of the terms of the encounter has been produced by narrative assignation: the narrative traveler and travelee coincide, respectively, with the political Same and Other as defined by metropolitan hegemony. Travel writing therefore is at the same time a (one-sided) product (of the real-) and a (metropolitan) producer of the (narrative-) contact zone. It locates itself in the frontier *narratively*. The writing of this incantation zone erases the zone of contact that forms the materiality of its representation. Further, its production is monologically situated in the metropolis and is aimed at home consumption. In contrast with travel, travel writing does not rehearse a (material) encounter (of the Other). In its stead, it performs an apparition (the other's). In this semiotics of empire, the act of thematizing the Other becomes both an erasure (of the Other as such) and an inscription (of the allegorized Other), by a seeing gaze that does not register its being seen. The conversion of the traveling eye to the writing gaze points to an inscription and erasure of materiality. The eye/I that travels is a most delicate and vulnerable organ. It can be seen, (and therefore) slashed, obscured, forever closed, obliterated. The gaze that writes is but its survived remnant, placidly and securely located outside the dangers of travel, out of bounds of the Other's grasp, (and therefore) indifferent to the Other's scrutiny. The gaze is but the eye's postscript, its safely arrived souvenir. The symbolic economy of this leap from travel to travel writing, implicit in the displacement from the eye to the gaze, forms the conditions of possibility of a movement from a body-bound to an embodied experience, allowing for the transformation of the contact zone into its incantational mutant. The very fact that in the experience of traveling this being seen, spoken to, challenged, and denied by the Other's very existence is inescapable, serves to highlight the allegorical operations that code that encounter as a self-affirming event. Travel writing, thus, is not about the apparition of the Other but about its domestication. It is not travel—its destabilizing, de-centering experience—but its exorcism. It is just as much about the production of others as it is a production of the Same. It is produced from and for home and, as such, in its myriad forms, travel writing has produced the domestic subject of Empire.

Mary Prince's History: the slave narrative as travel writing

The political economy of travel writing undergoes important changes with the appearance, in the late eighteenth century, of the slave narrative. As I will later argue, the advent of the slave narrative does bring the contact zone into travel writing. But it will do so, paradoxically, by removing itself from the genre to assume the shape of testimony, this new form of inscribing the historical experience of travel within narrative conventions being a result of the very negotiations of that contact.

The slave narrative emerges as a literary genre by the late eighteenth century. Most were published in London and New England. Reflecting the then ongoing controversies over the slave trade, they dealt with the wandering of exotic, well-educated, highly intelligent and resourceful African slaves of noble birth who undergo an experience of capture, enslavement, escape, freedom, and conversion to Christianity. The genre emphasized the dimensions of manly struggle and personal affirmation as inscribed within a romance of heroic survival. As Frances Smith Foster points out:

> . . . each of the narratives portrays an individual confronting a series of threatening incidents and having to rely quite extensively upon his courage and intelligence to survive. Sometimes this was manifest as rebellion or resistance, but at other times it was aggression. Many narrators sought adventure as a way of achieving personal satisfaction..[25]

Although dealing with slavery, the survival-aesthetic of the eighteenth-century slave narrative places its most striking effect upon its audience in the realm of the adventure of an individual's will to power, focusing upon the individual and his adventures to highlight his independence, daring, and curiosity, thereby downplaying the historical specificity of the slave's experience while stressing the archetypal dimension of the situations narrated. Slavery is presented as a loss of physical freedom, but its dehumanizing aspects are not emphasized.[26] By 1831 the polemic against the slave trade had been replaced by the abolitionist cause. The African-born freedman ceded his place to the American-born slave. Survival adventure is followed by the aesthetics of the sublime and sentimentality. The woman-slave emerges into the slave narrative.

The History of Mary Prince, a West Indian Slave, Related by Herself appeared in 1831. The first slave narrative told by a woman, it is situated between the eighteenth-century paradigm of the slave-narrative-as-survival-adventure just described (and epitomized by *The Interesting Nar-*

rative of Olaudah Equiano or Gustavus Vassa, the African of 1789), and the two diverging but complementary forms that the slave narrative was about to take: a (masculinist) sublime[27] paradigm (well represented by *Narrative of the Life of Frederick Douglass, an American Slave, Written by Himself* of 1845) and its (feminized) fully-fledged sentimental form (as crystallized in Harriet Jacobs's text *Incidents of the Life of a Slave Girl, Seven Years Concealed* of 1861). As Moira Ferguson remarks, the book itself was a form of hybrid:

> Her *History* . . . combines aspects of the eighteenth-century British slave narrative, the nineteenth-century US narrative, and the format of recorded court cases of slave abuse. Because of its rarity, Mary Prince's *History* is also sui generis, with no comparable account extant by a female West Indian slave.[28]

By now, the reception of the slave narrative has to be understood within the modes of consumption crystallized by the sentimental novel and travel writing. The slave's avatar is inscribed within the heroic economy of bourgeois values. The ambiguity of the hero, her being simultaneously Other and Same, allows for both identification and distantiation. The first makes possible the pathos of survival, the second opens the way for a safe space from which the domestic subject of Empire could break the constraints of Victorian morality with impunity. As a figure full of pathos, the slave joins the repertoire of heroic figures, outperforming them, as attested by the *Putnam's Monthly* review of 1855: "Our English literature has recorded many an example of genius struggling against adversity . . . yet none of these are so impressive as the case of a solitary slave, in a remote district, surrounded by none but enemies, conceiving the project of his escape, teaching himself to read."[29]

Impressive, we should add, because of the utter destitution of the slave, not because of his radical Otherness, but in spite of it. Aside from this particular dimension, the slave narrative's grounding in the ambiguous terrain of Same/other provided a space for the safe rehearsal of pseudo-masochistic, erotic, and heroic fantasies. As Robin Winks states:

> . . . the fugitive slave narratives were the pious pornography of their day, replete with horrific tales of whippings, sexual assaults, and explicit brutality, presumably dehumanized and fit for Nice Nellies to read precisely because they dealt with black, not white, man.[30]

Or, as Arna Bontemps puts it, in the case of North America:

> . . . they . . . created a parable of the human condition. . . . Their theme was the fetters of mankind and the yearning of all living things for freedom. In this context the perils of escape and the long journeys toward the North Star did not grow tiresome with repetition until a new myth, the Western, replaced the earlier one.[31]

Whereas scientific and sentimental writing allowed for the metropolitan thematizing of the Other as fact, land- or body-scape, the slave narrative seemed to bring a different dimension to the experience of metropolitan travel—to its recycling and allegorizing of the world, to its domination, disciplining, and enjoyment. It brought the Other into view as a gesticulating face, a subject of enunciation. It brought her home, it brought her into his listening, it created an other pathos. It was precisely the appearance of this "unmediated" presence[32] of the Other that captivated the public, what rendered the experience of reading the slave narrative as a form of travel. Not so much the vicarious travel to a different geography—this was already the case with most travel writing—but the traveling through an Otherness that seemed to make itself visible and willingly available for the reader's gaze. But paradoxically, as will be argued, Prince's text allows (and, in fact, invites) this voyeurisn not through an unveiling but through a multiple masking that hides, covers up, and erases, the slave's experience, travel, and masking practices.

The History of Mary Prince was edited and published by her employer at the time, Thomas Pringle, secretary of the Anti-Slavery Society. The book's appearance was followed by heated controversy between the antislavery supporters and the proslavery lobby. The debate involved both the accuracy of Prince's testimony and her moral qualities as a person—the confrontation ended in two court cases finally settled the same year that the Emancipation Bill passed the House of Lords.[33] The book itself, and increasingly so under each subsequent edition, reflects this court-case format by framing Prince's narrative with an annotation apparatus consisting of several parts: (1) a preface, attesting to the genesis of the publication and making general claims as to the editor's every effort to ascertain the accuracy of its contents. (2) A series of footnotes that intervene in Prince's text mostly in an explanatory and documentary manner. (3) A supplement, where Pringle relates: (a) the circumstances of Mary Prince's coming to the Antislavery Society, (b) the detailed and documented story of the editor's and the Society's intercession in her behalf, and (c) the reproduction of a body of letters that throw a most unfavorable light on Mary Prince, in each case followed by a point-by-point cross-examination and refutation of their validity by Pringle's critical reading of their inconsistencies and tergiversations. (4) Appended to every edition was the "Narrative of Louis Asa-Asa, a Captured African," prefaced by the editor. (5) A postscript to the second edition, informing of Prince's deteriorating state of health in the time between the first and second editions (the text announces that proceeds from its sale will go to her purse). (6) An appendix to the third edition that reproduces a letter from the editor's wife, Mrs. Pringle, to a Mrs. Townsend, one of the secretaries of the Birmingham Ladies' Society for Relief of Negro Slaves, testifying to the existence of marks on Prince's body (co-signed by three witnesses, including Susanna Strickland, Pringle's secretary and the person in charge of transcribing Prince's narrative).

The narrative itself is a recounting, from her present position as a house servant in Mr. Pringle's home in London, of the geographical displacements and working relations with the multiple owners that variously claimed her as their slave. The story narrates her first twelve years in the house of Captain John Williams Jr. and his wife, Sarah, where she happily spent the first years of her youth. With her sale in 1805 to Captain John Ingham (Captain I_) and Mary Spencer of Spanish Point she is made to part from her family and is subjected to a gruesome experience of exploitation. She rapidly learns the variety of tasks associated with her work and starts developing decision-making skills. After witnessing the sadistic practices of her masters, the torture of children, flogging, head-punching by her mistress, and the murder of a fellow slave, she escapes to her family (then living under the protection of Captain Darrell, an upper-class Bermudan politician) only to be returned by her father, after a short period, to the Inghams. Five years later she will be sold to Mr. D_ of Turks Island and Bermuda. As Ferguson puts it:

> Why they sold her when she was still a young, fit, industrious worker is hard to say, but a maintained posture of intransigence could explain her early release. Most slaves had only one or two owners in a lifetime, whereas Mary Prince had five before she freed herself. (7)

Following her new owner, she will travel 720 miles to Turks Island, where, under ghastly conditions, she is made to work in the old ponds and is, from time to time, punished by hanging from her wrists while stripped naked, and mercilessly flogged and beaten under the impassive gaze of her owner.

Whereas in the extremely harsh conditions of Turks Island Mary Prince had silently borne her punishment, once back in the comparatively more benign Bermuda, she actively reacts to her master's abuse and starts to impose certain limits to the amount of pain and humiliation she will undergo, particularly by refusing to accommodate Captain D_'s licentious whims, such as the demand that she wash him nude in the bathtub (the only incident of sexual harassment mentioned in the text). In Bermuda, she cares for D_'s daughter and works on the grounds, whereby she is able to make money on her own (something she will from now on always manage to accomplish, no matter how hard she is made to work for her owners or how deteriorated her health has become), saving with a view to her manumission. Unable to withstand Captain D_'s devious sexuality, she asks to be sold to John Wood, a Bermudan merchant who was moving to the more liberal Antigua, where she becomes a washerwoman and, under the tremendous loads she is made to wash, coupled with the change from Bermuda's tepid saltwater to cold Antiguan water, she becomes crippled with rheumatism and erysipelas. Tensions now arise with the black overseer, Martha Wilcox, while she develops a seven-year affair with the white Captain Abbot, followed by her marriage to pious and hardworking Daniel James, a free black carpenter. After asking the Woods for her manumission on several occasions and being variously refused, and while accompanying them to a visit to London in 1827, she eventually escapes and goes to work as a domestic to Thomas Pringle, whose friend Susanna Strickland, a recent Methodist convert, transcribes her story between 1829 and 1830. Mary Prince ends her narration by thanking her transcriber and the reverend Mr. Young for instructing her into the word of God. Her voyage thus finds its culmination (in truth, its silence, being constructed as the point of departure of her backward-looking traveling) in Christianity and wage labor, marking her territorial and institutional displacement as a passage into metropolitan capitalism.

The modern reception of the text, preoccupied with making it talk fully, has highlighted and celebrated what the text brought to the surface: the experience of slavery as seen from the slave's point of view, however surreptitiously and subtly contrabanded. In so doing, contemporary criticism has produced some perplexing conclusions. Henry Louis Gates, for example, states in *The Classic Slave Narratives:*

> Prince's account makes her readers acutely aware that the sexual brutalization of the black woman slave along with the enforced severance of a mother's natural relation to her children and lover of her choice—defined more than any other aspect of slavery the daily price of her bondage. (xv)

And yet, it is precisely the realms of sexual brutalization, sexual love, and maternity that are most evidently and uniquely either lacking or under-played in her narrative, a point that does not escape Ferguson's attention, although neither does it exempt her from highlighting Mary Prince's sub-tle bringing forward of sexuality as a particularly daring and transgressive intervention into the puritan taboos of the genre:

> Mary Prince manages to foil this taboo by encoding her abusive sexual expe-riences in accounts of jealous mistresses and a master who forced her to wash him while he was naked. (4)

Yet, the particular form of this inscription is purely negative (a perverse sexuality that is rejected), leaving the Other's desire, sexual transactions, and erotic imaginaries (that is, affirmative sexuality) out of the text. To this extent then, Prince's mention of sexuality confirms rather than foils the generic taboos of Puritanism by inscribing the text's libidinal economy within the disembodied and abstracting aesthetic of Puritan ethics and morality. Thus the political economy of the de-erotization of the contact zone by Mary Prince: Eros, the predilect performance of the sentimental novel, being quite a dangerous ground to be transited by the subaltern unless inscribed within the sexual economy of sentimental narratives writ-ten by the metropolitan self, where, as Pratt notes:

> The colonized heroes and heroines of European sentimental literature are rarely "pure" non-whites or "real" slaves. Like Joanna [narrator of *Incidents in the Life of a Slave Girl*], they are typically mulattoes or mestizos who already have European affiliations or, renewing an older motif, are "really" princes or princesses.[34]

Contrary to the contemporary reading of the text-as-unveiling, I suggest that the textual silencing of Prince's sexuality is part of a more general rhetorical politics of erasure that structure the narrative: the simultaneous erasure of travel, self, and Prince's masking strategies of survival will point toward the picaresque structure that formed the conditions of possibility of subaltern writing.

Erasure of travel: the traveler as travelee

To the reader's expectations, the slave's travel seemed to do away with the intermediary: the act of vicarious travel—the reader's—would seem to become doubly instantiated: travel through other spaces by an Other traveler. And yet, this doubling was a textual mirage. The Other's traveling does not textually register the space she travels as an other space, as a space in itself, but as an inscription into her body—which becomes, in the process, the true site of the reader's traveling gaze. The refraction of travel into the landscape of the traveler is a necessary condition of subaltern travel once inscribed within the symbolic economy of the center. In other words, from the point of view of the Same, the Other's experience is always already embodied. The reason for this particularity lays in the imputed otherness of the subaltern. It is this otherness that renders her speech-act not a conversation (even when addressed to the One) but a confession, a deposition, an unveiling to be paraded in front of the Same's critical gaze: her utterance will not be answered. It will be circulated among a dialoguing community that excludes her and that will either corroborate or deny it.[35] Whereas in the case of the European traveler, experience is rendered as knowledge, in the instance of the subaltern the opposite occurs: knowledge is rendered into experience. In other words, legitimation resides outside the authority of the Other, in the One's evaluative reading of the subaltern's discourse—in Prince's *History,* a fact crystallized in the formal structure of the book, particularly in the dialectic between the testimonial text and the annotation apparatus that frames it.

The subaltern traveler knows she is not entitled to such an affirmation of either the I that travels nor of the eye that surveys (these tasks would be left to the scientist, the naturalist, and the capitalist avant-garde).[36] The seen will only appear sentimentalized, as it affects her story—which is, after all, about slavery, hard luck, and victimization. The seen appears, therefore, as a function of a reduction: thus the conditions of discourse of the slave narrative, its erasure of the traveled as such, the negation of the traveled as objective description, and its substitution by subjectivized experience. Here the I does not affirm (even when it does): it shows, it lays bare for the one to see and evaluate. Not surprisingly, and replicating the obligatory market inspection that slaves underwent when about to be purchased, the text's preoccupation with ascertaining the truthfulness of Mary Prince's testimony will re-enact the public scrutinizing of Prince's body and the public circulation of its findings. Let me quote in full the contents of the Appendix to the third edition of the book,[37] as it illustrates many of the rhetorical mechanisms already discussed. In this appendix, Mrs. Pringle claims to respond to inquiries "respecting the existence of marks of severe punishment on Mary Prince's body" from Mrs. Townsend, one of the benevolent Secretaries of the Birmingham Ladies' Society for Relief of Negro Slaves:

'Dear Madam,

'My husband having read to me the passage in your last letter to him, expressing a desire to be furnished with some description of the marks of former ill-usage on Mary Prince's person, —I beg in reply to state, that the whole of the back part of her body is distinctly scarred, and, as it were, chequered, with the vestiges of severe floggings. Besides this, there are many large scars on other parts of her person, exhibiting an appearance as if the flesh had been deeply cut, or lacerated with gashes, by some instrument wielded by most unmerciful hands. Mary affirms, that all these scars were occasioned by the various cruel punishments she has mentioned or referred to in her narrative; and of the entire truth of his statement I have no hesitation in declaring myself perfectly satisfied, not only from my dependence on her uniform veracity, but also from my previous observation of similar cases at the Cape of Good Hope.

'In order to put you in possession of such full and authentic evidence, respecting the marks on Mary Prince's person, as may serve your benevolent purpose in making the inquiry, I beg to add to my own testimony that of Miss Strickland (the lady who wrote down in this house the narratives of Mary Prince and Ashton Warner), together with the testimonies of my sister Susan and my friend Miss Martha Browne—all of whom were present and assisted me this day in a second inspection of Mary's body.

'I remain, Dear Madam,
    'Yours very truly,
    'M. Pringle.'
'The above statement is certified and corroborated by
    'SUSANNA STRICKLAND'
    'SUSAN BROWN'
    'MARTHA A. BROWNE.'

Ironically, the multiple inspections, the proliferation of witnesses, the showcasing of Prince's inscribed materiality and its discernment, remain suspect. No matter how much the act of witnessing performed by all three signatories validates the existence of the marks on Prince's body, the operation fails to testify as to their origin, for which only her own telling can vouch. The text's efforts to fill the voids left by the Other's inaccessibility to self-representation, therefore, only come up to circumstantial evidence. More than to the truth of Prince's assertions, they point toward her suspect status. The text's strategies of legitimation, grounded as they are within the economy of metropolitan sameness, culminate in an unavoidable aporia. Once again, the archaeology of the Other's experience remains an interpretive act ultimately grounded in the Same, wherefore the undecidable character of its findings. Thus, the operations that Mary Prince's body is put through by the slave narrative's annotation apparatus serve to inadvertently reify it, making it other, disengaging it (no matter how momentarily) from its history by the same process that recognizes its production as historical. Through the intervention of the annotation apparatus, the history of abuse narrated by Prince (the traveled space of her past experience) becomes a traveling through her body (her present, the space of an already-arrived destination). Not the said (her story) but the act of saying it forms the basis of the *discovery*, an act more intimately attuned to its legal meaning than to its traveling homonym.

Instead of an eye that looks at the world as spectacle, the reception and framing of the slave's experience constitutes that experience as spectacle. The slave becomes a figure where the world colludes. She becomes that which is traveled upon: the traveler defers to the travelee. To give credible testimony she must be constructed as legitimate (Christian, moral, truthful), that is, as a face (in the metropolitan imaginary, as an instance of the Same). But, as already argued, this face is only a stratagem of the genre: it does not present an incognita, it does not interpellate as strangeness, inconmesurableness. It may (try to) talk, but as one of us. It mimics. It is a face that mirrors the One's gestures. In this context, the Other as traveler is an impossibility. Movement ceases to exist and is represented by its opposite: as an accummulation whose locale is the Other's body. To disengage that accummulated experience requires the reader's travel through the narrator's recollection, but all things revealed there will not be discoveries but recognizances, reaffirmations of an already existing knowledge. In this sense, her discourse does not produce knowledge, new paradigms, but information, to be freely circulated in the re-arrangement of diverse positions within an already determined field of knowledge—the slavery debate in nineteenth-century England.

Another consequence of this otherized subjectivity is that the subaltern can only travel by looking back. This looking back results in the effacing of the phenomenology of travel and the silencing of the Other's encounter with the Same. To travel otherwise, to travel while looking forward, would impose an ongoing, evolving hermeneutic. It would be tantamount to the production of the narrator's history as an ongoing, evolving present. The phenomenology of that traveling would capture the lived experience as a function of the narrator's subjectivity as it unfolds: it would be the slave doing the talking, viewing, reacting, and not her remnant, the converted freedwoman reminiscing. To travel while looking forward would also produce an Other hermeneutic, from which the Other looks at the metropolitan land- and body-scape as *her* Other. This impossibility explains why once Mary Prince arrives in England, description ends: the ethnographic task will only be allowed to the subaltern as autoethnography, which renders travel unnecessary.[38] Only by traveling while looking backward can that metropolitan encounter by the Other be rendered mute; only then can it be inscribed as a nonsignifying moment, where departure—exile's moment—is transformed into an arrival.[39] Travel-by-looking-back, therefore, points to the erasure of the subjective historicity of the subaltern, which helps explain the necessarily restricted sentimentality of her text.

Erasure of self: the politics of restricted sentimentality

In Mary Prince's *History,* sentimentality appears in a subdued form. This restricted sentimentality is a function of the subaltern's inaccessibility to subjectivity, a most necessary attribute of the sentimental narrator, since, as Pratt has noted:

> Sentimental writing explicitly anchors what is being expressed in the sensory experience, judgement, agency or desires of the human subjects. Authority lies in the authenticity of somebody's felt experience. Predicates tend to be attached to situated observers.[40]

Given the suspect character of Prince's testimony, the gap between experience and the subjectivity that legitimates it has to be bridged from outside her text: whereas experience is allowed to, and in fact required of, the female subaltern witness,[41] sentiment is not, as it asserts what should be only given a posteriori by the audience through sympathy. The conditions of possibility of that sympathy are grounded in the modest and unassuming character of the subaltern's voice: her narrative decorum (where one can find the reason for Mary Prince's textual taming of sexuality and narcissism). It is her lack of narcissism that allows and even compels the reader's gaze to fix itself upon her textual self. Symptomatically, in the editor's evaluation of Mary Prince's personal character (her nontextual persona), her sense of self—rendered as "a somewhat violent and hasty temper, and a considerable share of natural pride and self-importance" (115)—is identified as her chief fault, perhaps pre-emptying and anticipating the audience's reaction (for all textual purposes his own's) to the self-affirming character of any act of narrative from the status of subalternity, no matter how well modulated to humble itself.

The narrative commands through its silences, disguises, and omis-

sions—the sublime and sentimental tendencies that constitute its protagonist as a heroic model of female abnegation, intelligence, thrift, and containment; in other words, through a text that produces its other as an
instance of a striving toward feminine-bourgeois subjectivity. But the
restricted sentimentality of the narrative, while problematizing the subaltern's subjectivity (in fact, because of it) opens a contestatory space where
the confrontation of metropolitan social forces takes place. In other words,
The History of Mary Prince does more than simply play into the aesthetic of
sentimentality. While utilizing it restrictedly, it performs a rhetorical operation of political reconfiguration of the terms of its reception in its effort
to carry on a political intervention. It does so by displacing the narration,
from the reified forms of survival literature that the slave narrative had
acquired in the eighteenth century to the concrete discussion of slavery as
a form of economic production that brings about the degradation of the
human person. The text's move away from personal melodrama becomes
an assertion of societal problematics. Reader-narrator identification,
therefore, serves a purpose here different from that of the survival narrative. It is there to mobilize in the Other's behalf. It asks the reader to pass
judgment and mobilize his solidarity. The ultimate remoteness of its problematic (one that, structurally, has taken center stage) places this text as an
interlanguage of the contact zone. The use of the other to potentiate the
aesthetics of sensationalism and sentimentality is quite different from this
Other, picaresque use.

Radical associations and antislavery societies formed the material and
institutional basis of slave narratives, and the conditions of their possibility.
The slave narrative, on the other hand, is one of the enabling practices of
these societies. Therefore, although producing a restricted spectacularity of
the sublime (when viewed form the standpoint of the slave as person, as
social agent), this sublimation of the Other, this appropriation of the Other
within the limits imposed by the structures of imperialism, functioned,
within the political practice of the center (England), as an effectively radi-
calizing practice (the antislavery debate), constituting itself as an alternative
to the metropolitan economy of the sublime, insofar as it became embedded in and made possible an economy of cultural production and reception different from the bourgeois practices of monadic consumption. As
Andrew McCann intelligently conceptualizes the circulation of textual
production within the English radical associations of the 1790's:

> This is a very different economy of cultural production and reception from
> that implied by the practices of monadic consumption. It constructs, or

interpellates communal identity, and accordingly deploys socially situated knowledge, in a way that privatized reading practices alone could not. The public meeting itself becomes a mediating context making articulate oppositional knowledge possible in a way that does not manipulate isolated subjects in violation of their individual integrity, but that demonstrates the socially contingent nature of the isolated, monadic subject in the first place, and its relationship to forms of hegemony, exploitation and repression specifically designed to contain experience within the bounds of individuated subjectivity and hence to efface the possibility of collectively articulating the common experience of political disenfranchisement.[42]

Once placed within the context of textual production and consumption, that is, within the economy of the text's circulation in abolitionist discourse and practices, the production of the slave narrative could be seen as politically ambiguous or, better yet, ambivalent. On the one hand it instrumented and allegorized the Caribbean Other—by inscribing her in its restricted sublime and sentimental aesthetics—while, on the other, it created a text that, because of the particular form of its inception within the antislavery debate, allowed for the overcoming of monadic subjectivity. This operation was central to the counter-hegemonic, associational spaces of the English antislavery societies—an ambivalence, we might add, that was unavoidable, being grounded in the recycling of peripheral symbolic capital made to circulate within the socioeconomic structures and symbolic economy of the metropolitan center.

As already noted, the slave narrative forms part of this metropolitan economy by constituting and being constituted by the antislavery societies. From the perspective of the Other, being subsumed within the aesthetics of the abolitionist movement is a concession, but an act of political praxis nevertheless. The subaltern status of the subaltern subject in this symbolic economy does nothing but reflect the asymmetry in the development of antislavery forces in the center-periphery divide of the time. This geopolitical configuration preceded the slave's narrative, it was not created by it. It formed, in fact, the very conditions of possibility of the slave-as-narrator being able to speak at all. At the same time, the antislavery societies were the product of the development of the sociopolitical conditions of the metropolis as it encountered slavery and could hardly escape this overdetermination (it being, in fact, also its enabling circumstance). To ask otherwise of it, as it has lately been the case with deconstructivist criticism of the testimonial form, is to miss the connectedness of discourse and institutional dynamics, the historicity of textual production, the political savvy of the subaltern, and the creative and picaresque thrust of testimonial discourse.[43] The positioning of the Other within the symbolic economy of the slave narrative, then, is a willful act of political and rhetorical intervention. Based, as it is, on an aesthetics of concealment and display for the Other's Other, it is a picaresque act.

The picaresque genre, in fact, had been the textual simulacrum where the traveling experience of the subaltern Other—rendered as vagabondage— was inscribed during the sixteenth and seventeenth centuries. Not surprisingly, the picaresque novel, as genre, was characterized by three structural elements we have come to discern in the slave narrative: travel, subalternity, and autobiography.[44] A closer look at this genre will allow us to see the continuities and ruptures attendant to the subaltern traveler as she takes upon herself the task of narrating the experience of travel.

Erasure of the mask: the slave narrative as picaresque

The term "pícaro," before pointing to a literary character within a literary genre, referred to a subaltern subject attached in conditions of servitude to a powerful figure:

> Picaros were, at the beginning, servants and pages. The "kitchen picaro" soon became a very well defined type of servant. . . . In 1560 the term already applies to vagabonds and criminals. . . .[45]

The picaresque novel was to take this social type and make it into its protagonist. The pícaro's travels consist of a displacement through social institutions from a condition of subalternity. As a result of her subaltern status, to make this social mobility possible, the traveler needs to adopt a variety of masks and simultaneously suspend her values as a function of survival. Thus, the pícaro is a subject-in-institutional-transit. The instrumentation of the self and her body that makes that transiting possible presupposes a flexibility and a theatricality that forms the conditions of necessity of that mask—the theatrical semiotics of the pícaro being the underside to the symbolic economy of the sublime, with its aesthetics of rigidity and its rhetorical coincidence between signifier and signified: in the sixteenth century, the (hegemonic) knight is produced as a face (novel of chivalry), the (subaltern) page as a mask (picaresque novel), that is, as a face gesticulating within the realm of need, affirming its will to survival within a framework of asymmetrical power relations. Both imaginative operations constitute two sides of the same coin, that is, both express hegemony's construction of itself and the Other. They *represent* but in no way *express* the Other: the pícaro, as a hero who narrates her autobiography, does so from a hegemonic position—either by having repented of past deeds *(Guzmán de Alfarache),* or by having overcome her dereliction *(Lazarillo de Tormes).*

The sixteenth-century narrative fluctuation of the hero from knight to rogue (from the novel of chivalry to the picaresque novel) does not have so much to do with Aristotelian aesthetics (the moral character of the tale as appropriate to a particular genre) as with a movement through estates: when the hero traverses the threshold of the chivalric novel she does it as pícaro. The picaresque novel's historicization of the lower-class experience finds its rhetorical alibi (and one was necessary in the sixteenth century to justify a narrative prose that was to pay sustained attention to the everyday experience of the lowest strata of seignorial-monarchical society) in the autobiographical form,[46] as derived from the tradition of letter writing. The picaresque novel, as letter, did not only enable the telling of this lowly story, historicizing it. It provided verisimilitude to the text, conferring on to it documentary status (a necessary prerequisite of the novelistic form). In its classical form (as epitomized in *Lazarillo de Tormes*) the telling of the story is itself part of the narrative structure—explaining why the narrator has been summoned to write what it writes for her—thus legitimating itself as both text and genre.[47]

Thus, the picaresque, as a narrative apparatus, serves to make the Other's experience intelligible by replacing her voice by its simulacrum. One of the results of this rhetorical operation is to render transparent the picaresque structure of the Other's modus operandi—it is precisely as simulacrum that the pícaro's avatars, otherwise hidden, are narrated as picaresque, as an ostensible parading of its masking strategies in carnivalesque fashion. But whereas in the picaresque the narrator's voice is suspect by virtue of the very structure of the novel—performed by the dubious moral character of the pícaro, a fact that marks his enunciation as suspect (its irony is textually grounded and thus easily inferred)—the slave's testimony is not necessarily so branded, as it is structured by textual mediations that mutilate the total range of the slave's experience according to the needs of the genre's sublime and sentimental tendencies. In Mary Prince's case, the negation of the mask and erasure of the slave's picaresque strategies of survival do not follow structurally from the testimonial voice itself. They were, nevertheless, possibly suspected by the unsympathetic reader and, as we have seen, ambiguously highlighted by the text's annotation apparatus.

On the footsteps of the picaresque tradition of inscribing the subaltern's iruption into the world of the Same, the pro-slavery forces tended to construct the slave as picaro, as a being that hides her antisocial dispositions behind a multiplicity of strategies of concealment, posturing, and simulation. Mrs. Carmichael's *Domestic Manners and Social Conditions of the White, Coloured, and Negro Population of the West Indies,* a text published in 1833, only two years after Prince's *History,* is a case in point. There, the slave is represented as a guileless pícaro: "The first defect of character which struck me as very marked among negroes, was a love of deceit."[48] "Negroes will steal, cheat, and deceive in every possible way, and that with a degree of adroitness that baffles the eye and the understanding of any European. . . . They have not the slightest sense of shame" (263). She is lazy: "Employment is their abhorrence—idleness their delight; and it is from having so minutely watched their dispositions, habits, and method of work, that I have come to this conclusion, —that to overwork a negro slave is impossible" (96). Expert at avoiding work and feigning sickness, "Negroes have more imaginary diseases than any set of people I ever was amongst. . . . Monday morning is always a great day for the sick; all lazy or ill-disposed negroes come into the hospital at least once a week, and sometimes oftener" (204). Deft at stealing from her masters, "The elder negroes teach theft to their children as the most necessary of accomplishments; and to steal cleverly, is as much esteemed by them as it was by the Spartans of old" (264). The slave's cunning has no limits: "I never saw but one blind negro; and he, although blind to his master, and able to do nothing for him, could build a house for himself, and plant provisions" (207). As in a picaresque society, the relations of solidarity within the group of slaves are not based upon a collective sense of communitas but upon individual gain: ". . . there was no arrangement, cooperation, or agreement among the servants, save only one thing, and that was stealing; for a bottle of wine was hardly opened, until some clever hand whipped it away, and without any apparent fear of detection or sense of shame . . ." (36). They are sexually voracious, lacking in Christian values and indoctrination. The masking of the slave-as-pícaro rests in two complementary operations: the hiding of their true self (deceit) and the ostentation of a feigned persona (mimicry): to their children, "they are fond of teaching them to mimic, a talent which is conspicuous in negroes, and early teach them deceit" (25). The colored slaves do not fare any better in her text: "They are generally rather more polished than the negro, but I think they are, if possible, more artful" (83). "To obtain the truth from them is difficult beyond measure, since they, as well as negroes, will swear to anything" (85). "To speak the truth seems to them almost impossible, and they often invent so cunningly, that it is difficult to prove the falsehood of that which all the while you feel convinced is a tissue of lies" (86). In short, the masking imperative forced upon the subaltern's actions render her and her discourse suspect: "It is impossible for me to vouch for the truth of details coming from a set of people who, as a people, have so little regard for truth" (299).

Carmichael's narrative representation of the slave as pícaro,[49] a perspective undoubtedly shared by many readers, reminds us of the hermeneutic of suspicion under which a text such as Mary Prince's would be examined. The anticipation of such a paranoid reading is integrally built into the *History* by the editor's comments. But, although made to "vouch for the truth" of the story, the deployment of the editor's annotations create a (de)legitimating effect, bringing to the fore the ambiguous and suspect character of the narrator's voice and inscribing it into the narrative's very structure. The annotation of the slave's text underscores what it seeks to dispel, confirming the subaltern status of the narrator's voice within the political and rhetorical economy of the slave narrative. The annotation apparatus thus legitimates the text while de-legitimating its narrator—in fact, the very presence of this juxtaposition of voices within the book makes difficult the identification of *a* narrator, problematizing the source(s) of textual authority, a tension that confirms its being in the contact zone. While the restricted sentimentality of the narrative constructs the other as an instance of the European self (through the mediation of Christianity), the annotation apparatus' affirmation and validation of the story converts the witness into an Other, affirming the other's story while debunking her ontological status as a subject able to communicate her story unmediatedly, that is, constructing an impossibility: a subject devoid of self-representational capabilities. The *History,* therefore, is both structurally and contextually engaged in a discussion about the possible maskings of her protagonist.

But the picaresque masking reaches across the dynamics of the production of literature into the slave's self-production. It is a structural overdetermination arising out of the very existence of the subject's subaltern positioning within the logic of institutionalization—its reduction of the subject to a role. The location of the slave within the bounds of the institution of slavery made the confrontation of role economy unavoidable. But so does the location of the freedwoman within the bounds of the antislavery society. The subaltern's masking, therefore, is doubly instantiated: (1) in the everyday survival strategies of her life in slave society, and (2) in her writing within the bounds of the slave narrative. Her movement from periphery to center, from slavery to freedom, does not do away with the masking process: slavery ceases, but not subalternity.

As the institutional forces she is made to inhabit demand and impose an allegorical structure (typification) to the subaltern subject as the conditions of her (re)production and survival—she needs to play a functional role within the institution in order to exist at all—the subject's transactions adopt the form of a masking—that is, the asymmetry of power relations makes it necessary to circulate one's self under negotiated forms: those parts of the self that are (deemed) problematic to the institutional logic find their expression in an altered form. The mask, from this perspective, is an act of social *poesis* that allows the excessive materiality of the subaltern subject (Mary Prince's sexuality, her masking strategies, the subjective impressions of her traveling experience) to enter into the stage of the institutional semiotic universe as a legitimate part of its world—its appearance is, therefore, symptomatic (the investigation of its pathology being one of the chief preoccupations of Carmichael's paranoid hermeneutic). Mary Prince is thus caught in the institutional dynamics of colonial capitalism. Her travels through the various masters, regions, and Caribbean islands, as well as her participation in the production of her narrative—her insertion into slavery and antislavery institutions alike—subject her to a double erasure: that of the self (the erasure of her face) and that of the other (the effacement of her mask). The institution of slavery produces her as a mask while effacing her face to reduce her to labor power, thus producing her as other—the mask here renders any encounter with the Other as a pseudo-encounter; stripping away all claims, from the part of the subaltern, to interpellation; negating all possible testimony; foreclosing all possible confrontation. The antislavery society, on the other hand, contrabands her mask to produce her as a pseudo-face, thus erasing her Otherness—the encounter is here feasible but asymmetrical, as the face confronting the Same is not that of the Other, it is not expressive of the Other's totality but a simulacrum made to operate strategically. It confronts, but not radically; it does not confront as an incognita piercing through the metropolitan imaginary, but as a plea, reaffirming, in the process, the disputed identity of the Same (a split identity, no doubt, as attested by the metropolitan polarization with regard to the slavery debate).

Whereas, as I have previously noted, the picaresque images the Other's experience into a writing that displays and theatricalizes from the perspective of the Same, the subaltern's strategy is articulated in the opposite operation of concealment—of the subaltern's mask—and mimicry—of her master's ways and *sensibilité*. Parodying Gayatri Chakravorty Spivak's question: can the subaltern travel?, can the subaltern write? [50] Indeed. Her writing, by not saying what it means, by not (truth-fully) saying her experience does nothing but truly write. Her concealment is tantamount to her strategic deployment of her experience within the institution of writing. In fact, to ask of her to write her "experience" fully and faithfully (as a transposition of her lived history) would amount to denying her access to writing *tout court* (as writing is always already an act of omission, addition, and strategic deployment of the lived experience within the bounds of a particular institution and genre). There is found (by not being found out) her picaresque strategy. It is articulated as a double concealment: the absence of the pícaro in her narrative hides the picaresque structure of her voyage and its narration. If the picaresque effect is the result of one's gaze upon the pícaro (as character), the pícaro's tale (the pícaro as narrator), paradoxically, appears as testimony (if we have been had by this narrative strategy). The subaltern picaresque deployment is, therefore, not an act of parading of her body's experience (a revelation), but a well-articulated and modulated political and aesthetic act (a gesturing, a partial concealment, a showing, and a fabrication of sorts): it implies the selective instrumentation of her experience, a theatricality-for-the-Other-of-the-Other.[51] Here, contrary to the critics of the testimonial narrative's "mutilation" of the subaltern's voice—by the ethnographer, the editor, the sociologist—there is nothing missing. The lack of the for-itself is not really a lack but the result of the overdetermination of the spoken by the symbolic economy within which her discourse is made to operate—this, in fact, does not negate but affirms the speaking subject's agency: the act of saying is made expressly to operate within those coordinates; its being at all is due to the existence of the genre and, in the last instance, of the sociopolitical and aesthetic project that makes it possible and even desirable.

As previously noted, the radical difference between the picaresque novel and the slave narrative is found in the transparency of the picaresque structure as well as in the uses of its deployment. Whereas in the former the picaresque mechanism is made visible—deconstructing its hero's claims to respectability through suspicion and in spite of the pícaro's intentions[52]—in the latter the voice of the witnessing slave hides her masking act to the point of not being detected (the successful act of roguery is the one that passes for something else). The passage from the former to the latter points toward the literalization of the subaltern's appearance into writing. Ironically, then, the irruption of the pícaro into writing results in the pícaro's literary disappearance. The travestying of the slave's experience through the sublime and sentimental garments of the slave narrative is therefore not simply a lack, but a lack and an excess: the telling of a mutilated experience that silences and hides—the textual production of a mutilated body—but also a telling that creatively transforms in order to seduce, persuade, and interpellate—the production of a prosthetic body—formed, in part, by the armored prosthesis (her textual chastity belt) provided by the genre's interventions: the annotation apparatus, the typification from which Mary Prince's testimony is read, and the production of the textual sublime. Whereas the totality of the slave's experience would be tantamount to an expressive act of remembrance, an unveiling, a confession (an autobiography of sorts), its mutilated and augmented form (the testimony) is a performative one (a political theatricalization). The passage from the former to the latter, then, is achieved through the downplaying of the phenomenology of the experience of travel and the simultaneous underscoring of the point of arrival, a location from which the avatars of the slave's history will be judged, relived, and represented—in Mary Prince's narrative this location being that of the female Christian believer—its being narrated from the point of arrival casting her traveling eye backwards. The organicity obtaining between the narrated experience and the generic form that structure it are thus evident. Herein lies the historical and institutional (im)possibility of Mary Prince's travel writing. To the sympathetic reader, her mutilated body becomes the site of the voyage. To the paranoid hermeneut, it will be her excess baggage. In both instances it will not be the territory traveled by Prince but herself as travelee. Mary Prince's picaresque appropriation of writing, as an instance of the Other in the self-production of an otherness strategically located to bring about a confrontation of social forces within the space of metropolitan politics and its aesthetic imaginary, lays bare the possibilities, agency, and restrictions of the subaltern, once irrevocably installed, and writing, in the contact zone.

NOTES

1. In Mary Louise Pratt's book *Imperial Eyes: Travel Writing and Transculturation* (New York: Routledge, 1992).
2. The travel element of these texts is not located in their thematic content but in the strategic moves that make them possible. The slave narratives can be seen as travel writing in the sense that their locatedness imply and are made possible by the shifts produced by relocations that are both geographical as well as textual—the latter understood in the sense of the narrators' derelict circulation through the symbolic fields imposed by the

multiple agents that intervene in their narratives (transcribers, editors, implied and actual audiences).

3. For rhetorical convenience, I will be using the term "Other" (capitalized) to refer to the subaltern subject and "other" to refer to its metropolitan representation.

4. I follow Levinas' understanding of this unmediated confrontation. As Adriaan Peperzak notes in his *To the Other: An Introduction to the Philosophy of Emmanuel Levinas* (West Lafayette, IN: Purdue University Press, 1992): "Levinas understands Heidegger's attempt to think Being in the light of the expression *es gibt* (the normal German equivalent of the English 'there is' and the French 'il y a') as the celebration of a profound generosity by which Being would bestow light, freedom, truth, and splendor to all beings. The il y a does not, however, strike Levinas as particularly generous but rather as an indeterminate, shapeless, colorless, chaotic, and dangerous 'rumbling and rustling.' The confrontation with its anonymous forces generates neither light nor freedom but rather terror as a loss of selfhood. Immersion in the lawless chaos of 'there is' would be equivalent to the absorption by a depersonalizing realm of pure materiality" (18).

5. As Sander L. Gilman suggests in his *Difference and Pathology: Stereotypes of Sexuality, Race, and Madness* (Ithaca, NY: Cornell University Press, 1985): "The infant's movement from a state of being in which everything is perceived as an extension of the self to a growing sense of a separate identity takes place between the ages of a few weeks and about five months. During that stage, the new sense of 'difference' is directly acquired by the denial of the child's demand on the world. We all begin not only demanding food, warmth, and comfort, but by assuming that those demands will be met. The world is felt to be a mere extension of the self. It is that part of the self which provides food, warmth, and comfort. As the child comes to distinguish more and more between the world and self, anxiety arises from a perceived loss of control over the world. But very soon the child begins to combat anxieties associated with the failure to control the world by adjusting his mental picture of people and objects so that they can appear 'good' even when their behavior is perceived as 'bad.'

"With the split of both the self and the world into 'good' and 'bad' objects, the 'bad' self is distanced and identified with the mental representation of the 'bad' object. This act of projection saves the self from any confrontation with the contradictions present in the necessary integration of 'bad' and 'good' aspects of the self. The deep structure of our own sense of self and the world is built upon the illusionary image of the world divided into two camps, 'us' and 'them.' 'They' are either 'good' or 'bad.' Yet it is clear that this is a very primitive distinction which, in most individuals, is replaced early in development by the illusion of integration.

"Stereotypes are crude sets of mental representations of the world. They are palimpsests on which the initial bipolar representations are still vaguely legible. They perpetuate a needed sense of difference between the 'self' and the 'object,' which becomes the 'Other.' Because there is no real line between self and Other, an imaginary line must be drawn; and so that the illusion of an absolute difference between self and Other is never troubled, this line is as dynamic in its ability to alter itself as is the self. This can be observed in the shifting relationship of antithetical stereotypes that parallel the existence of 'bad' and 'good' representations of self and Other." (17-18)

6. See Eric J. Leed, *The Mind of the Traveler: From Gilgamesh to Global Tourism* (New York: Basic, 1991).

7. I have arbitrarily chosen to use the masculine form to describe the Same and the feminine to refer to the Other. I do not intend this use to be thought of as an essentializing gesture but one that metaphorically points to a historically located patriarchal system of domination and representation. Its purpose is intended as purely dramatic, performative, as well as stylistic (avoiding the profusion of he's and she's, his and hers).

8. In Adriaan Peperzak's explanation of Levinas's notion of the face: "The otherness of the Other is concretized in the face of another human. . . . I can see another as someone I need in order to realize certain wants of mine. She or he is then a useful or enjoyable part of my world, with a specific role and function. We all belong to different communities, in which we function more or less well on the basis of reciprocal needs. I can also observe another from an aesthetic perspective, for example, by looking at the color of her eyes, the proportions of his face, and so on. But none of these ways of perception allows the otherness of the other to reveal itself. All aspects manifested by a phenomenological description that starts from these perspective are immediately integrated by my self-centered, interested, and dominating consciousness. These ways of looking at them transform the phenomena into moments of my material or spiritual property. The sort of phenomenology based on these and similar observations is a form of egology." (19) Subsequent page references will appear in parentheses in the text.

9. For a discussion of the face-to-face, see Peter L. Berger and Thomas Luckman's *The Social Construction of Reality: A Treatise in the Sociology of Knowledge* (New York: Anchor, 1967), 28-34.

10. Anomie, in counter distinction to the face-to-face, produces: (1) a spatial and temporal discontinuity (where the Other is seen as belonging to a different historical time or another stage of civilization); (2) the Other's intermittence or lack of expressivity (which allows the Other's objectification); (3) an orientation of expressivity toward a third party that is not the Other (transforming communication into a spectacle); (4) a maximizing of discursive typification and a minimizing of the Other's existential presence (allowing for the reduction of the Other to a role, an institutional performativity, or a thing).

11. Michel de Certeau makes a very interesting analysis of this cannibalistic dynamic of Sameness over the Other in "Montaigne's 'Of Cannibals': The Savage 'I'." In *Heterologies: Discourse on the Other* (Minneapolis, MN: University of Minnesota Press, 1993), 67-80.

12. Certeau makes the following distinction: "Psychoanalysis and historiography . . . have two different ways of distributing the *space of memory*. They conceive of the relation between the past and present differently. Psychoanalysis recognizes the past *in* the present; historiography places them one beside the other. Psychoanalysis treats the relation as one of imbrication (one in the place of the other), or repetition (one reproduces the other in another form), of the equivocal and of the *quidproquo* (What 'takes the place' of what? Everywhere, there are games of masking, reversal, and ambiguity). Historiography conceives the relation as one of succession (one after the other), correlation (greater or lesser proximities), cause and effect (one follows from the other), and disjunction (either one or the other, but not both at the same time)." (4)

13. Certeau, 3-4.

14. It is important to see the complex character of discursivity in its relation with otherness. As Certeau explains: ". . . discourses constitute forms of actual social interaction and practice. As such, they are not irrational, but they are subject to the pulls and pressures of the situations in which they are used as well as to the weights of their own tradition. They must always handle the complex interplay of that which is of the order of representation and the nonrepresentable part which is just as much constitutive of them, their own other. . . . This other, which forces discourses to take the meandering appearance that they have, is not a magical or a transcendental entity; it is the discourse's mode of relation to its own historicity in the moment of its utterance." (xx)

15. Certeau, 18.

16. Certeau, 16.

17. For a discussion of these missionary aesthetics in connection to modes of institutional life, see Mario Cesareo's *Cruzados, mártires y beatos: emplazamientos del cuerpo colonial* (West Lafayette, IN: Purdue University Press, 1995).

18. Neither Certeau nor Levinas differentiate between Other and other, that is, between the real other and her phantasm made to circulate the symbolic economy of the Same. Although one cannot determine that this absence points to their identification, the void generated by the Other's disappearance renders Certeau's and Levinas's conclusions problematic.

19. As the Other has been inscribed into the discourse of the Same as a mutilated remnant, the archeological reconstruction of the Other's totality (and, therefore, the totality of the self) cannot be achieved through the rearticulation of the order of the Same under a purely textual paradigm. Even if

the critical discourse were to identify the Other's materiality found under the phantasmatic form of its inscription in the order of the Same, it would find but the logic of that transformation. It is, therefore, not sufficient to deconstruct a narrative order from its own assumptions. To be able to leave the egologic episteme it will be necessary to bring, from outside the text, the remaining vestiges of the Other's materiality. For a discussion of this type of hermeneutic, the need to bring about a pluritopic reading of texts, histories, and materialities, see Walter Mignolo's *The Darker Side of the Renaissance: Literacy, Territoriality, and Colonization* (Ann Arbor: University of Michigan Press, 1995). A purely deconstructivist logic or a psychoanalytical one will find the Same's lacunae and aporias. It will never be able to reconstruct the ecology of the encounter, its existential and material engagement.

20. See Pratt's "Arts of the Contact Zone," in *Profession* (1991): 33-40.

21. Pratt, *Imperial Eyes . . .* , 6.

22. Pratt, *Imperial Eyes . . .* , 6.

23. See John Beverley's *Against Literature* (Minneapolis: University of Minnesota Press, 1993), xiii. For a self-critique of his previous unprobematic acceptance of the notion of contact zone, consult Beverley's "Respuesta a Mario Cesareo," in *Revista Iberoamericana* (January-March 1996): 225-233. Also see my "Hermenéuticas del naufragio y naufragio de la hermenéutica: comentarios en torno a *Against Literature,"* in pages 211-224 of the same issue.

24. Thus, Pratt asserts: "In the midst of current scholarly critique of colonialist discourses, contemporary readers can scarcely fail to link this creation of a speechless, denuded, biologized body with the deracinated, dispossessed, disposable work force European colonialists so ruthlessly and tirelessly fought to create in their footholds abroad" (*Imperial Eyes . . .* , 53).

25. In Frances Smith Foster's *Witnessing Slavery: The Development of Ante-bellum Slave Narratives* (London: Greenwood Press, 1979), 45.

26. See Foster, 47.

27. See Robert Fanuzzi's "Douglass, the Sublime." Unpublished manuscript.

28. See Moira Ferguson's edition of *The History of Mary Prince: A West Indian Slave* (Ann Arbor: University of Michigan Press, 1997), 24-25.

29. Cited in Henry Louis Gates's *The Classic Slave Narratives* (New York: Penguin, 1987), xii.

30. Cited in Foster, 20.

31. Cited in Foster, 21.

32. Had the framing mediations of the genre been an evident intervention that distorted the authenticity of the testimonial voice, they would not have provided the pathos of an Other speaking. In other words, the interventions render the text readable but only by the simultaneity of its operations of textual inscription and erasure of the Other's voice and experience.

33. Ferguson, 28.

34. Pratt, *Imperial Eyes . . .* , 100.

35. Symptomatically, Mary Prince's deposition in the court case of Pringle v. Cadell, an action brought by the *History's* editor for libel against the London publisher of *Blackwood's Magazine,* follows this mechanism: "The libel was then put in and read. It extended to a great length, [and] professed, amongst other things, to expose what it termed the black system of falsehood against the colonists. The greater part of it consisted of animadversions on Mary Prince's statement.

    "Mary Prince was then called in and sworn. She is a negress of very ordinary features, and appeared to be about 35 years of age. She stated that she gave an account of her life to Mr. Pringle. *No other question was put to her by the plaintiff's counsel, and the other side declined to cross-examine her*" (Ferguson, 138, my emphasis).

36. Pratt has noted the complimentarity and contemporariness of these two paradigms in travel writing: "Sentimentality and *sensibilité* began asserting themselves in travel writing about the same time science did, from the 1760s on . . . [readers were] already primed in sentimental dramatizations of the contact zone, many of them generated by the abolitionist movement" (*Imperial Eyes . . . ,* 86).

37. I am quoting from Moira Ferguson's edition.

38. In this connection, and in the context of a metropolitan circulation of the text produced, the autoethnocentric traveling is a traveling in the Other-of-the-Other's behalf.

39. It is interesting to note, in contrast to Prince's absolute silence with respect to the phenomenology of her English experience, Mrs. Carmichael's comments, in her *Domestic Manners and Social Conditions of the White, Coloured, and Negro Population of the West Indies* (London: Whittaker, Treacher, and Co., 1833), upon the subject of slave expectations regarding the metropolis: "Negroes have often a strong desire to see England; and when you ask them what it is they particularly wish to see, it is either the cold of England, or the number of white faces" (320-21).

40. Pratt, *Imperial Eyes . . . ,* 76.

41. The gendered character of this limitation can be ascertained by the cases of such male heroes as Equiano and Douglass.

42. Andrew McCann, "Politico-Sentimentality: John Thelwall, Literary Production and the Critique of Capital in the 1790s." Unpublished manuscript.

43. Pratt similarly notes: "When such 'autoethnographic' texts are read simply as 'authentic' self-expression or 'inauthentic' assimilation their transcultural character is obliterated and their dialogic engagement with Western modes of representation lost" (*Imperial Eyes . . . ,* 102).

44. Juan M. Lope Blanch in *La novela picaresca* (Mexico: UNAM, 1958) provides the following succinct definition: "The picaresque novel is, in essence, a moralizing narration of the different adventures—misadventures—of a picaro, narrated by the protagonist himself" (12, my transla-

tion). And, for Angel Valbuena Pratt, in *La novela picaresca española* (Madrid: Aguilar, 1946), "In the picaresque proper, the most characteristic technique—in its exterior form—has to do with the adventures of a lad of many masters. It finds its most consummated form in *Lazarillo de Tormes* (12, my translation).

45. Blanch, 14 (my translation).

46. In the words of Américo Castro, cited in Francisco Rico's *La novela picaresca y el punto de vista* (Barcelona: Seix Barral, 1973), "As the biography of such a minuscule character would have lacked all justification (nineteenth-century Romanticism was still quite distant), the author ceded his word to the creature of his imagination. The autobiographical style is thus inseparable from the very operation of artistically treating a theme that had been, until then, non-existent or frowned upon . . . Lazarillo's autobiographic mode is organic to his anonymity" (21-22, my translation).

47. For a discussion of the picareque's formal use of this narrative strategy, see Franciso Rico's *La novela picaresca y el punto de vista*.

48. Mrs. [A.C.] Carmichael, *Domestic Manners and Socal Condtions of the White, Coloured, and Negro Population of the West Indies* (London: Whittaker, Treacher & Co., 1833), 257. Quotations in the text are from the second edition (New York: Negro Universities Press, 1969). Subsequent page references will appear in parentheses in the text.

49. Although Carmichael presents the slave as pícaro, her portrayal differs markedly from the one carried through by the picaresque novel. Whereas in the latter the pícaro's gaze is focused on the chaos of the surrounding world that his sardonic seeing deconstructs, in Carmichael's anti-picaresque position chaos attaches to the pícaro. The written word (ostensibly the author's), therefore, is not suspect (as it is in the pícaro's account, fictionally his own), losing its ambiguity and thus its distance and humor.

50. See Gayatri Spivak's "Can the Subaltern Speak? " In *The Postcolonial Reader.* Edited by Bill Ashcroft et al. (London: Routledge, 1995), 24-28.

51. "For the Other of the Other" and not for the Other of the self, because Mary Prince installs herself as other in the very act of writing. She writes for an Other (the English public) conscious of her being an Other (a freed Caribbean woman slave) to that Other and unwilling to become a self. Her self-renunciation is also her self-assertion. The strategic operation allows her affirmation not in the sphere of the narrative voice but in that of the political agency that makes it heard: not as voice but as the speaking body concealed behind it.

52. The narrator is a pícaro only insofar as a narrated character. As narrator it ceases to be one as soon as his writing reveals his truancy by giving up the mask. He becomes a pícaro-for-the-other by ceasing to be a pícaro-for-himself; that is when he becomes a narrator—not coincidentally, the picaresque is always narrated from the vantage point of either the pícaro's

repentance of past deeds or as a result of her overcoming of her subaltern condition. As Genaro Talens has pointed out in his *Novela picaresca y práctica de la transgresión* (Madrid: Ediciones Jucar, 1975): "A fundamental characteristic of the picaresque novel, insofar as discourse, is the transitory character and accessory function of the picaresque lifestyle. The pícaro is not an entity but a function of his social upward mobility. He exists to cease to exist. His only goal as pícaro is to cease being one" (31, my translation).

Chapter 5

WOMEN ADRIFT:
MADWOMEN, MATRIARCHS, AND THE CARIBBEAN

Ivette Romero-Cesareo

> *The sea, alas! It is the only place to which we can be faithful.*[1]
> —Adèle Hugo

Travel is an enterprise requiring a certain degree of camouflage. Travelers prepare for their encounters and negotiations with other social settings, languages, and physical surroundings, by donning protective lotions and garb, in an attempt to erase or *accentuate* the distance between Self and Other.[2] For women traveling through the Caribbean, this enterprise becomes a complex act, necessitating pretexts, smoke screens, and masks. The discourse of travel, then, whether written or spoken by/about mobile women, is difficult to control and categorize because of the diversity of voices, each imbued with varying strategies and intentions. When writing focuses on singular women travelers—the Nun of Alferez (Catalina de Erauso), pirates Anne Bonny and Mary Read, Josephine and Pauline Bonaparte (wife and sister of Napoleon Bonaparte, respectively), or Adèle Hugo (daughter of Victor Hugo)—each remarkable in her own way—the multiplicity of accounts and interpretations of their trajectories is astoundingly heterogeneous, rendering them legendary as much by hyperbolic renditions as by the impossibility of knowing which of the versions best reflects the circulating bodies behind the texts. These subjects of travel are made to clash with or conform to moral and aesthetic parameters, first provoking titillation, then reassuring that social order has been restored. When travelers do not write their own narratives, their travels and travails are presented to the reader as a prism, whereby the narrators' own journeys and frames of reference are reflected; the function of memory as self-reflexive exploration becomes the expedition of the "distanced" writer. In cases where the travelers *themselves* relate their ventures—the Countess of Merlin, Aphra Behn, Mary Carmichael, Mary Prince, Mary Seacole, Nancy Prince, Zora Neale Hurston, Katherine Dunham—one is still presented with multilayered narratives that often present contradictory tensions and stances.[3] The narrators perform a dance of veils where one pose counteracts another to reveal or disguise dissent, assume traditionally accepted personae, or break with previously set discursive models.

The three women studied here—Adèle Hugo, Céline Alvarez Baa, and Mary Seacole—represent three distinct types of travelers who undertook their voyages with varying objectives in mind. The first two are closely linked: Adèle Hugo leaves Guernsey to follow her lover across the ocean to Halifax, Nova Scotia, and then to Barbados in 1866 where, as legend has it, her lovesickness culminates in insanity.[4] Céline Alvarez Baa is the Trinidadian woman credited with rescuing a delirious and anonymous Hugo from the streets of Bridgetown; she travels to France to deliver the young woman to the arms of her celebrated father. Traveling in the 1850's, Mary Seacole (born Mary Jane Grant in 1805) is best known as the nurse who performed heroic deeds in the Crimean War. In her travel memoirs, *Wonderful Adventures of Mrs. Mary Seacole in Many Lands* (1857),[5] Seacole—who leaves her native Jamaica to journey through Haiti, the Bahamas, Cuba, New Granada (now Panama and Colombia), England, and all the countries from there to Crimea—provides multiple reasons for traveling. While her aim seems to be to make a living, she underscores her role as mother to all English soldiers overseas—the guise of motherly concern and duty being a commonly adopted reason for travel. In writings about women travelers, motherhood appears as a repeated trope, often deployed to discursively tame a "wild" woman wandering too far from the paths of femininity.[6] These three wayfarers stand at different points in reference to motherhood. Mary Seacole plays with this by listing the familiar terms used to address her—Mrs. Seacole, Dame Seacole, Aunty Seacole, The Mother of the Regiment, La Madre, La Mère Noire. She becomes everyone's mother and she hides behind this image to safeguard her reputation in her ambiguous role as a mobile subject. Alvarez Baa also travels as a surrogate mother—her motherly devotion is stressed in all accounts of her relationship to Adèle Hugo. Upon Adèle's arrival in France, for example, Victor Hugo, without having seen either woman, proclaims in his journal, "My poor, dear child! . . . The black woman who accompanies her, Madame Baa, is devoted to her" (12 February 1872).[7] Adèle, who never becomes a mother nor displays the nurturing qualities attributed to women of her generation, is absolved by virtue of her madness. However, her condition might also be interpreted as punishment for her excessive passion and refusal to adapt to conventional models of femininity.

Motherhood is rendered all the more problematic by the dimension of race. Hugo, Alvarez Baa, and Seacole represent different points of the color spectrum: white, black, and mulatto. When narratives about or by women travelers involve racially mixed groups, it is always the woman of color who becomes the nurturing mother willing to give her life for her white sons and daughters. Although all three women were apparently childless—neither Alvarez Baa nor Seacole were known to have children of their own[8]—only the black/mulatto women assume or are ascribed the "mammy" role.[9]

The notion of the sacrifices necessary for the continuation of a white dominant group is best exemplified in the story of Madame Lacouture.[10] Born in early-eighteenth-century France, Madame Lacouture travels to Louisiana and is shipwrecked off the coast of Florida with the captain of the ship, her son and daughter, and an African slave. For the sake of survival, the group ends up killing and eating the slave. Here, the white "lady" and mother cannibalizes the black male, who is stereotypically identified as a potential barbaric cannibal, in order to save her family. On the one hand, Alvarez Baa and Seacole seem to have internalized ideas of motherly self-sacrifice for the persistence of the white world, readily assuming prescribed roles set into place by slavery. On the other, the mothering role may be the passport or *passe partout* enabling them to negotiate physical and social boundaries and to pursue their own thirst for exploration. Both women were imbued in the expansionist and mercantilist energy of their time; they were highly mobile businesswomen involved in transporting and selling products wherever they traveled. Donning the mask of motherhood may have very well been a strategy allowing them to widen their range of movement and enterprise.

Adèle Hugo and Céline Alvarez Baa

> *This incredible thing, that a young girl, a slave to the point of not being able to go out alone for five minutes to buy paper, should walk on the sea, cross the ocean, leave the old world for the new world to join her lover: that I will accomplish.*
>
> —Adèle Hugo[11]

Although Adèle Hugo wrote feverishly for years,[12] her life story has become legendary partly because of the doubts regarding her credibility:

her consistent lying to her parents in order to freely pursue the object of her desire, the disguising of her true identity in her new surroundings (often living under different aliases: Miss Lewly, Mrs. Pinson), and the uncertainty as to when she started to succumb to dementia. Hugo related her *own* account about the circumstances preceding her trip to Halifax to two lawyers by the names of Lenoir and Motton.[13] Her father, Victor Hugo, went to live in Brussels and then to the island of Jersey after being exiled from France by Louis-Napoleon Bonaparte in 1851. There Adèle met Albert Pinson, with whom she fell deeply in love. After the Hugo family moved to Guernsey, she rarely saw Pinson, but they wrote to each other regularly, pledging their eternal love. Hugo claims that they were officially engaged, that they signed a marriage contract approved by her father— although Pinson's father did not approve of the marriage because Hugo was not Anglican—and that they were secretly wed with Pinson's promise that they would be married publicly in the Anglican church at a later date. After the contract, Pinson left for England for an indeterminate span of time. During his absence, he wrote to Hugo announcing that his regiment was being sent to Nova Scotia; he asked her to join him in England where they would get married in an Anglican Church and set sail for Halifax. Facing her parents' adamant disapproval of her marrying in England rather than Guernsey, she created such a scene that her mother finally consented, accompanying Hugo to England to prepare for the wedding ceremony. Upon arrival, they were astonished to discover that Pinson had already left the country. Insisting that she was already Pinson's wife before God, Hugo managed to convince her family that she should follow Pinson to Halifax, and although they tried to dissuade her, they finally acquiesced, sending her off with enough money for her trousseau. According to Frances V. Guille, editor of her journals, many of Hugo's assertions have not been confirmed; for example, none of the civil or parochial archives of the time record a formal marriage contract between Hugo and Pinson. It is important to remember that Hugo's disclosure of her identity and "true story" to the lawyers was instigated by the announcement of Pinson's impending engagement to another woman, a Miss Johnstone. This woman assured the lawyers that Pinson had visited her on many occasions, convincing her of his undying affection and devotion, and blaming circumstances outside his power as obstacles to their marriage. Hugo declared that she was Pinson's real wife and that she would keep him from marrying anyone else as long as she lived. She was in fact successful in separating the couple.

People who knew her in Halifax confirm some parts of her story; for example, her landlords assert that Pinson came to visit Hugo at least six times in their home. There was also suspicion of extortion; it is believed that Hugo gave away large amounts of money to Pinson to pay his gambling debts.[14] Much was said about her eccentricities: she was said to go out in the day dressed entirely in black, including her shawl, bonnet, veil, and umbrella. When there were balls at General Doyle's residence, Bellevue Mansion, she would wear one of her best dresses and demand to see Lieutenant Pinson; he would take her across the street to a pauper's cemetery where they would talk in the shadows, after which he would return to his flirting and dancing at the ball, leaving her to walk home alone. She was also known to disguise herself as a man to go out at night, with a top hat, boots, and a cane, most often to lurk behind the trees in a park across from the Bellevue mansion to spy on Pinson and his female companions.[15] These particularities of dress are emphasized in François Truffaut's *Adèle H.*[16] While Alvarez Baa and Seacole traveled under the guise of surrogate motherhood, Hugo's camouflage required cross-dressing to negotiate access to a man's [Pinson's] world.

Hugo's peculiarities were noted by all but accepted and even humored as her progressive disorder became obvious. Among the rumors about her, she was known to take her umbrella everywhere, often insisting on keeping it open indoors until she sat down; it was also said that she sometimes strolled about the city draped in long pieces of fabric affixed with pins. Paradoxically, her "marginalization" as a madwoman allowed her the freedom she had always sought. As an eccentric, romantic figure, she was able to dress as she wished, to travel at will, and to circulate freely within the spheres typically forbidden to her nineteenth-century sisters.

As a consummate traveler consumed by love, Hugo was always ready to undertake a voyage in pursuit of the object of her affection. Upon discovering that Pinson's regiment was to be transferred to Barbados, and supposing he would return temporarily to see his family in England before resuming his military duties, Hugo set out every eight days to survey the ships headed for Liverpool, baggage in tow, with the hope of joining him. In a span of six weeks, she packed and unpacked her bags constantly. Finally, she found out he had gone directly to Barbados and she immediately followed, declaring that she would go to the end of the world to be near him.

Although most accounts of Hugo's life attribute her desire to travel to her all-consuming love for Albert Pinson, her manuscripts attest to other reasons. On the one hand, it must be noted that her formative years were marked by forced travel due to her father's political exile from France. In an 1852 journal entry written in Jersey, Hugo muses about her family's nomadic state and uncertain future:

> If war broke out between France and England, what would happen to little Jersey? What would happen to the expatriates? What would happen to my father? In case of expulsion my father speaks of going to Gibraltar, an English possession. He would leave first with Charles, and would choose a small house, certainly close to the sea. The sea, alas! It is the only place to which we can be faithful. Later, perhaps Spain would receive us; we would go to Seville. Then, we, the nomadic family, if Turkey accepts us, will go to the Bosphorus, passing through Corfu.[17]

On the other hand, Hugo's desire for independence and her resistance to the restrictions demanded from women of her generation, are reflected in her manuscripts. After meeting Pinson, she profited several times from her mother's own trips to France to run away and seek out her beloved. It is difficult to determine whether her obsession with independence was provoked by Pinson or whether her obsession with Pinson was a good excuse to seek the independence she aspired to achieve. In either case, her writings show a strong determination to free herself from what she called the slavery imposed by her parents, in particular, her father. She was offended by her father's insistence that marriage was "the role of a woman" and her brother Charles's claim that it would be the only way to liberate herself, and countered these remarks by saying that marriage "is humiliating for a woman." When she asked her brother whether there would be any way to obtain "emancipation" from her father, he answered that legally, she would not be able to, but that she could always become a thief or prostitute. She answered: "Becoming a thief or prostitute is contrary to my conscience; I would not do it, while emancipating myself from my father is not contrary to my conscience."[18] She immediately made plans to free herself through writing music or literature. She claimed she would write a liberating book for women, a book addressed to the twentieth century, which would not be laughed at one hundred years from then (1854).[19] Hugo was able to escape familial restraints by fleeing from home, but she never managed to become financially independent nor to produce the book she set out to write.

In Auguste Joyau's *Héroïnes et aventurières de la mer Caraïbe* (Heroines and adventurers of the Caribbean Sea),[20] the lack of information on Hugo herself is noticeable although the account is titled "Adèle Hugo and the Three Masses." This information gap is due to lack of written material—the manuscripts and letters she wrote to her family from Barbados have not been found. The only information that has been included in biographies about her has been gleaned from a handful of letters written by her brother and from a few entries from her father's journals. Most of the narration focuses on how Céline Alvarez Baa saves the raving Adèle and nurses her back to health. One wonders then why the story is not called "Céline Alvarez Baa and the Three Masses," since Adèle Hugo has nothing to do with these three masses that Alvarez Baa dedicates to Victor Hugo upon his death.[21] The message that Joyau tries to convey is that the heroine of the story is Adèle Hugo, and although it is true that Hugo showed a great sense of independence and adventure by traveling alone in search of her lover, her survival also depended on the sympathy, generosity, and courage of other women—Mrs. Saunders in Nova Scotia and Alvarez Baa in Barbados—who took it upon themselves to care for this "helpless waif." In my reading of this account, Céline Alvarez Baa is the true heroine of the story, although she remains marginalized in all versions of the encounter between her and Hugo.

Perhaps because there is so little firsthand material about Hugo's perceptions of the Caribbean, chroniclers of her life have had to imagine and recreate the Barbados of the late nineteenth century, thus producing varied and contradictory scenarios. In most of these scenarios, a very pale,[22] delicate, romantic Hugo is presented against a backdrop of barbaric exoticism depicted by bright colors, noisy crowds, and pungent smells. While Frances Guille and biographer Henri Guillemin[23] constrain themselves to quoting the sparse comments found in letters by Hugo's brother François-Victor (who must also *imagine* a Barbados that his sister fails to describe and that he has never seen), other biographers indulge in creating a Barbados that better suits the tone of their narration. Joyau opens his narration by stating that of all Caribbean islands, Barbados is the one "whose past is the least charged with history." He portrays Barbados as a flat island with monotonous landscapes that barely maintain travelers' attention, and where, except for the beaches, everything is artificial. Joyau stresses that, because of its location, Barbados was never coveted by the Europeans. He adds that this is why "three centuries ago, when the English decided to take possession of it, neither the French nor the Dutch thought once of disputing their conquest" (168).

In Leslie Smith Dow's *Adèle Hugo: La Misérable,*[24] Bridgetown is seen as "a small but thriving colony known as Little England." This biographer stresses the island's prosperity and the fact that it was considered "the brightest jewel in the English crown" due to its abundant sugar production. While Joyau's Barbados is an inhospitable and barren strip of land, Smith

Dow's is the epitome of the exotic, tropical island. Upon Hugo's arrival, "sweating stevedores swarmed around her, loading and unloading goods. Turbaned women in bright red and blue dresses carried pots and packages majestically on their heads, while small children skipped blithely along beside them under the burning sun and the waving palms." Hugo is described as marveling at "her new landscape," while "a heady aroma of fried foods, slaughtered livestock and pungent seafood permeated the air. Sea urchins, dolphin fish, flying fish, kingfish steaks, cou-cou, spiced sweet potatoes, boiled pigs' heads and trotters, and other local dishes were offered up for sale by ample Bajan women stirring their big, iron buck pots suspended over open fires" (147). This description, conveying fertility and abundance with its endless list of tantalizing foods and overpopulated streets, provides the ideal setting for the arrival of the exotic Céline Alvarez Baa on the scene.

Truffaut's depiction of Barbados in his screenplay for *Adèle H* seems to balance both atmospheres. Initially, Hugo (portrayed by a wan and pale Isabelle Adjani) is shown walking through a crowded, noisy marketplace in what appears to be unbearable heat, while children run alongside her jeering and pulling at her tattered clothes. In other scenes she is seen wandering along dry, dusty, and notably empty cobblestone streets. It is interesting to note that to film these scenes of nineteenth-century Barbados, Truffaut chooses Dakar (fairly convincing, apart from the fact that everyone in the marketplace speaks French), broadly equating the Caribbean to Africa.

The descriptions of landscapes filled with an overabundance of exotic products, merry hard-working black bodies, and enough sun and color to provoke a sensory overload, harken back to an array of aesthetic traditions. The novelty and attraction of a cornucopia of tropical delights as well as allusions to the fertility of the land betray the priorities of the mercantilist, expansionist eye.[25]

Originally from Trinidad, ex-slave Alvarez Baa was a higgler[26] in Bridgetown, Barbados. In 1871 she finds Hugo walking aimlessly down the street with a haggard and expressionless look.[27] Noticing her incoherent speech and physical frailty, she decides to take her in and care for her. Little is known of how Alvarez Baa finds out that her charge is Victor Hugo's daughter. Some versions sustain that Adèle simply told her everything in a moment of lucidity, while others claim that Céline derived the information from the piles of papers Adèle feverishly wrote night after night. The latter version would disprove the descriptions of Alvarez Baa as an illiterate woman. Whichever the case, she manages to contact Victor Hugo and to describe the precarious state in which she has found his daughter. After the first exchanges, Alvarez Baa decides to take Adèle back to France personally. They leave Barbados and spend several months in Martinique, where Alvarez Baa must wait for Hugo to regain her strength before embarking on the voyage to Europe. Once in Paris, she remains close to Hugo until she is fairly strong and then returns to the Caribbean. Months later, Hugo's state seems to worsen and she begins to cry out for her "negress" (182). Called back from Barbados, Alvarez Baa agrees to return to her bedside and, once again, she undertakes the trip home only when she realizes nothing more can be done to help Hugo.

According to Victor Hugo's notes, "Mme Baa" refuses to remain in France because she is afflicted with homesickness for her island, her real home—Trinidad. Contrary to Hugo, who is unwilling or unable to undertake the trip home, and to Mary Seacole, who adopts England as her "home" (as we will see later), Alvarez Baa has strong ties to her country, and does not hesitate to embark on the return trip.

In most versions of the story, Alvarez Baa is portrayed as the quaint, eccentric other, preferring Caribbean "costume" to European styles. Hugo, of course, was no less eccentric, but she is always presented as a romantic heroine. Her eccentricities accentuate her poignant trajectory. According to an anonymous letter printed in the *New York Tribune* around 1885:

> Her [Adèle's] wardrobe added to the enigma; she did not wear the light robes of the tropics but heavy velours, silks and even sometimes furs. All of this was testimony to a home very far in the north, a lost home, and a spirit drowned in some strange fantasy.[28]

In this same letter, Hugo's nobility and beauty are emphasized. Guille's introduction to Hugo's journal states: "Physically, she was considered beautiful, tall, with an aquiline nose, black, wavy hair, dark complexion. . . . She was judged as an exceptional woman, with perfect manners; a sweet woman, whose face exuded goodness, whose eyes shone with tenderness; a woman who had certainly come from a distinguished and cultivated family, a woman who always behaved with dignity, with an irreproachable conduct."[29] What might be perceived as bizarre behavior is softened by statements about her beauty, charm, melancholy, sweet gaze, and by the assertion that everyone could see she was from a good family, had received an excellent education and moreover, that she needed to be protected. Perhaps only her dark complexion betrays her difference: madness. She presents an attractive enigma. Alvarez Baa, on the other hand, is simply a question mark. Although very little is known of her, she is never depicted as a mystery to be pondered upon. While all want to know what was going through Hugo's mind, there are no speculations on Alvarez Baa's thoughts. No one surmises about her beauty or lack thereof. She is simply described as a large woman. In most cases the qualities attributed to Alvarez Baa are strongly reminiscent of a domestic servant's. While Auguste Joyau describes her profession as a higgler, which offered her economic independence and great freedom of movement, he emphasizes her humbleness and total devotion to Hugo. For example, he imagines a scene in which Alvarez Baa undresses Hugo and puts her to bed, not leaving her side until she is fast asleep. Wittingly or not, Joyau repeatedly juxtaposes the term "the higgler" to "the lady" ("The higgler offered the lady a seat . . ."). Moreover, rather than crediting Alvarez Baa for her decisions regarding her patient, he prefers to say that she deferred to Hugo's wishes.

In other biographies, rather than ascribing the black mammy image, oblique remarks about Alvarez Baa's relationship with Victor Hugo portray her as a sexy, self-interested Jezebel, seducing him in order to ensure reimbursement for her trip: "Madame Baa already owed at least 1,000 francs and was dependent on [Victor] Hugo's good will if she wanted not merely to repay the money she had borrowed, but to go home again."[30] Although Victor Hugo was well-known as an incorrigible womanizer, there is little proof for the following elaborate musings by biographer Smith Dow: "Despite his age, Hugo was ever ready to fornicate, and even Sarah Bernhardt was not enough for him. He had yet another conquest in mind, the object was less famous, perhaps, but no less exotic, Céline Alvarez Baa." Smith Dow goes on to say that "[O]n February 23, 1872, Hugo had noted without fanfare in his journal that Madame Baa was 'black, nevertheless a lady in the colony,'" and he adds that this entry "gave only the slightest of hints that Hugo found her desirable"[31]—a very subtle hint indeed. Most biographers relish in gleaning proof of their supposed affair from another, less subtle journal entry; Victor Hugo writes a single phrase in Spanish: "la primera negra de mi vida" (the first black woman in my life).[32] It is not entirely implausible that Alvarez Baa was the first black woman Victor Hugo had ever *seen;* he makes several comments about how his grandchildren stared at her because of the novelty of seeing a black person for the first time.[33] But that single, cryptic phrase does not seem to justify the insinuation that: "Hugo failed to note Juliette Drouet's reaction to his latest love interest, nor did he observe how willingly his latest partner engaged in bedroom romping with her geriatric debtor."[34] As can be expected, there is no information that sheds light on Alvarez Baa's "romping." Despite abundant reports of Adèle Hugo's relationship with Pinson throughout all the years she traveled on her own, her claims to be married to Pinson in the eyes of God, and her modern declarations about women's emancipation, any mention of sex is carefully avoided. There is no reconstruction or elaboration of what transpires during Adèle and Albert's numerous meetings, and her love is portrayed as pure and incorporeal. Moral judgments are entirely suspended.

Extrapolations on Alvarez Baa's relationship with Victor Hugo are also based on their exchange of gifts: when she returns Adèle's jewelry, he gives her two gold bracelets, a brooch, and golden earrings as mementos of his daughter, while she gives him a small portrait of herself as a token of affection. On her second trip, she brings him a bouquet of colorful bird feathers. Much has been made of the latter gift perhaps because it is perceived as an emblem of the exotic (signifying the "multi-colored" fauna of the tropics) or because it echoes other "encounters" between celebrated European men and "native others" bearing feathers. In this case, the encounter is reversed: the new world, represented by Madame Baa, visits the old.

In all reconstructions of Adèle Hugo's life, praise for Céline Alvarez Baa is conspicuously absent. There is no direct mention of her courage, heroism, or adventurous spirit; there is no explanation of the fact that she was considered a "lady" because of her good standing as a merchant; there are no conjectures about the moral strength needed to face the racism of the late nineteenth century and the difficulties implied in traveling across the ocean to a world new to her while caring for a schizophrenic woman. Her mothering role is taken for granted as only too natural for a black woman.[35]

Adèle Hugo is engulfed in the shadow of her famous father in all accounts of her life—few things are said about her without reference to him. This is best exemplified by the final scenes of *Adèle H,* which consist of a succession of photographs of the crowds that attended Victor Hugo's funeral procession compared to a single photograph of Adèle Hugo's tombstone and the virtual silence surrounding her death in 1915. But Céline Alvarez Baa is mediated through *two* people, both Victor and Adèle Hugo. No one knows what she did after leaving France for the second time, or how, when, and where she died. We only know that she lit candles and paid for three masses for the soul of Victor Hugo. Her role is also best illustrated by her characterization in Truffaut's film. She appears only twice—once, telling the jeering children to "leave the French lady alone" and once, tending to a delirious Adèle. Nothing is mentioned about the existence of her own family or about the possibility of her having children in Trinidad or Barbados. In effect, Céline Alvarez Baa is written as Adèle Hugo's adoptive mother.

Mary Seacole

As I grew into womanhood, I began to indulge that longing to travel which will never leave me while I have health and vigour. (57)
—Mary Seacole

While, for the most part, Alvarez Baa is bridled with two stereotypical roles—that of the maternal, subservient woman and that of the sexually liberated, exotic Other—perhaps in an attempt to control her, Mary Seacole ostensibly attributes the role of motherhood to herself in order to justify her mobility, while occasionally revealing a more multifaceted and complex persona. In Seacole's case, it is the traveler herself who simultaneously presents herself on center stage and analyzes her place and role in society. She is successful in representing her problematic position in the intersections of gender, race, and class. In her book, *Wonderful Adventures of Mrs. Mary Seacole in Many Lands,* she does not give much information of her travels in the Caribbean islands, and since the selling feature of her autobiography is her exemplary presence in war-torn Crimea, she details her ventures and adventures in the coastal regions of Panama as a lead-in to that "larger" historical event.

In the first chapter of her narrative, Mary Seacole identifies herself as a Jamaican Creole, a female, and a widow; but it is the issue of race that she privileges in the first few pages. When she states, "I am a Creole, and I have good Scotch blood coursing through my veins," one is struck by the apparent pride she has in being part white, or having "good" blood, if one reads it literally. She seems to accept the standard prejudices of the English regarding the black and mulatto population by saying that she owes the "energy and activity which are not always found in the Creole race" to her Scottish blood. However, as we find her doing throughout her autobiography/travel narrative, she usually follows this type of biased comment with veiled irony or implicit reproach. For example, she states: "I have often heard the term 'lazy Creole' applied to my country people; but I am sure I do not know what it is to be indolent" (57). What follows is an enumeration of the qualities that have led her to travel far and wide: the impulse to be active, lack of idleness, an inclination to rove, and most important, a powerful will to carry out her wishes. These first paragraphs set the tone for the rest of the narrative, throughout which she moves back and forth between roles depending on her needs.

In describing her heroic journeys, Seacole projects herself through what has been considered the discourse prevalent in travel narratives written by men, always stressing her strong will, sense of purpose, exceptional moral and physical strength, and her overcoming of obstacles (illnesses, floods, mud slides, hostile terrain, war, plotting "natives"). These scenes alternate with depictions of herself as a well-mannered "English" lady, brewing a perfect cup of tea in spite of the odds, which is characteristic of many narratives by women travelers of the time, in particular white European travelers. But, she also seems to derive extreme pleasure in destroying the image of the meticulously dressed wayfarer by including numerous stories of mishaps: how she was covered from head to toe in mud during a long trek, or how she was drenched during a downpour.

What remains central to the text and is never contradicted by the narrator is her love of freedom. By stating early on that she is a widow and that her mother has died, she justifies her mobility. Furthermore, her profession is important because, although her main employment as a hotel-keeper and merchant was not rare for Creole women in the nineteenth century—both her mother and sister were hotelkeepers—she was the only mulatto woman known at the time to have traveled extensively to set up shops and/or inns in dangerous locales. After her mother's death, she travels to join her brother, also an innkeeper in New Granada, but she eventually leaves him to move around freely wherever she desires.

Seacole explains her desire to travel from an early age:

> As I grew into womanhood, I began to indulge that longing to travel which will never leave me while I have health and vigour. I was never weary of tracing upon an old map the route to England; and never followed with my gaze the stately ships homeward bound without longing to be in them, and see the blue hills of Jamaica fade into the distance. (57)

This quote betrays Seacole's desire to escape her reality as a colonized subject, allowing the Caribbean landscape to fade into the distance of memory. "Home" becomes England. However, she does not hesitate to illustrate the reality of her first "homecoming" trip, where she was vulnerable to jeers and insults. She carefully depicts the reception she is given because of her color, providing vivid recollections of the efforts of the London street-boys to poke fun at her and her companion's complexion:

> I am only a little brown—a few shades duskier than the brunettes whom you all admire so much; but my companion was very dark, and a fair (if I can apply the term to her) subject for their rude wit. She was hot-tempered poor thing! and as there were no policemen to awe the boys and turn our servants' heads in those days, our progress through the London streets was sometimes a rather checkered one. (58)

Judging by Seacole's witty prose, her use of the word "checkered" is hardly accidental. While we can imagine the contrasting situations the travelers encounter in London, we are also presented with a world in black and white.[36] Seacole often seems to fully endorse the empire, but she occasionally and very subtly casts doubts upon the picture she draws of English superiority, refinement, and generosity.

The narrator admits that some of her travels, especially those throughout the Caribbean, are often capitalist ventures motivated by the profit she makes by the "fast sale" of products she brings back: "Before I had been long in Jamaica I started upon other trips, many of them undertaken with a view to gain" (58). One must not overlook her enterprising character; Seacole was a hotelkeeper, a nurse, a doctor in folk medicine, a gold prospector, and a sutler,[37] selling provisions in war-torn Crimea. In fact, she relives and writes about her travels in order to survive financially. After the Crimean war, she goes bankrupt while living in London, and decides to earn her livelihood by writing her memoirs. This venture was unsuccessful, and despite several efforts by friends to collect funds for her, Seacole died penniless and lonely.

Another reason for Seacole's travels is to help others, for she has a true love of healing. She repeatedly stresses her skills and achievements in treating victims of cholera epidemics and war. Her comments on her vocation for healing, however, are sometimes problematic, echoing hegemonic views on the roles colonizers and colonized should play in the Caribbean context. In one instance, she suggests that Jamaican Creoles have a natural propensity to care for the English:

> I think all who are familiar with the West Indies will acknowledge that Nature has been favourable to strangers in a few respects, and that one of these had been in instilling into the hearts of the Creoles an affection for English people and an anxiety for their welfare, which shows itself warmest when they are sick and suffering. I can safely appeal on this point to any one who is acquainted with life in Jamaica. Another benefit has been conferred upon them by inclining the Creoles to practise the healing art, and inducing

them to seek out the simple remedies which are available for the terrible diseases by which foreigners are attacked, and which are found growing under the same circumstances which produce the ills they minister to. (108)

While advocating ideas amenable to British rule, she also claims a knowledge that the English cannot access. They must, in a way, be dependent on their "subjects."

Seacole also seems to travel as a representative of the English empire and to help the English soldiers overseas, whom she calls her "sons." While Adèle Hugo seeks her English soldier, following him from barracks to barracks, and from country to country, Seacole seems to follow an unknown, symbolic soldier throughout her travels—the faceless multitude of the British troops.

Seacole prefers to see herself as the "female Ulysses." In an interesting reversal of the classical male hero, this choice of mythological identification places her in a more empowered position, investing her "character" with decision making and drive. However, the names attributed to her change according to the varying degrees of her interlocutors' desire to control her and render her nonthreatening. Besides all the "motherly" labels mentioned at the beginning of this work, some insist on referring to her as the yellow doctress from Jamaica, the yellow woman from Jamaica with the cholera medicine, an elderly mulatto woman, a "coloured" woman, this little woman, the excellent lady, or the genial old lady. Although she seems proud to be called Mother Seacole, her motherly persona alternates with that of the adventurer. She constantly straddles two standpoints: the mother and the adventurer, the white and the black, the colonized and the colonizer.

Mary Seacole's shifting viewpoints are difficult to follow, especially where race and ethnicity are concerned. The internalization of racist views is apparent in the many instances in which she uses the word "nigger," offers cartoonish depictions of her "black" servants with white teeth bared, or disdainfully portrays them as superstitious cowards. However, when she is shocked into the position of the discriminated Other, she shows remarkable solidarity, quickly shifting positions and defending herself and the black diaspora.[38] She is quite aware of the prejudices that constantly surround her, although she is very careful not to accuse the English too directly; after all, her book is directed to English consumers. She consistently speaks of the virtues of the English compared to the uncouth hostility, and often savagery, of the Americans: "It was of no use giving them carving knives and forks, for very often they laid their own down to insert a dirty hairy hand into a full dish; while the floor soon bore evidence of the great national American habit of expectoration" (89). However, there are instances in which a direct accusation of the English finds its way into her critiques:

> . . . my experience of travel had not failed to teach me that Americans (even from the Northern states) are always uncomfortable in the company of coloured people, and very often show this feeling in stronger ways than by sour looks and rude words. I think, if I have a little prejudice against our cousins across the Atlantic—and I do confess to a little—it is not unreasonable. I have a few shades deeper brown upon my skin which shows me related—and I am proud of the relationship—to those poor mortals whom *you once held enslaved,* and whose bodies America still owns. And having this bond, and knowing what slavery is; having seen with my eyes and heard with my ears proof positive of its horrors—let others affect to doubt them if they will—is it surprising that I should be somewhat impatient of the airs of superiority which many Americans have endeavoured to assume over me? (67, emphasis added)

Here she purposely sides with all blacks, slaves and freed, from different continents, and the *Other* becomes both the Americans and the English, whom she is addressing when she says "*you* once held enslaved." She actually does not accuse the English of ongoing prejudice; instead, she cleverly diverts the attention from *them* by pointing to her own prejudices. When she refers to "others" affecting to doubt the horrors of slavery, one cannot help but wonder whether she is familiar with Mrs. Carmichael's sweetening of slavery in *Domestic Manners and Social Conditions of the White, Colored, and Negro Population of the West Indies* (1833).[39]

Seacole suspects she is the victim of English racism when she offers her services to nurse wounded English soldiers in Crimea. After going endlessly from office to office, suffering harsh rebuffs and humiliation, she gingerly confesses: "Doubts and suspicions arose in my heart for the first and the last time, thank Heaven. Was it possible that American prejudices against colour had some root here? Did these ladies shrink from my aid because my blood flowed beneath a somewhat duskier skin than theirs?" (126). In spite of her caution, the message is clear enough. The "ladies" to whom she refers are Florence Nightingale and her entourage. Seacole was neither able to get funding from the English authorities nor to join Nightingale's corps of nurses. She had to finance her own expedition to the Crimean front.[40]

Seacole's description of the "candid" racism demonstrated by an American makes English prejudice pale in comparison. While offering a toast in

Aunty Seacole's honor for her role in fighting a cholera epidemic in Panama, the speaker expresses regret that she is not white. You can get an idea of what he said by Seacole's fearless answer:

> Gentlemen—, I return you the kindness in drinking my health. Providence evidently made me to be useful, and I can't help it. But I must say that I don't altogether appreciate your friend's kind wishes with respect to my complexion. If it had been as dark as any nigger's, I should have been just as happy and as useful, and as much respected by those whose respect I value; and as to his kind offer of bleaching me, I should, even if it were practicable, decline it without many thanks. As to the society which the process might gain me admission into, all I can say is, that, judging from the specimens I have met with here and elsewhere, I don't think that I shall lose much by being excluded from it. So, gentlemen, I drink to you and to the general reformation of American manners. (98)

This is one of several instances where Seacole must react defensively. While she is surrounded by hard-drinking, violent men, her role as a nurturer and provider of comfort in the community assure her a certain level of safety and freedom. Her services are indispensable and she is accepted as long as she is needed.

Always aware of her shaky stature as a loved but not completely accepted English citizen, she does not adopt an official voice, but, when speaking of other colonized others, she comfortably assumes the imperialist ideology with gusto. Native Central Americans, whom she calls Spanish Indians, are treacherous and lazy compared to the industrious black population.[41] They seem all the more uncivilized to her because of their lack of clothing apart from a wisp of a loincloth, and she sarcastically states: "Perhaps . . . the thick coating of dirt which covered them kept them warmer than more civilized clothing, besides being indisputably more economical" (68). She considers "the natives" to be "constitutionally cowardly" because they "made not the feeblest show of resistance" during the cholera epidemic (78), and is disgusted by their religious fervor and superstitions as sole response to their suffering. Their passivity and acceptance of illness and death make them childlike, but not in the least endearing, in her eyes. Their barbarous nature is suggested by a description of their foods that vaguely alludes to cannibalism: "The native fare was not tempting, and some of their delicacies were absolutely disgusting. With what pleasure, for instance, could one foreign to their tastes and habits dine off a roasted monkey, whose grilled head bore a strong resemblance to a negro baby's? . . . They were worse still stewed in soup, when it was positively frightful to dip your ladle in unsuspectingly, and bring up what closely resembles a brown baby's limb" (46).

Seacole's musings on other women are much more complex. She focuses on two types of cross-dressing women travelers—gold-diggers going to or from California and dancers touring South America. In some instances Seacole seems to disapprove of the women who disguise their gender and to interpret cross-dressing as rejection of womanhood: "The women alone kept aloof from each other, and well they might; for, while a very few seemed not ashamed of their sex, it was somewhat difficult to distinguish the majority from their male companions, save by their bolder and more reckless voice and manner" (71). At times, she seems to resent the degree of freedom and power of the "unnatural,""indecent," cross-dressing gold prospectors, and she makes a point to set herself apart as a decent lady observing what to her seems to be an aberration:

> Although many of the women on their way to California showed clearly enough that the life of license they sought would not be altogether unfamiliar to them, they still retained some appearance of decency in their attire and manner; but in many cases (as I have before said) the female companions of the successful gold-diggers appeared in no hurry to resume the dress or obligations of their sex. Many were clothed as the men were, in flannel shirts and boots; rode their mules in an unfeminine fashion, but with much ease and courage, and in their conversation successfully rivaled the coarseness of their lords. I think, on the whole, that those French lady writers who desire to enjoy the privileges of man, with the irresponsibility of the other sex, would have been delighted with the disciples who were carrying their principles into practice in the streets of Cruces. (73)

When she writes of a cross-dressing woman traveler more notable than the anonymous female gold-diggers, Lola Montez, the Irish woman who became a "Spanish" dancer, Seacole cannot seem to choose between a purely moral judgment and a respect for power. She labels her as evil and wretched although her description of Montez reveals a degree of hidden admiration in spite of her apparent disdain: "Came one day Lola Montes [*sic*], in the full zenith of her evil fame, bound for California, with a strange suite. A good-looking, bold woman, with fine, bad eyes, and a determined bearing; dressed ostentatiously in perfect male attire, with shirt-collar turned down over a velvet lapelled coat, richly worked shirt-front, black hat, French unmentionables [trousers], and natty, polished boots with spurs"

(91). The veiled admiration might be a reaction to Montez' skill with her "handsome riding whip" when "an impertinent American, presuming—perhaps not unnatural—upon her reputation, laid hold jestingly of the tails of her long coat, and as a lesson received a cut across his face that must have marked him for some days" (91). The triumph of a female over a physically stronger male, especially an ill-mannered American, merits Seacole's attention and respect.

Seacole's own identification as a woman is very cautious. By telling her own story, she survives the eroticization imposed upon other women of color such as Alvarez Baa. She avoids all mention of her own sexuality and only occasionally comments on her "not altogether unpleasant" appearance, her plumpness, and the attention she attracted to herself throughout her travels: "time and trouble combined, have left me with a well-filled-out, portly frame, the envy of many an angular Yankee female" (131). Remarking on the way she turned the heads of the Greeks, Turks, English, and French in the Bosphorus, she says: "I accepted it all as a compliment to a stout female tourist, neatly-dressed in a red or yellow dress, a plain shawl of some other colour, and a simple straw wide-awake, with bright red streamers. I flattered myself that I woke up sundry sleepy-eyed Turks, who seemed to think that the great object of life was to avoid showing surprise at everything; while the Turkish women gathered around me and jabbered about me, in the most flattering manner" (132). She further sets herself apart from other roving women, especially the "Yankee female," by underlying her respectability:

> My present life was not agreeable for a women with the least refinement; and of female society I had none. Indeed, the females who crossed my path were about as unpleasant specimens as one would wish to avoid.

In the same section, she simultaneously stresses her moral and racial difference from other women travelers, particularly North Americans:

> With very few exceptions, those who were not bad were very disagreeable, and, as the majority came from the Southern States of America, and showed an instinctive repugnance against anyone whose countenance claimed for her kindred with slaves, my position was far from a pleasant one. (100)

The "instinctive repugnance" seems to be mutual, but despite her negative reaction to the traveling American woman, Seacole recognizes her contradictory feelings toward them:

Not that it ever gave me any annoyance: they were glad of my stores and comforts, I made money out of their wants; nor do I think our bond of connection was ever close; only this, if any of them came to me sick or suffering (I say this out of simple justice for myself) I forgot everything except that she was my sister and that it was my duty to help her. (100)

In a typically picaresque gesture, whereby she reveals her commercial motivation, Seacole admits to the practical fruits sown through her encounter with the other.[42] At the same time, she proclaims her solidarity with women, regardless of color or class boundaries, by considering them her "sisters."

Ultimately, what sets Seacole apart from Hugo, Alvarez Baa, and most of the women she writes about, is the freedom to portray herself as she wishes, to mask and unmask herself as she deems necessary.[43] In "When the Subaltern Travels: Slave Narratives and Testimonial Erasure in the Contact Zone," Mario Cesareo points out the contestatory rhetorical stances made possible to typically marginalized women (for example, ex-slave Mary Prince) through the adoption of varying poses and positionings in their travel writing:

The narrative commands through its silences, disguises, and omissions—the sublime and sentimental tendencies that constitute its protagonist as a heroic model of female abnegation, intelligence, thrift, and containment; in other words, through a text that produces its other as an instance of a striving toward feminine-bourgeois subjectivity. But the restricted sentimentality of the narrative, while problematizing the subaltern's subjectivity (in fact, because of it) opens a contestatory space where the confrontation of metropolitan social forces takes place. (118-119)

The text, he says, does more than play into the aesthetics of sentimentality:

[I]t performs a rhetorical operation of political reconfiguration of the terms of its reception in its effort to carry on a political intervention. It does so by displacing the narration from the reified forms of survival literature that the slave narrative had acquired in the eighteenth century, to the concrete discussion of slavery as a form of economic production that brings about the degradation of the human person. (119)

Although he is speaking specifically of Mary Prince's narrative and the English antislavery discourse that precedes Seacole's travel and writing, the same strategies are deployed by this woman who was born free. In the final analysis of her work, Seacole's true solidarity resides in her sense of justice; in this case, race supersedes gender. Although her apparent purpose for writing her autobiography is economic survival, her underlying agenda seems to be to denounce the suffering of people because of their color. She attacks the Southern United States for preserving slavery and she subtly points out that the English are not altogether devoid of racism, despite having abolished slavery far before the Americans. In a touching anecdote of great liberatory value, Seacole explains how the Central Americans were anxious to offer freedom and hints on how to escape to the slaves who accompanied American travelers:

> A young American woman whose character can be best described by the word "vicious," fell ill at Gorgona, and was left behind by her companions under the charge of a young negro, her slave, whom she treated most inhumanly, as was evinced by the poor girl's frequent screams when under the lash: one night her cries were so distressing that Gorgona could stand it no longer, but broke into the house and found the chattel bound hand and foot, naked, and being severely lashed. Despite the threats and astonishment of the mistress, they were both carried off and the following morning, before the alcalde [mayor], himself a man of colour, and of a very humane disposition. (102)

Throughout the account, Seacole opposes the mulatto alcalde's "humane disposition" to the vicious nature of the white mistress and celebrates his decision to pronounce the young slave a free woman despite the mistress' "fearful threats." Emphasizing the white woman's evil character, Seacole details her attempts to impede the slave's departure. "Then, with demoniac refinement of cruelty," the mistress threatens to torture the slave's young child, still in New Orleans, if the mother dared accept the offer of freedom. At this point in the narrative, Seacole includes herself in the liberating enterprise of the Gorgona townspeople: "but we knew very well that when the heat of passion had subsided, this threatener would be too 'cute to injure her own property; and at once, set afloat a subscription for the purchase of the child" (102). As part of the liberating front, Seacole not only enforces change in her encounter with an oppressor, but she also reinforces the action through her writing.

Seacole establishes her power as an authoritative narrator thus: "unless I am allowed to tell the story of my life in my own way, I cannot tell it at all" (185). Telling the story in "her own way" allows her to transcend the limitations of those who were written about. Adèle Hugo, Céline Alvarez Baa, and Mary Seacole have greater mobility than their nineteenth-century counterparts by virtue of their individual "differences" or "eccentricities." These ex-centric, or marginal, positionings enable them to circulate from margins to center and back again despite the physical obstacles and societal constraints. However, it is Seacole's *writings* that enable her to address and recomform the paradigms of both margins and centers.

NOTES

1. Frances V. Guille. *Le Journal d'Adèle Hugo.* Vol. I (Paris: Minard, 1968), 343. Subsequent page references will appear in parentheses in the text.

2. Writing about her life in Antigua and St. Kitts in 1774 and 1776, Janet Schaw proudly proclaims: "As to your humble Servant, I have always set my face to the weather; wherever I have been. I hope you have no quarrel at brown beauty." *Journal of a Lady of Quality; Being the Narrative of a Journey from Scotland to the West Indies, North Carolina, and Portugal in the Years 1774 to 1776.* Edited by Evangeline Walker Andrews and Charles McLean Andrews (New Haven: Yale University Press, 1934), 115. Such a statement is paradoxical, coming from an apologist for eighteenth-century slavery and plantation life; it indicates a desire to set herself apart from other European female counterparts, who strove to maintain their rosy cheeks and pale complexions, while closing the distance between herself and the dark-skinned people she believed had no human emotions and were born to bear pain. For an in-depth study of these contradictions, see Elizabeth A. Bowles, "Janet Schaw and the Aesthetics of Colonialism." In *Women Travel Writers and the Language of Aesthetics: 1716-1818* (Cambridge: Cambridge University Press, 1995).

3. I discuss notions of hybridity and contradictory discursive stances in "Travelers Possessed: Generic Hybrids and the Caribbean," forthcoming in *Anthropology and Literature: Estranged Bedfellows?* Edited by Rose DeAngelis (London and Newark: Gordon and Breach, 2000).

4. Romanticized descriptions of Hugo's illness as provoked by disillusion in love are standard fare.

5. Mary Seacole, *Wonderful Adventures of Mrs. Mary Seacole in Many Lands* (London: James Blackwood, 1857).

6. As Lizabeth Paravisini-Gebert discusses in this volume ("Cross-dressing on the Margins of Empire: Women Pirates and the Narrative of the Caribbean"), the highly eroticized concealment and disclosure of the breasts and the revelation of impending motherhood are crucial to rendering the pirates Anne Bonny and Mary Read palatable or manageable to their narrators/readers.

7. Quoted in Hubert Juin's *Victor Hugo: 1870-1885*. Vol. III (France: Flammarion, 1986), 127.

8. Alexis Sawyer, in *Sawyer's Culinary Campaign* (London: Routledge, 1857), describes a light-skinned young woman, Sarah, whom he believes to be Mary Seacole's daughter. On the one hand, he opposes her "whiteness" to Seacole's dark complexion—"an old dame of a jovial appearance, but a few shades darker than the white lily"; "La Mère Noire, although she has a fair daughter"—and, on the other, she emphasizes her "exotic" black-haired, blue-eyed beauty by calling her "the dark Maid of the Eastern War" and "the Egyptian beauty." See the Editor's introduction to Seacole's *Wonderful Adventures* (43).

9. See Patricia Hill Collins's "Mammies, Matriarchs, and Other Controlling Images." In *Black Feminist Thought: Knowledge, Consciousness, and the Politics of Empowerment* (New York: Routledge, 1990).

10. See Ferdinand Denis's *Les Vrais Robinsons: naufrages, solitudes, voyages* (Paris: Librairie du Magasin Pittoresque, 1863). Quoted in Richard Cortambert's *Les Illustres Voyageuses* (Paris: E. Maillet, 1866).

11. This segment of Adèle Hugo's manuscript is quoted in Frances V. Guille's *Le Journal d'Adèle Hugo*. Vol. I (Paris: Minard, 1968), 70.

12. Hugo's manuscripts, housed in the Pierpont Morgan Library, have been collected and edited by Guille as *Le Journal d'Adèle Hugo*. 2 Vols. (see note 11). A third set of manuscripts, written during her stay in Barbados, has never been found.

13. Guille, 128-30.

14. Halifax witnesses unanimously depict Albert Pinson as an avaricious villain: "He was considered completely selfish, insensitive, soulless, without ideals or ambitions other than easily obtaining the means to lead an indolent life" (Guille, 133). He was considered a *dandy* who had earned the mocking title of *le compte* (the count) in view of his snobbery.

15. Guille, 127-128.

16. François Truffaut, *The Story of Adèle H.* Translated by Jan Dowson (New York: Grove Press, 1976). This is the script of the film of the same title, directed in 1975 by Truffaut and starring Isabelle Adjani in the title role.

17. Guille, 343.

18. Guille, 69.

19. Guille, 69-70. Portions of Hugo's notes, quoted by Guille in her introduction, attest to her views on women's liberation: "This incredible thing, that a young girl, a slave to the point of not being able to go out alone for five minutes to buy paper, should walk on the sea, cross the ocean, leave the old world for the new world to join her lover; *that* I will accomplish.

"This incredible thing, that a young girl, who today does not have a piece of bread other than the one her father offers her in alms, would have, four years from now, gold in her two pockets, honest gold, gold of her own;

that I will accomplish. . . . This incredible thing, that a woman, nailed under the same roof to a man who loves her passionately, would leave him, without much ado, even without despair; *that* I will accomplish." (70) This excerpt reveals Hugo's desire to control her body (by choosing a lover or traveling across the seas), the wish to be financially independent, and the wish to be free of male domination, both her father's and her prospective lover's. Unfortunately, according to all accounts of her trajectory, she was only able to free herself by retreating into madness.

20. Auguste Joyau, *Héroïnes et aventurières de la mer Caraïbe* (Fort-de-France: Editions des Horizons Caraïbes, 1959).

21. A letter written shortly after Victor Hugo's death by a Dominican missionary from Trinidad confirms Alvarez Baa's dedication of the masses to Victor Hugo: "Some days ago a negress brought Father Marie-Joseph a small sum of money requesting a mass for the repose of Victor Hugo's soul. The priest was naturally surprised by this request and asked the woman how she came to know the French poet." She asserted that the poet's last words were these: "When you hear that I have died, would you please request three masses for me? She had promised him she would do it."

    "So when she learned of Victor Hugo's death, she cried for him saying: 'What a loss! He was such a generous man, such a good man! May God grant him peace!'" (Guille, 137).

    Apart from the first and last paragraphs, the body of the letter centers upon Adèle Hugo's story of lost love and madness.

22. Note that she is described as a tall, dark beauty in the North American (Nova Scotia) setting, while in the Caribbean setting she is imagined as a pale and fragile white woman.

23. Henri Guillemin. *L'Engloutie: Adèle, fille de Victor Hugo: 1830-1915* (Paris: Editions du Seuil, 1985).

24. Leslie Smith Dow, *Adèle Hugo: La Misérable* (Fredericton: Goose Lane Editions, 1993). Subsequent page references will appear in parentheses in the text.

25. For background and insightful analyses of eighteenth-century mercantilist aesthetics and colonial plantation culture, see Elizabeth A. Bowles, *Women Travel Writers and the Language of Aesthetics: 1716-1818,* 46-65.

26. A higgler, from the word "haggler," is a traveling salesperson who buys merchandise available in one region to sell in another region where these goods are not easily accessible.

27. François Guille's data show that Adèle Hugo arrived in Barbados in 1866. Very little is known about the five years between her arrival and her encounter with Céline Alvarez Baa.

28. Guille, 134-35.

29. Guille, 132.

30. Smith Dow, 162.

31. Smith Dow, 162.
32. Guillemin, 152.
33. As proof of Madame Baa's sexual encounter with the French writer, Hubert Juin points out an enigmatic notation (an underlined circle) that Victor Hugo used to mark an extensive list of women with whom he had purportedly had intimate contact; Madame Baa is one of those "marked" women. See Juin, 132-134.
34. Smith Dow, 162.
35. When Victor Hugo's granddaughter sees Madame Baa for the first time, she exclaims: "C'est une momomme." This illustrates how stereotypically black women were portrayed as mammies without regard for their real social standing. See Juin, 133.
36. We must observe the nineteenth-century usage of the word "checkered" in other contexts and in view of Seacole's systematic critique of North American slavery. Her wit and awareness of the power of language and its signifiers are evidenced by the following quote from an abolitionist's letter attesting to the horrors of slavery: "I beg in reply to state that the whole of the back part of her [Mary Prince's] body is distinctively scarred and, as it were, checkered with the vestiges of severe floggings." See Moira Ferguson's introduction to *The History of Mary Prince, A West Indian Slave, Related by Herself* (London: Pandora, 1987), 138.
37. A sutler is a merchant who follows an army, selling goods to the soldiers.
38. Seacole explains the prejudice of the people of New Granada (Panama and Colombia) against North Americans by contrasting the much-improved conditions of the black population in these areas to the lives of those who traveled north: "In the first place, many of the negroes, fugitives from the Southern States, had sought refuge in these and the other States of Central America, where every profession was open to them; and as they were generally superior men—evinced perhaps by their hatred of their old condition and successful flight—they soon rose to positions of eminence in New Granada. In the priesthood, in the army, in all municipal offices, the self-liberated negroes were invariably found in the foremost rank; and the people, for some reason—perhaps because they recognise in them superior talents for administration—always respected them more than, and preferred them to, their native rulers" (100).
39. Mary Carmichael, *Domestic Manners and Social Conditions of the White, Colored, and Negro Population of the West Indies.* 2 Vols. (London: Whittaker, 1833).
40. Ironically, Seacole now figures, albeit in a very marginal capacity, in the Florence Nightingale Museum in London, where one can find a small section dedicated to her work. Her autobiography is sold in the museum's shop.
41. Seacole's acquired baggage also weighs down her encounters with Spaniards, Maltese, Greeks, Turks, and Russians, whom she depicts as thieves, liars,

cheaters, or cowards. Only her Greek assistant, "Jew Johnny," and a generous Turkish pasha who helps her with her commercial enterprise, barely survive her harsh criticism. The rest are judged by the same (mostly negative) models of "orientalist" discourse prevalent at the time.

42. For an in-depth study of the picaresque elements in nineteenth-century travel and slave narrative, see Mario Cesareo's "When the Subaltern Travels: Slave Narrative and Testimonial Erasure in the Contact Zone" in this volume.

43. Some of these women did write. It would be interesting to compare, for instance, Lola Montez's autobiography to Seacole's.

Chapter 6

A "VALIANT SYMBOL OF INDUSTRIAL PROGRESS"?:
CUBAN WOMEN TRAVELERS AND THE UNITED STATES

Luisa Campuzano
Translated by Lizabeth Paravisini-Gebert

Among the profusion of travelogues written by European and American visitors to Cuba in the nineteenth century, there is a significant number of texts written by women.[1] These are works of great significance both for the information they contribute to our knowledge of everyday life on the island a century ago, and for their distinctive perspective, which incorporates details of the conditions under which Cuban women lived, and, by way of contrast, the parameters of women's lives in the writers' native countries. They are of special significance in the fields of cultural and gender studies for the ample documentation they provide about the conditions that inform women's writing in the period, and about the outcome of past projects for the education and emancipation of women.

These works include travelogues by a number of prominent North American women who, for a variety of reasons, traveled to Cuba between 1833 and 1890 and wrote with sometimes piercing insight about Cuban society and mores: Rachel Wilson Moore, a preacher for the Society of Friends, visited Cuba for health reasons in 1863; Eliza McHatton-Ripley, a Confederate supporter whose cotton plantation near Baton Rouge had been burned by the Union Army, ran a sugar estate in Cuba from 1865 to 1875; Louisa Mathilde Woodruff, a sentimental "authoress" from a Hudson

Valley village, whose novel *Shiloh* had enjoyed moderate success in the mid-1860s, spent many months in Cuba from 1879 to 1871; and Julia Newell Jackson, who traveled extensively through Cuba and Mexico, arrived in Havana around 1888. Some among them wrote about their travels from an eminently political perspective. The Peabody sisters (Sophia, wife of American writer Nathaniel Hawthorne, author of *The Scarlet Letter,* and Mary, wife of prominent educator Horace Mann), when visiting Cuba between 1833 and 1834, for example, saw in the possibility of the islands' annexation to the United States a hope for the end of slavery and the slave trade. Julia Ward Howe, a notable member of the women's suffrage movement and author of "The Battle Hymn of the Republic," who arrived in Cuba in 1859, glimpsed in all Spanish institutions and officers the heavy hand of an oppressive colonial regime whose laws and actions she equated with the iniquities of the Inquisition.

There are in the letters, diaries, and memoirs of these North American women travelers enough points of contact—thematic, ideological, structural, and philosophical—to persuade the scholar of the prevalence among them of a shared point of view on Cuba that cuts across literary genres. But there are also among them marked distinctions stemming from variations in social class, specific motivations for travel and writing, and the professional status of these various travelers. Although belonging to the privileged middle- and upper classes, there were significant differences in outlook and approach between middle-class and aristocratic women, as there were between wives accompanying their husbands—who tended to describe all that came within their purview for the mere pleasure it brought them—and those armed with a rigorous ideological, professional, or economic commitment who traveled and wrote in their roles as abolitionists, feminists, evangelists, teachers, or landowners. However, it is evident that there is in all of them a unifying trait that permeates their cataloguing and evaluation of the habits and customs, public and private institutions, and social and familial relationships that make up the cultural fabric of the island: their vision of Cuba and its inhabitants—particularly its women—as inferior and censurable Others whom it would perhaps be possible to redeem through education, hygiene, a new and true evangelization, the abolition of slavery, and even the annexation of the country to the United States, the last a project that is only explicit in two of these writers[2] but latent in most.

These "forms of female imperial authority," the civilizing mission common to all of them, the "white-woman's burden" they share, embody the glorified project of the north-European woman in the "contact zone." The Cuban cultural space, however, is not equivalent in the strictest sense to what Mary Louise Pratt calls the "colonial frontier"; when we take into account how Cuba and its economy fitted into the expansionist plans of the United States, neither could it be explained away through Pratt's concept of the site in which the "colonizers and colonized" establish relationships "usually involving conditions of coercion, racial inequality, and intractable conflict." It could be seen quite simply as the domain in which the "temporal copresence of subjects previously separated by geographic and historical disjunctures, and whose trajectories now intersect" takes place.[3] As far as nineteenth-century Cuba is concerned, it must also be remembered that the nuances of the relationships between Cuban women and visitors to the island were mediated by the deep historical and cultural links and strong economic ties between the Creole sugar-planters' class— the male and female travelers' "natural" informant on local conditions— and the metropolis. These differences will be subtler than those that characterize the colonizer/colonized dichotomy through which these travelers will fashion a self-image to represent them before the Other.[4] "I had not found the Cuban ladies and myself entirely in harmony," Louisa Mathilde Woodruff notes; "our education, religion, habits of life and thought, were so dissimilar that the maintenance of a certain degree of reserve had seemed a wise precaution against uncomfortable jarring of sentiment."[5] Take, for example, the practice of Catholicism in Cuba, which, perceived as ostentatious and irreverent by many of these travelers, becomes an effective means through which they can reinforce their own evangelical identity. In the writings of someone like American traveler Eliza McHatton-Ripley, the distaste of Catholicism is seen with perhaps less picturesqueness than in others, but certainly with the prototypical disdain that links religion to the political and economic system:

> The priests in the interior villages gather the children together and teach them that "Nuestra Señora de Cobre" is a patron saint of Cuba, because she miraculously appeared to two Negroes who were paddling about in a skiff, and pointed out to them valuable copper-mines on the coast. They are also taught their Paternosters and Ave Marias; occasionally a pupil is graduated who can read and write; but as a rule, the class that inhabits the country towns are very ignorant. An intelligent officer of the Spanish army, who had been stationed in the extreme eastern part of the island, told us he was astounded to see, during some raids upon insurgent camps, how primitive, indeed, how near to Adam and Eve, the country people remote from settlements were. He saw women, with even less adornment than Eve was constrained to wear, picking wild rice and digging roots in the wilderness. When they do not live in rocky caves, their abodes are rude huts that scarcely

deserve the name. Literally existing from hand to mouth, "they toil not, neither do they spin."[6]

Not even the most progressive among these writers could escape similar "forms of imperial female authority," since with greater or lesser emphasis, then as today, when North American feminists turn their gaze abroad they frequently seek to establish their authority over non-Western women, predetermining, however benevolently, the meaning and objectives of their lives.[7] This imperative accounts for the virulence of the opinions expressed in the pages of American feminist Julia Howe's *A Trip to Cuba,* for example:

> The ladies of Matanzas seem to possess a great deal of beauty, but they abuse the privilege of powder and whiten themselves with *cascarilla* to a degree that is positively ghastly. . . . In spite of this, they are handsome; but one feels a natural desire to rush in amongst them with a feather duster, and lay about one a little, before giving an available opinion of their good looks.
>
> . . .
>
> As to dress; although I have whispered for your good, my lady friends, that the most beautiful summer-dresses in the world may be bought in Havana, yet the Creole ladies themselves have in general but glaring and barbaric ideas of adornment, and their *volante*-toilette would give a Parisienne the ague.[8]

In counterpoint to the emerging United States colonial discourse vis à vis Cuba, of which these texts provide an example, and to the increasingly more precise configuration in the Cuban social imaginary of the United States as the most viable alternative to Spain as a possible model for the future nation—a privileged space of vertiginously developing modernity—a varied and practically unexplored body of texts by Cuban travelers to the North, written as much in favor of the United States as against, emerged in the second decade of the nineteenth century. These Cuban travelers were brought to various American cities sometimes by persecution or exile, sometimes for the purpose of studying American institutions—a true initiation ritual for future leadership groups[9]—and, later in the century, for the pleasure of visiting centers of leisure or culture, or for the purpose of fulfilling as correspondents both the curiosity of broad segments of the readership of Cuban newspapers and magazines as well as the political interest of the editors to which they sent their "letters."

However, in sharp contrast to the ample critical bibliography dedicated to French, English, or German visitors to the United States, books by Latin American travelers have only been included in studies that broach the broader theme of literary relations between the two Americas, such as those by Manuel Pedro González, José de Onís, Elizabeth Rezner Daniel, and John T. Reid.[10] In an ambitious book of essays intended to accompany the exhibit of portraits of travelers with which the National Portrait Gallery celebrated the bicentennial of the independence of the thirteen colonies, only Domingo Faustino Sarmiento (1811–1888), the Argentinean intellectual prominent in the struggle against dictator Juan Manuel de Rosas, and José Martí (1853–1895), the Cuban patriot who led the struggle for the island's independence from Spain, appear as representative of the South American continent. Likewise, in a recent anthology of travel writers, presumably very broad in scope, only Sarmiento is represented.[11] In another such collection, covering a period of over a 100 years and dedicated specifically to women who visited the United States—that is to say, to representatives, by virtue of their gender, of the margins of patriarchal culture—not one single visitor from Latin America is included, as if the editor, trapped in a net of conscious or unconscious hegemonic parameters, could not help marginalizing them further for ethnic or cultural reasons.[12]

As Julio Ramos has cautioned us, initially many of these texts attest to displacements through a symbolic topography, through paths that lead from chaos to order, from low to high, from barbarism to civilization, from the past to the future.[13] On the other hand, "the 'I' who travels bears with it all the spaces it has previously occupied, and is simultaneously here, there, and everywhere, recapitulating at every step a totality of knowledges."[14] No voyager travels blindly, but moves toward a country known, imagined, or previously constructed through readings and conversations. Therefore, voyages by Latin American men and women to the United States have often been mapped in advance, for better or worse, by previous visits to the old continent, or, like José de Onís had argued,[15] by prior readings of European authors who had described, in praise or censure, as the case may be, the historical process and the social institutions of that other America to the north. In part because of this, but above all because of Cuba's colonial condition, the appraisals of the United States offered by Cuban men and women travelers often takes place "by triangulation" and in a "reactive" manner—vis-à-vis Spain, as far as the economy, politics, or scientific and technical development is concerned; vis-à-vis France, as far as it regards culture. And in general, the literature of Cuban travel to the United States shows a marked political intention, since on many occasions what it preached about the North had an implicit or explicit correlate on the island.

My purpose in examining this unexplored body of texts by Cuban women travelers to the North—triply blocked from mainstream critical attention by the marginality in which traditional canon places travel literature, by their female authorship, as well as their peripheral geographical location—is also triple in nature. I seek to initiate their incorporation into the historical narrative of Cuban literature written by women, to contribute to the tracing of the map of the multiple and contradictory relations between Cuba and the United States (in which women have played an important but little-recognized role), and to throw my dry leaf into the pyre of scholarly debate in the United States about the relevance of considering the cultural production of our America in the field of American Studies, particularly when the elements of that cultural production refer explicitly to the United States.[16]

The texts by nineteenth-century Cuban women travelers that I have been able to identify, locate and study, are listed and discussed below. But first, a word on the criteria used in the organization and analysis of the texts. In the first place, it must be remembered that the experience of travel and the experience of writing are not always contemporaneous—that on occasion they are separated by months, years, sometimes decades. That is the case of many travel "books" or "impressions" or, as we know, of the "memoirs" or "autobiographies" that incorporate the narrative of authorial wanderings. The opposite is the case of "letters" sent by correspondents to the newspapers or magazines for which they write, or with actual correspondence—although the latter is usually published much later, if indeed it finds an editor. But in our case, as will be immediately apparent, the majority of these texts are the work of professional writers, produced either *motu propio,* or at the request—which is also the case with some nonprofessional writers—of editors or politicians interested in seeing the materials published as soon as possible, so that the dates of travel and publication either coincide or are relatively close. Only two appear much later. In the second place, as is evident from the reading of this group of texts, the sample does not consist only of traditional forms of the genre (chronicles or travel accounts) but includes other literary forms (such as poetry) or marginal genres (letters, memoirs) through which the experience of travel can be conveyed.

The Countess of Merlin and Gertrudis Gómez de Avellaneda, women who, although thinking of themselves Cuban, lived the greatest part of their lives and achieved significant literary reputations in Europe, were the first from the island to write about North America. For this enterprise they relied on experiences, readings, and perspectives born of their sojourns in France and Spain respectively, which set them apart from those of their male compatriots who had visited the United States before them or whose voyages coincided in time with theirs. This accounts for the emphasis and assuredness with which, from quite different ideological perspectives, they elaborate their respective narratives of the paradoxes and complexities of their attraction/rejection, love/hate reactions to the United States. The polarized nature of their warnings and praises will, with extremely rare exceptions of neutrality or indifference, always be present in Cuban women travelers' northward gaze.

The nine letters from the United States with which María de las Mercedes Santa Cruz y Montalvo, Countess of Merlin (1789-1852), opens her book on Havana, *Viaje a la Habana,* were not included in the Spanish version of the book nor have they been translated, as far as I know, into English, which is why they can only be found in the editions published in French in 1844, in Belgium, Holland, and France.[17] These letters describe the cities of New York, Philadelphia, Baltimore, Boston, and Washington, which she visited during the spring of 1840, when, newly arrived from France, she preferred to await a sailing boat that would take her directly to Havana, where she was returning after an absence of 40 years or so, instead of traveling by land to Charleston, from which she could take a faster steam freighter. That is, we have here a voluntary voyage, but not one of leisure; since, as we will see, her interest in the United States is intimately linked to the objectives of the book that motivate her return to her native country.

This Antillean woman of European education and habits, who in the preceding decade had published five critically well-received books, had been secretly commissioned by reformist compatriots belonging to the Domingo del Monte group—who had offered her all types of aid for the purpose, including access to their own writings and those of fellow supporters—to prepare a book on Cuba which, coming from her, then the best known of all Cuban writers, would have the resonance in Europe that their poor provincial voices could not attain. The book's aim was that of fostering the notion of the participation of the Cuban elite in the island's government, promoting the abolition of the slave trade, and encouraging a range of similar reform measures that would foster migration into Cuba and European investment in the island economy. These measures would help loosen somewhat the island's dependence on Spain, to which Cuba had to nonetheless remain connected given the peculiar demographic imbalances created by slavery and the middle- and upper-classes' fear of a slave revolt. On the other hand, her voyage and confrontation with Cuban relatives who had deprived her of her paternal inheritance—like the book that would result from it—would contribute to restore the Countess's financial situation, which had been seriously undermined in recent years.

A defender, then, of Cuba's remaining under the tutelage of Spain, and a defender, like many other contemporary European authors, of the principles behind the French Restoration, which had witnessed the return of a king to his throne, she articulates her preference for the monarchic system of government and her disdain for republicanism. The resulting vision of the United States that Merlin offers her compatriots is intentionally negative, as she makes explicit in the prologue she addresses to them—and which appears mutilated in the Spanish edition: "I have disguised nothing . . . of the social situation in which I found North America, a menacing situation both for the republics [sic] of Washington and for Europe, which would like to follow in its suite . . ." (4).

An aristocrat by birth, marriage, and relations, she detests the practices and habits she attributes to North American republicanism. On the one hand, she believes that collective freedom and equality have become a new sort of individual enslavement, since in its name she must sit amidst vulgar strangers in the theater, as she does when she attends Fanny Elssler's dancing debut. She had been applauded *avec fureur* as she seemed to unveil the art of the dance before her new American audience:

> The enthusiasm was overwhelming; I fancied myself in Rome and had difficulty recognizing those around me as the same Americans who speak only in one accent and trample about. But it was not long before these men, with their hats on their heads and their ordinary clothes, slumped on their seats, dropped their heavy thick-soled shoes on the floor, and nonchalantly rested their wool-stockinged feet on the backs of their neighbors' chairs, reminding me in the process that I was in the United States. (79)

The Countess exploits this episode to heap scorn on the undifferentiated masses from whom the republican system fails to protect her. They stand in stark contrast to the technological achievements of the nation. The concert hall is beautiful and well lighted, "but the principle of equality, intolerable slavery, demands that there be no assigned seats; so that most of the time the daughter is separated from the mother, the husband from the wife; all are placed, or rather, tossed about haphazardly" (79). Her description of the scene outside the theater, where the "chaos had reached its peak," emphasizes her rejection of habits that do not differentiate suffi-

ciently between social classes, as they deprive those like herself from avail-
ing themselves of the aristocratic accouterments that are the mark of a
superior class standing. "There is absolutely no police, since it is understood
that its presence could incommode the people in their freedom, as they
hurl themselves out of the foyer into the courtyard; no servants in atten-
dance, since that aristocratic practice would be too much of a shock to the
masses that should supply them but will not have them; no *commissionaires*
or pages who, in return for a slight compensation, would go find the carriages" (80). This absence of *commissionaires,* which she attributes to her
preconceived notion that "an American should not dedicate himself to the
service of another," leaves her at the mercy of the rabble, without the
"means of making her superior status known," which in turn leaves her
vulnerable to an attack from the mob (80).

The soirée at the theater described by the Countess serves as her opportunity to connect her negative notions of American equality—rooted in
her belief in a "natural" class order—with her ideas on the role of the
police as the defenders of the elites. The exit from the theater is described
as a "commotion the likes of which has never been seen": "people pushed
and jostled each other, blows rained and people tumbled" (81). Her
escort—her "knight"—finally succeeds in reaching their carriage, but
returns without his purse." She in turn, upon discovering that she has lost
her opera glasses, and wanting to reclaim them, is told that it would be useless to try to retrieve them. The police "only concerns itself with crimes,
and pays little attention to thefts: it would have too much to do" (81). The
police's inability to "serve" is equated here with the American disinclina-
tion to recognize class hierarchies and the upper-classes' intrinsic right to
expect their interests to come first. The same goes for the absence of separate accommodations in American travel conveyances, where she is forced
to travel in vehicles with 60 or 80 individuals "who chew on tobacco, spit,
and smell badly" (112) or to sail up the Hudson River "side by side with
pitiless yokels, a victim to their bad habits" (114).

On the other hand, she wonders what social equality can indeed exist
in a city such as New York in which money and, consequentially, the pride
and fear of its inhabitants, establishes the boundaries of neighborhoods
(73). The women in the United States strike her as superficial; the men are
vulgar, ill-educated, and dirty. The latter are, however, very hard-working,
very self-assured, and always in a rush, which is why she asks herself, finally:

Will American mores be the fate of all peoples to come, after all?—Are they
the unavoidable consequence of democratic principle?—And the European

nations, in drawing closer to the same political system, will they face the same consequences?—That cult of spirit and personality, which debases the soul and drags man's moral strength and power towards the life of the senses and the love of money, will it be the outcome of so many bloody struggles, of so many noble efforts?—The measure of human perfection, is it so short-sighted that it has already begun to retrace its steps?—And civilization, having come full circle, has it only managed to bring man back to his initial steps? (127-128)

The arrival in Cuba of the censured Spanish edition of *La Havane*, limited to only ten letters of the thirty-six included in the French edition, with a prologue by Gertrudis Gómez de Avellaneda and dedicated to General O'Donnell, governor-general of the island, coincided with the brutal repression of the so-called Conspiración de la Escalera (Conspiracy of the Ladder). This repression was waged by the latter to neutralize both the emerging colored middle class and the reformists, among them the members of the Domingo del Monte group who had encouraged the Countess to write her volume. As a consequence, the members of the group, seeking to evade responsibility and suspicion, rejected the book and accused her of plagiarism—even though there is proof of their previously having placed their own writings and ideas, and those of their supporters, at her service—and they used the most injurious terms to refer to her. Ironically, all this notwithstanding, Domingo del Monte himself, during his Parisian exile, did not hesitate for a moment in accepting her invitations or requesting her aid for himself and his friends.[18]

In 1864, more than a quarter of a century after the Countess's visit to Cuba, Gertrudis Gómez de Avellaneda (1814-1873), following the death of her second husband, prepares to return from Cuba, where she has lived for five years, to Spain, her country of residence since 1836. Faced with the certainty that she will never return to the New World, she takes advantage of the opportunity to beg her brother to accompany her on her first and only visit to the United States—a trip she had planned, to take with her husband—where she remains for two months. But, although she had earlier dedicated many pages to travel literature, on this occasion she conveys her impressions through another genre: the poetry that, in following her expressive capabilities, allows her to metaphorically focus everything that the United States signifies for her onto one feature seen during her trip— Niagara Falls, a space often celebrated in Latin American literature.

The title and first stanzas of her extensive poem "A vista del Niágara" (In view of Niagara)[19] would lead the reader to see it as yet another homage to José María Heredia (1803-1839), upon whose death Avellaneda had written one of her most important compositions; or else a tribute to what was already then a tradition among Latin American authors: that of dedicating a few paragraphs or stanzas to the famous waterfalls. But as we move further into our reading it becomes evident that that is not her intention, that this poem, like others in her collections, is written as a counter-discourse, in this case, as a contestation to Heredia.

Although from stanza to stanza the poem exalts this "sublime marvel," the divinity who created it, and Heredia, its singer, what the "humble" author admires most is "another portent / to human power a great monument," the bridge over the Niagara River:

Hail, oh lofty, indescribable bridge,
work of man that aims to emulate
the work of God next to which you scintillate!
Hail, valiant symbol
of industrial progress, whose heights
—to which more languid nations aspire—
like a king commands the young nation
that just yesterday, like a newborn in its mighty arms
seized liberty, and that today, bursting forth
surpasses the common stride,
to the astonishment of a world that beholds it as a giant!

The vertiginous and colossal development of the United States is for Avellaneda, the most famous Romantic of Hispanic literature, sufficient reason to situate the young nation at the forefront of countries with a longer and more victorious history. And the initial impulse for this evolution, in honor of which she intones an enthusiastic—and self-compassionate—*beatus ille,* is the freedom attained by its people:

Joyous the one who owes to fortune
to have found in this privileged region,
which I've come to know so late, a happy birthplace!
Happy the one who, at the dawn of life,
breathes your atmosphere, oh, American people!

But this freedom contributes not only to "industrial progress," but also to social advancement, as she underscores in the last verses of her final stanza, in which following her exaltation of the imposing presence of North American nature, she celebrates the political virtues of its people:

If you have—to extol your greatness—
prodigies like Niagara on your soil,
of whose superior grandeur you could boast,
you knew how to build upon it institutions
which the liberal genius, as a model,
can proudly unfurl before other nations.

But this text also speaks of its author. Toward the end of Heredia's "Oda al Niágara" (Ode to Niagara), the lyric voice fantasizes about the presence near the abyss of a "beauty" whom he would rush to protect with his embrace upon seeing her face "cover itself / with a slight paleness and be only more beautiful / in her sweet terror." But the woman who appears and speaks in the last verses of Avellaneda's poem, lamenting the advanced age at which she is making her acquaintance with this other America, is, despite the recent loss of her husband—which she does not cease to deplore in the first few stanzas—quite far from passivity or faintness. Instead of occupying the space of nature (of fear and the emotions), traditionally assigned to the female subject, it occupies, as we have seen, that space that then corresponded to man, the space of knowledge, as much of science and technology as of politics.

In a lecture given at the Institute of Literature and Linguistics of the Cuban Academy of Sciences in the 1970s, José Lezama Lima, approaching "A vista del Niágara" from the unsupported theory that Avellaneda "had a very sharp awareness of her limitations," suggested that the poet,

> when she finds herself in the presence of the great waterfall, does not even attempt to rival Heredia. She makes a brief reference to the cascading of the water, and then begins to speak of a bridge which had been built many years after Heredia's memorable visit. She never intended to rival Heredia in addressing the topic.[20]

However, one could surmise that if it is true that Avellaneda did not aspire to *rival* him, she did intend more than once to do something of greater transcendence: to *rectify* Heredia. And in the examples I have come across, this always happens in relation to what we could call the Romantic voyage, or with the transcription in Romantic code of the experience of travel. This is evidently the case of "A vista del Niágara," in which Heredia's exaltations of the portents of nature are complemented by Avellaneda's praise of the portents created by men, which he had disregarded. The same is the case with the poem "El viajero americano" (The American Traveler), whose revisionist reading of Heredia's "Teocalli de Cholula" has been proposed by Mary Louise Pratt.[21]

"A vista del Niágara" is the only one of Avellaneda's texts motivated by her visit to the United States. However, in the wake of this voyage to the United States she made significant modifications to her sonnet "Washington"—which had appeared in the 1841 edition of her *Poesías*—again with the purpose of underscoring the freedom and progress of the United States and its exemplary, paradigmatic significance for other nations. In "Washington" these qualities are underscored through comparison with the warrior-like virtues of the hero, while in "A vista al Niágara" it was done through the exaltation of the natural beauties surrounding the waterfalls. However, when looking at these texts, one must point out that this profession of liberal faith in Avellaneda does not mean that she sympathized with the ideal of Cuba's independence from Spain—neither did the Spanish liberals whom she counted among her friends—and, even less, with the possibility of Cuba's annexation to the United States.

By the summer of 1882, when a young woman from Matanzas, Dolores María Ximeno y Cruz (1866-1934), visited the United States in the company of an aunt, the concerns with North American notions of progress, republicanism, and the advances made by North American women so close to the hearts of the Countess of Merlin and Gertrudis Gómez de Avellaneda had crystallized into burning issues: feminism had been brought to the fore of cultural discourse in both Cuba and the United States by movements centered on women's rights to education and participation in politics; and relationships between the two nations were increasingly driven by American expansionist policies and the United States' clear designs on annexing Cuba and its sugar industry. The topics, as we have seen earlier, form the thematic core of the many books written by men and women visiting Cuba from the United States in the latter part of the nineteenth century—as they will likewise feature most prominently in the writings of Cuban travelers visiting North America. Dolores Ximeno y Cruz's *Memorias*[22] (written at the end of the 1920s, more than forty years after the event), tinged as they are by sadness and nostalgia by the death of her father, which took place just after her return to Cuba, nonetheless cannot avoid centering on those topics that her era seemed to impose on her. Not being a writer of great originality of expression, one can glimpse in her brief description of the nature and society of the North—in which she celebrates most warmly the respectful treatment received by women, not the freedom they enjoy—not so much her own personal vision as the clear allusions and imitations of the Cuban poetry of exile—José María Heredia, Juan Clemente Zenea—and the typical aesthetic depreciation of the United States in favor of Europe that was to be expected given her family's *integrista* (or pro-Spain) sympathies. What is perhaps most interesting to note in her writings is the imprint of the ideas that dominated the discourse of national identity in the early part of the twentieth century, such as the rejection of modernity and of the pace of life in large American cities, or the *arielista* recovery of the spiritual values of *latinidad* (or Hispanicity) and particularly of *lo hispánico,* in opposition to United States pragmatism. (In *Ariel,* published in 1900 by José Enrique Rodó, the author argued that the North American gift to the world was liberty, but that freedom could be marred by materialism and consequently needed to be tempered by the humanistic tradition of Latin culture, which in turn was imperiled by a lack of social order that could lead to chaos.)

Ximeno y Cruz's embryonic feminist and political perspective finds a fuller manifestation in the travel accounts written by Magdalena Peñarredonda y Doley (1846-1937), a young woman from Pinar del Río who would in time become a commander in the Army of Liberation and a liaison officer for General Antonio Maceo during the War of Independence of 1895, as well as one of the most notable newspaper reporters and fighters for the rights of women of the first third of the twentieth century. Peñarredonda y Doley, a proponent of Cuban independence from an early age, lived in the United States in the late 1880s, when the separatist cause was a chimera that few hoped would yield any results. From there she sent her "Cartas de Norte América" (Letters from North America) to *La Habana Elegante,* the Modernists' weekly magazine. (Modernism, in the Cuban and Latin American context, refers to a revitalizing literary movement of the latter part of the nineteenth century, akin to French Parnassianism and Symbolism, and characterized by its cult of beauty, its inclination toward historical themes, and the evocation of exotic locales and past ages.) In these letters, besides making known various aspects of the customs and notions of the United States, a country she admired because of the degree of freedoms attained by its women, she established constant comparisons to what was happening in Cuba, taking advantage of each available circumstance to denounce the errors of the colonial administration. Among these, she paid particular attention to Cuban economic migration to the United States, seen as beneficial to the development of the Floridian economy but as having a detrimental impact on the depopulation of the island and contributing to the decay of one of Cuba's principal sources of wealth: the cultivation and production of tobacco.[23]

The remarkable incisiveness of Peñarredonda y Doley's perceptions of political and economic relations between Cuba and the United States is seen most distinctly when contrasted against the lightness of tone of the letters from the United States written by Inés María de los Dolores Madan y O'Sullivan, Marquesa de San Carlos de Pedroso (1846-?), the daughter of a North American mother and a Cuban father, and a resident of France. Madan y O'Sullivan traveled to her mother's native country toward the end of the 1880s with the avowed objective of discovering who were the American young ladies and gentlemen who invaded Paris every summer looking for mates, alarming their potential mothers-in-law. Her discoveries surpassed her original plans. Written for the *Nouvelle Revue* and published as a book by the journal's own publishing house, its 300 pages do not once mention the name of Cuba nor refer to anything related to her country of origin, except for the "cigares de la Havane" smoked by the friends of the painter X.[24] However, Cuban poet and critic Julián del Casal dedicates a significant study to her travel book, which he describes as written by "a great Cuban lady." He seeks both to claim her for Cuban literary history and to foster the potential reader's enthusiasm through a review of the remarkable variety of topics of great interest and pertinence that it covers.[25]

An unlikely counterpart to Madan y O'Sullivan's silence about Cuban matters is to be found in the writings of the exceptional poet and artist Juana Borrero (1877-1896), who during her childhood had studied painting in the United States. In early 1896 Borrero and her family took refuge from the War of Independence in Key West. Her intense correspondence from exile gives evidence to the deepest indifference toward her environment, the result not only of her alienation from a homeland at war, but of her resulting separation from her beloved and the illness that soon thereafter would lead her to the grave.[26] Nothing seems to exist around her. She describes only her garret and the neighboring cemetery, which she sees from her window and visits during her constant trips to the post office. The rest is blurred, as is the case in most literature of exile.

Madan y O'Sullivan's physical and emotional distance from her father's native country and Borrero's ill health account for their apparent lack of awareness of those issues dominating public debate in Cuba. No such distance exists for Aurelia Castillo de González (1842-1920), a highly regarded writer and reporter, who in time would become one of the founders of Cuban feminism. Castillo de González traveled to the United States in 1893, having been commissioned by the newspaper *El País* to report on the Columbian Exhibition in Chicago, a popular destination for many Latin American travelers of the 1890s. Her "letters," published almost simultaneously by the newspaper and by the *Revista Cubana,* appeared in book form in 1895.[27] The most significant novelty of the Exhibition, from her point of view, consisted of a pavilion dedicated to a display of women's achievements. Like Gertrudis Gómez de Avellaneda before her, Castillo de González was a great admirer of North American technology, particularly when it was applied to the improvement of women's lives. She was dazzled by the use of technology to develop household appliances designed to improve domestic labor and family comfort, to which she dedicates many pages of her text. A wide variety of details of everyday life in the United States also receive considerable attention. However, it will be the respect and freedom attained by North American women, grounded on the country's more egalitarian educational system, that will become the central theme of her chronicles, which is perhaps the most relevant text about the United States produced by a Cuban woman.

The importance of the Columbian Exhibition as a vantage point from which to examine the social and educational progress made by North American women—particularly when compared to conditions for women in Cuba—is echoed by "La mujer en la vida contemporánea y su educación en los Estados Unidos" (Women in contemporary life and their education in the United States) by María Luisa Dolz (1854–1928), a pamphlet written to be read to the students, parents, and teachers of the elite school in which she taught. Her objective was to share her observations of her visit to the Columbian Exhibition in Chicago and to centers of study in other United States cities, and consequently to denounce the deplorable state of public education on the island.[28] The text aroused much commentary in the Cuban press, and was hailed as evidence of the arrival of the feminist movement on the island.[29]

Once the War of Independence ended with the intervention of the United States in 1898, around 1,300 Cuban teachers—of whom more than half were women—traveled to Harvard University in the summer of 1900 to acquire the training necessary under the new system of education, developed in the image and likeness of that of the United States. In the wake of the American takeover, new educational standards were imposed on the island, designed to build an alternative path of long-range domination over the island through the training of teaching teams, the reorganization of public education, and, by definition, the education of all of its future citizens according to U.S. patterns and models.[30] Two of these traveling teachers, in conjunction with sixteen other participants, wrote a brief, 100-page book that in great measure merely reproduced class projects, study plans, schedules, and travel guides to the United States and Boston. It also incorporated brief contributions from their American hosts, mostly expressions of support and encouragement. The work as such hardly presents directly or in personal terms the contributors' own experiences as travelers.[31] It does, however, manage to convey their positive assessment of the social condition of women in the United States. Perhaps the most engaging theme that emerges from this odd assortment of notes and texts is the Cuban women's resolution to imitate their American counterparts in all of those elements of their lives they deemed positive.

This approach to the texts through which the Countess of Merlin, Gertrudis Gómez de Avellaneda, and other Cuban writers report on their voyages to the United States allows us to discover something quite unexpected in women's literary production: the concentration of these writers' gaze on public life and on the system of government that sustains it, and the audacity of their political opinions.

Topics deemed female by tradition are absent from the earlier of these texts. Merlin's letters, as a matter of fact, contain barely any commentary on North American women. There is absolutely no reference to women in Avellaneda. But this does not mean that women are not present in them. In "A vista del Niágara," the lyrical voice—easily identified through biographical detail with the poem's explicit author—builds a persona whose vigor and decisiveness, despite her advanced age, is the very opposite of the fainting Romantic heroine. The self-portrait offered by the Countess seems different at first impression. Her continuous references to the lack of a sense of safety she experiences in the United States and her search for protection could be attributed to the "weakness" proper to her sex. But one soon discovers that that is not the case, that she does not fear for her feminine fragility, but for the scarce attention given to her social position and to her belonging to the nobility. It is therefore her aristocratic condition rather than her female condition that is jeopardized by the lack of due care. On the contrary, it is obvious that she spends her time in the country in perpetual motion, traveling widely in a short space of time and visiting not only the spaces traditionally associated with women or considered proper to feminine sensibilities, such as shops, museums or concert halls, but also schools, prisons, hospitals, and even the United States Congress. Later writers, particularly Magdalena Peñarredonda y Doley, Aurelia Castillo de González, and María Luisa Dolz, for example, insist on judging the United States as a nation from the perspective of the social and economic advances made by its women. Their travel accounts, however, although focused on women, elude "feminine" topics in favor of the political and critical "male" gaze.

Slavery and the black population do not appear in these texts either, which is even more surprising, since many of these authors, particularly the Countess of Merlin and Gertrudis Gómez de Avellaneda, had previously given the topic considerable attention. Merlin had not only dedicated many pages of her childhood memoirs, *Mis primeros doce años* (My first twelve years) to the memory of the domestic slaves of her Cuban childhood; but she addresses the topic in the very same book that opens with a description of her visit to the United States. In letter number XX, which was published in 1841 in the *Revue des Deux Mondes* and immediately translated and reprinted as a pamphlet in Madrid, she argues for the suppression of the slave trade but never proposes the abolition of slavery.[32] In that same year, and in that same city, Avellaneda published her abolitionist novel *Sab,* a work so transgressive in its articulation of the "double slavery of gender and race,"[33] that it was banned from Cuba by the Spanish authorities as long as their colonial rule lasted. But the most shocking element in Avellaneda's silence about slavery during her visit to the United States is the fact that her voyage coincided with the War of Secession between the North and South. However, if her approach depended solely on the re-elaboration of an already worn topic—that of Niagara and the celebration of the technical progress of the United States and the system of government that propitiates it—one can conclude that she aligns herself with the states of the North, representative of industrial progress and the "liberal genius" that fostered it. However, one should say in defense of both writers that the existence of slavery and racial discrimination in the United States—a topic of such interest to travel writers from other latitudes—is something that escapes most Cuban travelers, a "blind spot" in those who bear the imprint of a racism built upon centuries of African servitude.

In the long history of coincidences and dissonances, of encounters and evasions, of attraction and rejection between Cuba and the United States around which we have built our respective identities and learned to imagine each other, the texts written by women travelers from both sides of the

Strait of Florida occupy a very important place. To rescue them from oblivion can make a noteworthy contribution to our knowledge and understanding of each other.

NOTES

1. The most recent anthology covering this subject, which gathers texts by 35 men and women travelers of various nationalities (German, Italian, French, as well as British and American) is that edited by Louis A. Pérez: *Slaves, Sugar, and Colonial Society: Travel Accounts of Cuba* (Wilmington, DE: Scholarly Resources, 1992). See also *Viajeras al Caribe*. Selection, prologue and notes by Nara Araújo (Havana: Casa de las Américas, 1983). All the works by women writers I cite below focusing entirely or partially on Cuba are included in this volume, except for that by the Peabody sisters, whose *Cartas sobre Cuba* remains unpublished; other American collections of letters or memoirs about Cuba held in libraries or private collections; and scattered texts published in magazines and never published in book form.

2. See Francine Massielo's "Diálogo sobre la lengua: colonial, nación y género." *Casa de las Américas* (Havana). 34:193 (October–December 1993): 34. Ricardo Repilado, in his essay "Acerca de viajeros y novelistas" (from his book *Cosecha de dos parcelas* [Havana: Letras Cubanas, 1985], 367-385), and before him Louise Hall Tharp (*The Peabody Sisters of Salem* [Boston: Little, Brown & Co., 1950]), have studied the presence in Cuba of these singular representatives of New England's most important literary circle. Mary wrote when in her eighties a novel inspired by her Cuban experience: *Juanita, A Romance of Real Life in Cuba Fifty Years Ago.*

3. Mary Louise Pratt, *Imperial Eyes: Travel Writing and Transculturation* (New York: Routledge, 1992), 6-7.

4. Sara Mills, *Discourses of Difference: An Analysis of Women's Travel Writing and Colonialism* (London and New York: Routledge, 1991).

5. Louisa Mathilde Woodruff, *My Winter in Cuba* (New York: E. P. Dutton, 1871), 260.

6. Eliza McHatton-Ripley, *From Flag to Flag: A Woman's Adventures and Experiences in the South During the War, in Mexico, and in Cuba* (New York: D. Appleton and Company, 1889). Subsequent references will appear in parentheses in the text.

7. Aihwa Ong, "Colonialism and Modernity: Feminist Representation on Women in Non-Western Societies." *Feminism and the Colonial Discourse.* Special issue of *Inscriptions* 3/4 (1988): 79-93.

8. Julia Howe, *A Trip to Cuba* (Boston: Ticknor and Fields, 1860), 146, 231. Subsequent references will appear in parentheses in the text.

9. Julio Ramos, *Desencuentros de la modernidad en América Latina: Literatura y política en el siglo XIX* (México: Fondo de Cultura Económica, 1989), 145.

10. Manuel Pedro González, "Las relaciones intelectuales entre los Estados Unidos e Hispano América." *Universidad de la Habana* 8: 24-25 (1939): 84-110; José de Onís, *The United States as Seen by Spanish American Writers (1776-1890)* (New York: Hispanic Institute in the United States, 1952); Elizabeth Rezner Daniel, *Spanish American Travellers in the United States Before 1900: A Study in Inter-American Literary Relations.* Ph.D. Diss. University of North Carolina at Chapel Hill (1959); John T. Reid, *Spanish American Image of the United States, 1790-1960* (Gainesville: The University Presses of Florida, 1977).

11. *Abroad in America: Visitors to the New Nation, 1776-1914* (Reading, PA: Addison-Wesley Publishing Co., 1976); and Robert B. Downs (comp.), *Images of America: Travelers from Abroad in the New World* (Urbana: University of Illinois Press, c. 1987).

12. Marion Tinling, ed. *With Woman's Eyes: Visitors to the New World, 1775-1918* (Hamden, CT: Archon Books, 1993).

13. Ramos, 147.

14. Mónica Tamborenea, "La constitución de la subjetividad en los relatos de viaje en los "80," *Dispositio* XVII: 42-43 (1992): 309.

15. Onís, see note 10 above.

16. See Carolyn Porter, "What We Know that We Don't Know: Remapping American Literary Studies." *American Literary History* 6:3 (Fall 1994): 467-526.

17. Condesa de Merlin [María de las Mercedes Santa Cruz y Montalvo], *La Havane.* 3 Vols (Paris: Librairie d'Amyot, 1844). Subsequent references will appear in parentheses in the text.

18. See Salvador Bueno, "Introducción." In Condesa de Merlín [María de las Mercedes Santa-Cruz y Montalvo], *Viaje a la Havana* (Havana: Editorial de Arte y Literatura, 1974), 30-34, 376-377. See also Urbano Martínez, *Domingo del Monte y su tiempo* (Havana: Ediciones Unión, 1997), 375, 376-377.

19. Gertrudis Gómez de Avellaneda, *Antología poética* (Havana: Editorial Letras Cubanas, 1983), 234-239.

20. José Lezama Lima, "Conferencia sobre Gertrudis Gómez de Avellaneda." *Fascinación de la memoria* (Havana: Letras Cubanas, 1993), 153-165.

21. For another example of "counter-poems" by Avellaneda that have Heredia's texts as referent, see Pratt, 193-194, and her "Las mujeres y el imaginario nacional en el siglo XIX." *Revista de Crítica Literaria Latinoamericana* 19:38 (1993): 58-59.

22. Dolores María Ximeno y Cruz, *Aquellos tiempos . . . Memorias de Lola María.* Prologue by Fernando Ortiz (Havana: Colección Cubana de Libros Inéditos o Raros, 1928-1930). 2 vols.

23. Ximeno y Cruz, *La Habana Elegante* 6:31, 34, 40 (July–September 1888).

24. Inés María de los Dolores Madan y O'Sullivan, *Les Américains chez eux* (Paris: Librairie de la Nouvelle Revue, 1980).

25. Julián del Casal, "Libros nuevos. Los Estados Unidos por la Marquesa San Carlos de Pedroso." In *Prosas.* Vol. 2 (Havana: Consejo Nacional de Cultura, 1963), 179–181. This text was published originally in *La Discusión* (Havana), 1 July 1890.

26. Juana Borrero, *Epistolario.* 2 Vols. Havana: Academia de Ciencias de Cuba, 17.

27. Aurelia Castillo de González, *Un paseo por América. Cartas de México y de Chicago* (Havana: Imp. La Constancia, 1895). A second edition appeared in her *Escritos . . . .* Vol. 3 (Havana: El Siglo XX, 1913).

28. María Luisa Dolz, *La liberación de la mujer cubana por la educación* (Havana: Oficina del Historiador de la Ciudad, 1955), 35–47.

29. See Enrique José Varona, "El movimiento feminista en Cuba." *El Fígaro* (Havana) 10:19, 5 (May 1894), p. 198.

30. Louis A. Pérez, Jr. "El diseño imperial: política y pedagogía en el período de la ocupación de Cuba, 1899–1902." *Estudios Cubanos* 12:2 (1982).

31. *La escuela de verano para los maestros cubanos* (Cambridge, MA: Press of Edward W. Wheeler, 1900).

32. See Salvador Bueno, 34–38.

33. See Evelyn Picón Garfield, *Poder y sexualidad: el discurso de Gertrudis Gómez de Avellaneda* (Amsterdam and Atlanta: Rodopi, 1993), 53.

Chapter 7

COLONIZING THE SELF:
GENDER, POLITICS, AND RACE IN THE COUNTESS OF MERLIN'S *LA HAVANE*[1]

Claire Emilie Martin

Nineteenth-century autobiographical narratives have given us a curious perspective into the early manifestations of Latin American writing as well as into Latin America's emergence from colonial status to nationhood. Sylvia Molloy, in *At Face Value*, maintains that the autobiographical works of these new nations became a form of historical account, a personalized insertion of the authorial I/(eye) witness in the historical process. Thus, the personal, private history of the individual functions metonymically within the national discourse.[2] Travel narratives stemming from the autobiographical impulse of constructing the self through the travel metaphor confront us with a unique perspective into a privileged site of confluence where the individual voice acts (however reluctantly) as a vessel for a dominant ideology.

The works of Cuban-born María de las Mercedes Santa Cruz y Montalvo, Countess of Merlin (1789-1852) constitute a shrewd and engaging blueprint of a life in the making, not unlike the birthing process of the new American nations. The Countess' travel narrative, *La Havane*, represents her most conscientious effort to carve an intellectual position as a Creole amidst the Parisian as well as Cuban intelligentsia.[3] In its cumulative impulse toward a compendious literary assessment of Cuba's economic, social, political, and ethical situation, the Countess grafts onto her life story the dramatic events of Cuban life in the first half of the nineteenth century. *La Havane* offers to her twentieth-century readers a vantage point from which to witness the construction of subjectivity as inquiry about self-knowledge and self-invention, encompassing not only the individual, but also colonial Cuba and Europe. Thus, this essay positions Merlin at the confluence of national, racial, class, and gender contexts, in order to extract a richer and more accurate reading of her quasi-encyclopedic travel narrative, *La Havane*.[4] I chart the construction of a historical female subject out of the equivocal negotiating in which Merlin engages with her own status as colonized/er, female, and Creole. From this angle, the Countess of Merlin becomes less an individual than a "site" where these contexts meet.[5] Inevitably, as a by-product of the process of self-invention, the subject creates an opposing but complementary image, that of the Other. The construction of Self and Other becomes a historical/literary act of invention carried out by Merlin through her travel narrative. We can see it most clearly through two examples of this process: the invention of "Cubanness" through the landscape imagery of the island itself, and the description of the women of Havana.[6]

Between 1841 and 1844, Merlin published two major versions of her trip to Cuba: *La Havane*, [Havana], written in French, and *Viaje a la Habana*, [Voyage to Havana].[7] She also published Letter XX of *La Havane*, on the conditions of slaves in the Spanish colonies, in the famous *Revue des Deux Mondes*, and several others in *La Presse*. These publications were articulated as autonomous yet intimately related versions of the same experience, tailored to satisfy the interests and demands of different readerships. Thus, the publication of parts of the voluminous *La Havane* before its completion suggests the urgency of the political situation on the island, and Cuba's strained relations with the Spanish Crown and with foreign powers in the Caribbean. Sensing the volatile nature of her assessment of the situation in the colony, Merlin fragmented her narrative to capture the goodwill of the Spanish readership, the Cuban intellectual circles that welcomed her return to the island, and the European public. Given the wide-range differences in readership and interests that she hoped to reach, it becomes clear that the publication of interrelated materials during this short period followed her ambitious goal of engaging the international community in the debate around abolition, the cessation of the slave trade, and Cuba's teetering colonial status.[8]

The three-volume work, *La Havane*, stands as a literary homage to her homeland, a search for her identity as an exiled Creole in France, and an ideological positioning to guard the economic and political interests of her class (the Cuban saccharocracy). The full text includes 36 letters and an appendix containing letters on the slave situation in Cuba by the British Consul Mr. Turnbull and several influential Cubans. The letters that comprise the three volumes (over 1,200 pages long) shape a multilayered discourse that entangles itself in the profusion of historical narrative, essays on the political, economic and social systems governing the colony, and anecdotal and pictorial narratives. While unfolding the "petite histoire" with its charming scenes of colonial life, the text reflects a well-defined political agenda espoused by the Countess herself and many of the Cuban intellectuals of the time.

The same year, a translation of *La Havane* was published in Madrid in a much abridged form with a preface by her compatriot Gertrudis Gómez de Avellaneda. *Viaje a La Habana* includes only 10 of the 36 letters, and the appendix was omitted along with the name of the person to whom the letter was addressed. The resulting text was a diluted version of the original; it transformed the politically volatile issue of slave emancipation and slave trade into an uneasy absence. Merlin characterized this Spanish version as "divertida" (light and amusing); however, in reading *Viaje a La Habana* the reader cannot fail to notice the constant preoccupation with the role of blacks (slaves or freed) within Cuban society. There is also a singular attempt to erase any fears the Spanish readership harbored concerning the violent disposition of blacks and the possibility of a general uprising such as the one in Haiti. The dilemma of the black element in Cuban society became the matrix subtext of all three works. In both its conspicuous absence as well as in its obsessive presence, blacks (slave, cimarrón, or freed) were in the limelight of the economic, political, and philosophical debate on the island.[9] It is interesting to note that the most controversial aspects of the work seemed to remain unnoticed as many European readers saw it as no more than an entertaining piece of "exotica." On the other hand, the reaction and subsequent resistance to Merlin's works by Cubans surfaced shortly after the publication of some of the letters in Havana's newspapers. The extreme polarity of reception warns us about the complex dynamics between identity and representation. This study focuses first on the shifting of positionality that Mercedes Merlin engages in while in the process of "becoming" again a Creole to lend authority to her portrait of the colonial subject, and then primarily on the first encounter with her homeland and her people in the harbor of Havana.

Embarking on a trip that would take her to the United States and Cuba in 1840, the Countess of Merlin expresses an unmovable self-assuredness regarding her aristocratic lineage and class alliances. Much more problematic is the Countess's conflictive representation of Other and Self during her brief stay on the island of Cuba. Merlin engages in the process of colonizing her own self by adopting or appropriating a linguistic, a cultural, a political, and a racial position that is not fully hers, but that represents the self she so earnestly desires. She is, after all, a Cuban-born aristocrat writing in French; she belongs to a slave-holding and land-owning family, and defends the anti-abolitionist forces, but decries slavery as inhuman. She is an imperial apologist clamoring for more political autonomy and justice for the colony. The ambivalence in Merlin's writing suggests the validity of the notion of colonialism as a shifting paradigm, constantly renegotiated to maintain its rule, and its relatively stable official discourse. Yet, her ambiguous stance turns any reading of her work into an uneasy and unstable dynamic between the forces of Empire and the emergence of a "nationalist" impulse. *La Havane* constitutes a prescriptive work with ambitious guidelines noted in her dedication to Governor O'Donnell and to her compatriots: "Until now, Europe, so proud of her arts and laws has forgotten or ignored too much our Queen of the Antilles, her resources, her riches and her due place in the history of the Americas" (8). She appointed herself the "go-between," mediating and translating the colonial subject to her European readership, and in doing so she inscribed her conflictive self within the representation of Otherness. Her fragmented narratives respond to the realities of a discourse born in what Mary Louise Pratt, in *Imperial Eyes,* has termed the "contact zones," the sites of colonial encounters (4). *Imperial Eyes* is an attempt to show how travel narratives of Europeans about non-Europeans go about creating a "domestic subject" of Euroimperialism (borrowing Gayatri Spivak's term). Merlin's *La Havane* must be studied from this perspective as an example of "transculturation," as a phenomenon of the contact zone to be fully understood.[10]

As the construction of self evolves throughout her earlier works, including *Mes douze premières années, Memoires et Souvenirs* (My First twelve years, memories and remembrances), the Creole self begins to fuse with the emerging European one. Over a decade later, in *La Havane,* the process of assimilation is seemingly complete. It is with deep sorrow that Merlin confesses to her daughter that she feels like a stranger in her native land. This loss of Creole identity is dramatized in her futile attempts to conjure up images that will stand up to the realities she faces on her return to Cuba. She flatly admits that her memories are drawn from the heart. By the time she takes up her pen, Merlin has chosen her stance; a stance that is based on a "fence-sitting" positionality that confirms her authority as a Creole while maintaining her Europeanness. Her Creole self is constructed of images carefully placed within the narrative to lend her an usurped authority in the matters of the island. It is not a full-fleshed, authentic Creole self emerging from the pages of *La Havane,* but a rhetorical construct shrouded in the effusions of the language of Romanticism.

Merlin becomes a "traveler-theorist," holding a privileged perspective, claiming authority denied her as a woman in Europe, but that suddenly becomes attainable away from the colonizer's "home." In discussing the metaphorical and material significance of travel writing, Alison Blunt states that "[t]ravel is bounded by points of departure and destination, but in an arbitrary, retrospective way defined by perceptions of 'home' that can only arise with critical distance."[11] This residual reversal of authority and cultural positioning leads to a conflictive travel discourse aware of the precariousness of its situation. Like many women travelers before and after, the Countess of Merlin finds herself entrapped in a hierarchical system not of her own making but, that for the space and time of the narrative, accommodates her at the top. Therefore, she can once again shift her positionality when engaged in the act of seeing and writing about the colonial subject.

At first Merlin seems to oscillate between the two positions: her Creole self and her European one. As a daughter of the island she writes: "It seems to me that when I arrived to my country I came home. What a sacred right it is to live in one's native land!" (103); as a foreigner, she laments: "My heart is anguished to think, my daughter, that I come here as a foreigner" (102). Merlin, however, manages to steady her gaze and to look at the island with the borrowed spectacles of the colonizer subject, the "individual rational male" of contemporary travel narratives.[12] Georges Van Den Abbeele, in *Travel as Metaphor,* touches on the fact that "[w]estern ideals about travel . . . have generally transmitted, inculcated and reinforced patriarchal values and ideology from one male generation to the next."[13] The sum of these two traditional views on travel narratives seems to preclude women from assuming the role of travel-theorist at the risk of losing the liminality of their femaleness within the social and textual order. However, Merlin, like dozens of women travelers, does just that: she defies patriarchal order by writing about the colonial Other from the perspective of the enlightened male traveler. As we will study below, the initial act of apprehending, of penetrating and possessing the land and the people of Havana, demonstrates vividly the patriarchal and imperialist perspective spoused by Merlin. This perspective or point of view reminds us of another term coined by Pratt: the "anti-conquest," defined as "strategies of representation by which European bourgeois subjects seek to secure their innocence in the same moment they assert European hegemony." The main protagonist of the anti-conquest is the "seeing man" (7). Whether we choose "individual rational male" or "seeing man," it is apparent that Merlin as a woman-traveler must embody this most unseemingly stance. Yet again, the stance cannot be sustained for the whole length of the narrative, and it is at these junctures that the sentimental, autobiographically charged voice of the female traveler obscures the "seeing man."

We must move cautiously over this terrain, since this kind of narrative is highly interactive and maintains an improvisational dimension reflective of the negotiating present in all colonial encounters. Merlin succeeds in straddling cautiously between the two cultures; she presents herself as fragmented, between two worlds. Her excursions or displacements from her European self to the Creole one are brief and carefully noted as coming from circumstantial knowledge, experienced as detached (in time), and only in situations dealing with patriotic fervor and with heightened nationalistic pride. She does not fully submit to the ambiguous, imprecise quality of a self away from home and amid places, time, and languages. Her duality is carefully limited by the rhetorical use of "they" when referring to the Creoles, and by the use of her autobiographical self constructed as object, as Other, in contrast with the colonizer subject that she has adopted. This strategy results in an uneasy distancing of her Self as the object of autobiographical recollections from the imperial subject that is given to theorizing through the travel narrative. Craftily, she fashions herself a detached chronicler of imperialist discourse with an insider's expertise and knowledge on the colonial subject to be studied.

As traveler-theorist, Merlin reads the signs of the colonial system, interprets them, and bestows upon herself a hermeneutic task to "explain away" the island to the distinguished readership she herself creates. She remains in total control of her narrative by addressing each letter to a designated, and therefore fixed and dependent, reader/authority in whatever field she has chosen to write about. Merlin's task is an unambiguous one: she is homogenizing the colonized subject in order to serve several private, class, and "national" interests. Her portrait of race relations, of life in the city and the country, of the customs of Havana women, all point to a faceless, meek, and self-satisfied "colonial subject." Merlin smoothes the rough edges of colonial life in order to present a world of surfaces, as glossy and colorful as the memories she has previously shared with her readers.

Her return to Cuba in May 1840 in the frigate *Cristóbal Colón* offers a tempting parallel to the voyage of discovery and the act of taking possession by the Genovese. This is not lost on Merlin, who dedicates several pages to Columbus. She, too, places her gaze onto the Caribbean shoreline and discovers along with her readers the lusciously green mountains and exotic topography rhapsodized by the Admiral of the Ocean Sea. She, too, will describe to a European authority the wealth and service the land and its people represent. Both are caught in the process of "inventing" America that in the mid-nineteenth century is still the object of European desire and a reflection of its myopic imperialist policies.

In Letter XIII, entitled "Contemplación- Las cercanías de la patria-" [Contemplation- Nearing the Fatherland] Merlin salutes nature:

> I'm ecstatic! Since this morning I breathe the warm and lovely air of the tropics; this air full of life and enthusiasm, full of soft and sweet voluptuousness. The sun, the stars, the ethereal skies, all of it strikes me as bigger, more brilliant, more splendid. The clouds do not travel in the distance through the sky, but in the air close to our heads, with all the hues of the rainbow. The atmosphere is so clear, so radiant that it appears to be suffused in gold dust. (93)

In this passage, and a little later before the city itself, Merlin adopts the elegiac tone favored by the Romantic poets. The poetic exultation over this peculiar Caribbean nature implies a strong sense of Americanness that negates Europe and affirms America's uniqueness. Leaving the American landscape, or conversely, returning to it, produces a sort of revelatory state in which the narrative or poetic voice can re-attach itself to the land and its people. In these instances of sentimental bonding with America, Merlin discards the rational male persona that she inhabits in much of her narrative.[14]

The Countess catalogs the villages and towns as she sails parallel to the coastline. The use of the personal pronoun "we" becomes ubiquitous, announcing that Merlin has initiated the process of recovery and appropriation. The towns she describes, Santa Cruz and Jaruco, happen to be those connected with her illustrious family. Her brother, she declares, is "the chief justice of the town of Jaruco; that is to say its benefactor" (97). Insidious ideas of ownership and paternalism emerge from Merlin's writing as soon as she arrives at the lands she so clearly admires and covets. Forced to position herself again as the traveler, Merlin has to admit that the

memories do not adjust themselves to reality: "Nothing has the same proportions anymore" (99), she laments, but quickly recovers to continue to
catalog the landscape.

Merlin's arrival on the island initiates the dual movement of recaptur-
ing the past through memory and observing the present through ideology.
The description of the coastline and the city at dusk is drawn with emotion and with pride, but hardly with any true recognition. From the very
first moment that she glimpses Havana, Merlin is thrust into a game of
invention, of matching and fitting the scenes she sees with the memories
she has fashioned for herself during her exile. The scope of her sometimes
inaccurate views can only be apprehended when one is confronted with
the virulent criticism that her work provoked among her compatriots, and
the accounts of earlier and later travelers to the island.

Cautiously, Merlin gains her Creole identity as she describes for her
reader the city in terms of a welcoming lady: "There she is, with her balconies, her canopies and terraces. Doors and windows are open all day
long, and the gaze penetrates domestic life intimately; from the patio, wet
and covered with flowers to the girl's bed, with its linen curtains adorned
with rose-colored sashes" (100). The recurring images of openness, of
trusting hospitality exhibited by the people of Havana, are foreshadowed in
the airy and public character of the city's architecture. Merlin appears to
reassure her readers that there are no secrets for the curious and interested
traveler. Doors, windows, courtyards, and balconies invitingly embrace the
reader, and as the sailboat that carries the prodigal daughter approaches, the
whole city turns into a joyous welcoming spectacle: "We keep on moving,
and the balconies are swarming with people who observe us and greet us
with joy as we sail by" (101). In contrasting fashion, the descriptions of
Alexander Von Humboldt hardly seem to refer to the same city: "During
my residence in South America few of the cities presented a more disgusting appearance than this Havana. One walked through the mud to the
knees, and the many carriages . . . made walking in the streets both vexa-
tious and humiliating. The offensive odour of salted meat, or tasajo infected
many of the houses, and even some of the ill-ventilated streets."[15]

Robert Francis Jameson, a few years later (1821) describes in more detail
the city: "On passing the seagate you become sensible of one great source
of disease, from the insufferable stench of the stores of dried beef and fish
which are imported for the sustenance of the blacks. A multitude of narrow streets open to your eye, each contributing to the congress of smells,
by their want of sewers and paving."[16] Anthony Trollope writing in 1860

exclaims: "There is nothing attractive about the town of Havana; nothing whatever to my mind, if we except the harbour. The streets are narrow, dirty and foul."[17]

To the Countess, the vivid images of contrasting light and darkness and the presence of the black slaves insinuates the "foreignness" of the scene. The black and mulatto population permeates the air with the "savagery" of their music: "More than human melodies one would say it is a concert performed by evil spirits on a day of 'cattivo umore'" (102). The transparency of the air is disrupted, cut through like a knife by the chaotic and barbarian sounds of Africa in America.[18]

When first greeted by the uncle she does not recognize, the Countess initiates the process of reconstructing the present with the aid of the memories from the heart: "More than recognize him I imagine him, and I do not find a difference between these two emotions. It could be said that in this instant my heart becomes my sight, for I feel that my memory and my sight fuse into this striking revelation" (103). Soon, the movement from sight to memory to emotion becomes the medium for the ideological stance of the colonizer adopted by Merlin in spite of her avowed identification with the land and the people she is writing about. Merlin cannot hide the fact that her own family sees her as a "frenchified" curiosity, unaware of local customs, and even ignorant of idioms and colloquialisms. Undeterred, Merlin conjures up her Creoleness and proceeds to manipulate with shrewdness her blood alliances with the Cuban saccharocracy, her well-documented horror of slavery, and her imperial views on Cuba.

Memory toils to retrieve the forgotten past, and, confused by the arduous task, it recovers a world upside down that provokes the hilarity of Merlin's family: "I mix and confuse everyone, taking the son for the father, the nephew for the uncle and a hundred other mistakes that provoke general laughter and that reveal my ignorance" (106). The faces from childhood parade before Merlin, who gives equal treatment to family and slaves. This equalizing embrace of race and class conforms to a very simple narrative design. Merlin needs the black presence in the narrative to act as witness to her past as a Creole. The blacks' effusive show of emotion upon the sight of the foreigner confirms what Merlin is unable to offer to her readers: irrefutable evidence of her Cubanness. Each slave or freed slave is anointed with a privileged role in the development of Merlin's motherless childhood. However, the image of the black slaves becomes increasingly more problematic. Merlin depicts them as smiling and docile as readily as she conjures up images of primitive evil. The city has tamed them into beings abandoned to luxurious practices of complacent laziness. The countryside, on the other hand, intimates Merlin, has nurtured their savage nature.

Bent on legitimizing her authority, Merlin takes possession of all the objects she sees: "At the same time, it seemed to me that everything I saw belonged to me, that every person I met was a friend. . . . I liked everything, the fruits, the blacks who carried them on their heads to sell them; the black women who walked proudly in the streets at the rhythm of their hips" (104). Merlin wills herself into the world she has recreated, but is unable to sustain the identification with the Creole for very long. Her European perspective takes hold of her: "Here, I miss the active life of Europe, and sometimes I resent the fact of having distanced myself from my ancestors the Indians, because the 'dolce farniente' does not suffice to render me happy" (109). While distancing herself from the subject of her narrative, Merlin surely exaggerates in depicting the culinary habits of the people of Havana: "The people of Havana eat very little at each meal, like birds; one can see them at any hour of the day eating a piece of fruit or a sweet" (106). It is this particular passage that will provoke the bitingly ironic comments of her detractors.

On 21 September 1843, more than a year before the publication of the three volumes of *La Havane,* the Cuban newspaper *Faro Industrial de la Habana* included a translation of the letter the Countess of Merlin addressed to George Sand on the mores and habits of women from Havana. Excerpts from it were published in several other newspapers, adding to the heated polemic over the merits and accuracy of her observations. The reaction against the portrait of Cuban society and women's everyday life painted by the Countess was vitriolic, though she was not without defenders. In a series of articles published in the literary section of the *Faro Industrial de la Habana,* dating from September 1843 to 1844, a critic of Merlin, under the pseudonym Veráfilo (Lover of Truth) attacks with acerbic humor the author's description of Cuban life: "What does the author of this letter know about our customs . . . ? When has she studied them, when has she observed them? . . . The Countess is not making it up, as one might assume from her exaggerations, but she has confused everything because her febrile imagination wanted to store all into her memory, which it could not do."[19] The "habaneros" resist Merlin's project of classification and description of native life for European consumption and ridicule Merlin's letters as "daughters of her exaggerated God-given imagination at the service of her native land."[20] The ambiguity of "native land" lends the criticism its mordacity. She was born in Cuba, but she left and therefore is considered an outsider representing the European perspective from within which she observes and writes.[21]

Merlin's construction of the colonial Other proves deeply problematic for this self-appointed Creole torn between competing ideologies. Nowhere is this dilemma more starkly evident than in her description of the women of Havana in letter XXV, addressed to the French writer George Sand. While attempting to objectify the Creole women to present them to her European readership, Merlin is inevitably performing an act of self-invention. She becomes the object and the subject, the colonized and the colonizer, a character and an author.

Merlin, aware of the power of sexual, sensual, and exotic imagery on her European readership, resists one form of stereotype to succumb to another, and complies with racial prejudice by furthering the stereotype of blacks (in particular, women). Citing Homi Bhabha, Alison Blunt explains the function of the stereotype: "The stereotype is the main discursive codification of fixity and similarly reflects ambivalence because it is a form of knowledge and identification that vacillates between what is 'in place,' already known, and something that must be anxiously repeated" (23). For the white female colonial subject, Merlin tries to "untaint" the exotic image that the Caribbean seems to elicit from European readers. She starts her letter to George Sand denying the false representation of Creole women:

> Do not expect either pathetic and steamy tales, colored by the tropical heat, or tragic stories whose interests lie in irate jealousy and bloodied daggers. This chaste woman from Havana, in spite of her fiery soul and her passionate nature, does not know the fancy refinements of these affairs of the heart, or about their torments and fictional voluptuousness; or of the ripened fruits in warm hot-houses possessing neither perfume nor taste; or of imaginary passions, those parasitic plants that dry out the greenish vigor from the young sap. [22]

Chastity seems to be in constant struggle with the "fiery soul" and "passionate nature" of the women of Havana. Caught in her own mythmaking prejudices, Merlin strives to achieve a perfect blend of cool white purity and hot red passion, all in the delicate vessel of the Creole. To this end, as we shall see, the interplay between color and whiteness, light and shadow, heat and coolness becomes a thinly veiled representation of a colonialist racial discourse.

To further the image of purity and innocence, Merlin turns to the "infantilization" of the Creole woman's physical attributes. One cannot fail to notice the sexual undertones of such a description:"She has the tiny and delicate limbs of a child. Her feet, small and plump, don, or better yet, are delicately surrounded by white satin, for her shoes barely have soles and have never stepped on street pavement. The foot of this woman from Havana is not merely a foot, but nature's poetic luxury" (14). These are the feet of a woman-child, never allowed to wander away from the vigilant gaze of home, her soles never soiled from walking out into the world. Confinement and dependence are the ultimate virtues of Creole women, literally and metaphorically bound by white satin.

Merlin, acting as the surrogate eye, intrudes into the female Creole private space during periods of immobility, indulgent stillness, and defeated prostration caused by the extreme heat and by her naturally frail disposition: "She hardly walks, and spends a good portion of the day bathing or eating fruit; the rest of the day she spends swinging in a *butaca* [easy-chair]. . . . As soon as the sun's rays weigh heavily in the air, she is incapable of any activity whatsoever" (14).

The lazy, sensuous, and languid nature of the "habaneras" is contrasted with the other half of the stereotypical equation: the passionate, physical presence of the black woman. Both races are depicted as indolent seekers of worldly pleasures and portrayed under similar circumstances in a sort of female community, grooming and fanning themselves and each other. This fantastic scene first introduced female black slaves into the narrative, and is later mirrored by the Creoles adopting similar postures. As a matter of fact, the image of the harem instructs many of her descriptions of women, rarely seen as individuals or in isolation, but in small groups, devoid of labor, carefree, "innocent," flaunting their sensuous bodies to the voyeuristic gaze of the imperialist eye that Merlin has so faithfully served during her narrative. Females (either black or white) are described as passive beings awaiting the cooling breezes at sundown to erupt into a frenzy of movement, igniting with the passion of dance and music:

> In an easily understandable contradiction, the women of Havana love to dance; they spend whole nights moving their feet, excitedly turning round and round until they collapse from exhaustion.
>
> The traditional dance of Havana is executed with the whole body rather than with the feet; it is a mix of waltz with gliding steps and swings of such softness and undeniable voluptuousness that last until the fatigue felt by the dancers comes to the rescue of the musicians in the orchestra. (14–15)

The paradoxical superposition of images contributes to further the sexual potentiality of Creole women, at once too weak and childlike to refuse, and too passionate and irrational to disappoint. These frenzied activities of the body left to its own primeval instincts of movement, hunt, flight, and sex, separates the "civilized" European, imperial subject from the colonized one represented by blacks and the Creole women that Merlin describes to her readership.

Merlin suggests in her use of images of Creole women that many of the exotic and sexual traits that she observes in black women have been passed on, rubbed off in the constant exposure to the "black body": "The relentless public aspect of private family life, the constant presence of Negroes who remain nude until the age of eight, do not destroy in our young women but one sort of modesty: that of the sight, which does not offend the purity of their thoughts and the honesty that they always preserve" (16). While stressing the racial cohabitation, their love of music and dancing, their shared apathy, she is "darkening" the white woman to make her an easier object of imperialist desire; she is objectifying her, integrating her into "the totalizing conception of otherness" that obliterates race and bases itself on gender alone.[23] Merlin exposes the female Other; she reveals her and makes her available, as E. Shohat explains: "The process of exposing the female Other, of literally denuding her . . . [coming] to allegorize the Western masculinist power of possession, that she as a metaphor for her land, becomes available for Western penetration and knowledge."[24]

Merlin, while appropriating this sexually energetic imagery to "apprehend" the nature of island women, performs a linguistic and ideological "rape," much in the same way the European colonizer rapes native land and women. She is the viewing subject objectifying the natives. It is no wonder that the "habaneras" reacted furiously to Merlin's letters published in Havana's newspapers. They could not identify with the foreign image of themselves found in passages such as this one:

Because of the freedom that she has enjoyed from childhood and the constant and sweet warmth of the air, her limbs maintain the same original freshness and flexibility and give a velvet-like softness to her skin which is often a pale shade of white; but underneath one can perceive a warm and golden luminescence as if the sun had suffused it with its rays. Her movements, marked by a languorous voluptuousness, her deliberate and indolent walk, and her soft and rhythmic speech sometimes contrast with her vivacious physiognomy and with the fiery blaze that escapes from her large black eyes, whose gaze proves incomparable. She never exposes herself to the sun except when she travels. She only goes out at dusk, and never on foot. Aside from the inconvenience of the heat outside her house, her aristocratic pride does not allow her to mingle with the street crowds. (14)

Merlin constructs the Creole woman on the juxtaposition of bipolar imagery based on the elements of fire and ice, hot and cold, light and dark, movement and stillness. The resulting image is one of enticing exoticism, of threatening sexuality, of calculated elusiveness. The racial darkening of the colonial female subject is accomplished subtly. By emphasizing the warm and golden glow that penetrates her and that emerges from within and spills on the pale skin changing its shade, and by focusing on the fiery blackness of her large dark eyes, Merlin offers a safe object of desire for the scrutinizing gaze of the colonizer/reader.

The imagery of stillness seems to exacerbate the availability and vulnerability of the Creole, fashioned as a prey too slow to flee or too unaware of the danger. Even her speech is deliberately made into a childlike language constructed of slow rhythms, soft and faintly perceptible: "Nothing rivals the naive charm, the caressing words of our women, and the harmony that exists among the musicality of their voices, the original turn of phrase and their seductive gestures. Yet, there is no malice in their innocence nor anything untrue in their gaiety" (16). Lack of movement is also present in the black population of Havana. Merlin, aware of the political implications of her narrative on European readers, struggles to convey a static yet colorful tableaux of racial harmony skillfully erasing the menacing reality of slavery and the all-too-real threat of slave uprisings.

The stillness of the characters is further enhanced by the spatial parameters within which the Creole female thrives. Her space is carefully reduced to a minimum as women are briefly seen through door openings and windows framing their white beauty; balconies, patios, and the open carriage constitute the safe spaces, the dominion of Creole women, guarded against the intrusion of foreign gazes: "As the sun sets, the gracious sylph, all dressed in white and with flowers in her head, comes alive; she gets into the *volante* [Cuban open carriage] and goes to different shops; she never gets out since she makes the whole shop come to the foot board of her carriage" (14). The metaphor of confinement is transformed into privilege: she need not soil her satin shoes, for the world will come to rest at her feet.

The letter to George Sand concludes with the construction of the female Creole as wife and mother. The "infantilization" of women continues as Merlin praises the natural malleability and innate sweet disposition of

Creole women. She depicts them as a blank page on which men will write their own lives: "Since her ambitions, vanity or sensual longings are never consulted in choosing her future husband, the man she marries is always in accord with her age and tastes. She loves him, and does not arrive to the nuptial bed her heart in turmoil, her imagination beguiled by other unions and other desires" (17). This image of total female compliance is furthered by the critical views on motherhood that Merlin points out to her reader:

> The extreme youth of mothers and the precocious development of children do a great disservice to their early education. The child, from the very beginning treats her mother as a companion, and the inherent Creole insouciance deprives mothers of the energy to scold them and to validate their rights as parents. Due to this maternal weakness, the male child becomes domineering and capricious. The damage is lesser when we consider the daughter's education, for the sweet, loving and malleable character of the little girl turns itself tenderly onto her parents. It is then the early education of boys that often fails. (19)

The writings of Mercedes Merlin about Cuba proved to be motivated by a complex array of factors: literary aspirations, intellectual curiosity, philosophical convictions, political gain, and monetary compensation. Moreover, Merlin gave Europeans a reassuring image of colonial life, far away from their own troubled shores. Cubans were a content and generous lot who treated their slaves magnanimously, and who were oblivious to the political maneuvers of the European colonial powers. She also seemed to warn Europeans that if meddled with, this "island-paradise" would collapse in anarchy, or worse, it would follow the path of Haiti. It is difficult to ignore that at that time white Cubans lived in constant fear of slave rebellions, and were actively trying to recruit European immigrants to redress the racial composition of the island. The Countess, aware of this predicament, could not paint a bleak picture of racial, political and socioeconomic realities. In fact, she hoped the German translation of her work would convince some to join white Cubans in their economic prosperity and leisurely lives.

Merlin's correspondence to her lover and collaborator Philarète Chasles about the publication and promotion of *La Havane* makes clear that Merlin was fully aware of her intellectual appropriation of Cuba through her representation of the colonial subject, the imperialist stereotyping, and the liberal use she made of the literary works by some of the best writers from the island. She instructs Chasles to select "the most pertinent paragraphs, be they about politics, be they as stimulus for the foreign migration [of

German colonists], without forgetting the one [paragraph] that will allay their fears of yellow fever, etc."[25] It all points to a rather convincing portrait of a colonialist enterprise if it were not for a twist that places Merlin at the intersection of the construction of the colonial Other and the colonizer Self. She is after all writing to present the best aspects (in her mind) of the island to attract hard-working Germans to balance Cuba's racial composition, and, in the process, to transform the colony. She writes to convince Spain to allow some measure of freedom to Cuba, to recognize the island's treasures represented by the land and its peoples. She uses some of Cuba's best writers to add the native perspective she cannot lend her narrative. In spite of it, trapped in the web of her own shifting identity, Mercedes Merlin remains a European to the Creoles and a Creole to the Europeans.

Yet, letter XXV, as many others in *La Havane,* point to a subtext. There is in Merlin's nostalgic and hyperbolic memories a desperate attempt to bridge the two worlds, the two languages, while remaining firmly anchored in her privileged position as an adopted European. Perhaps not unlike the Inca Garcilaso at the beginning of the seventeenth century, she tries to validate Havana by comparing it to Paris, and in many instances by judging it superior in spite of its colonial status. Not only is Merlin reaffirming her voice within an American literary tradition, but, more problematically, she is also consciously disseminating a falsely embellished image of her native land to maintain its colonial status; an image that has, to some extent, prevailed in shaping the new mythologies with which Europeans make sense of the Americas.

The uneasy alliances that Merlin has created for herself in her travel narrative point to the conflictive nature of the relation between colonizer and colonized. This tension and ambiguity about the motives and the legitimacy of the Countess was brought to light by the Cuban intellectuals of the time who did not know how to evaluate Merlin's position regarding Cuba. First, she was received with accolades for her published work as a "hija de la Habana" (daughter of Havana). Once on Cuban soil, the warmth turned to icy irony when Cubans were forced to look at themselves through European-colored glasses. The images of colonial society, imperfect as they were, reminded them of all that was wrong in Cuba. And it was an outsider and a woman who did so at a time when the ferment of independence was already gaining ground.

The Countess of Merlin allows us to take into account the dissonant discourse of her imperialist ideology and her avowed longing to belong to the island. It is perhaps because of this unresolved tension that *La Havane* succeeds as a personal narrative, a travel, and a metaphor for the conflictive beginnings of the new American nations.

NOTES

1. Parts of this article have appeared in "Slavery in the Spanish Colonies: The Racial Politics of the Countess of Merlin." In *Reinterpreting the Spanish American Essay: Women Writers of the 19th and 20th Centuries.* Edited by Doris Meyer (Austin, TX: University of Texas Press, 1995), 37–45.

2. Sylvia Molloy, *At Face Value. Autobiographical Writing in Spanish America* (Cambridge: Cambridge University Press, 1991), 82–83. Molloy observes that "la petite histoire," that is, the personal narrative of childhood and family life, is relegated during this period to the margins of the autobiographical discourse. The first autobiographical works of Mercedes de Santa Cruz y Montalvo illustrate the inclusion of the self into the history of the island in order to weave a national/personal identity that will evolve throughout her works.

3. Mercedes Santa Cruz y Montalvo, Condesa de Merlín, *La Havane* (Paris: Librairie d'Amyot, 1844). Translated into Spanish as *Viaje a La Habana* (La Habana: Editorial de Arte y Literatura, 1974). All English translations are mine. Page references are to the 1974 Spanish edition and appear in parentheses in the text. It has been noted by several critics (Salvador Bueno, Domingo Figarola Caneda) that the financial gains derived from the publication of these volumes and their possible translations were the principal reason for their existence. In her private correspondence with her lover, Philarète Chasles, Merlin bitterly complains about her financial woes. However, to reduce the Countess' production of literary works to a mercenary cause would be to overlook the early attraction that literature and the world of ideas held in Merlin's life.

4. For an interesting study on the issues of travel, gender, and imperialism, see Alison Blunt's treatment of the English nineteenth-century traveler Mary Kingsley, *Travel, Gender, and Imperialism: Mary Kingsley and West Africa* (New York: The Guilford Press, 1994).

5. Blunt, 10.

6. Adriana Méndez Rodenas has lucidly written about the impulse toward "Cubanness" in Merlin in "Voyage to *La Havane:* The Countess of Merlin's Preview of National Identity." *Cuban Studies* 16 (1986): 71–99; and "A Journey to the (Literary) Source: The Invention of Origins in Merlin's *Viaje a La Habana.*" *New Literary History* 21:3 (Spring 1990): 707–731.

7. Merlin's works were translated into Spanish or English shortly after their publication in French. *Mes douze premières années* was translated by Agustín

de Palma in 1838; her *Les loisirs d'une femme du monde* was translated into English as *Memoirs of Madame Malibran*. The Countess herself was in the process of translating *La Havane* into English and considering a German version according to her correspondence with her lover and collaborator Philarète Chasles. Domingo Figarola-Caneda, in his volume dedicated to the Countess, *La condesa de Merlín* (Paris: Editions Excelsior, 1928), lists the translations and editions of Merlin's works he consulted in the libraries of Madrid, Paris, Brussels, London, Milan, and Berlin. Salvador Bueno corrects some of Figarola-Caneda's errors in "Una escritora habanera de expresión francesa." In *De Merlín a Carpentier* (La Habana: Unión de Escritores y Artistas de Cuba, 1977).

8. See Robert Paquette's study on the slave uprising known as "La conspiración de la escalera": *Sugar is Made with Blood: The Conspiracy of La Escalera and the Conflict Between Empires over Slavery in Cuba* (Middletown, CT: Wesleyan University Press, 1988).

9. Letter XX of *La Havane* appeared in the *Revue de Deux Mondes* as "Observations de Madame la Comtesse de Merlin sur l'état des esclaves dans les colonies espagnoles" [Observations by the Countess of Merlin on the Conditions of Slaves in the Spanish Colonies], and it was translated into Spanish and English shortly after the French publication. For a more detailed analysis of this essay and the question of abolition and slave trade in the Caribbean, see Claire Martin's "Slavery in the Spanish Colonies: The Racial Politics of the Countess of Merlin." In *Reinterpreting the Spanish American Essay*.

10. Mary Louise Pratt, *Imperial Eyes. Travel, Writing and Transculturation* (London: Routledge, 1992). Subsequent references will appear in parentheses in the text.

11. Blunt, 17.

12. Blunt, 18.

13. Georges Van Den Abbeele, *Travel as Metaphor: From Montaigne to Rousseau* (Minneapolis: University of Minnesota, 1992), xxvi.

14. Adriana Méndez Rodenas, in chapter 3 of *Gender and Nationalism in Colonial Cuba: The Travels of Santa Cruz y Montalvo, Condesa de Merlin* (Nashville, TN: Vanderbilt University Press, 1998) discusses the trope of discovery in Merlin's narrative.

15. Included in *Slaves, Sugar & Colonial Society. Travel Accounts of Cuba, 1801-1899*. Edited by Louis A. Pérez (Wilmington, DE: SR Books, 1992), 2.

16. Included in Pérez, 5.

17. Included in Pérez, 15. Merlin would find a kindred soul in the twentieth century in Alejo Carpentier's defense of the narrow, badly traced streets of Havana in *La ciudad de las columnas* (1970).

18. Like Alvar Núñez Cabeza de Vaca, Esteban Echeverría, Andrés Bello and all of those who write about entering into the "contact zone," the indigenous,

the black and mulatto elements are first perceived through sound as dissonant notes, as a chaotic noise that disrupts the harmony of nature. See José Piedra's discussion of Cabeza de Vaca's *Castaways* in this volume.

19. See Figarola-Caneda, *La condesa de Merlín,* 160-177.

20. Figarola-Caneda, 168.

21. Méndez Rodenas, *Gender and Nationalism,* 94-95.

22. All the quotations of Letter XXV to George Sand are taken from my translation of the text that appears in *Rereading the Spanish American Essay: Translations of 19th and 20th Century Women's Essays.* Edited by Doris Meyer (Austin, TX: University of Texas Press, 1995), 9-22.

23. Blunt, 30.

24. See *Writing, Women and Space: Colonial and Postcolonial Geographies.* Edited by Alison Blunt and Gillian Rose (New York: The Guilford Press, 1994), 30.

25. *Correspondencia Intima de la Condesa de Merlín.* Edited by Domingo Figarola-Caneda. Translated by Boris Bureba (Madrid, Paris: n.p., 1928), 54-55.

Chapter 8

TRAVELS AND IDENTITIES IN THE CHRONICLES OF THREE NINETEENTH-CENTURY CARIBBEAN WOMEN

Aileen Schmidt

Translated by Lizabeth Paravisini-Gebert

The labor of rescuing forgotten women's voices and experiences, and the analysis of the feminine imaginary, are—for those of us for whom literature is a scholarly discipline—not only professional obligations but above all political and ideological commitments. During the last three years I have dedicated my research to the investigation of the autobiographical discourses of Puerto Rican and Cuban women of the nineteenth and twentieth centuries, from which work stems this exploration of their incursions into travel literature, examined here from within the perspective of gender ideology and the autobiographical stance. I am interested, above all, in how women's literary expression is determined by cultural representations of sexual difference and by the hierarchies of power and influence that these differentiations produce in social life. I am particularly motivated by the need to formulate new evaluations of the autobiographical text to challenge the premises of universality and representativity that characterize male autobiography.

Narrated life can adopt a multiplicity of forms: the classical autobiography, diaries, letters, chronicles and narratives of travel, memoirs, testimonies, and oral histories. For women in particular, the practice of autobiographical writing is an exercise in freedom. Writing about themselves and their lives represents the validation of a discursive authority that allows for public self-interpretation within the patriarchal culture, a way to exercise new instances of power. Autobiography unveils a desire for transgression: in narrating their experiences, women assume control of their own self-representation, ceasing thereby to continue being represented solely by the objectifying male gaze.[1] Self-representation is one form of inscribing the female subject: transgressing its historical marginality, it affirms itself as an agent of language and history. The most notable aspect of female autobiographical writing is that it serves as a vehicle for women's assertion of themselves as subjects conscious of their own history.

As in all travel literature, travel chronicles propitiate the expression of women's voices, voices so often silenced or distorted. To have a voice is to insert oneself into history. Autobiographical writing offers a space to validate women's knowledge. The articulation of the experience of travel through letters, memoirs, chronicles, and diaries constitutes a transgressive gesture: the subjectivity that writes and writes itself affirms itself through writing. The chronicler positions herself as owner and possessor of her reality, and from her consciousness of herself as a traveler assumes authority over the experiences that will inform her account. The narrative of her experiences is a form of self-knowledge, of understanding herself, and, consequently, of self-validation. The narrating subject constructs itself as it gives an account of its passage through the world, of its travels. The female traveler situates herself by her own will in history; she claims for herself a protagonist's role that the "official history" has denied her because of her gender.

The expression of women travelers in Our America has manifested itself in the form of chronicles, letters, diaries, novels, and memoirs. When we examine the nineteenth century, we find women who dared not only to travel, but to relate their experiences. They are the forgers of a literary tradition that deserves our attention and that finds its precursors in Peruvian writer Flora Tristán, author of *Peregrinaciones de una paria* (Pilgrimages of a Paria, 1838) and the Argentinean Eduarda Mansilla de García, whose *Recuerdos de viaje* (Memories of Travel) was published in 1882. Among the many Cuban women writing about their travels, we find the Countess of Merlin, author of *Viaje a La Habana* (Voyage to Havana, 1844), María Luisa Dolz, author of three travelogues, *Visita a la Exposición de Chicago* (Visit to the Chicago Exposition, 1893), *Visita a la Exposición de París* (Visit to the Paris Exposition, 1901), and *Viaje a Alemania y la Exposición de Lieja* (Voyage to Germany and the Liege Exposition, 1906). This tradition is bolstered in the twentieth century by the writings of Renée Méndez Capote, whose *Hace muchos años, una joven viajera . . .* (Many years ago, a young woman traveler . . .) was published in 1893; Ofelia Rodríguez Acosta, author of *Europa era así. Crónicas de viaje* (Europe was like this. A Chronicle of Travel, 1941); Teté Casuso, author of *Recuerdos de un viaje a Europa* (Memories of a trip to Europe, 1951) and *Panorama de México* (Panorama of Mexico, 1938); and Dulce María Loynaz, author of *Un verano en Tenerife* (A Summer in Tenerife, 1958), among others. We also have published accounts by European and North American women who traveled to Latin America and the Caribbean, including Maria Calcott Graham, Mary Nugent, Fanny Erskine Inglis, Fredrika Bremer, Louisa Mathilde Woodruff, and Margherite Arlina Hamm.

The works of Cuban travelers Aurelia Castillo de González and Catalina Rodríguez de Morales, and of Puerto Rican poet Lola Rodríguez de Tió, on whom I wish to focus here, articulate the reformulation of their personal experiences through letters and chronicles that construct identities mediated by the circumstances of exile. The common element in their writing is that of forced migration, the political exile that separates them from their everydayness. Each of them will approach her situation differently. Their works articulate with equal determination a national identity and an artistic/literary identity: they write as women anchored in their Cubanness and Puerto Ricanness.

Castillo de González, Rodríguez de Morales, and Rodríguez de Tió not only recount their experiences as travelers; as they narrate, they simultaneously configure their identities. Even though the particular circumstances of their exiles differ, the cause is essentially the same: the repressive practices of Spanish colonialism. In exile, national identity and gender identity become sites of struggle for these women. Their subjectivities constitute themselves from within the various discourses available in their particular historical moment and, as result, must confront systems of power of diverse forms—political, economic, social, cultural, and domestic.

In these contexts, writing evolves into a space of freedom that represents, without doubt, an exercise in decolonization, both public and social. Castillo de González, Rodríguez de Morales, and Rodríguez de Tió validate themselves even from their political and gender marginality, which is why the act of narrating their lives is an instance of power, an act of resistance. Rodríguez de Tió assumes herself as a political woman, as a creator of culture, always from a position of national affirmation. Writing from a contestatory identity, she always positions herself at the point of resistance. Castillo de González and Rodríguez de Morales are more careful, as we will see in their texts, but no less firm. The three authors were exiled for political reasons, and their writings were significantly affected by their exile. Active in the literary, cultural, and political activities of their period, they challenged the feminine paradigms of their society, paradigms anchored in patriarchal notions that destined women to the roles of mother and wife.

A glance at the texts that served as models for the education of women in the nineteenth century allows us to understand how the differences that defined the situation of women and justified their subordination were configured and institutionalized. Thus, for example, in the second half of the century, the Gobierno Superior Político de la Isla de Cuba demanded the use of "Cartas sobre la educación del bello sexo" (Letters on the education of the beautiful sex) to help form "the future women of the nation,"[2] emphasizing the observance of moral rules and domestic duties, and restricting women to the home.

Evelyn Picón Garfield has identified two Spanish treatises of the sixteenth century as the source of the dominant ideas on the condition of women in Spain and its colonies: *Instrucción de la mujer cristiana* (The instruction of the Christian woman, 1528) by Juan Luis Vives, and *La perfecta casada* (The perfect married woman, 1583) by Fray Luis de León.[3] Nineteenth-century Cuban newspapers (those addressed to a feminine audience, such as *La Moda o Recreo Semanal del Bello Sexo, Guirnalda Cubana,* and *El Almendares*) offered them as authorities in the definition of virtuous conduct in women. Both authors considered women to be the cause of all the evil and sin in the world, and, as a consequence, advocated their confinement to the home. They insisted on the undesirability of a broad and thorough education for women, arguing that they only required the learning of such notions as would allow them to become honest mothers. They deemed women to be physically, intellectually, and morally inferior to men. Other authors from the nineteenth century, such as the Spaniards Severo Catalina, Francisco Alonso y Rubio, and the Cuban Manuel Costales, all widely read in Cuba, echoed these notions of women's intellectual and physical inferiority in their writings.

The prominent figure of Gertrudis Gómez de Avellaneda, novelist, poet, dramatist, and journalist—the most prolific and best-known Hispanic writer of her time—signaled an exception and a rupture with that misogynistic tradition. She founded and edited (between February and August 1860) the bimonthly *Album Cubano de lo Bueno y lo Bello* (Cuban album of the good and beautiful), the first Cuban publication published by a woman, the pages of which she used to argue in favor of a recognition of women's far-ranging capabilities, particularly in two series of articles written by Gómez de Avellaneda herself: "Galería de Mujeres Célebres" (Gallery of Celebrated Women) and "La Mujer" (Woman).

The situation in the Puerto Rican press was not much different: the first publications addressed to a feminine audience (*Guirnalda Puertorriqueña. Periódico de amena literatura y modas. Dedicado al Bello Sexo,* 1856, and *La Azucena,* 1870) validated women's traditional roles and posited the feminine tropes of the era. Their discourse in defense of morality and domesticity will find its counterpart in the publications directed by Ana Roqué de Duprey, suffragist, feminist leader, prolific author (she cultivated various genres and fields), and founder and editor of various newspapers for women published between 1894 and 1918. In these publications she voiced her ideal of female emancipation, argued in favor of women's suffrage, and, in their production (from writing to typesetting and printing), employed a predominantly female staff.

Aurelia Castillo de González (born in Camaguey, 1842-1920)—known in Cuba as "our Madame de Sévigné,"[4]—poet, prose writer, and typographer—was also a biographer and editor of the works of Gertrudis Gómez de Avellaneda. Her chronicles of travel were published originally in the newspaper *El País* (1887-1891 and 1893) and appeared later in book form as *Un paseo por Europa* (A voyage through Europe, 1891) and *Un paseo por América* (A voyage through America, 1895), both published in Havana. The author gathered her writings and incorporated texts by other authors related to her life and work for the edition of her complete works, *Escritos de Aurelia Castillo de González* (Writings of Aurelia Castillo de González), of which 60 copies were printed in 1913. The six volumes of her collected works gather reviews, prologues and book introductions, chronicles, poems, fables, and essays on social themes, among which those dealing with women and social justice figure prominently. A text dedicated to Lola Rodríguez de Tió, to whom she was bound by close ties of friendship, "Para las *Cartas a Lola*" (For the Letter to Lola, 1894), bears particular mention in this context.

Aurelia Castillo was a cultural figure of great significance—among her many accomplishments, she was named honorary member or president of various literary societies and centers, in addition to being a member of the Academia Nacional de Artes y Letras de Cuba. A woman of the vanguard, "she distinguished herself in activities traditionally reserved for men: she was an active contributor to newspapers, which was in itself a challenge to colonial conventions; she interested herself in philosophical polemics, not in a passive manner, but actively participating in debates in lyceums and salons."[5] A victim of the historical situation of the colony, she was sent into exile on two occasions. In 1875 her husband, a Spanish military officer, was repatriated to Spain as a result of his public protest against the death by firing squad of a Cuban patriot. From this first exile they returned to Cuba at the end of the Ten-Year War. In 1896 her activities in support of Cuban independence took her once again into exile. After this second banishment she lived in the Canary Islands and Barcelona, before returning to Cuba in November of 1989.

Catalina Rodríguez de Morales (born in Madruga, 1857-1894) was the first Cuban woman to win first prize in a literary contest. Her poem "Oda al Trabajo" (Ode to work) was the winner of the 1865 Juegos Florales (Literary Contest) of Matanzas. Following the trajectory mapped by the celebrated Gertrudis Gómez de Avellaneda, she also headed the publication of an important journal in Matanzas, *El Album: Revista Quincenal de Literatura, Ciencias, Bellas Artes e Intereses Generales* (The Album: bi-monthly review of literature, the sciences, the arts, and general topics). In her "Introducción," the segment that serves as a prologue to the first issue of *El Album,* Rodríguez de Morales offers what amounts practically to a feminist manifesto in which she argues in favor of the education of women and defends their participation in the press:

> Here we are ready to struggle against the diverse aggravations that journalism entails in Cuba. . . . In former times, which we could properly refer to as the iron age, it was enough for us to be instructed in matters pertaining to the domestic sphere in order to have us believe that we could thus fulfill our mission in the world; this is what men demanded of us. . . . In *El Album,* we will have much to say about this issue, presenting studies about women in Europe and the United States, countries which, without doubt, have reached a degree of illustration much superior to ours.[6]

The chronicles of her travels through Colombia in 1875 were published in the "Páginas íntimas" section of *El Album* (1881-1882), under the title "Impresiones de viaje." In them she narrates her hazardous voyage on the

Magdalena River on her way to Bogotá. In addition to her poetic and jour-
nalistic work, she wrote a comedy of manners (*Hijo único*/Only son, 1884)
and the *Libro de las Niñas* (The girls' book, 1891, conceived as a collection
of readings adapted for girls attending elementary schools).

The travel writings of Lola Rodríguez de Tió (born in San Germán, 1843-
1924), considered Puerto Rico's most notable female literary and political
figure of the late nineteenth and early twentieth centuries, appeared in the
newspapers *La Crónica* (Caracas, 1877, 1878), *El Eco de Las Lomas* (San Germán, 1880), *La Patria* (New York, 1898), *La Provincia* (Havana, 1900), and
other Cuban and Puerto Rican publications, as well as in her published
diary. A pioneer in many fields, she was the first woman to address a public audience in Puerto Rico, having, in 1873, given the graduation speech
at a college in Mayagüez.[7] A poet and pro-independence fighter, her travel
chronicles are intimately linked to her situation as a political exile. She was
banished from her home island for the first time in 1877. Her husband,
Bonocio Tió, was exiled for having denounced the iniquities of the Spanish Governor of Puerto Rico. She lived for three years in Caracas—where
she acted as matron of honor at Eugenio María de Hostos's wedding—
before returning to Mayagüez. Her second "destierro" (in Spanish, literally,
"uprooting," the term she preferred) took place in 1889, when the couple
went to live in Havana. While in Cuba she and her husband participated
intensely in cultural and political activities, going as far as helping José
Martí in his struggle for Cuban independence by hiding weapons in their
home in Havana. They lived in Havana until 1885, when she again had to
go into exile when she was accused of sedition by the Cuban government.
She traveled then to New York, where she collaborated with the Partido
Revolucionario Cubano and was elected president of the Rius Rivera
Club, whose members were Cuban and Puerto Rican expatriates. In New
York she found a very solid Antillean community. It must be remembered
that since 1860, some young Puerto Rican professionals, members of the
enlightened elite who supported the pursuit of economic and social
reforms, had begun to seek voluntary exile in New York after the failure
of their endeavors. Others, victims of official repressions, had come to
New York after being deported. There was in New York at the time great
revolutionary effervescence among Cuban and Puerto Rican patriots,
whose numbers were swelled by other Latin American exiles. Rodríguez
de Tió and her husband remained in New York until they returned to
Cuba in 1899. There, she consolidated her position as an intellectual figure
of note and lived until her death in 1924. She traveled on occasion to

Puerto Rico, but her sojourns in her home island were always brief—the longest having taken place in 1915, when she remained for five months.

The popularity of Romanticism in Europe in the second half of the nineteenth century offered women more alternatives for self-expression. The exploration of subjectivity unquestionably propitiated women's participation in the literary world. Authors as important as Mary Shelley, Madame de Staël, and George Sand became models for Spanish, Cuban, and Puerto Rican women just beginning to publish their work. The discourse of Romanticism favored autobiographical writing since it considered the representation of the individual subject, distancing it from the paradigms of rationalism, uniformity, and order. Personal experience, axis of the outer gaze, is articulated from the subjective as a characteristic element of Romantic literature. In validating the individual subject, Romanticism likewise valued originality, diversity, and freedom, both personal and creative. Truth would no longer be objective, but personal and entirely subjective. In Romantic aesthetics, emotions and the imagination are the vehicles for the expression of intimacy. The creative process develops out of the relationship between consciousness, experience, imagination, and the representation of the self, in a dialectics of continuous formulation and reformulation of identities.

By definition, all narrative discourse presupposes elements of fiction. Chronicles of travel are sometimes considered a type of fiction, but they are a different sort of fiction, incorporating both history and the imagination. The narrator's memory is always selective in its remembrances. Fictionalizing is founded precisely on this process of selection. Consciousness situates itself in the present to interpret the experiences of the past. Both what the consciousness decides to exclude and its interpretation of that which it wishes to make public will inform the representation of that life. Writing itself, constructing itself, the subject creates and recreates itself, anchored at all times in the historical spaces inhabited by these women chroniclers. The subject's history is always that of a concrete life.

Through the narrative of their experiences, these authors elaborate the self-representation of personal experience, and, simultaneously, their self-interpretation. In travel literature, fictionalization dialogues with the "true and objective" narrative of events. It is not a matter of simply narrating events, but of articulating the past through selective memory and reproducing some incidents through language. The narrative subject matter of all chronicles will always be informed by the tangents between the imagination, desire, fantasy, and experience. These tensions condition the instances of representation in which writers of autobiographies inscribe themselves. It is through—and starting from—these dialectics that they construct themselves as protagonists, narrators, and authors. It is precisely the dialectics that empower the validation of feminine subjectivity, the instrument and at the same time the product of autobiographical writing, and which operate against the grain of the social structures that have limited women's participation in literature. Dialectics that feed literature, produce knowledge, and constitute a taking of power; a creative response and a site of struggle against historic limitations; dialectics that allow these writers, consequently, to redefine the boundaries that patriarchal culture has imposed on their identities.

The autobiographical subject constitutes itself from a variety of positionings, practices, and levels of representation. There is not one single and unique way to articulate it—to pretend such a thing would be to homogenize the differences between women. A narrated life is always an interpretation of personal experience, a system of signification on which the narrative structure is mounted. The subject is constructed discursively, but above all historically. In the chronicle of travel, as in all autobiographical discourse, textuality is nourished by personal history. It is a concrete life that is narrated and interpreted, enriched by the imagination of the protagonist/narrator. The personal and unique vision of women's everyday practices is the most notable resource of all types of autobiographical writing. As Begoña Huertas has argued, "the gaze centered on the details of domesticity and everydayness rescues not the evident, distinctive aspect of events, but their subjective hues."[8]

These "subjective hues" are precisely the gaze I wish to privilege. Women's travel chronicles emphasize the unique and personal perception, a particular form of feeling and experiencing reality. The referentiality of the world of men has always been imposed upon women in a further effort to limit them. Domesticity and everydayness is the space in which the structures of domination affirm themselves with greater force. The decision to narrate their lives is an instance of rupture with the diverse manifestations of patriarchal control—the affirmation that their lives themselves and the narratives that they construct around them are of value.

The chronicle of travel is not merely a discourse of the private sphere: the subjective articulates material, historical, and economic relationships.[9] Self-representation is a fundamentally political issue: we are dealing with an identity that is articulated against the authority and privilege of patriarchal society. Identity is not merely a rhetorical artifice, but rather a material and historical subject that assumes itself as such. The chronicler legitimizes antihegemonic spaces through a strategy of affirmation of her subjectivity. Writing becomes a contestatory practice, a seizure of power for the protagonist/narrator who, from the will of her consciousness, assumes control of her life and decides to interpret it, breaking the literary and cultural barriers against her gender. Narrating oneself is an affirmation of power.

Chronicles of travel were a very popular vehicle for the expression of subjectivity in Our America throughout the nineteenth century. Despite the abundant corpus of chronicles written by women, their narratives have not received much attention. The exclusion of women from the canon of travel literature (Homer, Herodotus, Lord Byron, Alexander von Humboldt, Domingo Faustino Sarmiento, and others) is another instance of gender oppression. Female chroniclers in most instances do not position themselves as witnesses to history, nor do they present their lives as paradigms, as male chroniclers do; they seek rather to give the reading public a unique vision—that of their personal experience. What is truly notable is the desire to present subjectivity, to display their perception of the world, and not the voyage in and of itself.

Lola Rodríguez de Tió, like Aurelia Castillo de González and Catalina Rodríguez de Morales, wrote many of her travel accounts in the form of letters. The use of letters as a means of expression proper to women is a tradition dating back to the Middle Ages, to which critics like Olga Kenyon attribute an 800-year history.[10] Since the sixteenth century, letters have become an instrument allowing for the calling of attention to women's needs. Among the functions fulfilled by letters, Kenyon mentions those of informing, educating, discussing philosophical themes, serving as entertainment for relatives and friends with descriptions of domesticity and society, spreading news, offering accounts of travel, giving advice, and maintaining personal and familiar affective relationships (ix). This plurality of themes and styles turns these letters into multivalent discourses. As thus they can be conversational, descriptive, dramatic, philosophical, spiritual, or propagandistic letters, but they are always transgressive, since they emerged from the margins of the great narratives of history, offering the inscription of a marginal, non-authoritarian, antihegemonic subject.

Lola Rodríguez de Tió's prose has not received the same attention that has been given to her poetry. Even less attention has been given to her autobiographical texts,[11] her chronicles and impressions of travel, and pages of her diary, published almost in its entirety in Cuba, Venezuela, and New York. The predominant trait in her autobiographical writing is the expression of a clear and combative national consciousness, a conviction that in her times had heroic dimensions. The affirmation and defense of the independence of Puerto Rico is the impetus for all of her actions and the constant inspiration for her writing. In her life and discourse there is a clear interaction of the private and public subjects—both spaces complement each other. Rodríguez de Tió's discourse is always political, but it is also always emotional and intimate. She writes with the language of sentiment. The affective gesture is the conduit for her deeply rooted revolutionary spirit. Her discourse is anchored in feminine interiority and thus enriches the public debate of her age with a new language, a different expression from those of the authorized voices of public men, of the leaders and politicians of reputation. Rodríguez de Tió's project constructs the nation from within personal and intimate space. Thus she writes with tenderness about her daughter and tells with emotion about her unconditional support of her husband, while in the same text she assumes herself as a patriotic fighter and situates herself as an active agent in social movements.

In Rodríguez de Tió's writings, the word nation (*patria*) is the emotional, discursive, and political axis (she even named her daughter Patria). The expression of her love for her nation is always exalted, poetic, and painful, not only by reason of her exiles, but as a reaction to Puerto Rico's condition of political subordination. She writes with anguish in her letters of her "expatriación"[12] and "proscripción,"[13] while in other texts written from New York and Havana she speaks of emigration, exile, and uprootedness.[14] Of her first exile, en route to La Guaira, Venezuela, and "overcome by the most profound sadness," she writes:

> The nostalgic ache begins to invade me and despondency takes a hold of me . . . the contemplation of the land which during other voyages had brought a mysterious happiness to my soul this time will be a reason for sadness because it will come to remind me that they are not the shores of my native island. . . . [T]hat remains behind with all its charms and memories. To think that the mercilessness of fate can hide them from me forever . . . possessed by pain, my constant companion since I left Puerto Rico.[15]

Her travel chronicles of Venezuela, "the nation of spirit and intellect," gather what the author calls "impressions" in which she manifests her admiration for the free and sovereign country.[16] Rodríguez de Tió recognizes its "social progress" and its "feast of civilization" as the natural expression of a free and happy people.[17] This modern gaze appears also in the writings of Aurelia Castillo de González, who celebrates the "progress" of Europe and the United States. Rodríguez de Tió's trip to Mexico, which took place when she was very young, years later merited "a delicious page of memories for my soul, always open to the sweet emotions of reverie!"[18] Once again we observe the recognition of the "progress" of an American nation. Her admiration for Mexican literature and her emotion before the spectacular nature of the landscape conform her memory of "one of the most beautiful regions of America." It is of interest that in this text the Romantic imagination, eloquent in the exaltation of the emotions, ardent in its description of nature, and poetic in its longing and nostalgia for the indigenous past, dialogues freely with the modern gaze of the author, that which allows her to appreciate the virtues of development and celebrate the cultural advances of modernity (in literature, science, and journalism).

Her Americanist and Antilleanist consciousness, which earned her Antonio Maceo's comment that "with women like Lola revolutions could be made," is clearly observable in her chronicles about Venezuela, Cuba, Mexico, and Puerto Rico, in which her love for Latin American history and culture are evident. It manifests itself equally in her everyday occupations: in Cuba, for example, she was a recognized writer and cultural figure, a contributor to the principal publications of the period. Her home was a popular gathering place for literary debates. In Caracas, she had distinguished herself as an inspector of private schools, a position to which she was appointed by the country's president, and was an elected member of the Academy of Arts and Letters. During the time she lived in Caracas, she published admiring commentary on Venezuelan social reality. Thus, for example, she celebrates "all the spectacles, all the works of art and social welfare which signal in this most beautiful portion of the Latin American continent a step in the magnificent path towards social progress . . . in this most agreeable city of Avila, which has welcomed our proscription with truly fraternal feelings."[19] She declared on more than one occasion than in Venezuela she found "a new homeland." We must not forget that Rodríguez de Tió, in open opposition to Spanish colonial repression, wrote the patriotic verses of the *danza* "La Borinqueña," a version of the Puerto Rican national anthem known as the "revolutionary" anthem.

Cuban chroniclers Catalina Rodríguez de Morales and Aurelia Castillo de González narrate their travels through Switzerland, France, Italy, Mexico, the United States, and Colombia. The latter travels with her husband, retired from military life since 1878, and publishes her impressions in the form of letters that give testimony to her ample culture and the broad variety of her interests. Her chronicles are marked by her artistic temperament; one is surprised in reading them by the delight in detail, the sophisticated appreciation of all art objects, the inspired gaze that meets all new spaces. The structure of *Un paseo por Europa* gathers the letters published originally in *El País* (in which she narrates her impressions of France, Italy, and Switzerland), together with a handful of poems and a section called "De Regreso" (Upon my return), written in 1891 after her return to Cuba, and in which she hurls a strong invective against the Spanish government and the demoralization of Cuban society for which she held it responsible. The letters on the Americas were published for the first time in *El País* and later in the *Revista Cubana*. The 1895 book includes ten letters on Veracruz, Mexico, Toluca, San Luis Potosí, San Antonio, St. Louis, and Chicago.

Castillo de González's chronicles cover a more extensive period of time than those of Rodríguez de Morales, which are limited to a single trip to one country. Castillo de González traveled more extensively, hence the broader discursive scope and historical spaces her writing encompasses, which afford her greater opportunities to editorialize and reflect on a historical figure or event. On the other hand, Rodríguez de Morales' chronicles are centered on the narration of a specific, dangerous, concentrated experience. Her narrative is more dramatic, more urgent, more immediate. The author always assumes herself as an exile, a reluctant traveler, contrary to Castillo, who positions herself always as the acute commentator, the free and tranquil voyager who enjoys fully the experience of her tour, of her "paseo," as the titles of her collections of chronicles accurately describe.

Both writers wish to be read, but, above all, they wish to be believed. They proclaim the authenticity of their stories, insisting in the sincerity of their emotions. Anecdotes, emotions, and reflections are intertwined in their texts. Thus Rodríguez de Morales will describe with surprising minuteness the variety of flora and fauna between Barranquilla and Honda, taking care to document each detail of her voyage on the steam ship *Tequendama*. Castillo de González, conscious that her duty as a chronicler is that of relating her "impressions of travel," tells us that she "is in the habit of sending notices about what she sees to a newspaper" and "every nation, every city she visits, if one is to write about them, should be considered in its distinctive character."[20]

As opposed to Rodríguez de Tió, they assume the discourses of femininity of their times: both configure themselves, before all else, as wives, insisting always on the fact that they do not travel alone, but are accompanied by their husbands. The use of "we" is not a mere artifice of the narrative voice, but reveals their social and moral placement. If they are indeed protagonists and chroniclers, the husbands are defining figures of their identities as women. In the same way, there appear in their letters other tropes of femininity, such as modesty, sentimentalism, attention to detail, and sensitivity to the sufferings of others.

The contradiction between their realities as travelers and writers and their self-positioning as dedicated wives, "ladies of the house," becomes quite revealing. They are audacious women who subvert tradition, although they never question openly the parameters that limit women's lives. Aurelia Castillo celebrates the advances made by women in the United States, but does not denounce the subordination of women in Cuba.[21] Despite the fact that they are both educated, cosmopolitan women of great sophistication, they fail to address their own situation critically, which confirms how difficult it is for women to disengage from the discursive practices of their historical moment. Aurelia Castillo, for example, celebrates the advances of women in the United States and expresses her admiration for the fashions, usages, and everyday practices of North American women, but never openly denounces the oppression of women in her own country. Instead, she comments obliquely on the difference in the perception of women in both societies.

> What a pleasure it is to see women here driving their carriages, either alone or accompanied by a friend or a young daughter! . . . without losing one tiny bit of their reputation, without anyone paying attention to what they are doing, free and happy, and as virtuous and respectable—those who want to be so—as the best and most modest woman in our more reclusive and bothersome conditions.[22]

The extraordinary fact is that the mere act of traveling and writing presupposes a personal conviction that their discourse is important. Thus, their letters reflect their resistance to patriarchy and the constructions of femininity that patriarchy imposes on them, even when that resistance is not articulated consciously. These audacious writers who write about their lives, or, better yet, who write their lives, configure themselves as autobiographers in the process of naming themselves, in the process of defining themselves as object and subject of the narrative. Various forces, not always harmonious, operate in this creative and existential process: the confessional imperative or the need to narrate, the desire to communicate, the self-validation through the affirmation of subjectivity, modesty, silence, self-censure, denial, sublimation, idealization, and other tensions that are the product of the conventions of femaleness signified by gender identity and an androcentric literary canon. The narrative subject matter of her chronicles, as in all autobiographical discourse, will always be informed by the tangents between the imagination, desire, fantasy, and experience.

Thus, for example, when Rodríguez de Morales assumes control of the care of her sick husband, confronting and overcoming the most difficult circumstances (cold, hunger, poverty, solitude, dangers in the jungle, etc.), she cannot disengage herself from the behavioral paradigms of the married woman and assumes a weak and dependent public stance. It is fascinating to discover in her narrative instances of emancipation; examples, despite herself, of her strength and determination.

> My ailing beloved, a thinking man and botanist as he is, was delirious with the discovery of the virtuous plant, and I, not able to dismiss my foolish female fears, was delirious at the perils we were facing, made worse before my eyes by the illness of the only companion on which I counted on such a long voyage through unknown terrain. Each one of us was thus on familiar terrain.[23]

A defender of modernity and admirer of progress, Castillo possesses a modern gaze, while Rodríguez de Morales's gaze is a Romantic one, dazzled by the magnificent nature of the Colombian jungle. There she will live the earthy adventure par excellence, traversing American rivers and jungles, experiencing unknown climates, and facing constant dangers. On the other hand, Castillo, impressed by the universal expositions of the turn of the century in Paris and Chicago, expresses her desire for Latin American nations to embrace the European and North American advances, thereby inserting themselves into modernity. In her voyages she will privilege "modernism" and high culture, elements for which she searches in each city visited.

> The secret of Paris and New York—to mention cities I know well—to attract and retain our attention, consists of the great potentiality for life they exhibit in their constant renovation, in not showing any attachment to what exists from the moment they can replace it with something better.[24]

Her admiration for the vitality of urban centers, for the rapid replacement of ancient and useless structures through architectural and technical renewal as synonymous with modernity, suggests her desire for transformation in Cuban society. Her fascination for modern construction reveals a desire to toss out everything that is obsolete, of shaking the foundations of the patriarchal structures of colonial society, eliminating all barriers to freedom, not only architectural, but political, moral, and social.

An experienced traveler, she always incorporates into her text allusions to different cities and to her frequent travel experiences, nuanced by incisive and profound commentary on philosophical, social, and cultural topics. Her judgments of some historical personalities and events (the French Revolution or the veiled criticism of the metropolis for the paltriness of the exhibits on Cuba, Puerto Rico, and the Philippines in the Spanish Pavilion of the Paris World Exposition)[25] give testimony to a political expression with a liberal bias. Castillo presents herself always as a defender of justice and honor, although occasionally she gives evidence of a trace of racism, especially in her opinion of the indigenous population of Mexico, which surprises because it presents a difficult to understand contradiction given the liberal consciousness otherwise professed by the author.[26] The meaning of judgments such as the following points to a prejudiced vision for which we do not have any explanation other than the dogmatism of the European-derived values adopted by the privileged sectors of Creole society:

> I hate to say this, because they inspire pity in me, but the truth is that they are horrible. Their skin is not so much bronzed as it is almost black, their faces are broad, they have very dark bristles for hair and are of short stature. Besides this, which is already ugly and repugnant, we must add their going around in a perfect state of uncleanliness, half-covered in rags that barely provide any coverage, loaded with children more appalling still than the parents (the fact of children possessing less grace than the parents being so rare), offering dishes of their own peculiar making and begging for alms, always begging, and I suspect that in order to get them they exaggerate their nakedness and that of their children and exhibit, as it is done in other parts of the world, to the detriment of human dignity, their imperfections and sickness.[27]

Like Lola Rodríguez de Tió, however, Castillo's artistic conscience is nurtured by a patriotic conscience: "The person who writes owes to those who pay him the honor of reading him the truth, and the person who loves his homeland owes it any sacrifice."[28] It is a sentiment echoed by

Rodríguez de Tió, who always links the sense of what is beautiful to the search for truth and the struggle for freedom:

> This book that gathers on its white pages my impressions, which tomorrow will be memories consecrated by affection and time, I dedicate to my daughter . . . searching . . . to inscribe between the lines my love for truth, beauty, and that which I love so sweetly, freedom![29]

Aurelia Castillo positions herself as a voice critical of political abuses, of primitivism and social injustice, when she inserts into some of her chronicles commentary of a strong ideological content. On 14 March 1891, she writes from Guanabacoa (a region a short distance from Havana):

> Heavy is the responsibility that falls to the Metropolis, dark enough are the charges that can be brought against it. It brought us slavery; it resisted every possible effort to eradicate it; it brazenly neglected our culture . . . it has made us accustomed to fraud in the administration and despotism in government; it obstinately refuses to recognize this country's coming of age . . .[30]

In 1890, Castillo was returning to Cuba after "three long years of absence." As all exiles, she longed to return to her homeland and her family. She was returning full of admiration for the progress and lifestyles she had observed in European cities, strengthened in her democratic ideals, and with the greatest enthusiasm for transforming Cuban society. Her return was, however, a great disappointment due to the demoralization that plagued the country. In the passage just quoted she denounces the Spanish colonial government for the political, moral, spiritual, and emotional control that keeps Cuba from developing toward the maturity of nationhood. She criticizes Cuba's infantilization as the result of Spanish domination and expresses nostalgia "for freedom, progress, and order." Indifference and frustration had depleted the Cubans' will to struggle, and Castillo finds herself obliged to warn her readers about the dangers of the historical moment through which Cuba is living.

We see, thus, how Castillo, after presenting to her readers a diversity of topics related to her visits to European cities, cannot relinquish her patriotic obligation and ideological positioning, and decides to conclude her chronicle with a warning to her people. She evidences hence the sagacity and courage of a writer who decides to evade no topic, even when doing so can only bring conflict and risk to her personal safety.

Catalina Rodríguez de González presents herself as an involuntary traveler. A victim of political situations she never explains, she finds herself forced into exile with her husband. One must note that this reticence (a sort of self-censorship that provokes some silences in her narratives) about her personal circumstances can be observed also in Castillo de Morales, who was banished on two occasions and who does not mention the fact openly in her chronicles. In her letter of 15 July 1881, Rodríguez de González expresses nostalgia for "the nation and the family," but the certainty of her convictions strengthens her and the majesty of nature helps her forget "the bitter tribulations of my life." She presents herself as a woman accustomed to "the eventualities suffered in exile." In her letter of 15 August 1882 she observes that "they did not know that she had been educated in the school of grief." She sees herself and her husband as "outlawed Cubans," but reticence and fear for their safety impede her articulation of a discourse of clear political content.

Aurelia Castillo presents herself as an experienced and cosmopolitan traveler, one with varied interests, while Catalina Rodríguez assumes herself as an exile, never as a free and unworried traveler. Her letters concentrate on the narration of the dangers her exile entails, privileging a highly emotive voice that gives form to a Romantic narrative. Her account is imbued with anguish, fear, and numbness before a strange and intimidating nature. On different occasions during her voyage the narrative is exoticized by the threat of wild animals (lions, jaguars, monkeys, and crocodiles). These threats are often suddenly followed by moments of astonishment before the exuberant nature, so different from that of her country, and the author's discourse is aglow with marvel and emotion:

> Those immense mountains, those exhausting climbs and descents on which the traveler's life is at the mercy of the legs of the mules who bear them; and above all, the lions and jaguars who roam those regions. The frightful descriptions they had given us of the trip to Santa Fe were capable of forcing anyone less enthusiastic to retreat. . . . The fresh breeze blowing at that moment, the blue and crystalline sky . . . the thick and perfumed vegetation . . . I felt enchanted by the beauties of such wondrous nature, and had forgotten the crocodiles, the snakes, the Guarinó rapids and the dangers of the Andes . . .[31]

This sense of wonder, however, is confined to nature, for as is the case with Castillo, when Rodríguez de Morales has her first contact with

Colombian Indians on a remote "caserío" on the banks of the Magdalena River, her comments bear the burden of a racist attitude imbued from her upbringing in Cuba's pigmentocracy:

> Those Indians of both sexes, unwashed, rough of feature and living in base ignorance, are not to be envied by even the most savage creatures of Creation.[32]

I have already commented on the disdain of Cuban travel chroniclers toward the Other, in this case, the Indian, whom they do not recognize as a part of their historical space or their Latin American reality, and with whom they recognize no link. The alterity due to racial difference was an integral part of the discourse of the Creole class in Cuban society, one of the most complex and unbending sectors of what was by all standards a rigid class structure.

But the welfare and condition of the Latin American Indian was not of primary importance in Rodríguez de Morales' letters, whose greater concern was to articulate the consciousness of an exile who suffers dramatically the loss of her country. This concern is one shared with our other travelers, and recalls the pain and anguish of exile in the texts of Lola Rodríguez de Tió:

> Oh! the sorrows I suffered in that unfortunate voyage have had a great influence on my character, true happiness has never returned to my heart. From then on my soul has been prey to a profound sadness which I have never been able to overcome.[33]

Such sorrow reminds us of that of the Puerto Rican chronicler when faced with the dislocations of exile:

> Exiles, deceits, reversals of fortune that are the result of expatriation . . . nothing was enough to obscure the ideal of freedom that shone in the depths of my conscience with the brilliance of a star . . . overwhelmed by my infinite sadness . . . ![34]

Conclusions

The validation of the feminine subject is the fundamental sign of travel literature written by women. I have attempted to underscore the importance of the travel chronicle as a liberating discourse for women and to recognize at the same time the historical value of personal experience. Women travel writers articulate their identities while they generate their own narrative. The female subject is continuously configuring itself, remaking itself in the practice of thinking, remembering, and writing itself: it continuously creates itself. They are voices that procure the authority of individual experience; as they write, they authorize themselves; they do not have to wait to be authorized by the canon.

The autobiographical narratives of Lola Rodríguez de Tió, Aurelia Castillo de González, and Catalina Rodríguez de Morales are expressions of an antihegemonic literature that allows us to know the female experience of political exile in the nineteenth century. Their discourses on the nation, each different from the other, are examples of how the trajectory of the feminine subject contributes to the formation of a concept of nationhood. The way in which each of them articulates the experience of migration offers us a broad repertoire of signs that defy any homogeneous definition of national and gender identity. Identities are always a space of multiple possibilities, never a fixed or static instance. Chronicles of travel constitute an instance of affirmation for women, one in which they confront the marginality and victimization assigned to them. The literary expression of the private sphere is a proposal for the configuration of the feminine subject, rich in its multiple discursive and political registers.

NOTES

1. See Sidonie Smith's *A Poetics of Women's Autobiography: Marginality and the Fictions of Self-Representation* (Bloomington and Indianapolis: Indiana University Press, 1987).
2. Emilio Godínez, "La mujer cubana y el acceso a la cultura." *Revolución y Cultura* (Marzo, 1979): 37.
3. Evelyn Picón Garfield, "Periodical Literature for Women in Mid-Nineteenth Century Cuba: The Case of Gertrudis Gómez de Avellaneda's *Album Cubano de lo Bueno y lo Bello,*" XV International Congress, Latin American Studies Association, Miami, 1989.
4. Domitila García de Coronado, *Album poético fotográfico de escritoras y poetisas cubanas* (Escrito en 1868 para la señora doña Gertrudis de Avellaneda) (Havana: Imprenta de "El Fígaro, 1926), 137.
5. Denia García Ronda, "Poesía femenina cubana del siglo XIX." In *Mujeres latinoamericanas: Historia y cultura. Siglos XVI al XIX.* Vol. II (Havana/Mexico: Casa de las Américas/Universidad Autónoma Metropolitana-Iztapalapa, 1997), 287-294.

6. Catalina Rodríguez de Morales, "Introducción." *El Album: Revista Quincenal de Literatura, Ciencias, Bellas Artes e Intereses Generales.* Primera Serie, Vol. 1 (15 July 1882): 1.

7. Carmen Leila Cuevas, *Lola de América* (Hato Rey: Ramallo Bros., 1969).

8. Begoña Huertas, *Ensayo de un cambio: La narrativa cubana de los '80* (Havana: Casa de las Américas, 1993), 50.

9. See Linda S. Kaufman, *Special Delivery: Epistolary Modes in Modern Fiction* (Chicago and London: The University of Chicago Press, 1992), xxi.

10. See Olga Kenyon, *800 Years of Women's Letters* (Boston and London: Faber and Faber, 1992). Subsequent references will appear in parentheses in the text.

11. See Lola Rodríguez de Tió, *Obras completas.* Vol. IV (San Juan, P.R.: Instituto de Cultura Puertorriqueña, 1971).

12. Rodríguez de Tió, "Cartas caraqueñas" (June 1877). See *Obras completas.*

13. Rodríguez de Tió, *La Crónica,* June 1877.

14. See letters of 12 October 1898 and 17 June 1900 in *Obras completas.*

15. Rodríguez de Tió, *Obras completas,* 100-102.

16. Rodríguez de Tió, *La Crónica,* 6 September 1878.

17. Rodríguez de Tió, *La Crónica,* 3 April 1878.

18. Rodríguez de Tió, *El Hogar* (Cuba), 18 February 1902.

19. Rodríguez de Tió, *El Hogar* (Cuba), 18 February 1902, 98.

20. Aurelia Castillo de González, *Un paseo por Europa. Cartas de Francia (Exposición de 1889). De Italia y de Suiza, Pompeya (Poemita)* (sic) (Havana: La Propaganda Literaria, 1891).

21. See Castillo's *Un paseo por América. Cartas de Méjico y de Chicago* (Havana: Imprenta La Constancia, 1895), 63-64.

22. Castillo, *Un paseo por América,* 63.

23. Catalina Rodríguez de Morales, "Carta VIII," *El Album* I:7 (15 October 1882): 100.

24. See Castillo's *Un paseo por Europa,* 142.

25. See Castillo's letters of 3 November 1889 and 17 September 1889 in *Un paseo por Europa.*

26. See Castillo's letter of 15 July 1893 in *Un paseo por América.*

27. Castillo, *Un paseo por América,* 41.

28. Castillo, *Un paseo por Europa,* 214.

29. Lola Rodríguez de Tió, *Obras completas,* 63.

30. Castillo, *Un paseo por Europa,* 214,

31. Catalina Rodríguez de Morales, "Impresiones de viaje. Pajinas [sic] íntimas." *El Album* I:1 (15 July 1881): 12-13.

32. Rodríguez de Morales, "Impresiones de viaje. Pajinas [sic] íntimas," 29.

33. Rodríguez de Tió, *Obras completas,* letter of 30 October 1882, 114.

34. Rodríguez de Tió, *Obras completas,*188-189.

Chapter 9

JOURNEYS AND WARNINGS:
NANCY PRINCE'S TRAVELS AS CAUTIONARY TALES FOR AFRICAN AMERICAN READERS

Cheryl Fish

W hen Nancy Gardner Prince stood on the deck of the *Romulus,* leaving Boston for Russia in 1824, she must have felt the presence of all that was divine and terrible as she looked out to sea. A freeborn African American woman from Massachusetts who had worked as a domestic and had been a part of Boston's tight-knit black community, Prince was about to leave the United States for the first time. Her experiences as a traveler—narrated in two travelogues and several shorter pieces—constitute important yet neglected components in the emerging discourse of the Black Atlantic. Her departure from the United States crystallized many important developments in her life that until recently had been silenced, marginalized, or simply ignored by critics and historians. Moreover, her journeys and subsequent accounts of them, as presented in her hybrid travelogues, add a significant gendered dimension to the Black Atlantic tradition and point to a complex narrative strategy through which we can study the transnational agency of black women.

Prince's travels to Russia and Jamaica in the first half of the nineteenth century do not fit the dominant workingman's paradigm of *sailor,* exemplified in fiction by Herman Melville and in nonfiction by freed slave Olaudah Equiano. Nor is Prince's example consistent with the antebellum image of a slave mother who might throw herself overboard because her baby has been sold, like Lucy in *Uncle Tom's Cabin.* Prince did not don a disguise, as did light-skinned Ellen Craft, who "passed" as a white male slave owner accompanied by her husband William as they traveled north in their flight from slavery. Nancy Prince may not have been a slave, but neither did she share the race and class privilege or the absolute sense of security exhibited by Sophia Peabody, a young white New Englander (and the future Mrs. Nathaniel Hawthorne), when she declares herself exhilarated by the freedom and the sea air onboard *The Newcastle* as she traveled to Cuba in 1833 to improve her health.

If all these models fail to account for Nancy Prince's rationale for traveling and for the generic importance of her narratives in the scholarship on transnational cultural studies and Black Atlantic exchange, we must examine what was at stake for her as she journeyed out of New England. For Prince was free to travel away from her home, but did so within the limited parameters of viable social and economic roles open to black women. First, she traveled as a wife—accompanying her husband to Russia, where he was to assume his duties as a Tsarist guard. And then she journeyed as a widow—traveling to Jamaica to do missionary work, to help educate and uplift emancipated Afro-Jamaicans, and raise funds for a manual-labor school for orphans she had planned to establish in Kingston. Of her desire and motivation to leave New England for Jamaica in 1840, she wrote:

> My mind, after the emancipation in the West Indies, was bent upon going to Jamaica. A field of usefulness seemed spread out before me. . . . I hoped that I might aid, in some small degree, to raise up and encourage the emancipated inhabitants, and teach the young children to read and work, to fear God, and put their trust in the Saviour.[1]

Prince's travel narratives include a pamphlet on Jamaica, *The West Indies, Being A Description of the Islands, Progress of Christianity, Education and Liberty Among the Colored Population Generally* (published in Boston in 1841), three self-published editions of *A Narrative of the Life and Travels of Mrs. Nancy Prince* (1850, 1853, and 1856), and several letters to the abolitionist press. These works present us with a complex, cross-cultural discourse on mobility, emigration, and the work of uplift in varying colonial contexts.[2] The slave experience is presented and "troped upon" (in her writing), as part of a dialectic on what it means to be a free and mobile ethical subject with a complex relationship to nationality, class, and public discourse. Prince had strong abolitionist sentiments, and particular incidents in her work point to the contingent nature of freedom for mobile blacks, a freedom contingent on laws, luck, and location. For instance, when her boat was detained in Key West en route from Jamaica to the United States, Nancy

Prince and the other blacks "were obliged to remain on that broken wet vessel" (76) because various laws required free blacks to be put in custody or risk being beaten or enslaved in a Southern state. Thus, as I argue elsewhere, narratives of journeys by freeborn blacks are significant genres through which other experiences and identity formations for Africans in the Diaspora have been produced and read.[3] In this essay, I shall focus on the significance of embedded warnings to African American readers regarding emigration schemes that characterized Prince's hybrid writing about Jamaica, and how her mobility created the various contexts through which I read her interventions.

Nancy Prince was humble about her own contributions and, perhaps as a result, was virtually ignored by her abolitionist peers; her published narratives were advertised in *The Liberator*, for instance, but never reviewed or mentioned. (The neglect is not just a thing of the past; a recent example of groundbreaking scholarly work, Paul Gilroy's *The Black Atlantic* [1993], excludes black women as cultural agents.[4]) I, however, shall claim Prince as a traveler, ethnographer, educator, and evangelist of the greatest importance, one who foresaw transnational alliances between the Americas and Europe emerging out of the work of uplift, alliances that might disrupt certain discourses of racial stereotyping, colonial power, and the mechanisms of slavery, even if she occasionally aligned herself with certain aspects of the Western imperialist tradition.[5] Her evangelical New England voice registers outrage at the scenes of empire and emancipation in Jamaica, taking to task those who fail to live up to her sense of Christian ethics or what she considered to be the democratic ideals of the American Declaration of Independence.

Prince had begun her *Life and Travels* with a brief narrative of her origins, which encompass the American paradox of captivity and escape, slavery and freedom, interracial mixing and the genealogical memory on which to base her claim to ethical American citizenship. Her maternal grandfather, Tobias Wornton, "or Backus, so called . . . was stolen from Africa, when a lad," and was both a slave and a soldier in the Revolutionary Army, serving at the battle of Bunker Hill.[6] An unnamed maternal grandmother, "an Indian of this country . . . became a captive to the English, or their descendants" (5). These opening pages detailing her familial origins also ground Prince's identity as a rational, Enlightenment subject whose "I" is understood as a sovereign individual, an African American "daughter of the American Revolution," whose ancestry and position establish her as a reliable narrator. This knowledge of and pride in one's lineage is commonly missing from slave narratives, which more often than not open with a description of the location where the slave was born, but lack any knowledge of his or her birthdate, and offer little of family history. And in another departure from United States slave narratives, generally written to incite Northern white readers with antislavery sentiments into action in the abolitionist cause, Prince discursively negotiates with a readership that cuts across race and gender, a literate public of black New Englanders and committed white abolitionists.[7] She anticipates and expresses the anxieties that signify the complex realities of her black readers' lives as free subjects who have great advantages over their enslaved brethren, yet as Americans experience racism, discrimination, mob violence, and the threat of enslavement. Just as Harriet Wilson turned to a fictional third-person autobiography for *Our Nig* (1859), Prince uses a hybrid genre—that is, one that intersperses elements from other genres—to address the hypocrisy of Northern whites in their treatment of blacks. But she does so by incorporating a secular travelogue into larger cautionary tales that rely heavily on biblical allegory.

As a person who spent time living and traveling in Russia and Jamaica, Prince positions herself in relation to varying kinds of Otherness. She goes from being an exotic black in a position of relative privilege in St. Petersburg, running her own sewing business and even employing journeywomen in the Tsar's court, to observing and interacting with freed Afro-Jamaicans as a wandering evangelical black American who has to cope with scheming philanthropists, violent rebellions, and the possibility of danger and bodily harm. To account for the varying relationships that Prince constructs for herself in relation to location, institutions, natives, work, and homespaces, I have coined the term "mobile subjectivity." This is a fluid and provisional epistemology from which to advocate individualism within a context of collectivity or intersubjectivity, especially as it relates to being a productive, ethical citizen.[8] Mobile subjectivity contextualizes the narrator's subject position in relation to specific persons, ideologies, locations, and geographical space. Through movement of the body in time and space, temporary dwelling, and locally engaged work, Prince becomes what James Clifford calls a "participant/observer,"[9] one deeply involved in the conflicts and causes she witnesses, and her travel accounts consciously and unconsciously advocate particular agendas.

In representing her travels, Prince combines elements of the itinerant preacher and the colonial missionary (both of whom emphasize enlightened self-improvement and civilizing through Christianity), with the discourse of the adventurer/explorer, including accounts of dangerous journeys, incidents of deceit, and gaining access to the means necessary for

survival. These varying strands are juxtaposed, often through the use of displacement and synecdoches, weaving stories of personal stability and instability, sin and virtue, chaos and order, in a text that harkens back to the
Bible and epic literature. As Frances Smith Foster reminds us in her study
of literary production by African American women, "this literature is an
entity, an interstice, a nexus, and it is not deductible simply by identifying
its components."[10]

After living in Russia with her husband, who served in the Tsar's Guard
for nine years, Prince came back to Boston for health reasons; her husband
passed away before rejoining her. She does not detail how she survived in
New England, but we know she worked as a seamstress at various times in
her life, as perhaps she did upon her return to the United States. She was
involved in the abolitionist movement, but was recruited by an American
missionary to travel to Jamaica to observe, educate, and enlighten the newly
emancipated slaves.

Prince resided in Jamaica from December 1840 through July 1841, and
then returned in May 1842 and stayed until August. Her pamphlet on
Jamaica was published in Boston in late 1841; its title, *The West Indies, Being
a Description of the Islands, Progress of Christianity, Education and Liberty Among
the Colored Population Generally,* recalls that of a missionary report from the
field; some of its diverse purposes and uses are therefore not immediately
obvious.[11] The pamphlet, for instance, offered testimony by Prince to complement fundraising appeals she made in the Boston abolitionist newspaper, *The Liberator,* under the headline "To the Benevolent," asking for
clothes and money to support her proposed manual-labor school in
Kingston.[12] The title indicates her focus on the conditions of the colored
population in Jamaica, but she addresses her reader as "an inhabitant of
New England," a regional American identity encompassing male and
female, black and white. She pays special attention, although not always
directly, to addressing anxieties of black readers at a time when questions
surrounding their location, mobility, and opportunity for a better life were
being raised in the abolitionist press. According to Floyd J. Miller, the
nationalist-emigrationist debates that addressed whether or not blacks
should leave the United States, where the Fugitive Slave Law was in effect,
did not really intensify until the 1850s and 60s.[13] But Prince's text engages
with and anticipates significant questions about what constitutes a commitment to citizenship for African Americans. Was it really most prudent
to leave New England, or to remain in place? Where was the greater economic and educational opportunity? Would there be more respect for
blacks (instead of racist treatment) in a country with a black majority, such

as Jamaica? Colonization schemes that had at their heart the removal of blacks from the United States were realities in the lives of free blacks as vital as limited employment opportunities and the possibility of mob violence and kidnapping. Although it was not uncommon to find post-Emancipation narratives written by white supporters of abolition who had traveled to the Caribbean and found the freed slaves to be industrious, and who had noted improvements since emancipation, these writers did not address or anticipate the wide array of concerns Northern black readers might have had about their own status in these post-Emancipation societies.[14] Even narratives written by African Americans about the viability of emigration to a particular Caribbean or African location differed markedly from Prince's account. They focused quite sharply on their "relocation" agenda and did not necessarily offer the kind of comparative international hybridity (between Russia and the Americas, for example), sassy back talk, and dialogic voices that have the effect of complicating Prince's stated objectives.[15] Her works, as we will see, are *sui generis*.

From merely reading the titles of Nancy Prince's narratives and gleaning the generic constraints she drew on from autobiography, spiritual narrative, and descriptive travelogues, one would not immediately perceive her embedded warnings and her often powerful attacks against institutions, such as established English missionaries in Jamaica and their commodification of religion, or against the deceit and greed of other philanthropists and ship captains. Prince's power as a narrator comes precisely from her position both inside and outside the American society she wished to condemn.[16] Prince claims the typical foundation of most travel writing—proclaiming a "truth" based on empirical observation—but her narrative authority is enhanced by a struggle that comes in part from the tensions between marginality and defiance, which at times blur the boundary between Self and Other that is one of the staples of Western travel writing. As Nancy Hartsock's notion of "standpoint epistemology" helps us see, writing from the margins can expose the falseness of the view from the top, and can transform those margins (as well as the center), by intervening in the center's domination and by valorizing other ways of seeing.[17] Prince weaves diverse voices into her narratives to illustrate the ideas she wants to convey to readers, or to present harsh and threatening notions in a more palatable format. For instance, she focuses on the lives of the newly emancipated slaves, with whom she often identifies as a black woman victimized in her own country and in her travels; her defiance and exposure of corruption and deceit become cautionary allegories for blacks and examples of misuse of power that their white allies in the struggle might note.

Prince illustrates how individual moral character is often sacrificed, or in flux, during the process of acculturation. One tactic she employs intermittently is to let the freed blacks speak for themselves, in order to convey with greater immediacy how they were taken advantage of by both the Baptist ticket and the class-leader system, where money is charged for "being baptized; they receive a ticket as a passport into the church" (73).[18] A former slave tells her how they would like to hire teachers to educate themselves but "our money is taken from us so fast we cannot" (54). Prince is impressed by the sarcasm the Jamaicans use in calling the missionaries and class-leaders "Macroon hunters," punning on the name of a Jamaican coin, mack, and also on the outlaw maroons she mentions with admiration.

In an interesting dialogue that can be read as Prince's attempt to illustrate why she adopted what we would call an ethnographic gaze to examine the emancipated Jamaicans, she tells readers: "They wished to know why I was so inquisitive about them. I told them we have heard in America you are lazy and that emancipation has been no benefit to you; I wish to inform myself of the truth respecting you and give a true representation of you on my return" (11). Hence, Prince tries to account for her encounters with otherness in what Mary Louise Pratt calls the contact zone while she simultaneously sketches out her agenda of "true representation" in the process of becoming what I am calling a "resistant truth teller."[19] This is a form of agency authorized by the moral sanction granted to her by her allegiance to a form of a political, evangelical Christianity. In her narratives, she embedded her critiques of emigration schemes, of the established practices of abolitionists and missionaries, and of the unfair treatment received by black travelers; but because of constraints placed on black women as public activists, she wrestled with her desire to be both outspoken and modest, a form of gendered double-consciousness. What might be revealed and what needed to remain veiled are bound up in the expressed and unexpressed restraints put upon black women to prove their respectability. As Anne M. Boylan suggests, "Unlike white women, especially of the middle class, black women could not presume they would be seen as 'virtuous' because they are women. Unlike black men, they had no special claim to leadership roles among their people."[20]

Prince struggled with her desire to claim authority and aid the cause of racial and religious uplift, and as she moved in various communities within Jamaica, she witnessed practices and policies that gave her cause for critique, even as she must have realized she needed the support of certain institutions and persons. The contradictions that seemed to arise between her ideals and realities are expressed textually as she juxtaposes or elides incidents and information. It is in this mediating role that we can read a mixture of nationalistic and biblical allegory emerging in her critical voice. Prince mixes her own voice with the voices of others, both black and white, in positions of marginalization and power, to open a transgressive space for herself and to critique Northern hypocrisy in the United States.

It may seem puzzling that in a work published and sold by supporters of the abolition movement, only one long paragraph in Prince's narrative is devoted to her work and activities in the antislavery society during her seven years in Boston before traveling to Jamaica. She merely hints at the sharp divides that had developed over the question of women's participation as speakers and equal members of the antislavery movement.[21] Nancy Prince appears to have had ambivalent feelings about women's participation in the abolition movement; while she sided with the faction that supported women's more public participation, it appears that she was concerned that the "woman question" could preempt or detract from the antislavery crusade. Interestingly, she displaces her ambivalence over this divide by writing in eliding terms about the antislavery society: "There has been a great change in some things but much remains to be done," she comments before turning to the language of moral sanctity: "Man has disobeyed . . . and become vain in his imagination. . . . The sins of my beloved country are not hid from his notice" (43). Yet it is telling that one of the first incidents Prince narrates of her arrival in Jamaica involves a dispute with a black female class leader in Reverend Abbott's missionary station in St. Ann's Harbor. Prince refuses to "yield obedience" because the class-leader's "method" displeases her, and she finds a lack of "necessity of being born of the spirit of God before we become members of the church of Christ . . ."(46). When Prince tells Abbott, an English Baptist, about her dispute, he seems angry that she had confronted the class leader; he had wanted her only to address him. Then she includes a comment from Abbott: "I do not approve of women's societies; they destroy the world's convention; the American women have too many of them" (47).

Part of the tension here comes from the difference between English and American abolitionists—by "world's convention" he most likely meant the World Anti-Slavery Convention, held in London in June of 1840, just months before Prince departed for Jamaica. At this convention, seven American women delegates were refused seats, because the participation of women went against the traditions of the British antislavery movement. In challenging the class-leader's moral conduct, Nancy Prince displays her own ambivalence about women's leadership in the context of a religious tradition outside her own New England brand of Christianity—that of Afro-Jamaican Myalism. For the class-leaders, in general, "were spiritual guides similar to those in Myal groups."[22] Nancy Prince may have found the method used by the class-leaders too full of "superstitions," as the idea of spirit was elevated above written gospel, which was dear to her. She does not mention the race of the class leader, but almost certainly she is black, as Abbott's congregation was composed almost exclusively of black workers.[23]

I read Nancy Prince's refusal to "yield obedience" to the female class leader, and ultimately to Abbott, in several contradictory ways: as a moment of personal defiance, her will and body in conjoined agency; as an American refusing to submit to the English Baptist missionary system; and as a revelation of her lack of tolerance for difference during a time when Christian and Myal elements were being blurred in religious practices of the Jamaicans. On the other hand, there are times in the narrative when Prince describes aspects of their religious practice with tolerance and respect, minimizing the differences she witnesses, as she does not express familiarity with Myalism or Obeah. She would probably want to downplay these Afro-Jamaican practices to emphasize instead qualities about the former slaves that would meet with the greatest approval by an American readership. In addition, both Myalism and Obeah were illegal.[24] Her refusal to follow another form of religious teaching and her incorporating Abbott's comment about American women might also serve as a safe way to blend her critique of the English missionaries and the colonial practice of using blacks in order to raise money and gain power, with her ambivalence about the actions of the white women in Boston. When the split occurred between the Boston Female Anti-Slavery Society, both sides tried to secure the support of African American members, although blacks were generally not in leadership roles. According to Debra Hansen, the African American women were more interested in developing programs that directly assisted the black community than in debating policy issues that consumed the white women.[25]

Prince's mobility and "heroic" independence allowed her to walk away from a disagreeable situation—she compared the religious meeting house she disapproves of to a "play house," and narrated how her presence inadvertently interrupted English Baptist business as usual—"I gave several Bibles away, not knowing that I was hurting the minister's sale"(47). It is here that she uses her mobility to set up shifting subject/object positions to make her strongest case for black industriousness and to warn black readers about misleading information they had been receiving in the press concerning the benefits of emigration compared to the advantages of remaining in New England.

At the time Prince's pamphlet was published, advertisements and letters appeared in the abolition press by blacks and whites, expressing both advantages and disadvantages to be derived from emigrating to the West Indies. When the Fugitive Slave Law was passed in 1850, African Americans such as Martin R. Delany advocated emigration to places like Central and South America as part of a black nationalist movement removed from United States slavery and the perpetual threat of recapture and reenslavement.[26]

The emigration question was taken up in another kind of narrative in this period, what I am calling a "speculative emigration narrative," such as one written by Nathaniel Peck and Thomas S. Price, two respected free blacks from Baltimore who went to British Guiana and Trinidad to determine if there were advantages to be had in relocating to one of those places. They concluded that in both countries, particularly Guiana, there were "many advantages over the United States for the industrious man of colour."[27] A letter by an unsigned writer, published in *The Colored American,* accused Peck and Price of being "simple-minded" and taken in by the planters, "whose interest it is to import emigrants to these colonies to produce wealth for them, and who therefore flatter them."[28] Therefore, the debates were highly politicized and connected to larger questions about power, co-optation, and control of wealth and resources after slavery.

Planters and magistrates were anxious to import immigrant laborers to the emancipated West Indian islands to work on plantations, since emancipated Afro-Jamaicans were determined to be free of former masters. John Candler, an English Quaker who traveled to the West Indies a year before Prince did, notes the desire of an agent-general of Jamaica to induce laborers to come to Jamaica, but he claims "There is in fact no need of immigration: the population is fast increasing by birth, and will supply the labor market as fast as capital is ready to give labour its profitable direction."[29] However, an act had been passed in April 1840 to encourage immigrants to come to Jamaica. Alexander Barclay, Commissioner of Emigration, promised free passage, constant and steady employment, and "comforts enjoyed by the laboring classes . . . exceeded by none in the world."[30] Rather than focusing on wages, which were probably higher in New England than in Jamaica, Barclay emphasized that free colored people would enjoy the rights and privileges of free men denied to them in the United States.[31] Barclay was also instrumental in bringing indentured laborers from Sierra Leone and St. Helena to Jamaica in 1841.[32]

Here is an example of a notice in The Liberator, offering opportunities and free passage, which a number of free blacks in New England would have read. It also reminds us that Garrison's paper printed notices and ads that he did not necessarily agree with:

> *The undersigned, having been appointed Agent under the Immigration Act of the island of Jamaica, hereby gives notice, that he will provide with a free passage to Jamaica, such persons as may be disposed to avail themselves of the advantages offered by emigrating to that island, where ample employment is to be found for mechanics, agricultural and other laborers, and provision made for their support on their arrival. Many other and peculiar inducements exist for the colored emigrant. Further information may be obtained by personal application to the Agent.*
>
> Edmund A. Grattan, H.B.M. Vice-Consul
> No 5 Lewis's wharf, Boston[33]

Nancy Prince seemed particularly sensitive to the exaggerated promises and empty rhetoric used to lure blacks to Jamaica. Her description of the realities in Jamaica are a striking contrast to the ads:

> How the mistake originated, I am not able to say, but on arriving here, strangers, poor and unacclimated, the debt for passage money is hard and unexpected; it is remarkable that wherever they come from, whether fresh from Africa, from the other islands, from the South or from New England, they all feel deceived on this point. I called on many Americans and found them poor and discontented, ruing the day they left their country, where, notwithstanding many obstacles, their parents had lived and died, which they had helped to conquer with their toil and blood, "Now shall their children stay abroad and starve in foreign lands."[34]

This passage seems to suggest both a practical and a more deeply rooted rationale for staying home: for African American families, there is a particular irony in having sacrificed their lives in slavery, hoping it would be better for their children. To leave your country, despite the hardships, only to starve abroad, would be particularly bitter. Prince suggests that the sacrifices made with African blood and toil give African Americans a particular motive to stay and to fight for the right to prosper in the United States;

as an abolitionist, she would also want free blacks to stay home to support the cause of their brethren still in bondage.[35] She focuses on the economic difficulties of the emigrants, while commenting elsewhere on the self-sufficiency and industriousness of her "injured brethren in Jamaica." "They have bought land and built houses. They raise all kinds of vegetables. . . . They have no need to let themselves on plantations. They are extremely kind to each other, and have shown an excellent capacity to take care of themselves."[36] This suggests it is prudent to work the land in your own nation; self reliance comes through kindness and mutual, communal support as well as land ownership. Here, Prince's secularly oriented economic voice is emphasized, contrasting her other, providentially oriented voice that we had seen scolding the class leader and the American abolitionists.[37]

Prince cautioned black readers against immigration schemes in her narratives, while William Lloyd Garrison and his supporters used the pages of *The Liberator* and *Pennsylvania Freeman* for the same purpose, embedding warnings in obituaries.[38] Thus, both tried to create obstacles to Barclay's efforts to attract free blacks to Jamaica.[39] A notice on the death of James G. Barbadoes, one of the leading black abolitionists in the Boston community, stated that "contrary to the advice of his friends, he emigrated with his wife and family to Jamaica. . . . They soon sickened with the fever of the country, and two of his children died. And now the last intelligence from there informs us of his own decease by the same malady."[40] Mr. Barbadoes was among the emigrants who went from this section of the country last year to the island of Jamaica, hoping to better his condition; but in common with them, he soon found that he had been duped by flattering representations that had been held out by persons in the pay of the West Indian proprietors.[41] The tone of these obituaries also reveal a patronizing, paternal voice on the part of Garrison and friends in cautioning the African American community; Prince first calls emigration schemes a "mistake"—her tone is one of surprise and sympathy, then anger, as she describes "a thousand young women and children, living in sin of every kind. From thence I went to where there were seventeen men. . . . I went to the Admiral's house, where emigrants find a shelter until they can find employment, then they work and pay for their passage" (51).

In numerous references throughout her writing, she expresses her own anxiety about bodily harm and death, but distinguishes her purpose from that of her fellow African Americans. Theirs appears to be economically motivated, while hers is a higher, uplifting enterprise that gives her authority to speak as a servant of God. She is a traveler, a mobile female subject in the Black Atlantic, temporarily serving various communities, distinguished from the would-be emigrant seeking a new home. The remainder of Prince's *Life and Travels* shifts between Jamaica and the United States, as she returns to the States to raise money for her proposed free labor school in Kingston. In passing, she mentions that Lucretia Mott was enthusiastic about her plan, and that money was raised in New York, Philadelphia, and Boston (55). When Prince returns to Jamaica, she finds it too dangerous to stay, and comes up short of funds. Her voyage home presents us with loss, confusion, dislocation, theft, and danger, which is contrasted with final redemption and acceptance in God, her savior, as the conclusion of her narrative finds her "broken up in business, embarrassed and obliged to move, when not able to wait on myself. This has been my lot. . . . I have thought of my case like that of Paul's, when cast among wild beasts . . . but blessed be the Lord who hath not given me a prey to their teeth" (85).

As a final example of Nancy Prince's complex agency and defiance, we find her once again aboard ship, issuing another warning to her black readers about the unofficial crime of black mobility. This one is a testimony on the double standards, bodily harm, and death-threatening conditions that African Americans are forced to endure in their travels. It comes in the form of a letter to *The Liberator:*

> I wish to give publicly . . . to the particulars of the harsh treatment I suffered onboard the steamboat Massachusetts, Capt. Comstock, on her passage from New York to Providence. . . . I purchased my ticket . . . and took my seat with the other ladies . . . but two colored chambermaids . . . told me "that was no place for me—I must go out of that" . . . and behaved with great rudeness and violence. I then went to the captain's office and on finding I had not paid full price, told him I wished either to have a cabin ticket or to have my money returned. He refused to let me have either, and I should have left the boat . . . had not my lameness rendered me unable to walk. I was therefore compelled to pass the entire night on the forward deck. . . . I could find no place to sit except in a passage where there was a constant draft of cold air. About ten o'clock, I again went to the cabin, and requested the chambermaids to find a bed for me elsewhere. . . . This they refused to do, answering me with great impertinence. In consequence of this exposure, I took cold, and have ever since been much worse. My object in writing and publishing this is that it may serve as a caution to colored people to beware of that boat and to show the recreant conduct of the colored girls who deserve exposure for pursuing such a course.[42]

Prince warns colored readers in general about this particular route, while exposing the specific chambermaids (although unnamed) and captain. Unlike the Afro-Jamaicans who "are extremely kind to each other," the colored chambermaids have failed to show respect and kindness to the elder, Nancy Prince, and have contributed to her illness. The exposure of this incident may also be related to unstated anger and shock over the death of Susan Paul, the accomplished daughter of the Reverend Thomas Paul, who had converted Prince to Baptism when she was a teenager. According to Shirley Yee, Susan Paul had died of an illness contracted aboard a steamboat to New York; segregationalist policies barring her from the "ladies cabin" forced her to stay on the lower deck.[43] It also harkens back to Prince's own youth, when she worked as a servant in a number of houses in New England. Nancy Prince's letter is a vehement first-person account, full of anger, although it is prefaced with comments from Garrison, validating Prince as "a highly respectable colored female."

In a column called "Colored Travellers," another case of mistreatment and exposure on deck is highlighted, this time to a colored clergyman. The "meanness and absolute villainy" of the steamboat proprietors and railroad conductors on the route from New York to Boston, via Stonnington and Providence, are noted. The conclusion, most likely by Garrison, is that "Shame is at least one step in the ladder of true reform."[44] Nancy Prince, however, did not include the details of this incident aboard ship, or of another defiant act in which she led a group of women and children in a rock-throwing incident to apprehend a slave catcher,[45] in her *Narrative of Life and Travels.* Perhaps she felt she could not afford to shame too many of her potential readers, upon whose support she was relying for sales of her narrative. To include such acts of defiance and activism would have created a self-portrait of a resistance that contradicted the image of a physically frail but spiritually empowered Nancy Prince the reader is left with at her narrative's end.

Thus, Prince publicly exposed the culprits in another venue, revealing a complex strategy for narrative presentations of the Self. Mobile subjectivity and the flexible genre of travel narrative allowed her to be didactic, heroic, veiled, and faithful to her vision. Her voice deserves to be part of the emerging discourse on the Black Atlantic and on cross-cultural interventions made by women during the antebellum period and beyond.

NOTES

1. Nancy Prince, *A Narrative of the Life and Travels of Mrs. Nancy Prince, Written by Herself.* 2nd edition. In *Collected Black Women's Narratives.* Edited by

Henry Louis Gates (New York: Oxford/Schomburg Library, 1988) (reprint of 1853 edition), 43, 45. Unless otherwise stated, all references will be to this edition and will appear in parentheses in the text.

2. Several recent full-length studies and articles on the writing produced by African American women in the antebellum years have included Nancy Prince. See *A Stranger in the Village: Two Centuries of African-American Travel Writing.* Edited by Farah Griffin and Cheryl Fish. (Boston: Beacon Press, 1998); Frances Smith Foster, *Written By Herself: Literary Production by African American Women, 1746-1892* (Bloomington: Indiana University Press, 1993); and "Adding Color and Contour to Early American Self-Portraitures: Autobiographical Writings of Afro-American Women." In *Conjuring: Black Women, Fiction and Literary Tradition.* Edited by Marjorie Pryse and Hortense Spillers (Bloomington: Indiana University Press, 1985). See Carla L. Peterson, *Doers of the Word: African American Women Writers in the North, 1830-79* (London and New York: Oxford University Press, 1995) and "Doers of the Word: Theorizing African-American Women Writers in the Antebellum North." In *The Other American Traditions.* Edited by Joyce Warren (New Brunswick, NJ: Rutgers University Press, 1993). Hazel Carby included Nancy Prince's *Narrative of the Life and Travels* in her study of the development of black women's fiction, *Reconstructing Womanhood: The Emergence of the Afro-American Woman Novelist* (London and New York: Oxford University Press, 1987). Useful introductory essays to editions of Nancy Prince's *Narrative* were written by Ronald G. Walters, *A Black Woman's Odyssey Through Russia and Jamaica: The Narrative of Nancy Prince* (New York: Markus Wiener, 1990) and Anthony G. Barthelemy, "Introduction." In *Collected Black Women's Narratives* (Oxford/Schomburg Library, 1988). Dorothy Sterling and Bert James Loewenberg and Ruth Bogin included excerpts from Prince's *Narrative,* with brief commentary: See *We Are Your Sisters: Black Women in the Nineteenth Century.* Edited by Dorothy Sterling et al. (New York, 1984) and *Black Women in Nineteenth Century American Life: Their Words, Their Thoughts, Their Feelings.* Edited by Bert James Loewenberg and Ruth Bogin (University Park: Penn State University Press, 1976).

3. In "Voices of Restless (Dis)continuity: The Significance of Travel for Black Women in the Antebellum Americas," I discuss Mary Seacole's travel writing as well as Nancy Prince's. They represent two varying narratives of mobility and the desire to "trespass" and intervene at sites of empire building and war. *Women's Studies: An Interdisciplinary Journal* 26: 5 (1997): 475-495.

4. Paul Gilroy, *The Black Atlantic: Modernity and Double Consciousness* (Cambridge, MA: Harvard University Press, 1993).

5. Sylvia M. Jacobs has written about some of the tensions that arise between the work of uplift and Western "civilization" in her collection on African American missionaries in Africa. See *Black Americans and The Missionary*

Movement in Africa. Edited by Sylvia M. Jacobs (Westport, CT: Greenwood Press, 1982).

6. Although there is no Tobias Wornton listed in the list of black servicemen from the Revolutionary War records, there is a "Boston, Bachus" who served as a Private in the Massachusetts Third Regiment. There are also men listed with names like "Boston, Caesar," and "Boston, Negro," which seems to indicate that because many black soldiers were slaves, they were not listed by their full Christian names. *List of Black Servicemen, Compiled from War Department Collection of the Revolutionary War Records.* Compiled by Debra L. Newman (Washington: National Archives and Records Service, General Services Administration, 1974).

7. The black population of Boston totaled approximately 2,000 in 1850. That year's census reported that only 14 percent of the city's black adults were unable to read and write, a number that dropped to 8 percent by 1860. Massachusetts-born blacks had a high rate of literacy because of a strong system of public education within the state, but literacy in some cases referred to a rudimentary knowledge of reading and writing. (See James Oliver Horton and Lois E. Horton's "The Affirmation of Manhood: Black Garrisonions in Antebellum America." In *Courage and Conscience: Black and White Abolitionists on Boston.* Edited by Donald M. Jacobs [Bloomington: Indiana University Press, 1993], 12-13.)

8. I am borrowing the notion of intersubjectivity from Jessica Benjamin, who uses it to refer to a space of mutual recognition of subjects, replacing the subject/object divide with a form of tension between contradictory forces. In intersubjectivity, the need for recognition and independence is simultaneous; the "other" is outside our control, and yet we need him. (See Benjamin's *Bonds of Love: Psychoanalysis, Feminism, and the Problems of Domination* [New York: Pantheon, 1988], 220-21.) Mobility would shift the terms of the contradictory forces, as they depend upon circumstance and varying power relations; for Prince, the ethical dimensions of individualism within the collective, or the lack of such dimensions, drives her narrative and perception of the "other."

9. See Clifford James, "Travelling Cultures." In *Cultural Studies.* Edited by Paula Treichler et al. (New York: Routledge, 1992), 98.

10. See Foster's *Written By Herself,* 15.

11. Nancy Prince, *The West Indies, Being A Description of the Islands, Progress of Christianity, Education and Liberty Among the Colored Population Generally* (Boston: Dow & Jackson, 1841). All subsequent references will appear in parentheses in the text.

12. The connection between her fundraising appeals and the sale of the pamphlet is made evident in an advertisement in *The Liberator,* addressed "To the Benevolent." Donations in money, children's books, or clothing solicited from "the benevolent and liberal" by Mrs. Nancy Prince "being about to

establish a manual labor school for orphans and outcasts" at Kingston, Jamaica. They were to leave donations at Miss Ray's house or the offices of the newspaper, where "may be found a pamphlet on the present state of Jamaica, written by Mrs. Prince" (12 November 1841).

13. Floyd J. Miller, *The Search for a Black Nationality: Black Emigration and Colonization, 1787-1863* (Urbana: University of Illinois Press, 1975), ix.

14. For instance, some of these points were addressed by American missionary David Ingraham in letters to *The Liberator,* and by Englishmen Joseph Sturge and Thomas Harvey in their book *The West Indies in 1837; Being the Journal of a Visit to Antigua, Montserrat, Dominica, St. Lucia, Barbados, and Jamaica, Undertaken for the Purpose of Ascertaining the Actual Conditions of the Negro Population of Those Islands* (London: Hamilton, Adams & Co, 1838).

15. For a discussion of texts written by women in the Caribbean, see Bridget Brereton, "Text, Testimony and Gender: An Examination of some Texts by Women on the English-Speaking Caribbean, from the 1770s to the 1920s." In *Engendering History: Caribbean Women in Historical Perspective.* Edited by Verene Shepherd et al. (New York: St. Martin's Press, 1995).

16. See Hazel Carby's *Reconstructing Womanhood,* 42.

17. Hartsock is quoted in Sidonie Smith and Julia Watson's "De/Colonization and the Politics of Discourse in Women's Autobiographical Practices." In *Decolonizing the Subject: The Politics of Gender in Women's Autobiography* (Minneapolis: University of Minnesota Press, 1992), xx.

18. According to Robert J. Stewart, the class-leader and ticket system was actually the invention of John Wesley and the Wesleyans in England, but in Jamaica it was used "in a more limited and tightly controlled way than that employed by the Baptists" (*Religion and Society in Post-Emancipation Jamaica* [Knoxville: University of Tennessee Press, 1992], 7). In the Baptist system, missionaries set up a class house in areas where church members lived and appointed a black member of the community as leader; they might be former slaves, and literacy was not a requirement for membership.

19. Mary Louise Pratt, *Imperial Eyes: Travel Writing and Transculturation* (New York: Routledge, 1992).

20. Anne M. Boylan, "Benevolence and Antislavery Activity Among African-American Women in New York and Boston, 1829-1840." In *The Abolitionist Sisterhood: Women's Political Culture in Antebellum America.* Edited by Jean Fagan Yellin and John C. Van Horne (Ithaca, NY: Cornell University Press, 1994), 133.

21. What she leaves out is that by the fall of 1839, the Boston Female Anti-Slavery Society (BFASS) had divided into two factions over the "woman question," one that sided with William L. Garrison and his followers, and the other that sided with the more conservative clerics. The clerical faction used the argument that sexual integration and the full participation of women as speakers would distract abolitionists from their original goal

(Debra Gold Hansen, "The BFASS and the Limits of Gender Politics." In *The Abolitionist Sisterhood*. Edited by Jean F. Yellin and John Van Horne. Ithaca, NY: Cornell University Press, 1994, 54).

22. Abigail B. Bakan, *Ideology and Class Conflicts in Jamaica: The Politics of Rebellion* (Montreal: McGill University Press, 1990), 53.

23. Joseph J. Gurney, *Familiar Letters to Henry Clay of Kentucky Describing a Winter in the West Indies* (New York: Mahlon Day & Co., 1840), 101.

24. Philip D. Curtain, *Two Jamaicas: The Role of Ideas in a Tropical Colony, 1830-65* (Cambridge, MA: Harvard University Press, 1955), 169.

25. Debra Gold Hansen, "The Boston Female Anti-Slavery Society and the Limits of Gender Politics." In *The Abolitionist Sisterhood*, 46.

26. See *Witness for Freedom: African American Voices on Race, Slavery, and Emancipation*. Edited by C. Peter Ripley et al. (Chapel Hill: University of North Carolina Press, 1993), 20.

27. Nathaniel Peck and Thomas S. Price. *Report of Messers. Peck and Price . . . Delegates to Visit British Guiana and the Island of Trinidad for the Purpose of Ascertaining the Advantage to Be Derived by Colored People Migrating. . . . (Baltimore: Woods & Crane, 1840), 23.

28. See the letter, as reprinted in *The Liberator*, 13 November 1840.

29. John Candler, *West Indies: Extracts from the Journal of John Candler, Whilst Travelling in Jamaica*. 2 Vols. (London: Harvey and Darton, 1840/1841), II, 37.

30. Alexander Barclay, *Remarks on Emigration to Jamaica Addressed to the Colored Citizens of the United States* (New York: James Van Norden & CO., Printers, 1840), 8.

31. Mary Elizabeth Thomas, *Jamaica and Voluntary Laborers from Africa, 1840-65* (Gainesville: University Presses of Florida, 1992), 19-20.

32. Monica Schuler, *"Alas, Alas Kongo": A Social History of Indentured African Immigration into Jamaica, 1841-65* (Baltimore: Johns Hopkins University Press, 1980), 11.

33. *The Liberator*, 27 August 1841.

34. *West Indies*, 12 and *Narrative*, 51.

35. See Thomas, *Jamaica and Voluntary Laborers*, 22.

36. See Prince's "Letter to the Public," published in the *Anti-Slavery Standard*, 25 May 1843.

37. See Houston Baker, *Blues, Ideology and Afro-American Literature* (Chicago: University of Chicago Press, 1984), 43.

38. See also William Lloyd Garrison, *Thoughts on African Colonization* (New York: Arno Press, 1969) [Reprint of 1832 edition].

39. See Thomas, *Jamaica and Voluntary Laborers*, 22.

40. *Pennsylvania Freeman* (reprinted in *The Liberator*, 20 August 1841).

41. *The Liberator*, 6 August 1841.

42. Prince, Letter to "Mr. Garrison." *The Liberator*, 17 September 1841.

43. Shirley J. Yee, *Black Women Abolitionists: A Study in Activism, 1828–1860* (Knoxville: University of Tennessee Press, 1992), 19.
44. *The Liberator,* 13 August 1847.
45. John T. Hilton, "Reminiscences." *The Woman's Era,* 4–5 August 1894.

Chapter 10

DECOLONIZING ETHNOGRAPHY:
ZORA NEALE HURSTON IN THE CARIBBEAN

Kevin Meehan

At the height of the Great Depression, in 1936 and 1937, African American novelist and folklorist Zora Neale Hurston traveled to Jamaica and Haiti on consecutive Guggenheim grants in order to study Caribbean folk religion.[1] It was during this period that Hurston produced her best known piece of writing, the novel *Their Eyes Were Watching God*.[2] After her time in Haiti was cut short by a mysterious stomach ailment—caused, perhaps, by a *bocor* or Vodou priest who was guarding his turf against the anthropologist's prying gaze—Hurston returned to the United States, where she completed *Tell My Horse: Voodoo and Life in Haiti and Jamaica*, a nonfiction text based on her Caribbean fieldwork.[3] Successive generations of African American anthropologists have faithfully preserved her legacy as an anthropologist and a Caribbeanist, but outside this community of scholars the primary transcript of Hurston's Caribbean sojourn has languished in relative obscurity since its publication in 1938.[4] With the recent re-issue of *Tell My Horse*—in two separate editions offered by Harper Collins and the Library of America—and given signs that under the influence of feminist and colonial discourse theory a new wave of interpretive scholarship on this text may be emerging, the time for reconsidering and reclaiming Hurston's neglected Caribbean narrative has certainly arrived.[5]

After providing a brief overview of the structure and contents of *Tell My Horse,* I want to suggest the important contributions Hurston makes to the theory and practice of anthropological writing and cultural decolonization. Though Hurston employs a wide range of writing styles, *Tell My Horse* is best read through—and against—contemporary theories of ethnographic representation. Hurston exposes the implicatedness of ethnographic projects (including her own) in imperialist political economy and moves to decolonize ethnography by manipulating it away from a tendency to represent native populations as exotic and dependent Others. Hurston challenges this dominant rhetorical strategy by portraying informants who undercut the ethnographic authority of her narrator and by scripting delineations of Caribbean culture in which fables of self-reliance displace fables of dependency. Also a part of Hurston's decolonizing project are the gendered and gendering cultural descriptions that make up the core of her ethnographic practice. *Tell My Horse* stands out in the history of critiques of colonial discourse by offering harshly critical narratives about the limits of decolonization for women in the Caribbean. Hurston uses her ethnography, then, both to criticize dominant narratives of decolonization and to expand the scope of cultural decolonization by equating this goal with the struggle to author a female subject. Hurston is able to project this complicated vision of inter-American solidarity, shaped by the intersections of race, class, gender, and nationality, because she simultaneously invokes more than one tradition in Caribbean travel writing. On one hand, *Tell My Horse* echoes the signal tropes of a dominant—and dominating— line of commentary that stretches from Columbus down to Hurston's contemporary and fellow Boasian anthropologist Melville Herskovits. At the same time, *Tell My Horse* also derives its perspective and rhetorical strategy from a dissident tradition of African diasporan travel and cultural production radiating outward from the Caribbean in all directions across the hemisphere. The representative figures in this tradition include maroons, enslaved Africans who were trans-shipped within the Americas, present-day migrant workers, and luminary African American travelers such as Frederick Douglass, James Weldon Johnson, and Langston Hughes, all of whom spent significant time living in and writing about the Caribbean. What unifies this dissident tradition, and its expressions both written and nonwritten, is a denunciation of impoverishment and imperialism, a celebration of the liberating potential of Caribbean civilization, and a commitment to advocating Caribbean sovereignty.

One of Hurston's most neglected book-length works, *Tell My Horse* is a generic hybrid, a travelogue/ethnography that recounts more or less chronologically her two-year sojourn in the Caribbean during 1936 and 1937. Placing this voyage historically, it comes at the peak of Hurston's prolific career. With support from the Guggenheim Foundation, Hurston vacated a position in the Federal Theatre Project in New York City, where she had helped to organize the celebrated Harlem unit. Proposing "to make an exhaustive study of Obeah (magic) practices . . . to add to and compare with what I have already collected in the United States," Hurston traveled briefly to Port-au-Prince, Haiti, then to Jamaica, in April 1936, where she resided mostly with the Accompong Maroons, and finally to Haiti, in September 1936. It was during a seven-week period following her second arrival in Haiti, when she was learning Haitian Creole and making local connections, that Hurston wrote *Their Eyes Were Watching God*.[6] Like every American who came to Haiti at this time, Hurston's presence there was overshadowed by the 19-year occupation of the country by U.S. Marine Corps forces from 1915 to 1934. In terms of overall regional history, which had been marked since the Spanish-American War by four decades of direct U.S. military intervention in the Caribbean, her trip came during a period of relative cooling off that was prompted by economic depression at home and the installation of pro-U.S. dictatorships in Haiti and the Dominican Republic. This was the time of "Good Neighbor" vs. "Big Stick" policies in the region.[7]

Tell My Horse reads like a compendium of the styles and strategies employed by Hurston throughout her career. The writing in it ranges from subtly rendered history and portraiture to incisive (albeit debatable) political analyses, from bodacious accounts of Hurston's travel adventures and striking ethnographic description of religious ceremonies to straightforward folklore cataloguing. The text of *Tell My Horse* is divided into 18 chapters spread out across 3 sections. The first 4 chapters deal with Jamaica and focus on the effects of British colonialism, such as social stratification, racial ideologies, and sex/gender relations; female initiation ceremonies; the Accompong Maroons; and peasant burial rites/duppy stories. The last 13 chapters deal with Haiti and are divided into 2 parts: "Politics and Personalities of Haiti," which includes political analysis, a historiography of the Haitian state written in a mytho-prophetic voice employed by Hurston in her novels to recount black history in epic form, and a troublingly ambiguous account of the 1915 U.S. invasion; and "Voodoo in Haiti," which provides a taxonomy of Vodou deities and numerous descriptions of Vodou culture in process. There is an appendix that catalogues the music and drumming of Haitian folk dances, and one chapter, titled "Women in the Caribbean," which bridges Haiti and Jamaica in Hurston's commentary. I mention this transitional chapter last in order to emphasize that it warrants special notice for the way it breaks new ground—methodologically, epistemologically, and politically—by positing gender as a category that can critically mediate cultural-political divisions in the Caribbean.

The existing criticism on *Tell My Horse* is sharply divided. Gwendolyn Mikell, who wrote the entry on Hurston for an encyclopedia of women anthropologists, describes Hurston's ethnography as "pioneering, her methodological approaches solid and almost avant-garde."[8] Léon-François Hoffman, one of the deans of Haitian literary scholarship, called it "the first respectful treatment of vodun" in American letters.[9] At the other end of the spectrum, Caribbeanist critic J. Michael Dash criticizes Hurston for a long list of offenses, including her evocation of "sensationalist travelogues of white American visitors to Haiti," her "dismaying apology for the Occupation," and her "alarming and racist references to the weaknesses of the Haitian character."[10] Hurston's biographer, Robert Hemenway, sees the stylistic diversity of *Tell My Horse* as a fatal flaw: he dismisses it as her "poorest book, chiefly because of its form."[11] A major reason for this uneven reception (and certainly this is the biggest challenge in reading *Tell My Horse*) is difficulty in situating Hurston's roving narrator and the comparative cultural commentary that issues forth from this first-person narrative voice. The problem is that the narrator is ambiguous about her position(s) within a social setting structured by imperialism. Like every anthropological voyage before and since, Zora Neale Hurston's Caribbean sojourn occurred against a backdrop of European and North American domination of the region. In addition to the historical context provided by a particular event such as the U.S. occupation of Haiti, anthropology as a discipline is mired generally in the project of empire-building, leading one critic to dub anthropology "the child of imperialism."[12] Politically, economically, and culturally, imperialist domination constitutes a direct condition of possibility for Hurston's fieldwork experience. Her response to the history of imperialism in the Caribbean, however, vacillates between criticism and seeming embrace.

At times, the narrator is an incisive critic of the legacy of European colonialism—a Frantz Fanon 20 years earlier and with feminist-oriented gender consciousness—who attacks colonialist discourses and social practices. In Jamaica, for instance, where Hurston claims "it is the aim of everybody to talk English, act English and *look* English" (16), racism and patriarchy combine under British colonialism to the detriment of black women, who are trod upon systematically in the native bourgeoisie's "stampede whiteward" (16). Hurston's narrator labels Jamaica "the Rooster's Nest" because, as she explains:

[b]lack skin is so utterly condemned that the black mother is not going to be mentioned nor exhibited. You get the impression that these virile Englishmen do not require women to reproduce. They just come out to Jamaica, scratch out a nest and lay eggs (19).

Hurston's critical point of view on race, gender, and power in a colonial setting strongly echoes the earlier writing of African American travelers to the Caribbean region. Indeed, there is a long history of cultural exchange and advocacy, particularly between Haitians and African Americans, and it is important to situate *Tell My Horse* as a highly developed expression of this discursive and political legacy. The Haitian Revolution (1791-1804) immediately impressed African Americans, and the memory of it was kept alive during the nineteenth century in speeches, pamphlets, and visits to Haiti by black abolitionists such as William Wells Brown, James Redpath, and Frederick Douglass. Even before word of the uprising in colonial Saint-Domingue reached North America, though, Haitians had established a North American presence during the American Revolution by fighting as French soldiers in the battle of Savannah. This military experience proved invaluable to the Haitians when their own war of independence erupted a decade later and they faced and defeated Spanish, British, and, finally, two separate French expeditionary forces. Haiti fired the dreams of African Americans, particularly those with revolutionary leanings. In Charleston, South Carolina, Denmark Vesey, leader of one of the most detailed plans for antebellum revolt, was himself of Caribbean descent, and lived for a year in Saint-Domingue before coming to Charleston in 1783.[13] Forty years later, Vesey's co-revolutionists firmly believed that they would receive support from Haitian as well as African sources for their efforts to overturn white supremacist rule in majority black South Carolina. Throughout the mid-nineteenth century, Haiti was frequently viewed by colonization societies as a place where free blacks from America might emigrate. Actual emigration to Haiti reached a peak in the late 1850s under the influence of James T. Holly, an Episcopal minister who moved to the island with his family and took up permanent residence. Holly gallicized his first name (later accounts refer to him as Jacques) and accepted a standing offer of Haitian citizenship to any person of African descent. J. T. Holly survived well into the twentieth century, and his letters to correspondents in North America constitute a rare sympathetic perspective on society and politics in turn-of-the-century Haiti.[14]

Within Hurston's lifetime, the contacts between Haitians and African

Americans increased dramatically. Frederick Douglass, having worked hard to deliver the black vote to Republican Benjamin Harrison in the presidential election of 1888, was appointed as high consul to Haiti, where he served from 1889 to 1891. Douglass's public talks from the time recognize the dignity of Haitian people, who walk, he says, "as if conscious of their freedom and independence."[15] His diplomatic dispatches, meanwhile, demand respect for Haiti from the international community and paint scenes of bustling development in Port-au-Prince. In one description of the Haitian capital, Douglass notes:

> the manifold projects for improving streets, roads, and wharves, and . . . the increasing number of private dwellings in process of erection both within and without the limits of Port-au-Prince. The sound of the hammer and the trowel is heard late and early. Soon an electric cable from Port-au-Prince will connect the cable at Môle St. Nicolas and thus bring Port-au-Prince *en rapport* with the outside world.[16]

Ultimately, Douglass resigned his commission in 1891 over U.S. attempts to bully Haitians into leasing Môle St. Nicolas as a naval base and coaling station. In his sensitivity to and advocacy for Haitian interests, Douglass's career is a unique chapter in U.S. diplomatic history, and Haitians later acknowledged his support by choosing Douglass as their representative at the 1893 Columbian Exhibition in Chicago (despite the fact that African Americans were excluded from the proceedings). Immediately prior to Hurston's arrival, Langston Hughes had visited Haiti during his own travels through the Caribbean and wrote the moving protest essay, "The White Shadows in a Black Land" as well as "The People Without Shoes," which later was incorporated as a chapter in Hughes's autobiography, *I Wonder as I Wander.* Before that, James Weldon Johnson had spearheaded a determined effort by black intellectuals in America to influence U.S. policies during the American Occupation.[17] Beginning in 1920 (though planned as early as 1918), Johnson made several trips to Haiti in his capacity as N.A.A.C.P. field secretary and contributed scathing, Walter Rodney-like reports to *The Nation* and *The Crisis.* In his 1920 series "Self-Determining Haiti," Johnson details the role of the National City Bank of New York in pushing for the 1915 invasion, exposes the barbarous behavior of the Occupation forces, asserts the vibrancy of both peasants and elites in Haiti, and discusses the problems of underdevelopment and illiteracy (interestingly, Johnson calls for literacy training in Haitian Creole, which he says "must not be thought of as a mere dialect."[18]

These reports inform Hurston's sense of the Haitian political economy in *Tell My Horse,* and though typically she constructs her narrative
in such a way that it is the Haitian characters who challenge her narrator's own American-biased perceptions, she herself clearly was aware of
the revisionist angle expressed by Johnson. In one exchange, Hurston's
informant in Port-au-Prince disputes the notion that American forces
intervened to make Haiti pay its foreign debts to America and France
(84-85). Instead, the informant claims that this $40 million debt was
foisted upon the Haitians *after* the invasion, a sequence and a figure also
cited in an unsigned 1926 article in *The Crisis* that was almost certainly
penned by Johnson.[19] Following this colloquy, as she rips into the
hypocrisy of efforts by Haitian president Sténio Vincent to characterize
himself as a national liberator (the Marines had departed during his
tenure), the narrator of *Tell My Horse* insists that "the N.A.A.C.P., *The
Nation* and certain other organizations had a great deal more to do with
the withdrawal of the Marines than Vincent did and much more than
they are given credit for" (86).

This argument is supported by Brenda Plummer's analysis of the role of
black newspapers and lobbyists in helping to end the U.S. Occupation and
moderate the level of brutality inflicted on the Haitians by Marine forces
drawn primarily from Southern states.[20] Hurston also uses the exchange
with her anonymous Port-au-Prince informant to register critical commentary on the 1937 massacre of Haitian *braceros,* or migrant sugar cane
workers, at the Haiti-Dominican Republic border.[21]

While Hurston thus takes her place in a long tradition of African
American commentators who respond to Caribbean societies critically but
with sympathy and solidarity, at other times, the narrator seems thoroughly
invested in Yankee imperialism. For instance, the chapter describing the
U.S. Occupation treats this passage of history as a positive development in
nation building, as the chapter title, "Rebirth of a Nation," indicates. Readers might be tempted to read a veiled ironic reference to D. W. Griffith's
infamous film here, but certainly on the surface, Hurston's narrator
unabashedly celebrates the arrival of U.S. warships in Port-au-Prince with
marines on board, claiming, "The smoke from the U.S.S. *Washington* was a
black plume with a white hope" (72). Meanwhile, her pronouncements on
Haitian character, such as her contention that lying is a "habit [that] goes
from the thatched hut to the mansion" (82), situate this text in another long
line of commentators—those European and North American travelers to
the region who, beginning with Columbus, find some pathological flaw in
Caribbean identity and who, as well, stress the necessary and inevitable

dependence of Caribbean natives on the modernizing influences of superior, colonizing forces.

Columbus initiated the European discourse on Haiti and the Caribbean with his 1493 *Letter,* a text that inaugurates the imperialist tradition of depicting Caribbean society as tainted by underdevelopment, ignorance, and superstition. Human settlements in Juana (Cuba) are described in the *Letter* as primitive and undeveloped. There are "no towns or cities situated on the sea-coast, but only some villages and rude farms," and farther inland the native settlements are "small and without any government."[22] Columbus finds the Taino natives of Hispaña (Hispaniola) "by nature fearful and timid" yet "of simple manners and trustworthy." Though they trade gold for baubles "like persons without reason," nevertheless they are "of excellent and acute understanding," and ready to accept Columbus as divine. "They firmly believe," Columbus writes of the Taino, "that all strength and power, and in fact all good things are in heaven, and that I had come down from thence with these ships and sailors." The idea of native ingenuousness functions as a crucial factoid in Columbus's attempt to sell the Spanish crown on a colonizing mission based as much on the promise of Christianizing pagan souls as on the prospect of gold.

By the time of Moreau de St. Méry, who wrote about colonial Saint-Domingue on the eve of revolution, indigenous people had long since been replaced by mulattos and blacks as the focus of white travelers' proto-ethnographic observation.[23] Numerous commentators precede Moreau in detailing the interracial mores of Saint-Domingue, which was known popularly as the "Babylon of the Antilles" and the "second Sodom."[24] It is, however, Moreau's monumental *Description topographique, physique, civile, politique, et historique de la partie française de l'île Saint-Domingue* (1797/98) that contains, in its descriptions of Vodou rituals, the first extended treatment of Caribbean popular culture. Moreau responds to Vodou, which he refers to as vaudoux, with both fascination and revulsion, characterizing it as "this system of domination on the one side and of blind submission on the other" (54). In spite of the secrecy that, according to Moreau, surrounds the practice of Vodou, he offers a full description of a ceremony. Moreau's text emphasizes the physical aspects—the dress and particularly the bodily movements—of those possessed during the ritual:

> Faintings and raptures take over some of them, and a sort of fury some of the others, but for all there is a nervous trembling which they cannot master. They spin around ceaselessly. And there are some in this species of bacchanal who tear their clothing and even bite their flesh (58).

There is no mention of Vodou as a spiritual system with a fully developed theology. In Moreau's denunciation of Vodou as a "dark cabal" and "terrible weapon" (59), achieving simultaneous expression are the anticlerical and antiroyalist sentiments of a French Enlightenment thinker along with the anxiety of a French colonial overlord living in a society about to explode:

> The members propose some plans, they stop some overtures, they prescribe some action which the Voodoo Queen supports, always as the will of God, and which do not always have public order or public tranquillity for their object. . . . After all, voodoo is not a matter of amusement or enjoyment. It is rather a school where those easily influenced give themselves up to a domination which a thousand circumstances can render tragic. (57-59)

While admitting the power of Vodou (even white interlopers are liable to be possessed at a ceremony), Moreau insists on the perception of popular religion as sinister and pathological.

In nineteenth- and early-twentieth-century travel writing, pathological designations continue to apply to descriptions of Vodou. They also are extended, though, to describe Haitian culture generally in texts that strive to evaluate Haiti's commercial possibilities in the wake of nationalist revolt and a French embargo. Where Moreau had emphasized the threat posed to colonial civil society by what he views as a morass of popular superstition, British writer John Candler typifies the trope, still current in Hurston's time, that majority rule in postrevolutionary Haiti results in a reversion to the jungle. Writing in 1842, Candler's *Brief Notices of Hayti: With Its Condition, Resources, and Prospects* laments the demise of the plantation system, particularly on Haiti's southwest peninsula. "The old mountain estates are fast declining," Candler writes, describing the land as "ruinate."[25] Believing, like most of his European and North American contemporaries, in hastening Haiti's return to a subordinate position in the world system, Candler emphasizes the potential for re-establishing an export economy based on coffee and sugar. The fact that Haitian peasants are not pursuing cash crop strategies, or not pursuing them as diligently as he thinks they might, leads Candler to assert "the natural indolence of the people" (159). Still, Candler is optimistic that modern improvements are possible: "education and the spread of gospel truth only, were needed to make this land one of the finest on the face of the globe" (143-44).[26]

The European and North American tradition of commentary reaches its nadir in the narratives of U.S. voyagers whose presence in the Caribbean increases after 1898 and the Spanish-American War. In 1906, traveling to destinations in the Caribbean he had helped subjugate during the previous decade while serving as a high-ranking officer in Cuba and then as Commander-in-Chief of U.S. forces in Washington, Theodore Roosevelt described Haiti in a letter to his son. Noting the "green, jungly shores and bold mountains" of these "great, beautiful, venomous, tropical islands," Roosevelt is gripped by a vision of "the desperate fighting, the triumphs, the pestilences, all the turbulence, the splendor and wickedness, and the hot, evil, riotous life of the old planters and slave owners."[27] The colonial past constitutes an unstable foundation upon which have sprung nightmarish contemporary social relations characterized by "the decay of the islands, the returning of Haiti into a land of savage negroes, who have reverted to voodooism and cannibalism." Throughout the 1910s, 1920s, and 1930s, images of Haiti and Haitians, brought back to American readers in press accounts and sensationalist novels, travel diaries, and memoirs of Occupation officials, deviate hardly at all from the fantasy projection recorded in Roosevelt's letter. A list of some of the titles will suggest the contours of the public imagination where Haiti was concerned: *Diane, Voodoo Priestess, Where Black Rules White, The Magic Island, A Puritan in Voodoo Land, The White King of La Gônáve, Cannibal Cousins,* and *Black Baghdad.* These images reinforced an elusive but iron-clad veil of cultural difference that had been effectively thrown over Haitian society by white American writers. The key to this discursive veil is a pattern of binary oppositions that will sound depressingly familiar to any student of modern ideologies of race and gender. As Dash argues in *Haiti and the United States,* Haiti and Haitians were consistently coded as Other by U.S. commentators seeking to textualize Caribbean encounters for white readers in America:

> Haiti seems always to have had the lure of the extreme case, whether it was virgin terrain, a garden of earthly delights where the black race could begin again or the closest and most histrionic examples of Africa's continental darkness. These alternating stereotypes of a void waiting to be filled or a flamboyant, inexcusable blackness constitute a binary model of difference that fixed the relationship between the United States and Haiti, between diametrically opposed poles of mind and body, culture and nature, male and female. Haiti is negative or feminine and marginalized in a symbolic order devised by the United States. From the nineteenth century what beckons or revolts Americans is Haiti's impenetrable mystery, its strangeness, its unpredictable "Otherness." Haitians are meant to be marvelled at, studied, converted, rehabilitated and ultimately controlled (2-3).

Even Melville Herskovits, the esteemed scholar of New World African survivals, and Hurston's one-time associate at Columbia University, participates in this pattern of representing Caribbean culture as pathological. Herskovits' *Life in a Haitian Valley,* published just a year before *Tell My Horse,* is the most important anthropological text on Haiti authored by a U.S. writer prior to Hurston's text. In the chapter "What Is 'Voodoo'?," Herskovits vigorously attacks the popular North American prejudice that, largely due to the excesses of Vodou, Haitians live "in a universe of psychological terror."[28] Debunking these popular misconceptions, Herskovits identifies Vodou as "a complex of African belief and ritual governing in large measure the life of the Haitian peasant" (139). Even more specifically, in Mirebalais, the village where Herskovits did his fieldwork, Vodou signifies "a form of sacred dance accompanied by spirit possession or merely a dance" (139). At the margins of his text, however, Herskovits reiterates the dominant North American image of Haitian society as pathological, thus complicating his own positioning as a humanist and cultural relativist. "Some Wider Implications" is a speculative chapter at the end of *Life in a Haitian Valley* in which Herskovits connects his analysis of Haiti with "larger problems" (300) in cultural studies. In particular, a study of Vodou might, he suggests, illuminate aspects of the so-called "Negro problem" in the United States, since understanding Haitian society can "throw light on the way in which American Negroes have met and are meeting their own social situation" (303). Herskovits reverts to traditional imperialist travelogue rhetoric when he attempts to describe Haitian psychology and refers to "the characteristic instability of attitude and emotional expression found in the Haitian" (298). Beneath a culturalist gloss on the unhappy collision of French and West African customs, Herskovits is recycling the old colonialist anxieties about miscegenation:

> As regards the Haitian, it must be recognized that the two ancestral elements in his civilization have never been completely merged. As a result, his outwardly smoothly functioning life is full of inner conflict, so that he has to raise his defenses in order to make his adjustment within the historical and cultural combination of differing modes of life that constitute his civilization (299).

While, as a group, these texts authored by white U.S. writers exhibit a hyper-race-conscious character that gives them their own national cultural specificity, they should also be seen as part of a larger tradition of depicting Caribbean culture as flawed and in need of outside assistance. Hurston's own narrator, when she celebrates the stabilizing influence of the U.S. intervention in Haiti, or when she generalizes about the Haitian character, voices this triumphalist ideology of empire that stretches back through Roosevelt, Candler, and Moreau, to Columbus.

Can we possibly sort out the conflicting tendencies of this problematic narrator, who inscribes both the liberating tradition of African American travel writing and the oppressive weight of imperialist culture in the Caribbean? The solution, I would argue, begins with realizing that Hurston's narrator is not the locus of authority—or the sole locus of authority—in the text. In fact, there is a constant parade of informants who talk back to the roving narrator, criticizing her judgments and refusing—more and more frequently as the narrative unfolds—to cooperate with her fieldwork inquiries. As such, this ethnographizing narrator functions more as a persona, as a character in a larger (ethnographic) drama. Once we dethrone (so to speak) Hurston's roving narrator, we can then look for clues as to the narrative politics of this background drama, which, in my reading, has a strong counter-imperial message. In fact, Hurston adapts and adopts the language of Vodou spirit possession as a strategy for staging scenes of social protest, and in her descriptions of Caribbean culture, fables of self-reliance increasingly come to displace the fables of dependency that mark the early part of the text. Moreover, as I will suggest in the conclusion of this essay, her ethnography derives much of its decolonizing force from the emphasis placed in the text on exposing the gender politics that shape Caribbean culture. On several levels, then, Hurston actually reconstructs an anti-imperialist ethnographic rhetoric that repudiates the instrumental marketplace logic that would convert Haitian and Jamaican cultures into exotic spicy morsels and/or manipulable scientific data. Ultimately, Hurston refuses to serve up Haiti or Jamaica—either in easily digested popular stereotypes or authoritative ethnographic pronouncements. She not only presents, then, a criticism of ethnography and the dominant tradition of representing Caribbean culture; Hurston also elaborates a model for decolonizing cultural production.

About halfway through the text, after a mytho-prophetic account of Haitian history and a catalogue of Vodou deities and their characteristics, Hurston begins to present scenes of Vodou culture in process. At this point, she has traveled to the Isle de la Gônave, located in Port-au-Prince Bay, about 30 nautical miles northwest of the Haitian capital. This location was made notorious in the cultural mythology of the American Occupation with the arrival of Faustin Wirkus, a Marine Corps sergeant who, in 1923, was parachuted in to oversee tax collection and was, in time, allegedly crowned king by the island's ten thousand inhabitants. Hurston has disparaging things to say about Wirkus, who, in a sensationalistic autobiography, styled himself "the white king of la Gônave." What interests me here, though, are the stories she records concerning some stone relics scattered about the island, left behind by the long-since-exterminated aboriginal population. The stones are priceless to the Haitians, who consider them to be sacred, inhabited by *loas*, or Vodou spirits, yet American Marines— Wirkus' subordinates—are collecting the stones for their own use as souvenirs, marketable trinkets, or museum pieces. In itself, this scenario captures much of the logic of unequal exchange that characterizes cultural imperialism;[29] one of Hurston's stone tales, however, reveals a particular form of indigenous backlash against the American bureaucratic war machine.

> We heard about one famous stone that had so much power that it urinated. It was identified as Papa Guedé, who had ordered it to be clothed, so it wore a dress. It attracted so many people and caused so much disturbance indoors that the owner had it chained outside the door. One of the American officers of the Occupation named Whitney saw it and finally got it for himself. It was a curious idol and he wanted it for his desk. The Haitian guard attached to Whitney's station told him that it would urinate and not to put it on his desk but he did so in spite of warning and on several occasions he found his desk wet and then he removed it to the outdoors again. They said he took it away to the United States with him when he left. (136)

While somewhat oblique as a criticism of the Occupation (even though the implications of pissing on state papers seem straightforward enough), this vignette inscribes a narrative politics of resistance that emerges more explicitly when the identity of the *loa* inspiriting the prodigious stone is traced throughout the text. Papa Guedé is described in a subsequent chapter as:

> . . . the deification of the common people of Haiti. The mulattoes give this spirit no food and pay it no attention at all. He belongs to the blacks and the uneducated blacks at that. He is a hilarious divinity full of the stuff of burlesque. This manifestation comes as near a social criticism of the classes by the masses in Haiti as anything in all Haiti . . . he bites with sarcasm and slashes with ridicule the class that despises him. (219-220)

Even more important in deciphering the narrative politics in *Tell My Horse*, though, is the fact that Hurston's title links her text with the protest

of Papa Guedé's servitors. "Tell my horse" is an English-language equivalent of the Haitian Creole phrase "parlay cheval ou," which is uttered by
devotees to signal the onset of spirit possession by Papa Guedé. The loa
mounts a subject "as a rider mounts a horse," and, guided by the spirit-rider
"the 'horse' does and says many things that he or she would never have
uttered un-ridden" (221). Hurston also insists that serving Papa Guedé can
be a means for expressing veiled or coded protest by those who "are feigning possession in order to express their resentment general and particular.
That phrase, 'Parlay Cheval Ou,' is in daily, hourly use in Haiti and no doubt
it is used as a blind for self-expression" (221). In my view, this identification with the *loa* of social protest serves as the crux of Hurston's larger
text-building strategy: "tell my horse" is a blind for Hurston's own self-
expression, allowing her to criticize not only the U.S. presence, but also the
locally compounded practices of race, class, caste, and gender oppressions
that Caribbeans inflict on one another. In Hurston's hands, then, ethnography becomes "possessed": she makes it speak in a language of indigenous
protest. In addition, though, I think we should view *Tell My Horse* as a critique of ethnography as a form of knowledge and see Hurston as working
to produce a dissenting form of transnational culture grounded in African
diasporan manipulations of the public sphere. The key elements in the production of African diasporan spheres are both explicit criticism of oppressive social relations and a "critique of the commodity form to which black
humanity was reduced during the slave period."[30]

To specify how this oppositional framework applies in Hurston's case,
we have to recall the description of anthropology as "the child of imperialism" and consider how ethnography collaborates (in the pejorative sense)
at a crucial moment in the history of Empire by coding and commodifying indigenous cultures—producing them in ways that maintain a subordinate relationship to metropolitan power.[31] Working mostly with Latin
American models, Armand Mattelart has characterized the postcolonial
process generally as one of global restructuring beyond the network of
nation-states. Formerly colonized territories and the people who live in
them are both objects and subjects in this struggle—players as well as the
prize vied for by multinational capital. Mattelart defines the terms of the
struggle of "third" world peoples as a fight between dependency and self-
reliance. In particular, this period of restructuring political economies
beyond the framework of nation-states is characterized by the increasing
use of cultural technologies to help solve the political problems that inhibit
the further accumulation of capital:

. . . the culture industry, and in a broader sense the information industry, is increasingly considered in our societies not only as an economic way out of the crisis (notice that information has been set up as an essential factor of production, a basic resource), but equally as a political way out of the crisis [in accumulation] (one no longer talks only of the information industry but also of the information *society*). As a producer of consensus between groups and classes, as much at the national as at the international level, it is called upon to participate in the restructuring of attitudes or to use the words of [Zbigniew] Brezinksi, who takes his desires for reality, to allow a "new planetarian consciousness" to be elaborated.[32]

Even progressive and radical ethnographers must contend with the way in which anthropological labor helps manage the transition from direct colonial rule to indirect neocolonial domination (interestingly, *Tell My Horse* looks at examples of both) by packaging indigenous cultures. In this vision, ethnography figures as a culture or information industry apparatus that serves the interests of multinational capital by commodifying or streamlining ethnographized cultures for smoother insertion in a revised global order. This insertion can occur through any number of forms, ranging from ethnographic films, (such as "Dances With Wolves," which smoothes over the U.S. government's genocidal treatment of Native Americans by eulogizing the demise of indigenous culture through the eyes of a white liberal whose discursive memorial seeks to expiate guilt), to country profiles for the World Bank or Agency for International Development, to CIA studies on how to manipulate local leadership most effectively.[33] Within the specific framework of representations of Caribbean culture, what links ethnographic writing like Herskovits' and even Katherine Dunham's with the history of European and North American travel culture from Columbus to the present, is the production of a symptomatic vision of the Caribbean "natives" as dependent in some way on "first" world society.[34] Sometimes childlike, sometimes savage, always archetypally underdeveloped, Caribbean societies consistently appear in ethnographic travel documents as desperately needing, if not desperately seeking, outside intervention of some kind.

Against this backdrop of predatory transnationalism, however, Hurston presents instead a pattern of dissident transnationalism. If, as anthropologist and cultural theorist Johannes Fabian argues, anthropological writing is "a praxis of representation in a context of power," *Tell My Horse* also must be seen as a textual practice that reconfigures the typical power relations enacted by anthropological texts.[35] Hurston disengages from ethnography's codification/commodification program by constructing an ethnographic drama in which fables of Caribbean dependency are displaced by fables of Caribbean self-reliance, thus short-circuiting anthropology's institutional logic. Though there are many series of scenes that establish this pattern, I will confine myself to two anecdotes concerning the use of fire, which I take to be an archetype for the Promethean, politically charged force of technology in the colonial encounter. When she arrives at the Maroon compound in Accompong, during the Jamaican leg of her journey, Hurston honors the community as a site of successful black liberation, yet she notes critically the stagnation produced by centuries of isolation from the flow of world events:

> Standing on that old parade ground, which is now a cricket field, I could feel the dead generations crowding me. Here was the oldest settlement of freedmen in the Western world, no doubt. Men who had thrown off the bands of slavery by their own courage and ingenuity. The courage and daring of the Maroons strike like a purple beam across the history of Jamaica. And yet as I stood there looking into the sea beyond Black River from the mountains of St. Catherine, and looking at the thatched huts close at hand, I could not help remembering that a whole civilization and the mightiest nation on earth had grown up on the mainland since the first runaway slave had taken refuge in these mountains. They were here before the Pilgrims landed on the bleak shores of Massachusetts. Now, Massachusetts had stretched from the Atlantic to the Pacific and Accompong had remained itself (22).

Hurston finds the present-day Maroons "very primitive" (23)—what amounts to an historical cul-de-sac. A clear sign of this stagnation is the fact that

> there was not a stove in all Accompong. The cooking, ironing and whatever else is done, is done over an open fire with the women squatting on their haunches and inhaling the smoke (23).

Very quickly, this arouses an interventionist impulse in Hurston and leads to her most active engagement with Caribbeans in the entire narrative:

> I told Rowe [the leader of the Maroons] that he ought to buy a stove himself to show the others what to do. He said he could not afford one. Stoves are not customary in Jamaica outside of good homes in the cities anyway. They are imported luxuries. I recognized that and took another tack. We

would build one! I designed an affair to be made of rock and cement and Colonel Rowe and some men he gathered undertook to make it. We sent out to the city and bought some sheet tin for the stove pipe and the pot-holes. I measured the bottoms of the pots and designed a hole to fit each of the three. The center hole was for the great iron pot and then there were two other holes of different sizes. Colonel Rowe had some lime there, and he sent his son and grandchildren out to collect more rocks. His son-in-law-to-be mixed the clay and lime and in a day the furnace-like stove was built. The kitchen house lacking a floor anyway, the stove was built clear across one side of the room so that there was room on it for pots and pans not in use. The pot-holes were lined with tin so that the pots would not break the mortar. Then we left it a day to dry. We were really joyful when we fired it the next day and found out that it worked. Many of the Maroons came down to look at the miracle. There were pots boiling on the fire; no smoke in the room but a great column of black smoke shooting out of the stove pipe which stuck out of the side of the house (23-24).

Beyond Hurston's justified pride in Maroon history, despite her politic sensitivity to cultural values shaped by economic class position (the Maroons had seen stoves as "imported luxuries"), and beneath a strong argument for pan-African solidarity (conveyed in the final image of rising black smoke), which suggests that successful black liberation in the twentieth century demands a hybrid union of intellectual and physical labor, the details in this anecdote coalesce into what is, fundamentally, a fable of dependency. Hurston narrates from the position of a semidivine Prometheus bringing fire and general modernizing technical skills to lesser mortals. The Maroons occupy this latter position as recipients of the Promethean gifts and confirm the asymmetry of the contract by viewing as a "miracle" the process that Hurston has just laid out in detail for readers to whom (presumably) the account will make logical sense. To be fair, the new stove looks more like an enlightened case of sustainable, appropriate technology than a suspect case of profit-motivated technology transfer, but my reading emphasizes the message—encoded in an ostensibly friendly encounter—that Caribbean development depends, necessarily and in this case happily, on the modernizing North American culture that Hurston bears.

This visit must be read against another fire tale that appears very near the end of *Tell My Horse*. After a night of touristic partying at the home of one of her patrons in Port-au-Prince, Hurston and her host receive an invitation to attend a different kind of party in Aux Cayes, a city on the southern coast of Haiti.

[The invitation] had been passed along by word of mouth of market women until it came to the young woman in Port-au-Prince. . . . What kind of ceremony was it going to be? It was to be a ceremony where food was to be cooked without fire. Real food? Yes, a great pot of real food—enough to feed all of the people attending the ceremony—would be cooked without fire. Was such a thing *possible?* The young woman asked for a cup and saucer, a fresh piece of laundry blue, a cup of cold water and a fresh egg. No, she did not wish to acquire the egg herself for fear that we might believe that she had one prepared. Dr. Reser [Hurston's host] went out and got one himself and gave it to her. She placed it in the cup at once. Poured some of the cold water on it and covered the cup with the saucer and made a cross mark on the saucer with the bluing. Then she bowed her head and mumbled a prayer for a few minutes. None of us could catch the exact words of what she said in that prayer. When it was over, she lifted the saucer and offered the egg to Dr. Reser with a diffident smile and told him to break it. He refused on the grounds that he had on his best gray suit and did not wish to have it spattered with egg. She assured him time and again that the egg would not spatter over his clothes. At last he broke the egg very carefully and found it done. That was startling enough. But the realest surprise came when the egg was found to be harder in the center than anywhere else. The young woman now begged him to eat the egg. He was so reluctant to do so that it was necessary for her to coax him a great deal, but she prevailed at last and he ate the egg. Then she assured him that he would never die of poisoning. He would always be warned in time to avoid eating poisoned food or touching poisoned surfaces. Would he now accept the invitation to the ceremony? He would with great unction and avidity (250).

Hurston and Reser duly attend the ceremony, which she describes in great ethnographic detail, noting the physical makeup of the hounfort, the menu for the feast, the clothing of the Vodou servitors, the music and dance steps associated with the ritual, and so on. At length they eat the food, but Hurston's "first" world appetite for anthropological data is still not satisfied. She writes:

How was the food cooked? I do not know. Dr. Reser and I tried bribery and everything else in our power to learn the secret but it belongs to that small group and nothing we could devise would do any good. Dr. Reser knew the girl who had boiled the egg in cold water very well indeed. I would say that they are very intimate friends. He concentrated upon her finally, but all she would say was that it was a family secret brought from Africa which could not be divulged. He kept at her and she yielded enough to say that she could not tell him until he had been baptised in a certain ceremony. He went to the trouble and the expense to have the baptism. After that was over, she returned to her original position that it was an inherited secret which she could not divulge under pain of death. So this is how far we got on with the food-without-fire ceremony. (251–52)

At this point, we might ask, did Hurston *really* see the egg boiled in cold water, or the feast cooked without fire, and, if we can't trust this story, what about the rest of *Tell My Horse*? Yet, what is ingenious about the narrative is that, like the young woman from Aux Cayes, it resists such prying interrogative demands. The dynamics of Hurston's blocked attempt to decode the text of the indigenous ritual transfer to (and serve as an allegory for) readers' attempts to unpack the information in Hurston's ethnography. Like the African family secret at the heart of the Vodou ceremony, the truth content of Hurston's account is not so much put into doubt as it is put beyond the reach of instrumental reason, manifested here in the fieldworkers' attempt to gain—by "bribery and everything else in our power"—access to the local technical know-how contained in the ritual.

Instead, what we are left to chew on is the fact of this indigenous resistance and its implications for reading the narrative politics in *Tell My Horse*. As I suggested earlier, my inclination is to see this as a fable of self-reliance that displaces the earlier fable of dependency used by the narrator to encode her encounter with the Accompong Maroons. Hurston's engineering skills are ultimately irrelevant in a cultural setting where Haitians are technologically self-sufficient and cannily able to fend off two ethnographers and their insistent demands.[36] In this Haitian fire tale, it is the Caribbeans, not Hurston, who appear semidivine, and no amount of ethnographic sleuthing will rationalize or secularize their feat. The food-without-fire description not only blocks the narrator's gaze, and that of her readers, it also repudiates the modernizing program of "first" world social science. It is, then, as a form of grassroots cultural resistance that the alleged magical aspects of Haitian folk religion assume their meaning in Hurston's text. *Tell My Horse* does not present a romanticized picture of Vodou as primitive magic, nor as an essential marker of savage identity in the bush. Rather, Vodou becomes coded as magical in the context of an encounter with predatory "first" world science. Actually, the possibility that Vodou practices have scientific—rather than magical—status is something that Hurston considers in her chapter on zombies. In it, she records a conversation with a Haitian doctor who speculates that "many scientific truths were hidden in some of these primitive practices that have been brought from Africa" (205). As in the case of the food-without-fire incident, though, these "scientific truths" are withheld: despite attempts by the Haitian doctor to unlock the secrets of the peasant herbalists, "never had he been able to break down the resistance of the holder of those secrets" (205). For Hurston, asserting the magical aspects of Vodou must be seen as a strategy of representation, that is, as an effort to describe the ethnographic encounter in a way that preserves the resistance status of Haitian peasants.

All of this brings us back to questions of representation: how Caribbean cultures have been imagined, and for whom. Once released into the marketplace, *Tell My Horse* does not perform as expected (that is, by serving up the ethnographized culture for easy consumption). Caribbean people are not presented as exotic morsels—that is, as noble savages, or bloodthirsty savages—neither are they transformed into manipulable data for social planners. What they "are" is strategically left indiscernible. Combined with the black liberationist itinerary, the anticolonial and antisexist protest, and the movement toward depictions of Caribbean self-reliance as the text moves geographically from Port-au-Prince into the Haitian countryside, the inscriptions of *Tell My Horse* enact a formal logic that radically reworks ethnography, orienting it toward pragmatic liberation via African diasporan cultural politics.

Up to this point, I have concentrated on showing how Hurston decolonizes ethnography by making it speak in a language of indigenous social protest, and by disrupting the institutional practices of an imperialist cultural marketplace. But I have considered only in passing the role of gender analysis in her anthropology. Yet, gendered and gendering cultural descriptions are at the core of her ethnographic method, and since *Tell My Horse* expands the scope of decolonization by equating Hurston's research with the struggle of authoring female subjectivity, it is both appropriate and necessary to now centralize the question of gender and decolonization. Hurston's work in *Tell My Horse* places her precisely at the intersection of postcolonial cultures and their inscription by women writers. In addition, her nearly unique status as a black female anthropologist in the 1930s—at once an anthropological insider by virtue of her talents, training, and ambition, as well as an outsider by virtue of closeness to the experience of her informants and exclusionary racial and sexist social practices—creates possibilities for North American and Caribbean dialogue with the potential to mediate, or at least illuminate in important ways, the divisions separating "first" and "third" world women. To conclude my argument for the importance of *Tell My Horse* as a theoretical and practical model of cultural decolonization, I will look at how Hurston explores the legacies of colonialism in the Caribbean from the standpoint of female sexuality—particularly through the use of stories about failed romance—while examining closely how her rhetoric articulates and negotiates the tension between a feminist kind of solidarity, on the one hand, and, on the other, a "first" world/"third" world division.

In Hurston's decolonizing ethnography, gendered cultural descriptions play a crucial mediating role and deserve special attention. Her dialectical formula, "It is a curious thing to be a woman in the Caribbean after you have been one in these United States" (57), asserts a relation between Hurston's identity and that of her informants on the basis of gender (experiencing what it means "to be a woman"). Simultaneously, it differentiates Hurston from her informants at the level of national community and regional geopolitics. In addition, this formula presumes a similarity between the highly differentiated social terrain in Haiti and Jamaica, both of which are subsumed under the regional heading "the Caribbean." Thus, gender is posed as a category that can mediate social divisions in the Caribbean as well as enable communication (and, potentially, coalition) through the international division of labor separating North Americans and Caribbeans, as well as Caribbeans from one another.

Much of what Hurston writes in *Tell My Horse* deals with the struggle for control over female sexuality and how the cultural definition of "woman" is constructed and contested within the matrix of Caribbean colonial culture. Consequently, gendered cultural descriptions permeate Hurston's accounts of Caribbean mores. A curry goat feed given in her honor in St. Mary's Parish, Jamaica, is noteworthy because it "has never been done for another woman" (11). The feast itself is described as "utterly masculine in every detail" (11) and Hurston's catalogue of the menu is full of phallic representations: cock soup, ram goat, and banana dumpling. Particularly in the first five chapters of *Tell My Horse,* her insistent gendering of social texts centralizes the focus on sexism in a way that allows Hurston to explore and criticize women's oppression as a foundation of Jamaican society. Thus, for example, Hurston gives repeated, extensive treatment to the official and unofficial institutions that help to maintain a sexual division of labor among the groups she visits. Hurston writes:

[I]f she is of no particular family, poor and black, [a Caribbean woman] is in a bad way indeed in that man's world. She had better pray to the Lord to turn her into a donkey and be done with the thing. . . . It is just considered down there that God made two kinds of donkeys, one kind that can talk.

The black women of Jamaica load banana boats now, and the black women used to coal ships when they burned coal (58).

In addition to exposing a racialized sexual division of labor that brutalizes black Caribbean women, Hurston focuses extensively on marriage customs. Marriage rites constitute a key cultural arena in which sex, class, and color caste ideologies play out in ways that reproduce a rigidly hierarchical Caribbean social weave. Through marriage to richer and/or lighter-skinned women, propertied men insure inheritance and color privilege. Because rich men will not marry outside their class, upper-class women have a comparative benefit—even over their Yankee counterparts—in that their standard of living is guaranteed (as long as the Caribbean native bourgeoisie remain capitalized). Yet the price of this security for women is complicity in a system in which "all women are inferior to all men by God and law" (58). In addition to being coerced by an external social machinery (legal statutes, property and paternity laws, etc.) women are taught to internalize the proper behavior and consciousness through a variety of rituals. One extended passage records a Jamaican prenuptial initiation rite that concludes with a strict interpellation code being drummed into the bride-to-be: "The whole duty of a woman is love and comfort. You were never intended for anything else. You are made for love and comfort. Think of yourself in that way and no other" (20).

Hurston's early hintings at the male hypocrisy enshrined in marriage customs (12) are confirmed subsequently in the chapter "Women in the Caribbean." She recounts several anecdotes from both Haiti and Jamaica that describe the fate of women who are separated from men by class and/or color. As Hurston discovers, "the man has no obligation to a girl outside of his class. She has no rights which he is bound to respect. What is worse, the community would be shocked if he did respect them" (59). Rich and/or mulatto men court and seduce poor and/or black women only to abandon them in favor of more appropriate marriage partners (60–62). Though the selection criteria and standards of behavior for men toward marriageable women are influenced by color, and certainly work to confine darker-skinned women to the most disenfranchised conditions, it is economic class, in Hurston's understanding, that intensifies the oppressive nature of marriage institutions. In borderline cases in which there is the possibility of a man treating a woman with some decency, it is class pressure that reinforces exploitative action on the part of men. One union between a middle-aged couple from a working-class background stands out as a telling exception to the litany of woeful marriage stories in *Tell*

My Horse (14-15), suggesting again that economic status has a critical role in determining how individual experiences will be articulated within the framework of gendered and racialized social institutions.

In her investigation of how culture shapes the sexual life of women in the Caribbean, Hurston also highlights various forms of resistance against rampant sexism. Possession by the Haitian *loa* Papa Guedé—the voice of strong social protest—permits one woman to cry out, before committing suicide, against the heterosexism that has censured her lesbian identity (222). The premarital female initiation rite Hurston observes in Jamaica constitutes a form of women's solidarity existing in the interstices of patri-archal sex-role formation. Though appearing at first glance to be the ulti-mate socialization of women (by women) as male sex objects—Ishmael Reed in his foreward to *Tell My Horse* characterizes this scene as depicting "the cultivation of Geishas for the delight of prospective grooms" (xiv)—it is worth reconsidering this ritual, in which a community of women stimulate the bride-to-be with an aphrodisiacal ganga tea and "light-fin-gered manipulation down the body" (19) until she "swoons" in orgasm. Could we not re-read this ritual as a counter-institution establishing the priority of a woman-identified path to female sexual fulfillment?

On the whole, Haitian women seem to suffer less extreme sexist abuse than their Jamaican counterparts, in Hurston's account. Interestingly, the use of gendered descriptions tapers off in the Haitian portion of the book, indicating perhaps that Hurston experienced a less sexist fabric of daily life. The gendered difference between Jamaica and Haiti is evident in the name-tag epithets Hurston assigns to each country: Jamaica, as we have seen, is "the Rooster's Nest," while Haiti is termed "the black daughter of France" (93). In Haiti, gender appears most centrally in Hurston's descrip-tions of androgynous cultural expressions within the realm of Vodou. Stones identified with Papa Guedé are dressed in grass skirts, while cross-dressing is emphasized as an element in the rite associated with Guedé's "cousin," Baron Samedi. Erzulie Freda thoroughly confounds gender cate-gories. Although she is described as the quintessence of bourgeois senti-mentality and heterosexuality (Hurston's Erzulie embodies "the ideal of the love bed"), typically it is men who are the mounts for this Erzulie. In choosing her own "husbands," Erzulie also reverses the marriage power dynamics criticized at length earlier in *Tell My Horse*.[37]

Overall, Hurston's sense of gender politics in Haiti squares with the commentary of other observers who have noted the egalitarian aspects of Vodou culture with regard to gender, and the economic and social power of Haitian market women.[38] Hurston portrays vivid scenes of empowered

Haitian women, who typically combine a position as mambo, or Vodou priestess, with prominent political or economic activities. Examples include the "feast without fire" passage (analyzed earlier), in which the invitation to attend the feast is "passed along by word of mouth of market women" (250), as well as an earlier chapter titled "The Black Joan of Arc" (93–101), which recounts the military and political triumphs of Celestina Simon, a mambo who rules the country along with her father for a brief period beginning in 1908. While there is a sexual division of labor in Haiti, gender differences appear to be defined more by complementarity than by power imbalances.

At the same time, Hurston does not romanticize or idealize the conditions of women in Haiti. Celestina falls from power in an ironic twist after repudiating a Vodou-sanctioned "marriage" to a sacred goat, Simalo, in order to pursue marriage to "a man of position and wealth" (97). The marriage plot fails, Celestina and her father are thrown out of the presidential palace, and she lives out her days as "an elderly woman living in poverty in the South" (99). And, as Hurston's "Women in the Caribbean" chapter implies, the problem of patriarchal legal codes extends throughout the region—*including* Haiti. When looking at Hurston's portrayal of the effects of Haitian law, it bears emphasizing that as the focus in *Tell My Horse* moves from the urban center to the outlying rural regions, the conditions seem to improve for women, with scenes of women's oppression giving way to scenes of active and empowered women. Here again, Hurston re-evaluates the opposition between Westernized bourgeois social structures and African-influenced peasant structures that forms the basis of so much European and North American travel writing on the Caribbean and especially Haiti.[39] Throughout her text, Hurston consistently teases out the sexual politics of social formations in which both Jamaican and Haitian women struggle for control over their bodies. On what basis, though, does Hurston connect with the condition of Caribbean women? What kind of solidarity is it that allows her to perceive and expose Caribbean gender politics?

While gender functions in *Tell My Horse* as a dialectical category that can throw into relief interlocking social divisions based on race, color, class, and nationality, Hurston never minimizes those differences in order to assert a simple or transparent feminist solidarity. Rather, Hurston continually marks her position as a woman from the United States. The opening passage of "Women in the Caribbean" goes on from the initial statement, "It is a curious thing to be a woman in the Caribbean after you have been one in these United States," to specify North American gendered life in terms that seem to deny the oppression of U.S. women: "The majority of the solid citizens strain their ears trying to find out what it is that their womenfolk want so they can strain around and try to get it for them" (57). With characteristic jagged harmony, this statement celebrating women's good fortune in the United States is placed side by side with her extended, muckraking account of sexist political economy in the Caribbean. "Of course," Hurston writes, "all women are inferior to all men by God and law down there," and her depiction of "sex superiority" is replete with stories of rape, abandonment, and "[t]he old African custom of polygamy"— though she also claims, concerning marital infidelity in the Caribbean, that "the finer touches of keeping mistresses come from Europe" (58). In one of the few passages containing actual bodily description, Hurston details the physical effects of neo–slave labor on black women in Jamaica. The narrative focuses on "their big toes thickened like a hoof from a life time of knocking against stones" (59) and concludes with the comment, "everywhere in the Caribbean women carry a donkey's load on their heads and walk up and down mountains with it" (59).[40]

If we read back from these descriptions to the ebullient, bodacious passages concerning the life of women in the United States, the latter images seem even more incompatible with the stark picture of poverty, physical pain, and emotional abuse suffered by Caribbean women. Such passages function, I would suggest, as indicators of the narrator's own relative privilege. Yet it is crucial to pick up on a level of dissembling that makes Hurston's claim to privilege more a narrative mask than a statement of objective fact. Even a surface acquaintance with her U.S.-based writing confirms that Hurston has compressed a meaningful, ironic silence into the phrase "after you have been a woman in these United States." Specifically, what is silent here—what goes without saying, because for Hurston to say it would dissemble on her relative privilege—is an awareness of women's oppression in America.[41] This goes without saying also because it is not necessary to articulate such oppression for the "you" that is mentioned several times in this chapter, "Miss America, World's champion woman" (57). Silence about women's oppression in America is thus a gendered silent crux in *Tell My Horse* that signifies to those who can read its (apparently) absent text. Self-ironizing rhetoric (which operates throughout *Tell My Horse*) helps to validate descriptions of women's experiences in the Caribbean by making clear Hurston's awareness that she occupies a different location within the social machinery of imperialism than the place(s) occupied by her female informants. Much of the impact of Hurston's decolonizing critique, I would argue, stems directly from this ironic rhetoric and its effectiveness in registering the difference between "first" and "third" world women's experiences.[42]

Recognizing Hurston's self-conscious awareness of divisions within the category "woman" is a prerequisite for grasping the utopian aspects of *Tell My Horse,* which center around possibilities for dissident transnational communication and the political corollary of coalition across colonial barriers. Her ability to articulate differences in the construction of gender roles presumes an underlying identification with the oppressed conditions she encounters among Caribbean women. Not only is the narrative driven—made possible—by a silent presumption of the oppressive conditions of gendered life in the United States; clearly, Hurston is also experiencing abuse and condescension in interactions with many Caribbean male informants, and this becomes another ground of solidarity with Caribbean women. When she is accosted by Jamaican interlocutors—"darkish men who make vociferous love to you but otherwise pay you no mind" (57)—Hurston's analysis is informed by an awareness of her own vulnerability to being scripted into the role assigned for women in the Caribbean. With an irony that, in this case, directly conveys her anger rather than veiling it, Hurston writes:

> If you try to talk sense, they [Caribbean men] look at you right pitifully as if to say, "What a pity! That mouth that was made to supply some man (and why not me) with kisses, is spoiling itself asking stupidities about banana production and wages!" It is not that they try to put you in your place, no. They consider that you never had any. (57-58)

The shared reality of living gendered female experience as alienation, negation, and displacement figures as a possible condition for Hurston being able to see and write about kinds and degrees of difference among Haitian, Jamaican, and North American women. Despite the distance introduced between herself, seen as a "first" world anthropologist, and her informants, seen as super-exploited "third" world laborers and household slaves, Hurston produced a text that stands as a mediating commentary not only within the Caribbean (it bridges between the two legs of her journey by incorporating stories from both Haiti and Jamaica), but also between the Caribbean and North America. Even today, at a point in time when strategies for progressive anti- and counter-imperial coalition across national and regional boundaries are desperately needed, *Tell My Horse* stands out as an inspiring example of how such connections might be elaborated. Perhaps most important for present-day readers and writers, *Tell My Horse* exposes the tension between theory and practice of representing colonial encounters and, ultimately, subverts the existing production modes of high theory in the process. Hurston accomplishes this by displacing social science discourse in favor of spirit possession, and by voicing a critique of ethnography as an institutional practice designed to reinforce stereotyped conceptual models of dependency and modernization. When we add to this an awareness of how gender analyses negotiate "first" world/"third" world divisions between women, it becomes clear that Hurston herself is addressing the role of cultural theory as a key problem in articulating cross-cultural dialogue. Because, moreover, Hurston insists in her ethnography that we focus on writing as a form of social action, the vision of her as politically naive or hidebound needs seriously to be re-examined.43 The writer who emerges from Tell My Horse is adept and even radical (especially when it comes to global issues) in her ability to navigate the literary marketplace, to negotiate the cultural politics of Caribbean-American relations, and to comment on these realms from her position as an African American woman anthropologist. The resulting style in *Tell My Horse*—hybrid and authority-subverting—constitutes not a structural flaw, but rather what Johannes Fabian terms a "critical epistemological diagnosis" of the ethnographic endeavor, that is, "a struggle with the 'means of production' of discourse that include autobiography, political economy, relations of power, scientific canons, and literary form" (765). The implications of this critique, as spelled out by Fabian, are profound. He writes:

> Perhaps we dare not say what we dare not hope: power relations must change. What can experimenting with genres or the critique of writing accomplish toward that end? Well, to begin with, they can help, have already helped, to undermine the kind of objectivity and the neutral nature of scientific prose. But is there a guarantee that oppressors will be less oppressive just because they become self-conscious? Consciousness-raising can only be preparatory to a critique which might have a chance of being truly subversive (768).

While Hurston was not a writer committed to frontline political organizing, her layered, resistant writing in *Tell My Horse* reminds us how cultural representations and the institutions within which they are promulgated form a key link in maintaining oppressive imperialist power relations, as well as necessary sites of anti- and counter-colonial resistance. This is a lesson that must be learned by anyone interested in decolonizing ethnography as a rhetorical and as an institutional practice in which diverse cultures come to terms.

NOTES

1. The writer wishes to thank the Africa and the Americas Committee of the University of Maryland at College Park, which supported this essay in earlier stages with a travel grant to visit the Zora Neale Hurston Collection at the University of Florida.

2. Zora Neale Hurston, *Their Eyes Were Watching God.* Foreword by Mary Helen Washington (New York: Harper Collins, 1990).

3. Zora Neale Hurston, *Tell My Horse: Voodoo and Life in Haiti and Jamaica.* Foreword by Ishmael Reed (New York: Harper Collins, 1990). Page references will appear in parentheses in the text.

4. For some sense of Hurston as a forerunner of contemporary African American anthropology, see St. Claire Drake, "Anthropology and the Black Experience." *The Black Scholar* (Sept.-Oct. 1980): 2-31. See also several essays by Gwendolyn Mikell, "The Anthropological Imagination of Zora Neale Hurston." *Western Journal of Black Studies* 7 (1): 27-35; "When Horses Talk: Reflections on Zora Neale Hurston's Haitian Anthropology." *Phylon* (Sept. 1982): 218-30; and especially her entry, "Zora Neale Hurston." In *Women Anthropologists: Selected Bibliographies.* Edited by Ute Gacs, et. al. (Urbana: University of Illinois Press, 1989), 160-166.

5. The current intersection of feminism and the critique of colonial discourse with anthropological writing begins with the special issue of *Inscriptions* edited by Deborah Gordon in 1989, *Feminism and the Critique of Colonial Discourse/Inscriptions* 3/4 [1989]. Kamela Visweswaran's essay, "Defining Feminist Ethnography" (*Inscriptions* 3/4 (1989): 27-46), which includes reference to Hurston's work, focuses not on Hurston's anthropological writing per se but rather on anthropological aspects of the novel *Their Eyes Were Watching God.* Fran Bartkowski's "Travellers vs. Ethnics: Discourses of Displacement" (*Discourse* 15.3 [Spring, 1993]: 158-176). Deborah Gordon, "The Politics of Ethnographic Authority: Race and Writing in the Ethnography of Margaret Mead and Zora Neale Hurston." In *Modernism and Anthropology.* Edited by Marc Manganaro (Princeton, NJ: Princeton University Press, 1990), 146-162, and Graciela Hernandez, "Multiple Subjectivities and Strategic Positionality: Zora Neale Hurston's Experimental Ethnographies." In *Women Writing Culture.* Eds., Ruth Behar and Deborah A. Gordon (Berkeley: University of California Press, 1995). All offer examples of critics reassessing *Tell My Horse* in light of feminist and postcolonial scholarship. While Bartkowski, Gordon, and Hernandez begin the process

of reclaiming Hurston's anthropology (as opposed to her fiction) for mainstream radical theory, none of the three delves deeply enough into the narrative and institutional politics enacted by Hurston's text.

6. Robert Hemenway, *Zora Neale Hurston: A Literary Biography* (Champaign-Urbana and Chicago: University of Illinois Press, 1977), 226-231.

7. Thomas Fiehrer, "Political Violence in the Periphery: The Haitian Massacre of 1937." *Race and Class* 32:2 (1990): 4.

8. Gwendolyn Mikell, "Zora Neale Hurston." In *Women Anthropologists: Selected Bibliographies,* 218.

9. Léon-François Hoffmann, *Essays on Haitian Literature* (Washington, D.C.: Three Continents Press, 1984).

10. J. Michael Dash, *Haiti and the United States: National Stereotypes and the Literary Imagination* (New York: St. Martin's Press, 1988), 59. Subsequent references will appear in parentheses in the text.

11. Hemenway, 248.

12. Lynn A. Bolles, "Anthropological Research Methods for the Study of Women in the Caribbean." *Women in Africa and the African Diaspora.* Edited by Rosalyn Terborg-Penn, Sharon Harley, Andrea Benton Rushing (Washington, D.C.: Howard University Press, 1989), 65. An African-American anthropologist herself, whose own research follows Hurston's by analyzing the organizing and agency of working-class Caribbean women, Bolles offers this incisive critique of anthropology as a discipline: "Established in the late nineteenth century, during the height of social Darwinism, anthropology has been used to serve the colonization efforts of the British, to document the U.S. government's maintenance of Native American reservations, and to romanticize the exotica of black America" (65-66). At the same time, Bolles argues for the progressive potential of anthropology as a form of knowledge that is "at once wholistic, comparative, particularistic, and general." Thus, Bolles also claims the following: "Despite its less than constructive history, however, anthropology has the ability to serve as a positive social force for advancing equality among people" (66). My contention in this essay is that Hurston manifests both the liberating and oppressive tendencies in anthropological research and writing, though I argue that ultimately she places more emphasis on decolonizing strategies and techniques in *Tell My Horse.*

13. See *The Trial Record of Denmark Vesey.* Introduction by John O. Killens (Boston: Beacon Press, 1970), xi, xv, 13.

14. See, for example, the letter excerpted by Brenda Gayle Plummer, which provides an illuminating account of gun-toting politicians in the Haitian parliament. Holly's letter, which characterizes the legislators' use of firearms as a case of militant democracy, is a powerful antidote to the tendency among American commentators to see Haiti in terms of reversion to savagery (*Haiti and the Great Powers, 1902-1915* [Baton Rouge and London: Louisiana State University Press, 1988, 20]).

15. Quoted by Philip Foner in *The Life and Writings of Frederick Douglass, Vol. 4: Reconstruction and After* (New York: International Publishers, 1950), 132.

16. Quoted in Foner, 133.

17. James Weldon Johnson, *Along This Way* (New York: Viking, 1933), 344ff.

18. James Weldon Johnson, "Self-Determining Haiti." In *Speech and Power: The African-American American Essay and its Cultural Content from Polemics to Pulpit, Vol. 2*. Edited by Gerald Early (New York: Echo, 1992), 214. Originally published in *Nation* 111, 4 parts, (August 28-September 25, 1920). Johnson dignifies the urban poor and peasants in Haiti, comparing both groups favorably to their U.S. and European counterparts. In Johnson's view, Port-au-Prince slums "are no less picturesque and no more primitive, no humbler, yet cleaner, than similar quarters in Naples, in Lisbon, in Marseilles, and more justifiable than the great slums of civilization's centers—London and New York, which are totally without aesthetic redemption" (212). Johnson sounds a similar note when describing a typical scene in the countryside. Peasant dwellings, he writes, "rarely consist of only one room, the humblest having two or three, with a little shed front and back, a front and rear entrance, and plenty of windows. An aesthetic touch is never lacking—a flowering hedge or an arbor with trained vines bearing gorgeous colored blossoms. There is no comparison between the neat plastered-wall, thatched-roof cabin of the Haitian peasant and the traditional log hut of the South or the shanty of the more wretched American suburbs. The most notable feature about the Haitian cabin is its invariable cleanliness" (213).

19. James Weldon Johnson, "Haiti: What Are We Really Doing There?" (unsigned article). *The Crisis* (July, 1926): 125-127.

20. Brenda Gayle Plummer, "The Afro-American Response to the American Occupation of Haiti, 1915-1934." *Phylon* 43:2 (1982): 125-143.

21. Writing in *Race and Class,* Thomas Fiehrer decries the extent to which this incident has been continually swept under the carpet by journalists and scholars since it occurred in 1937. Between 10,000 and 20,000 Haitian workers died at the Haiti–Dominican Republic border when Dominican troops killed Haitians en masse under orders from then-Secretary of the Interior Joaquín Balaguer (until recently President of the D.R.). The massacre came at a moment when jobs—even for Dominicans who normally shunned the cane fields—were scarce due to economic depression. Fiehrer's analysis summarizes the situation in this way: "In short, the Haitians became an eyesore—driving down Dominican wages, depleting rural resources (especially timber, their preferred fuel) and insulting the Euro-caucasian self-image of most Dominicans" (10). Hurston lambasts Haitian leaders, particularly Sténio Vincent, for failing to deploy the Garde d'Haiti that had been created as a surrogate police force by the U.S. Marines. She writes: "Does President Vincent think it better to allow the Dominicans to kill a few thousand Haitian peasants than to arm the peasants and risk being killed

himself? . . . Are his own people more to be feared than Trujillo? Does he reason that after all those few thousand peasants are dead and gone and he is still President in the palace?" (88). The point here is that, by bringing the 1937 massacre to the surface in her narrative, Hurston places herself in a line of descent from other critical African American travelers such as Weldon Johnson and Douglass.

22. Christopher Columbus, *The Letter of Christopher Columbus on the Discovery of America* (New York: Trustees of the Lennox Library, 1892), 2-3. All subsequent quotations in this paragraph are from pages 5 and 6.

23. Médéric-Louis-Elie Moreau de Saint Méry, *Description topographique, physique, civile, politique, et historique de la partie française de l'île Saint-Domingue* (Paris: Guerin, 1875). Moreau himself is a complicated figure in the history of Caribbean travel writing. Actually a native of the region, he was born in the French Caribbean island of Martinique and lived and worked for many years as a jurist in Saint-Domingue. Moreau was active in politics in France and achieved some notoriety as the person who distributed arms to the revolutionary militia before it stormed the Bastille on July 14, 1789. As a travel writer, Moreau also stands out as a commentator on the United States, where he lived and journeyed after fleeing France under threat of being guillotined. His *Voyage aux Etats-Unis de l'Amérique,* though unpublished in any form until this century, preceded Alexis de Tocqueville's classic text by three decades. Despite his Caribbean roots, Moreau's lascivious fascination with mulatta women and his contempt for the culture of the enslaved black majority mark him as an outside, European-identified commentator.

24. Joan Dayan, "Codes of Law and Bodies of Color." *Penser la créolité.* Eds., Maryse Condé and Madeleine Cottenet-Hage (Paris: Karthala, 1995), 41-67. 42

25. John Candler, *Brief Notices of Hayti: With Its Condition, Resources, and Prospects* (London: Thomas Ward & Co., 1842), 144. Subsequent references will appear in parentheses in the text.

26. Despite Candler's one-way vision of modernization, and although he clearly sympathizes with the elite families who host his travels through the countryside, sometimes it is possible to read *Brief Notices of Hayti* against the grain and recover a vision of small farmers improving their lot by triumphing against the old plantocratic regime. Candler's description of Fourcy, an estate in the southwest, offers just such a possibility. He writes: "Owing to the cheapness of good land, the labourers, who work for hire, already reduced in number by the civil wars, are now still further diminished; and a proprietor, if he wish to secure the services of those who have long laboured for him on the moiety system, must be content to allow them even greater advantages than that system affords. The few remaining labourers on Fourcy not only take their half of the 10,000 lbs of coffee which the plantation yields, but appropriate to themselves almost the whole of the

provisions which the land furnishes, sending down only a few of the rarer vegetables, beans, peas, and artichokes, to their master, for his table at Port-au-Prince, and supplying his need only when he comes to reside for a few days in the country. This he knows very well, but has no alternative but to bear it lightly" (144).

27. Quoted in Plummer, *Haiti and the Great Powers,* 2-3.

28. Melville Herskovits, *Life in a Haitian Valley.* Introduction by Edward K. Brathwaite (New York: Octagon, 1975). Subsequent references will appear in parentheses in the text.

29. Henry Schwarz, "Provocations Towards a Theory of Third World Literature." *Mississippi Review* 49/50 (1989): 178.

30. Paul Gilroy, *There Ain't No Black in the Union Jack* (London: Hutchinson, 1987), 198.

31. When Hurston published *Tell My Horse* in 1938, colonial networks were still very much the order of the day, despite cracks in the system and constant resistance in the colonies. Far from criticizing close links between the production of ethnographies and the restructuring of capitalist empires, be they British, French, or Yankee, many anthropological luminaries, such as Evans-Prichard in East Africa, were actively enlisting indigenous populations in service of European or U.S. global militarism (see Edward Evans-Prichard, "Operations on the Akobo and Gila Rivers, 1940-41," quoted at length in Clifford Geertz's *Works and Lives.* Stanford, CA: Stanford University Press, 1988, [50 ff.]). Moreover, while Hurston's mentor, Franz Boas, created a progressive—even avant-garde—niche in the Anthropology Department at Columbia University, Boas's doctrine of cultural relativism (one of the keys to subverting the triumphalism of European and North American writing on the Caribbean) has its ideological limits. Eric Ross critically assesses the way in which cultural relativism resituates on the terrain of "culture" the biological determinism of earlier evolutionary social theories. The result, in Ross's view, is a kind of cultural separatism that winds up reproducing, at the level of ideas, the deterministic views that Boasians initially sought to escape (see his "Introduction." In *Beyond the Myths of Culture: Essays in Cultural Materialism.* Edited by Eric B. Ross [New York: Academic Press, 1980], xx-xxi). In practice, meanwhile, Boas and his students did not always exercise the respect for ethnographized cultures that their ideology proclaimed.

32. Armand Mattelart, *Transnationals and the Third World: The Struggle for Culture* (South Hadley, MA: Bergin and Garvey, 1983), 14, original emphasis.

33. In 1963, for instance, prior to his much-praised study on the Balinese cock-fight, Clifford Geertz authored one of these CIA-funded monographs on social organization in Indonesia (Peter Dale Scott, *Coming to Jakarta: A Poem About Terror* [New York: New Directions Books, 1988], 118-122. In *Works*

and Lives, Geertz conveniently places the end of what he calls anthropology's "scholars in uniform" phase in the 1950s.

34. Katherine Dunham's travels and writings constitute another extremely complex case study in Caribbean travel writing. Trained by Hurston's contemporary and fellow Boasian, Melville Herskovits, Dunham came to the role of participant-observer, like Hurston, as an African American woman, a creative performer, and an intellectual with anthropological training. Like Hurston, Dunham visited the Accompong Maroons, publishing a personalized account in her monograph, *Journey to Accompong* (New York: Holt, 1937). Dunham, like Hurston, also did extensive fieldwork in Haiti. For both women, the "ancestral tie" played a part in mediating their encounters with informants (Dunham, *Dances of Haiti* [Los Angeles: Center for Afro-American Studies, UCLA, 1983], xxiv. Orig. publ. as "Las Danzas de Haití," *Acta Anthropologica* II:4 (1947), and *Les Danses de Haiti* [Paris: Fasquel Press, 1957].) In Dunham's case, most Haitians—particularly the dark-skinned peasants of the countryside—welcomed her with a special intensity as if "the welfare of the entire Negro race might be improved if these unfortunates to the north could be acquainted again with the rituals of ancestor worship" (xxiv). In addition to her well-known dance productions and schools in New York City and East St. Louis, Dunham has contributed numerous items to the anthropological literature on the Caribbean, and Haiti in particular, focusing primarily on sacred and secular dance traditions. Stylistically, her engagements represent fairly typical examples of what was then emerging as a model of ethnographic practice. Apart from an occasional foray into experimental writing, such as the "Footnote on Going Native" in *Journey to Accompong* (51-52), Dunham sticks to the stylistic straight and narrow. She consistently cites "authoritative" scholarly sources to contextualize and buttress her own judgments. Dunham registers the trope of dependency when she asserts the inevitable passing of Maroon society (161). In short, Dunham's work—in its orthodoxy—offers a clear sense of the professional expectations Hurston flouted when she produced *Tell My Horse.* While Hurston's text contains passages that are more or less "orthodox," such as the chapter on "Voodoo and Voodoo Gods," she chooses to omit footnotes and a bibliography. When she references "authorities" they are often local figures rather than "first" world scholars. Hurston's writing seems geared more toward successful character portraiture than with legitimizing her narrative through methodological rigor. And unlike Dunham, who returns from Accompong with a stash of indigenous musical instruments (some of which are irreplaceable), Hurston resists accumulating such artifacts. As we have already seen, after 1939, Hurston was rejected by the scientific community, presumably for her refusal to conform to disciplinary standards.

35. Johannes Fabian, "Presence and Representation: The Other and Anthropological Writing." *Critical Inquiry* 16:4 (Summer, 1990): 767.

36. This is especially interesting in light of Hurston's reputation as a successful folklore collector in the field. While Hurston and Reser's failure to secure the ritual formula is part of the narrative politics that block the reader's gaze, this could also be a sign of Hurston's own foreignness in the Caribbean. Part of her success in getting informants to offer up data was due to Hurston's ability to establish rapport with singers, musicians, storytellers, rootworkers, and everyday people. For example, the songs collected by Alan Lomax and Mary Elizabeth Barnicle in 1935 for the Library of Congress were for the most part acquired thanks to Hurston's mediations (Hemenway 211-212). Displaced from her most familiar surroundings, Hurston did not enjoy this instant rapport in the Caribbean.

37. The best critique of Hurston's treatment of Erzulie—a *loa* whose manifestations also include the vengeful Petro *loa* Erzulie-gé-Rouge—is given by Joan Dayan, who insists that we see the class/caste subtext in these two different Erzulies, and digest the fact that Hurston's account emphasizes the bourgoise/mulatta Erzulie Freda. See Dayan's "Caribbean Cannibals and Whores." *Raritan* XI:2 (Fall, 1989): 64-65.

38. Patrick Bellegarde-Smith, *Haiti: The Citadel Breached* (Boulder, CO: Westview, 1990), 22-29; Gerald Murray, "Population Pressure, Land Tenure, and Voodoo: The Economics of Haitian Peasant Ritual." In *Beyond the Myths of Culture: Essays in Cultural Materialism.* Ed., Eric B. Ross (New York: Academic Press, 1980), 300; David Nicholls, *Haiti in Caribbean Context: Ethnicity, Economy and Revolt* (New York: St. Martin's, 1985), 121-129.

39. Patrick Bellegarde-Smith's commentary on the sexual politics of bourgeois law vs. Vodou culture is relevant here: "Because the Haitian legal system is based on Western models imposed by colonial invaders, it lacks the centrality of Haiti's African heritage as attenuated by centuries of slavery; the position and status of women were more elevated in the Afro-Haitian peasantry than in the Franco-Haitian elite. The vision of androgynous gods in the Vodun belief system presented opportunities for the advancement and empowerment of women and homosexuals that might otherwise not have existed" (*Haiti: The Citadel Breached* 27).

40. Hurston's description here provides a stark contrast to James Weldon Johnson's aestheticization of Haitian market women in "Self-Determining Haiti." In an essay that elsewhere is informed by a sharp critical awareness, Johnson delivers the following exotic image: "Perhaps the deepest impression on the observant visitor is made by the country women. Magnificent as they file along the country roads by scores and by hundreds on their way to the town markets, with white or colored turbaned heads, gold-looped-ringed ears, they stride along straight and lithe, almost haughtily, carrying themselves like so many Queens of Sheba" (213).

41. "Sweat" and *Their Eyes Were Watching God* are primary counter-texts to the representation in *Tell My Horse* of women's life as privileged in America. ("Sweat." In *I Love Myself When I Am Laughing, and then Again When I Am Looking Mean and Impressive: a Zora Neale Hurston Reader.* Edited by Alice Walker. Introduction by Mary Helen Washington [New York: The Feminist Press, 1979].) Nanny's harsh wisdom in *Their Eyes,* "De nigger woman is de mule uh de world so fur as Ah can see" (14), is a folk-inflected distillation of Hurston's grim commentary on the lot of black women in the Caribbean. Hurston's physical descriptions of Delia in "Sweat"—"her poor little body, her bare knuckly hands" (*I Love Myself,* 198), "her knotty, muscled limbs, her harsh knuckly hands" (199)—and Joe Clark's speech in which he likens her to thrown-away "cane-chew" (201), echo the portrait of the Jamaican rockbreaker in *Tell My Horse* (59). Hurston's use of sugar cane as a metaphor for dehumanization is a key comparative link with Caribbean expressive traditions. As in the Caribbean, this registers symbolically the collective memory of slavery—of a plantation economy and the struggles to resist the plantation's oppressive material and psychological order. In many Caribbean countries, and in the works of many Caribbean authors (e.g., Joseph Zobel and Simone Schwarz-Bart), the plantation economy endures along with its conditions of enslavement and resistance, despite nominal emancipation. In "Sweat," the reference to cane-chew resonates in a similar way: it points toward the continuing threat of chattel status for black women, despite the nominal political autonomy represented by Eatonville's all-black citizenry and government.

42. African American texts dealing with U.S. society often employ ironic humor to articulate protest and criticism, convey painful social realities, or misdirect hostile readers. When Hurston takes this strategy off-shore to the Caribbean, other purposes emerge. In the colonial encounter, self-ironizing comments gesture toward the narrator's nationality (the ground of her relative material privilege vis-à-vis Caribbean women). Many commentators, perhaps because they focus on the assertion of U.S. national identity, but miss Hurston's ironic rhetoric, have not been able to see *Tell My Horse* as an example of progressive social criticism. When she adapts the rhetoric of black humor to convey the double and triple oppressions of women in the Caribbean, it is important not to gloss over the scathing nature of Hurston's critique.

43. This work has begun with Deborah G. Plant's new publication, *Every Tub Must Sit On Its Own Bottom: The Philosophy and Politics of Zora Neale Hurston* (Urbana, IL: University of Illinois Press, 1995).

Chapter 11
EPILOGUE

HAITI'S UNQUIET PAST:
KATHERINE DUNHAM, MODERN DANCER, AND HER ENCHANTED ISLAND

Joan Dayan

On October 24, 1801, Victor-Emmanuel Leclerc, First Counsel Napoleon Bonaparte's brother-in-law, was named commander-in-chief of what would be the largest expeditionary army ever to sail from France. The mission? To reclaim France's most lucrative colony and to restore the institution of slavery; or, as Napoleon commanded Leclerc, to leave no epaulette on any black shoulder. In 1791, black slaves in Saint-Domingue began the revolt against the colonial masters, a struggle that would end in 1804 with the founding of the world's first black republic.

In the eyes of the so-called civilized world, this revolution turned the profitable "pearl of the Antilles" into what Thomas Carlyle called a "tropical dog kennel."[1] It is chilling to read accounts of the cruelties inflicted by the French in their last-ditch effort to reinstitute slavery and regain their most prosperous New World market. General Leclerc was accompanied by Napoleon's youngest sister, Pauline Bonaparte Leclerc, and their son. Nine months later, as he lay dying of yellow fever, he recognized that Bonaparte had underestimated the bravery and skill of the rebels. "We have in Europe a false idea of the country in which we fight and the men whom we fight against."[2] Those men were not only the celebrated "Black Jacobins"— Toussaint l'Ouverture, Henri Cristophe, and Jean-Jacques Dessalines—but also the black guerrilla leaders, often unnamed in the standard histories. Leclerc's successor, General Donatien Rochambeau, is accredited by most accounts as the consummate villain of the doomed expedition to Saint-

Domingue. He joined magnificence and abjection, pleasure and pain in creating spectacles of brutality, including a virtual Roman circus, where dogs imported from Cuba ripped into black flesh.

As a vessel of beauty and splendor in the midst of a colony become one vast charnel house, Pauline Bonaparte Leclerc remains an emblem of the old regime in the last days of Saint-Domingue. General Leclerc built her a luxurious retreat on Isle de la Tortue, where a bejewelled Pauline indulged in lace, linen, silk, and sex. Yet, it is Habitation Leclerc, her estate not far from what is today one of Haiti's worst slums—Carrefour—that remains intact. Idealized as a Venus or goddess in the midst of what Leclerc's secretary De Norvins recorded as an "infernal bacchanal" of "fierce songs and barbarous howls," Pauline Bonaparte Leclerc testifies to a strategic feminization of the tropics: the white lady necessary to the invention of the black threat.[3]

Opulence and charm on one side, demonism and ferocity on the other. Haiti is one of those places all too easily represented by extremes. The first black republic threatened white interests, economic and ideological, so it was ridiculed as a dubious icon of civilization or a certain proof of savagery, most powerfully rendered as a woman alternately idealized and denigrated. A country that perhaps more than any other has complicated the simple racialized divide between black and white, French and African, Vodou and Christian, Haiti nevertheless continues to conjure these distinctions.

Dancer, choreographer, and anthropologist Katherine Dunham wrote *Island Possessed,* her story of visits to Haiti during a 30-year period (from 1936 until 1966), which was published in 1969.[4] Twenty-five years later, when Dunham's beloved Haiti faced the worst political crisis of its long and troubled existence—the coup that deposed Jean-Bertrand Aristide, Haiti's first democratically elected president—*Island Possessed* was finally republished. Its appearance during the horrific aftermath of Aristide's exile, as his followers' bodies were skinned and trussed up like sacrificial animals, left rotting in the streets of Port-au-Prince, is nothing short of a resurrection. For Dunham takes us back to a Haiti that is no longer. For readers familiar only with the sensationalized Haiti of violence and poverty, Dunham's memoirs emphasize complexities all too often ignored in more popular representations.

In her autobiography, *A Touch of Innocence,* Dunham tells of growing up in a racially mixed family in Chicago at a time when "an influx of Southern negroes" resulted in "prejudice against anyone with even slightly dark skin."[5] Before entering the University of Chicago to study anthropology in 1927, she lived in an area she describes as a "borderline area of the far South Side, . . . where a community of people neither black or white, but mostly passing for white, had penetrated beyond the barriers set up against their darker brethren" (62). For Dunham, arriving in Port-au-Prince, Haiti, in 1936, just two years after its occupation by the United States (1915–1934), the pride of the Haitian black majority—those Haitians who speak Creole and practice Vodou—led her to choose the first black republic as her spiritual home.

Dunham first visited Haiti on a fellowship from the Rosenwald and Guggenheim Foundations to study dance and ritual in the Caribbean and Brazil. About 16 months later, Zora Neale Hurston would also arrive on a Guggenheim; she published her own account of "voodoo and life" in *Tell My Horse* (1938).[6] In Dunham's determination "to study the dance of an African-Indian culture that had not been destroyed by the process of Western acculturation," she encountered Vodou and the components of African American dancing that would be recreated in her revolutionary dance technique. Between 1938, when she returned from her first Haiti stay, and 1939, she formed a professional dance company that would become the first group of black dancers to appear in nightclubs in the late thirties. For many white audiences the idea of blacks dancing meant minstrel shows and "chittlin' hopping," but Dunham created a technique and style that would redefine dance in the Americas—a revolutionary movement that celebrated African culture in the New World. African Caribbean possession ritual and dance ceremonies invigorated ballet and modern dance, even as they recorded the folk and oral traditions of the Diaspora.

The recollections of *Island Possessed* depend for their effect on the language of extremes so often a part of Haitian historiography. Yet Dunham's candor, wit, and courage in not only reiterating but in *questioning* what has become a kind of rhetorical fatality make her memories vital to our understanding of how this mythologized Haiti diverts our attention from economic exploitation, color prejudice, and political greed. Whether she is initiated into Vodou, married to a spirit, or celebrated as a "brown" performer at the Rex Theater in Port-au-Prince on the same program with a Parisian *vedette* in the 1930s, there is always a downside to the experience. For Dunham, possible plenitude just as easily gives way to rot. And yet, these loaded terms do not retain their usual meanings. In her hands, they become something like relics, trappings that must be exorcised. Her stories, like her acquisitions, seem to court doom.

Throughout her somewhat enigmatic reconstruction, Dunham takes great liberties with the empirical facts usually employed by ethnographers or historians. The disembodied souls of Haiti's colonial past haunt her book, as well as more recent "heroes" of contemporary Haitian history, including Presidents Sténio Vincent, Dumarsais Estimé, Paul Magloire, and François Duvalier. Then there are the African and New World spirits of the Rada and Petwo rites, tales of *lougawou* (vampires), she-devils, and shape-shifting spirits called *baka,* not to mention the stories of her various Haitian contacts—mulatto elites, newly empowered blacks, and the peasantry, "the true people of Haiti" (248). We are privy to the tragic exile in 1950 of Dumarsais Estimé (who would become Duvalier's idol), hunted and impoverished in Jamaica. While describing the excitement of her first encounters with this visionary politician (who never allowed her, she wryly notes, to touch his pistol and holster), she flashes forward to the failure of his dream for Haiti.

Dunham writes as if driven by her memories. It is thus fitting that Habitation Leclerc, or "Chez Pauline," as it was sometimes called, is the locale that occupies an eerie presence throughout this book. Pauline's place becomes the site for beauty, sweetness, torture, and suffering. Although Dunham bought Habitation Leclerc in 1949, about 13 years after her first visit, this ruin that will not die haunts her ritual of recollection. Possessed by the property she has herself acquired, she writes of "the predestined unhappiness of the master of Leclerc" (238). She senses that "some deep, insoluble sadness" came into her life when she bought the estate, and thinks that the closing of two Dunham schools and the end of the Dunham Company resulted from her becoming "the mistress of a property with a curse on it" (239, 240). She recalls "the malaise which I alone seemed to feel, and which came from the very pavements and huge trunks of trees and overripe fruit and arrested motion of small lizards, which seemed to be listening to some sound or cry of death or agony" (243).

In *Island Possessed,* the dancer, social reformer, and educator from the tough streets of Chicago, Illinois, demands that her readers acknowledge her as the "mistress" or "proprietor" of the 30-acre property Habitation Leclerc, where wander the unquiet dead of colonial Saint-Domingue: a ragged black man, hands tied behind his back, begs for help and then runs toward the "slave cell"; a lady in a white trailing gown and white bonnet strolls near Pauline's pool; the demons of Rochambeau's victims roam; and the Gran' Boeuf of Leclerc, "a full eighteen feet high and with glowing red eyes" (the Jamaican "rolling calf" transported to Haiti) menaces those who dare cross his path at night (250). Feeling the need to exorcise the evil spirits frequenting Leclerc, Dunham calls upon Kam, her godmother and "high priestess" from the north of Haiti. Kam identifies the "slave house" or "cell" as one of the centers of "evil emanation," still haunted by the victims of Leclerc and Rochambeau's atrocities. Dunham's descriptions of Kam's exorcism locate the tortures and trappings of slaves, come back as restless spirits and finally laid to rest, in what Haitians call "Nan Guinée," the idealized Africa of the Diaspora.

In October 1994, the *New Yorker* printed a short piece called "Miss Dunham's Haitian Home."[7] When the United States entered Haiti in "Operation Restore Democracy," one of the places they invaded was a garden in Habitation Leclerc that they suspected doubled as a training facility for terrorists loyal to Jean Bertrand Aristide. "They found no arms—found nothing at all, in fact, except a few slack-jawed gardeners and a cast of Haitian musicians and dancers rehearsing a voodoo-inspired number" (48). We should recall Dunham's 47-day hunger strike following the coup that deposed President Aristide. An outspoken supporter of Aristide in exile, she exposed the cruelty of President Clinton's forced deportation of Haitian refugees, as well as his empty rhetoric. Further, she brought this dehumanizing treatment to the attention of many who might have continued to ignore the plight of those the media called "the Haitian stampede," the Haitian "hordes," or "containers of contamination."

This raid was not the first time that Habitation Leclerc was suspected as the center of political or magical operations. Beginning in the late fifties, Dunham ran a medical clinic at Habitation Leclerc. Duvalier would soon suspect it was a cover for traitors plotting to overthrow his government. Another time, a neighbor, who must have objected to the Vodou drums played for tourists at Leclerc, charged "Madame Dunham" with "importing venomous serpents with the subversive intention to destroy the government by overrunning the island with them" (*Island,* 183). These same snakes, now swollen to "dragon size," Dunham explained, were said to have swallowed children as well as a woman riding a goat. President Duvalier "decreed their banishment" instead of immediately destroying them. Dunham regrets that, once placed in the government farm at Damien, they probably died of starvation.

The shadows of the colonial masters that lurk in the compounds of the New World gods account for the disorienting effect of *Island Possessed.* Dunham understands this, and she makes sure that her readers are confronted, again and again, with the shades that give substance to contemporary Haiti. Whether she speaks of those she calls "culture heroes"—among whom she includes François ("Papa Doc") Duvalier, identified for her with Jean-Jacques Dessalines, the founder of the Haitian Republic—or those she seeks as healers, spirit guides, or lovers, Dunham summons the buried history of Saint-Domingue as template for understanding the economic exploitation, political cunning, and color prejudice that still plagues Haiti.

Unlike the press and the media, Dunham does not use the figure of "Papa Doc" Duvalier as a bogey man to detract from the economic and social ills that have been persistently exacerbated by United States interests. As she notes, writing before American bankrolling of army generals became standard practice, Duvalier never allowed the United States to buy him off: "[H]e is not nor ever has been motivated by avidity for material things or good living at the expense of the populace. Today there is so much to hide behind, so he may have the largest bank holdings in Switzerland or Montevideo, but I doubt this" (*Island,* 167). Comparing "Papa Doc" to Jean-Jacques Dessalines (who was also singled out as "savage" by the "civilized" world), readers get a different picture of Duvalier from that projected by the mainstream media. Admitting Duvalier's brute despotism, Dunham asks, "The American press stresses political murder, torture, and assassination; but then are we not, as the French have pointed out, *tous assassins?*" (*Island,* 171).

Dunham's own history in a racist United States no doubt gave her a deep awareness of the paradoxes of performance in a prejudiced society. She knew that no matter how much an audience appreciated her onstage in such shows as *Tropic, Le Jazz Hot,* and *Carib Song,* racial discrimination would affect her reception in hotels and even determine the complexion of her audiences. In her biography of Dunham, Ruth Beckford recalls that Dunham not only performed dances of liberation, but consistently fought hotel authorities and the "black-in-balcony-only" policy of segregated theaters in the South, as well as in New York City, in Chicago, and on the West Coast.[8] Reflecting on the United States occupation of Haiti, Dunham recalls in *Island Possessed* that the "State Department . . . sent raw Southerners in as marines to put peace into the troubled little black island, going through one of its characteristic blood baths, and made hell out of purgatory. Haiti was good practice ground for what goes on now between black and white in the United States of America" (73).

I should remind readers that what has happened in Haiti since "Papa Doc" passed on—and especially since the coup that overthrew Aristide—is far more serious in its effects than Duvalier's dictatorship. What Dunham gives her readers, then, is an entry into spots of time, anchored in her visits to Haiti, each more troubling than the last. She first met Duvalier in 1956 (a year before he was elected president) and saw him for the last time in 1962 (as he consolidated his dread militia, the tontons macoutes, and his Presidency-for-Life). And yet, she is correct in her admission that "[i]t is impossible for me to think of what is happening in Haiti as due to one man, and this is why comparative history interests me" (*Island,* 172).

Dunham's comparative history is anchored in what she describes as "the mulatto-black dichotomy"—so unlike the sense of "blackness" in the United States—which she uses to account for "the continuous unrest of the country," and calls "a national psychosis" (*Island,* 173). She sets up this color opposition by explaining how colonial history created an elite mulatto class that acted as a buffer between the white masters and black slaves. Although her meditation on this divide as the source of the "anarchy" of contemporary Haiti is, generally speaking, accurate, it fails to account for the nuanced subtleties that complicate any simple splitting between black and mulatto. Granted that light skin, "good" hair, and facial characteristics survive still as determinants of class and social standing, in the history of Haitian political struggles, blacks have sometimes sided with mulattos, and vice versa. Where does Dunham place herself in the vexed color and class distinctions of Haitian history? *Island Possessed* recuperates what some would deem embarrassing categories and stereotypes. For example, Dunham draws our attention to the special brand of Haitian mulatto woman: a "blend of beauty hard to find elsewhere," a description that resonates with earlier travel writings and natural histories that singled out this image of the appropriately bleached out, honey-colored, or nut-brown women of the islands (220).

Further, William Seabrook's sensational *Magic Island* (1929),[9] published for the delectation of readers in the United States who sought justification for the occupation of Haiti, makes its appearance felt in Dunham's references to the "magic island," and "this possessed and obsessed island" (*Island,* 5). There is danger in this recourse to the strange and the magical. Stories of zombies, snakes, and red-eyed evil spirits, though peripheral to the beliefs and practices of Haitian socioreligious life, have always appealed to foreigners. Making Haiti and its inhabitants the stuff of legends obscures the less easily articulated facts of race and class as they play out in daily life in the postindependence Caribbean. How and why Haiti is so heavily metaphorized matters a great deal. During the occupation of Haiti by the United States, tales of cannibalism, sorcery, and zombies helped to justify the presence of the marines, and representations of Vodou have continued to have serious political consequences. If misery and poverty continue, with the United States aiding and abetting the rapacious local elite and military thugs, journalists blame something vague and threatening called "voodoo theocracy."

Since Vodou is always cast as undermining democracy, some of Dunham's most poetic representations might seem to buttress the image of a bestial and demonic Haiti, especially when she suggests the possibility of human sacrifices. And yet, Dunham (despite numerous attempts to confine her, as in the cinematic folk fable *Cabin in the Sky,* or to celebrate her only as the exotic dancer of rumba rhapsodies and tropical variations) cannot be easily pigeonholed.[10] Unlike Maya Deren in *Divine Horsemen* (1953), who presents her spiritual encounters as idealized surrender, Dunham describes her experiences as varied, gritty, and sometimes banal: "Squatting over the calebasse, the gourd shell cut in half which served as a chamber pot for each of us in turn, was an ordeal for me" (*Island,* 78). She offers her readers no easy entry into an experience that is ambiguous at best. What saves her evocation of the "true folk or primitive setting" from exoticism is her involvement in what she observes: those moments when she discards her pose as the center of ethnographic authority, admits her confusion "on a fringe border of belief and non-belief," and joins with those who ritually remember the heritage of a lost Guinea (*Island,* 105).

Island Possessed begins with the ghosts of color, the conumdrums of racial distinctions that force elite women into corsets of propriety and denial, turning them into ghostly inversions of the stereotypical mulatto concubine. Dunham refers her readers to the most astute of colonial historians and ethnographers, the Creole lawyer from Martinique, Médéric Elie Moreau de Saint-Méry and his still unsurpassed *Description of the French Part of the Island of Saint-Domingue* (1797-1798).[11] His "colored nomenclature" consisted of 11 categories and 110 possible combinations from absolute white (128 parts white blood) to absolute black (128 parts black blood). In colonial Saint-Domingue, the maintenance of white supremacy in the midst of ever lighter mixed offspring depended on this taxonomic debasement: a cult of whiteness that necessitated inventing new names for those who possessed "drops" of "black blood.

In her first pages, Dunham, aware of her presence in Port-au-Prince as a "young woman not yet placed sociologically or socially in the community," wonders where she would end up in Moreau de Saint-Méry's "scheme of things" (6). In the complexity of Caribbean color distinctions, would she be called "griffon," "marabou," "mulatto," or just "sang-mêlé"? She prefers to think of herself as "noir": "not exactly the color black, but the quality of belonging with or being at ease with black people when in the hills or plains or anywhere and scrambling through daily life along with them" (4). Though she demurs that the meaning of *négritude* is not exactly clear to her, her definition of black comes closer to Dessaline's radical revamping of color taxonomies in the 1805 constitution than to the sometimes mystifying linguistic invention of négritude. Instead of the tripartite division of whites, people of color, and blacks, Dessalines created one all-consuming category for Haitian identity: Haitians, no matter their color, would henceforth be known "only by the generic word black" (*Island,* 207).

But it is Dunham's description of the sisters Rouzier, the keepers of the aristocracy of skin and owners of the Hotel Excelsior in Port-au-Prince, that is the most stunning entry into what it means to be a "respectable" woman in Haitian society—at least in the 1930s. These sisters, Dunham says, "were indisputably mulatto and wore rice powder to accentuate an already egg-shell color," drawing our attention to the fact that "mulatto" in Haiti designates one among many nuances and does not simply denote (as in the United States) the mixture of black and white (*Island,* 7). Dunham recognizes some of her relatives in the "faded aristocracy of Haiti," working, yet "remaining genteel." As the intrepid anthropologist, returning in the early morning from ceremonies in the countryside, inviting her black peasant friends to call on her at the hotel, Dunham clearly enjoys her own classification as an "unplaceable," her ability to jostle received notions of status and acceptability in Port-au-Prince.

Dunham's book becomes more personal as she tries to recover the details of her quandaries and pleasures in the company of the Vodou spirits and their devotees. The story of her initiation in 1936, her experience of the *lave tèt* ritual, occupies nearly 90 pages. Her evocation is extraordinary, for she weaves all kinds of experiences from many time periods into the space of this one event. Placed on her side on the cold dirt floor of the *ounfò* or temple, dressed in new baptismal clothes, she joined eight other candidates, ranging in age from seven to seventy, all lying in spoon fashion: "There we lay, scarcely breathing, waiting, listening, senses alert, packed like sardines much as the slaves who crossed the Atlantic, motionless as though chained, some of us afraid" (79). This difficult ritual that she describes as "forcing into us the meaning of the vaudun" (spirits or *lwa*) is also a descent into the past: a journey back to Africa and a sending of the gods as vessels of slave history.

In the Cul-de-Sac plain, under the guidance of the *mambo* (or priest-esses) Dégrasse and Téoline, Dunham admits her discomfort, annoyance, and intermittent sense of the banality of the three-day proceedings. Only later does she confess that "my feeling was closer to belonging to some-thing all encompassing than I have known since" (137). Her response to the constraints of service is best expressed through the sacrificial headwrap. A mixture of cornmeal, feathers, *orgeat* (an almond-based syrup), chicken feathers, blood, herbs, and raw eggs matted her hair; for a full week after the initiation—the period of "arising"—she had to wear the wrap. She hid it from the suspicious eyes of her friends at the Hotel Excelsior with a blue headkerchief and sometimes a straw hat.

The spirit who claimed Dunham in mystic marriage was Danbala (Damballah), the snake god of the fresh waters. This is a surprising recla-mation—but intriguing as key to the logic of love in Vodou—since Dun-ham does not hide her fear and revulsion of snakes: "standing before the altar of decision with circumspection and belief each as strong as the other; with revulsion . . . because I was hungry and a little faint and because I don't like the company of snakes" (111). After her initiation, she is given to Danbala in marriage amid "drumming, singing, and exalting." She describes the demanding ways of the spirits in her elaboration of this sacred bond, reminding her readers that "the burden of being 'married' to a loa is best avoided. The demands are rigorous, the jealousy constant, the punishment for mishaps severe, and there is no divorce" (70). Like her obsession with Habitation Leclerc, her pact with Danbala is on her mind throughout these pages. She writes that in no other attachment has she "been so punished for infidelity as by my Haitian serpent god, the rainbow holding his tail in his mouth and supporting the sky to keep it from falling to earth" (111). Dunham often loses what she should most covet and mis-places what is irreplaceable. She loses the "ring of tiny diamonds and rubies," which was not to be removed after her marriage to Danbala. She can't find the *po-tèt,* the sacred china pot that houses the spirits, and she loses to fire the sacred drums of Ville Bonheur, village of the Black Virgin of Haiti.

In her moving biography of Dunham, Beckford describes the neigh-borhood suspicions of "the Black Witch of Tenth Street" in East St. Louis. Although Dunham has fought consistently to educate, form dance schools, and work for the rights of the disadvantaged in the ruins of the city, the evidence of many gods in her home has produced as many legends about her house in the States as about Habitation Leclerc in Haiti. What is most fascinating about *Island Possessed* remains Dunham's nearly jubilant courting of disaster as she serves virgins, saints, and gods from Cuba, Brazil, and Haiti. Her refusal to limit her choices, her willing embrace of the syncretism that is so much a part of African-based religions in the New World, taking on the entire range of images of the Diaspora in her dance and in her writings, make the reading of this book both disturbing and transformative. Even when she refers to herself histrionically as "Iphigenia tied to the mast" with "the black race broiling on hot coals below" (Eric Fromm's portrait of her), she counters such exclusive romanticism by her willingness to submit to the risks of the life of the spirit, mixing the gods and risking their anger in testimony to a longed-for "reconciliation" of "their wandering, jealous siblings of different nations but of the same ancestors" (69, 272).

NOTES

1. Thomas Carlyle, "The Nigger Question." *Frazer's Magazine* (December 1849).

2. See Paul Rossier, *Lettres du Général Leclerc: Commandant en Chef de l'Armée de Saint-Domingue en 1802* (Paris: Société de l'Histoire des Colonies Françaises et Librairie Ernest Leroux, 1937).

3. Jacques Marquet de Montbreton de Norvins, *Souvenirs d'un historien de Napoléon: Mémorial de J. de Norvins.* 3 vols. Edited by Léon de Lanzac de Laborie (Paris: Plon, 1896).

4. Katherine Dunham, *Island Possessed* (Chicago: The University of Chicago Press, 1994). Subsequent references will appear in parentheses in the text.

5. Katherine Dunham, *A Touch of Innocence* (New York: Harcourt, Brace and Company, 1959), 50. Subsequent references will appear in parentheses in the text.

6. Zora Neale Hurston, *Tell My Horse: Voodoo and Life in Haiti and Jamaica* (New York: Harper & Row, 1990).

7. "Miss Dunham's Haitian Home." *New Yorker,* 17 October 1994, 48ff.

8. Ruth Beckford, *Katherine Dunham: A Biography* (New York: M. Dekker, 1979).

9. William Seabrook, *The Magic Island* (New York: Harcourt, Brace, 1929).

10. *Cabin in the Sky,* a 1943 film based on the stage show of the same name and directed by Vincente Minnelli for MGM, featured, in addition to Dunham, Ethel Waters, Eddie "Rochester" Anderson, Lena Horne, and Louis Armstrong.

11. Médéric-Louis-Elie Moreau de Saint-Méry, *Description topographique, physique, civile, politique, et historique de la partie française de l'île Saint-Domingue* (Paris: Guerin, 1875).

CONTRIBUTORS'
BIOGRAPHICAL NOTES

Luisa Campuzano is Professor of Arts and Letters at the University of Havana. A classicist by training, she is the author of numerous books, among them *Breve esbozo de poética preplatónica* (1980), *Las ideas literarias en el Satyricón* (1984, for which she received the Premio de la Crítica), *Quirón o del ensayo y otros eventos* (1988), and *Carpentier entonces y ahora* (1997). In addition to her many articles, she is the editor of *Mujeres latinoamericanas: historia y cultura* (two volumes, 1998-1999). Campuzano is the Director of the Centro de Estudios de la Mujer at Casa de las Américas and editor of the Cuban journal *Revolución y Cultura*.

Mario Cesareo is an Associate Professor of Hispanic Studies at Vassar College. The author of *Crusados, beatos y mártires: emplazamientos del cuerpo colonial* (1995), he has also published on Hispanic and Lusophone colonial literature, the Argentinian novel of the 1970s, Chilean shantytown culture, Spanish Baroque, theater semiotics, Latin American cinema, and the aesthetics of civil rights and African American liberation movements in North America.

Joan Dayan is Regents Professor of English at the University of Arizona. She has published extensively on American Romanticism and Caribbean literature and culture. As an Americanist she is best known for *Fables of the Mind: An Inquiry into Poe's Fiction* (1987); as a Caribbeanist, she has published, in addition to numerous articles, a seminal critical study on René Depestre that accompanied her translation of *A Rainbow for the Christian West* (1977), and most recently, *Haiti, History, and the Gods* (1996). She is presently at work on a study on codes of deterrence and the law in the Arizona prison system.

Cheryl Fish is an Assistant Professor of English at the Borough of Manhattan Community College (CUNY). She is the editor of *A Stranger in the Village: Two Centuries of African-American Travel Writing* (1998). She has also published a variety of articles on African American travel and women's travel. She is currently completing a critical study of women's travel in antebellum America. She is also a poet.

Richard Frohock is an Assistant Professor of English at Oklahoma State University. His interests lie in the fields of Restoration and eighteenth-century and early American literatures. He has published on Aphra Behn and is at work on a study of fictional constructions of New World settings in the seventeenth and eighteenth centuries.

Claire Martin is Professor of Spanish and Chair of the Romance, German, Russian Languages and Literature Department at California State University, Long Beach. She has published in the field of nineteenth- and twentieth-century Spanish American literature and is the author of *Alejo Carpentier y las crónicas de Indias: orígenes de una escritura americana* (1995) and of numerous articles on women writers such as the Countess of Merlin, Teresa de la Parra, Marta Brunet, and Isabel Allende. She is completing a two-volume work on nineteenth-century women writers in Latin America in collaboration with Cristina Arambel Gruiñazú.

Kevin Meehan is an Assistant Professor of English at the University of Central Florida, where he teaches courses on World and Caribbean literatures and cross-cultural studies. He has published in the areas of Caribbean and African American studies, multi-ethnic U.S. literature, gender studies, and race theory. He is at work on a study of Jean-Bertrand Aristide.

Lizabeth Paravisini-Gebert is Professor of Hispanic Studies at Vassar College, where she directs the Latin American Studies Program and is a participating faculty in the Program in Africana Studies. She is the author of *Phyllis Shand Allfrey: A Caribbean Life* (1996) and *Jamaica Kincaid: A Critical Companion* (1999), and co-author of *Caribbean Women Novelists: An Annotated Critical Bibliography* (1993). In addition to numerous essays, she has published a number of co-edited anthologies: *Green Cane and Juicy Flot-*

sam: *Short Stories by Caribbean Women* (1991), *Pleasure in the Word: Erotic Writings by Latin American Women* (1993), *Remaking a Lost Harmony: Short Stories from the Hispanic Caribbean* (1995), *Sacred Possessions: Vodou, Santería, Obeah, and the Caribbean* (1997), and the forthcoming *Healing Cultures: Art and Religion as Curative Practices in the Caribbean* (1999). She is at work on a book about the eruption of Martinique's Mont Pelée volcano in 1902.

José Piedra is Professor of Romance Languages and Literature at Cornell University. Known for his insightful and original explorations of the interrelations of gender, race, and Spanish-Caribbean history, his numerous essays have appeared in *Callaloo, Dispositio, New Literary History, Transition, Diacritics,* and *Modern Language Notes,* among others journals and collections.

Ivette Romero-Cesareo is an Assistant Professor of Modern Languages at Marist College, where she teaches Caribbean and Latin American literature. She has published on a variety of topics in the fields of Caribbean literatures and art, cultural studies, and women's studies in journals such as *Callaloo, Journal of Caribbean Studies,* and *Anales del Caribe.* She is presently completing a book on women's testimonial narrative in the Caribbean.

Aileen Schmidt is Professor of Spanish at the University of Puerto Rico (Bayamón). She has published a variety of essays in the fields of gender studies, gender issues in higher education, and women's literature in the Caribbean. She is now completing a book of feminist readings of autobiographical literature in Cuba and Puerto Rico in the nineteenth and twentieth centuries.

Index

Abbott, John, 66
abolition, abolitionist, *see* slave(s),
    slavery
African(s), 27, 54, 227
    captives, 79
    models, 7
    nobles 48
    slaves, *see* slavery, slaves
Alferez, Nun of (Catalina de Erauso),
    135
Alvarez Baa, Céline, 4, 136, 139,
    141–5, 153–4, 156, 158
Amazons, 11–12, 32
Amerindians, *see* Native Americans
anti-slavery, *see* slavery, slaves
Aristide, Jean-Bertrand, 281, 284
Avellaneda, Gertrudis Gómez de, 166,
    170–3, 176–8, 185, 206, 207, 208

Balaguer, Joaquín, 274
Barbadoes, James G., 236
Barclay, Alexander, 234
Behn, Aphra, 3, 41–9, 55, 62, 64, 136
Berg, Elizabeth, 91
Berger, Thomas, 129
Bernbaum, Ernest, 42
Besson, Maurice, 67, 71

Beverley, John, 107, 131
Bhabha, Homi, 193
Black, Clinton, 67, 69
Blacks, *see* race, racism, *see also* slavery,
    slaves
Blanch, Juan M. Lope, 132
Blunt, Alison, 193
Bonaparte, Louis-Napoléon, 138,
    281–2
    Pauline, 6, 135, 281–2
Bonny, Anne, 1–4, 59–79, 81–3, 85–93,
    135, 156
Bontemps, Arna, 111
Borrero, Juana, 175
Bremer, Fredrika, 205
Bridie, James, 80, 82
Burke, Edmond, 52
Byam, Deputy-Governor, 49, 51, 53,
    57

Cabeza de Vaca, Alvar Núñez, 3, 10,
    20, 22–8, 30–2, 36, 200
Calico Jack, *see* John Rackam
Candie, Michel, 82, 85, 96
Candler, John, 253, 256, 275
cannibalism, cannibals, 11–12, 30, 32,
    104, 130, 137, 151, 254

Caribs, *see* Native Americans
Carlova, John, 87–9
Carlyle, Thomas, 281
Carmichael, Mrs. Mary 123–5, 132, 133, 136, 150
Casal, Julián del, 175
Castillo de González, Aurelia, 5, 175–6, 178, 205–6, 207, 212, 214–22
Castro, Américo, 133
Casuso, Teté, 205
Certeau, Michel de, 104, 130
Cesareo, Mario, 154, 160
Charles II, 42
Chasles, Philarète, 197, 199, 200
Cheyfiz, Eric, 52, 53
Christ, 15, 17
Christian, P., 78
Christophe, Henri, 281
Clifford, James, 228
colonizer/colonized, 2, 44, 114, 149, 163, 187–8, 191, 193, 195, 198, 230, 252, 256
colored, coloured, *see* race, racism
Columbus, Christopher, 9, 11, 14–15, 17–18, 24, 52, 58, 189, 246, 251–2, 256
contact zone, 4, 105–8, 114, 127, 162, 200
Craft, Ellen, 225
Craft-Fairchild, Catherine, 65
Creole, creoleness, 7, 146–9, 183–8, 191, 193, 195–8, 218, 247, 250, 258, 283, *see also* race, racism
cross-dressing, 61–3, 65–8, 72, 77, 88, 92–3, 152–3
Crusades, 17
Curley, Thomas, 63

Daniel, Elizabeth Rezner, 165
Dash, J. Michael, 248, 254
Dayan, Joan, 278
Defoe, Daniel, 59, 61–3
Delany, Martin R., 234
Deren, Maya, 288

Dessalines, Jean-Jacques, 281, 284, 289
Diaspora, 100, 149, 227, 264, 283, 285, 291
Dolz, María Luisa, 176, 178, 204
Dorantes de Carranza, Baltasar, 32
Doroteo, Teodoro, 38
Douglass, Frederick, 110, 132, 246, 249, 250, 275
Dow, Leslie Smith, 141–2, 144
Dugaw, Diane, 62
Dunham, Katherine, 6, 136, 258, 281–91
Duvalier, François, 284–7

Equiano, Olaudah, 110, 132, 225
Erauso, Catalina de, 135
Estebanico the Black, 37–9
Estimé, Dumarsais, 284

Fabian, Johannes, 259, 271
Farquhar, George, 62
Fanon, Frantz, 248
females, *see* women
Ferdinand, King, 19
Ferguson, Moira, 110, 114
Foster, Frances Smith, 109, 229

Garfield, Evelyn Picón, 206
Garrison, William Lloyd, 235–6, 238, 241
Gartner, Anne, 88
Gates, Henry Louis, 113
Gilman, Sander L., 128
González, Manuel Pedro, 165
Gooch, Steve, 85–7
Goreau, Agnes, 57
Graham, Maria Calcott, 205
Grant, Mary, 136, *see also* Mary Seacole
Greenblatt, Stephen, 58
Guille, Frances, 141, 143
Guillemin, Henri, 141
Gurney, Claud, 80
Guffey, George, 42, 56, 57

Hamm, Margherite Arlina, 205
Hanway, Mary Ann, 64
Hawthorne, Nathaniel, 162, 226
Hemenway, Robert, 248
Heredia, José María, 171–3, 180
Herskovits, Melville, 245, 255, 258
Hoffman, Léon-Francois, 248
homosexuality, 33–5, 89
    see also sexual practices and sexuality
Howe, Julia Ward, 162, 164
Hughes, Langston, 246
Hugo, Adèle 1–2, 4, 135–46, 154, 156
    Charles (brother), 140
    Victor (father), 135, 140–5, 158
hybrid, hybridity, 110
Hurston, Zora Neale, 6, 136, 245–79

Indians, see Native Americans
Inglis, Fanny Erskine, 205
Isabella, Queen, 9, 19

Jacobs, Harriet, 110
Jackson, Julia Newell, 152
Jameson, Robert Francis, 190
Jekel, Pamela, 88
Johnson, Charles, 59, 61, 66–8, 74–7,
    78, 90, 92, 93
Johnson, James Weldon, 246, 250, 274,
    275, 278
Jong, Erika, 90–2
Joyau, Auguste, 140, 144

Kindersley, Mrs., 64
Kofman, Sarah, 91

Lacouture, Madame, 137
Laqueur, Thomas, 65
Leclerc, Victor-Emmanuel, 281–2
Leed, Eric, 101
lesbianism, 77–8, 83
    see also sexuality
Levinas, Emmanuel, 105, 128, 129, 130
Lezama Lima, José, 172
Loynaz, Dulce María, 205

Madan y O'Sullivan, Inés María de los
    Dolores, 175
madness, 1, 143, 145, 158
madwomen, 1, 143, 145
Magloire, Paul, 284
Mann, Horace, 162
Mansilla de García, Eduarda, 204
marginalization, 2, 4, 139, 154, 165,
    230, 232
Marlbourough, Duke of, 63
Maroons, 58, 84, 96, 231, 247, 260–3
Martí, José, 10, 165
Martin, Colonel, 51, 53–4
Mattelart, Armand, 258
McCann, Andrew, 119
McHatton-Ripley, Elizabeth, 161, 163
McNaughton, Colin, 72
Méndez Capote, Renée, 205
Merlin, Countess of, 5, 136, 166–70,
    173, 177–8, 183–, 190–202, 204
Metzger, Lore, 57
Middle Passage, 39, 100
Mignolo, Walter, 131
Mikell, Gwendolyn, 248
Miles, Margaret R., 68
Molloy, Sylvia, 183
Montez, Lola, 152–3, 160
Moore, Raquel Wilson, 161
Mora de Hornachos, La 3, 10, 22,
    23–5, 27, 35–9
Moreau de St. Méry, Médéric-Louis-
    Elie, 252, 253, 256, 275, 288
Morgan, Mary, 64
motherhood, 65–8, 71, 73, 76, 136–7,
    156
Mott, Lucretia, 237
mulattos, see race, racism, see also
    women, mulatto

Narváez, Pánfilo, de 22–6, 27, 36
Native Americans, 28–36, 43–55, 51–2,
    55, 56, 105, 147
    Caribs, 11, 43–55, 50, 51–3
    Colombian, 221

Native Americans (*continued*)
  Mareames, 29–35
  Native Central Americans, 151, 155
  slaves 53, 105 (*see also* slavery, slaves)
  Taínos, 252
negress, *see* women, African-American, mulatto, *see also* race, racism
Nightingale, Florence, 150
Nugent, Mary, 205

Onís, José de, 165
Osborne Anne, 88
other(s), Other(s), self and, 2, 10–11, 13, 25, 27, 38, 135, 100–5, 108–11, 114–33, 135, 146, 149–50, 163, 184, 186–7, 193, 195, 198, 230, 246
l'Ouverture, Toussaint, 281

Pacheco, Anita, 56, 57, 58
Paravisini-Gebert, Lizabeth, 57, 156
Peabody, Sophia, 162, 226
  Mary (sister), 162
Peck, Nathaniel, 234
Peperzak, Adriaan, 103, 128, 129
Penarronda y Doley, Magdalena, 174–5, 178
picaresque, 4, 62, 91, 119, 121–7, 132–4, 154, 160
pícaro, 121–27, 132–4
Piedra, José, 92, 200
Pinson, Albert, 138–40, 145, 157
Plummer, Brenda, 251, 273
Pratt, Mary Louise, 2, 51, 100, 105–7, 114, 118, 131, 132, 163, 173, 186, 188, 231
Pratt, Angel Valbuena, 133
Price, Thomas S., 234
Prince, Mary, 2, 4, 109–34, 136
Prince, Nancy, 2, 5, 136, 154, 225–238
Pringle, Thomas, 111–12, 132
  Mrs., 111–12, 115–16

Rackam, John (Calico Jack), 59, 60–1, 65–6, 73, 76, 81, 86–7, 89, 93
race, racism, 43–55, 109–27, 137, 146–152, 154–5, 159, 163, 178, 191, 193, 201, 264–7, 284–9
Radclife, Ann, 64
Ramos, Julio, 164, 165
Read, Mary, 1–4, 59–71, 74–93, 135, 156
Rediker, Marcus, 61–62, 74
Religions, religious practices, 44, 49
  Animist, 31
  Baptist (or Evangelical), 227, 233, 238, 241
  Catholic, 31, 163
  Christian, 11, 13–14, 16–17, 24, 30, 37, 83, 107, 109, 117, 123–5, 127, 233
  Muslim, 16
  Obeah (or Myalism), 233, 247
  Vodou, Voudoun (Voodoo, Vaudoun), 245, 247, 252–8, 267–8, 278, 283–91
Rico, Francisco, 133
Rieuze, Catherine de, 83, 85
  Guillaume de, 83
Rochambeau, Donatien, 281, 284
Rodríguez de Morales, Catalina, 5, 205–6, 208, 212, 214–15, 221–2
Rodríguez de Tió, Lola, 5, 205, 207, 209–10, 212–22
Rodó, José Enrique, 174
Rodríguez Acosta, Ofelia, 205
Romanticism, 133, 171–2, 177, 189, 210, 220
Roqué de Duprey, Ana, 207
Rogers, Captain Woodes, 74, 82
Roosevelt, Theodore, 254, 256
Rosas, Juan Manuel de, 165
Ross, Mother, 63

San Carlos de Pedroso, Marquesa de, 175
Sand, George, 192, 196, 210

Sarmiento, Domingo Faustino, 165, 212
Schor, Naomi, 91
Seabrook, William, 287
Seacole, Mary, 4, 136, 143, 146–55, 159, 239
self, *see* other(s), other(s)
sexual practices and sexuality, 18, 26, 32–7, 75–7, 81–3, 88–92, 110, 113–15, 128, 159, 195, 267
Shakespeare, William, 9, 14, 62
Shannon, David, 71, 73
Shaw, Janet, 156
Shay, Frank, 78, 80
Shelley, Mary, 210
slavery, slaves, 43–55, 65–7, 74, 78–80, 84, 100, 105, 109–20, 123–7, 137, 150, 154–5, 157, 159, 167, 178, 185, 191–2, 227, 232–8, 241, 254
Smith, Captain John, 52–3, 56
Snell, Hannah, 64
Spivak, Gayatri Chakravorty, 126, 186
Stael, Madame de, 210
subaltern, 118–21, 124–7, 134
Symbolism, 174

Talens, Genaro, 134
Thrale, Hester Lynn, 64
Tourneur, Jacques, 88
Tristán, Flora, 204
Trollope, Anthony, 190
Truffault, François, 139, 142, 145

Van Den Abbeele, Georges, 187
Vincent, Sténio, 274, 284
Von Humboldt, Alexander, 190

Warren, George, 42
Wheelwright, Julie, 74, 75

whiteness, *see* race, racism
Wilson, Harriet, 228
Winks, Robin, 110
women,
  African-American, 6–7, 109–14, 123–7, 136, 143–4, 154, 158, 195, 225, 227–238, 239, 245, 264, 266–72
  Afro-Hispanic, 12, 22–3, 27, 35, 37–9
  Black, *see* African-American women, *see also* Africans, slaves, slavery
  Creole, *see* Creole, creoleness, *see also* mulatto
  cross-dressing, *see* cross-dressing
  Cuban, 163–181, 203
  Indian, 28–9, *see also* Native-Americans
  Mulatto, 137, 146–9
  North American, 177, *see also* Yankee women
  Puerto Rican, 203, 207, 209–10
  Spanish, 28, 35, 206
  White, 137, 142–5, 155, 158, 162–3, 169, 266, 270
  Yankee, 152–3, 266
Woodruffe, Louisa Mathilde, 161, 163, 205
Wycherley, William, 62

Ximeno y Cruz, Dolores María, 173–4

Yolen, Jane, 65, 70, 73
York, Alison, 88

Zenea, Juan Clemente, 174